Table of Contents

Acknowledgements   v

Introduction: *The Necessity of Rethinking the Constitution*   vii

PART I: CONSTITUTIONAL REFORM   1

1. ROBERT MARTIN
    A Lament for British North America   3

2. H.D. FORBES
    Trudeau's Moral Vision   17

3. CHRISTOPHER P. MANFREDI
    On the Virtues of a Limited Constitution:
    Why Canadians Were Right to Reject the Charlottetown Accord   40

PART II: CONSTITUTIONAL INTERPRETATION   61

4. RAINER KNOPFF and F.L. MORTON
    Canada's Court Party   63

5. BRADLEY C.S. WATSON
    The Language of Rights and the Crisis of the Liberal Imagination   88

6. KAREN SELICK
    Rights and Wrongs in the Canadian Charter   103

7. ANTHONY A. PEACOCK
   Strange Brew: Tocqueville, Rights, and the Technology of Equality   122

8. JOHN T. PEPALL
   *What's the Evidence? The Use the Supreme Court of Canada
   Makes of Evidence in Charter Cases*   161

9. GERALD OWEN
   Disclosure after Stinchcombe   177

10. SCOTT REID
    *Penumbras for the People:
    Placing Judicial Supremacy Under Popular Control*   186

PART III: CONSTITUTIONAL THEORY   215

11. BARRY COOPER
    Theoretical Perspectives on Constitutional Reform in Canada   217

12. TOM DARBY and PETER C. EMBERLEY
    *'Political Correctness' and the Constitution:
    Nature and Convention Re-examined*   233

13. ROBERT MARTIN
    *Reconstituting Democracy:
    Orthodoxy and Research in Law and Social Science*   249

Postscript: *The 1995 Quebec Referendum, Liberal Constitutionalism,
and The Future of Canada*   271

Notes on Contributors   276

Index   279

Acknowledgements

This book would have been impossible without the diligence and co-operation of all contributors. I am especially grateful to Rainer Knopff, Christopher Manfredi, Robert Martin, and Bradley Watson, who reviewed portions of the manuscript. The generous financial assistance of the Lynde and Harry Bradley Foundation of Milwaukee, Wisconsin, which has supported me as a Bradley Research Fellow since 1993, afforded me the opportunity to work on this manuscript at length. I would also like to thank Ralph Rossum, James Nichols, Jr, James Ceaser, Charles Kesler and Joseph Bessette for their assistance throughout. Jeffrey Strype and James Howie of Thomson, Rogers (Toronto) provided me with the opportunity I needed to get this project off the ground. Dianne Sydij and the late Arthur Loranger, also of Thomson, Rogers, gave me extensive help in the library and on the computers. The Center for Politics and Economics, Claremont Graduate School, and the Department of Government, Claremont McKenna College, have helped me in many ways since 1992. Gwen Williams has provided secretarial assistance above and beyond the call of duty. Freya Godard's copy-editing of the manuscript was nothing less than superb. Euan White, the acquisitions editor at Oxford University Press, had confidence in this project from the start, and his skill at navigating the manuscript through the various stages of production would make even the most adept kayaker envious.

Introduction:
The Necessity of Rethinking
the Constitution

The 1992 referendum on the Charlottetown Accord and the 1993 federal election seemed to mark the culmination of an ambivalent, if not divisive, period of Canadian constitutionalism. Yet these developments could not be interpreted in isolation. As much as anything, they appeared to be the off-spring of a conspicuous transformation in the process and substance of Canadian constitutional politics brought about by the 1982 Charter of Rights and Freedoms. As Alan Cairns has observed, the Charter has not only engendered a change in Canada's constitutional order: it has engendered a change in Canada's constitutional discourse.[1] The interpretive enterprise of Charter review and the symbolic politics it has generated have had consequences extending far beyond the purview of Canadian courts and the parties to constitutional litigation. The problems that plagued constitutional reform in the late 1980s and early 1990s, and that resulted in the precipitous demise of the Charlottetown Accord as well as that of the federal Progressive Conservative Party itself, seemed intimately related to the politics of judicial review under the Charter. Was there a common thread linking the problems of Canadian constitutional reform, interpretation, and theory? The contributors to this volume believed there was and the essays that follow attempt to address these themes with a view to rethinking them in the context of Canadian liberal constitutionalism.

A constitution is many things. It has authority and provides for government. It establishes the structure of government, the powers government possesses, how these are to be allocated among the various branches and institutions, how the balance between power and liberty, government and individual rights, is to be maintained, and how the constitutional design may be amended through means other than violent revolution.[2] More generally, a constitution is composed of parts that have a purpose and that serve a broader constitutional whole. A constitution, in a sense, is a rational whole, the reasonableness of which can be assessed. Writing in the United States, Allan Bloom has remarked, 'The Constitution, of all public documents, invites rational discourse. It was written by a group of wise statesmen who believed in the necessity, goodness, and power of reason in the establishment of just regimes.'[3] Does the Canadian constitution lend itself to such an interpretation?[4] Does its authority originate in reason rather than tradition, history, revelation, or prejudice? Ironically, at the very time one would have thought it most imperative that Canadians resort to rational discourse on the constitution, the very possibility of it seems to have been denied.

The Charlottetown round of constitutional negotiations, for instance, centred on the idea that a constitution is a compromise between competing, if not incompatible, interests; that it should not look or cannot look beyond these interests to what might be good in a liberal democracy. The idea that there could be any common good that all Canadians might agree on was generally denied by the advocates of constitutional reform and their partisans in the media and legal academies. The underlying assumption was that reason is not something shared by all but is the product of will or arbitrary preference. It is bound to one's language, colour, religion, culture, and sex. It is a function of power. Hence we had to have proportionate representation of interest groups in the constitutional negotiations (and eventually in the constitution itself) since otherwise there would be bias. Representatives could not speak on behalf of those who did not share their biological, racial, sexual, or cultural characteristics because they did not possess those pre-rational attributes that determined their thought.

Statesmanship itself assumed a new role during the Meech Lake and Charlottetown rounds of constitutional negotiations, the assumption being that politics is determined by culture and not the other way around. Thus the constitution was perceived as having to reflect social preferences rather than as providing an institutional structure that might guide those preferences. To have proposed an institutional structure that would have produced culture as the residue of a good social order maintained by good institutions would have turned the assumptions underlying the Meech Lake and Charlottetown constitutional discussions on their heads.

If anything, those discussions reflected as much a crisis about how to think about the constitution as they did the difficulty of reaching consensus on constitutional reform. Canada's constitutional difficulties, which are not limited to constitutional reform but apply equally to constitutional interpretation, specifically, the interpretation of the Charter and its place in Canadian politics, can be traced directly to opinions dominant in Canadian universities and, in partic-ular, the law schools. The media, government, interest groups, elementary and high school teachers, as well as other retailers of ideas, receive their opinions first and foremost from the universities. With respect to the constitution, the dominant opinions come from the law schools. But what are those opinions?

The dominant ideological strains in the law schools—materialism, post-materialism,[5] and feminism—are not particularly friendly to liberal constitu-tionalism. Canvassing law review articles, one might get the impression that the rule of law, the idea that citizens are equal before the law and that the law must be impartially applied to all, is anathema to many legal academics. Law, like politics, is often portrayed as the offspring of power. The exercise of political power cannot be distinguished independently of the will of those who wield it, and as such the distinction between power and authority, force and right, is understood to be anachronistic. There are no objective standards of truth or rationality independent of the actions of political actors by which we may assess their actions or which may guide their actions.[6] 'Objectivity', Catharine MacKinnon has written, 'is liberal legalism's conception of itself. It legitimates itself by reflecting its view of society, a society it helps make by so seeing it, and calling that view, and that relation, rationality.'[7] Sheila McIn-tyre, a law professor at Queen's University, agrees. 'Law rationalizes power.'[8] Defending substantive equality against the formal equality of liberal democ-ratic theory, McIntyre asserts that, whereas the 'formalists argue theoretically among themselves about the ideal balance between the conflicting principles of liberty and equality, those pursuing equality of results focus upon the power conflicts between actual social groups. . . .'[9] The projects advanced by substantive equality 'collapse the distinction between public and private, political and personal by revealing the degree to which what counts as ratio-nality depends on and serves the interests of those who have power.'[10] The distinction between private actions and public actions, originally conceived as the precondition of free government, is deconstructed, replaced by a vision of society that ties reason to status and that shifts the focus of concern more to who is advancing the issues than to the issues themselves. As McIntyre explains, the substantive 'method discloses whose inequality is systematically enforced in whose interest. . . . It also demonstrates how situated power shapes individual perspective and, in particular, how the perspectives of the powerful define and shape individual and cultural definitions of value in a way which rationalizes existing unequal distributions of power.'[11]

Michael Mandel, of Osgoode Hall Law School, advances a similar line of argument with respect to the Charter, maintaining that the Charter has changed the form of Canadian government by making it less, not more, democratic.[12] '[T]he Charter has *legalized* our politics.' Where it 'has had an effect, that effect has been to strengthen the already great inequalities in Canada.'[13] The Charter, on Mandel's reading, is another instrument in the arsenal of liberal constitutionalism that will maintain, if not exacerbate, the social and economic inequalities in Canada. It is not that the language of the Charter is skewed against the disenfranchised or disadvantaged. Rather, the problem is that judicial review is inherently abstract and conservative. Judges are selected from the legal profession, and 'the profession is still almost entirely the domain of the white and upper class.'[14] Moreover, since judicial review involves formal rules and is backward-looking, courts having to justify their decisions as deriving from *principle*, not *policy*—which is the prerogative of the legislative branches to develop—judicial reasoning ends up 'making things acceptable', serving as a 'form of legitimation'.[15] 'Arguments of principle are forced to derive their premises from *existing* arrangements (principles must have "institutional support"). They must start from, take for granted, and indeed *justify* basic social arrangements.'[16] Since there are 'great inequalities' in Canadian society, judicial review under the Charter serves to legitimize the existing unequal relations of power and property. For Mandel, as for his colleagues at Osgoode Hall, Harry Glasbeek,[17] Alan Hutchinson, and former Osgoode professor, Andrew Petter,[18] the Charter will not realign social and economic relations of power in the manner they desire. To achieve this, something more radical is needed.

Joel Bakan, of the University of British Columbia Faculty of Law, again admonishes those who think the Charter will be used to promote progressive social change that they may be mistaken. For one thing, '[t]he oppressed and disempowered groups who are the supposed beneficiaries of progressive Charter litigation will, because of their lack of resources, be the least likely to have genuine access to the courts.'[19] For another thing, judicial ideology will tend away from, not toward, progressive reform that may threaten the status of powerful groups. There is an 'affinity between attitudes and beliefs of judges and the interests of litigants who represent the social and economic élite. . . . Judges are for the most part white, male, wealthy, and they are always lawyers. . . . [They] do not represent the Canadian population, not in terms of class, race, ethnicity, gender, culture or education.'[20] If judges are to represent the Canadian population adequately they will have to be part of the groups over which they preside. Otherwise their decisions may not be impartial. Again, the assumption is that the capacity to judge, like the capacity to reason, is tied to status.

The examples here could be multiplied. The point, however, would remain the same: liberal constitutionalism, as well as what we understand by reason, are under attack. Despite prevarications to the contrary, the materialists, postmaterialists, and feminists are not marginalized in the law schools, however much they may be unrepresentative of Canadian society as a whole. These groups constitute the mainstream of legal academic scholarship, a rigid orthodoxy that has had an unparalleled influence on constitutional reform, interpretation, and theory in Canada. In a recent collection of essays, Bakan and David Schneiderman observe, 'A quite heated debate has developed among activists and academics on the utility of the *Canadian Charter*'s rights in advancing progressive social change.'[21] This is true, but as two of the contributors to this book, F.L. Morton and Rainer Knopff point out, the debate over the efficacy of the Charter and its implications for Canadian politics has been monopolized by progressives. The field of battle has been reserved almost exclusively to the materialist and postmaterialist camps, to those who think the Charter is a variant of liberal constitutional politics that will fail in any serious way to redistribute wealth or power and to those who see the Charter as an expedient tool by which to aggrandize a progressive platform.[22] These new ideologies dominate Charter scholarship, and challenges to their interpretations are rare and often not warmly received.[23]

Anyone who has attended a Canadian law school over the last generation—and many of the contributors to this volume have—has witnessed a sea change in legal education. But it is not only the law schools that have been affected by the new ideologies. So have Canadian legal élites.

The Canadian Bar Association (CBA), for instance, recently financed and promoted the CBA Gender Equality Task Force, chaired by former Supreme Court Justice Bertha Wilson. The task force was charged with studying the barriers faced by women in the Canadian legal profession. In its report, released in August 1993, the Wilson task force found direct and systemic discrimination in the legal profession, government legal departments, corporations that employed lawyers, administrative tribunals, the judiciary, and faculties of law. But the report's findings were suspect even before the report was released. Writing in *The Lawyers Weekly* in October 1992, Robert Martin, a contributor to this book, queried whether the CBA was spending its money wisely in financing the task force.[24] 'Is there one lawyer in Canada,' Martin asked, 'who cannot predict, in detail, everything the official report is going to say?'[25] Martin was referring, among other things, to Bertha Wilson's famous speech at Osgoode Hall Law School in February 1990,[26] where she declared that male and female judges bring very different perspectives to their judicial duties. Wilson reaffirmed that opinion in a recent interview in the CBA's *National* magazine. Responding to a question about the apparent feminist bias of the CBA's task force, Wilson demurred: 'It's very simple. The assumption out there is that male is neutral. We challenge that. Yes, our perspective is female. Yours is male. The big point is a white perspective is not neutral, a male perspective is not neutral, a heterosexual perspective is not neutral. . . It's just a matter of being balanced.'[27] In the same interview Wilson added that she and other members of the task force, shortly after convening it, felt that its scope should be expanded:

> As a result of our consultations, we became aware that our mandate was not broad enough. Gender bias includes bias against black women, Aboriginal women, disabled women, lesbian women. There's a large segment of women that suffer double, triple discrimination . . . and (a woman) can't tell if she's being discriminated against because of sex, race, or disability. She just knows she's a victim of discrimination.[28]

Wilson's comments and the findings and recommendations of the task force drew quick and sometimes pointed responses. Vancouver lawyer Greg Lanning described Wilson's comments in the *National* as 'high-sounding vacuousness', inquiring, 'what exactly is the female perspective on offer and acceptance?'[29] In British Columbia, the Chief Justice, as well as the chief provincial court judge and over a dozen female judges rejected the report's findings in a series of newspaper articles and television interviews, denying that they had encountered gender discrimination in the provincial judiciary or in the province's administration of justice.

Despite attacks on the report, the CBA executive proposed that the task force's recommendations be implemented, although with qualification. Outgoing president Cecilia Johnstone remarked in an interview, 'The idea is not necessarily a wholesale adoption of the report, but to use it as a catalyst for change.'[30] At the time of writing, the CBA has adopted 229 of the report's 256 recommendations in original or amended form.[31]

At the same time as the gender equality task force was conducting its investigations and drafting its report, the CBA's provincial divisions were sponsoring continuing legal education courses on how to develop feminist litigation strategies. In June 1993, the CBA Ontario (CBAO), the largest division of the CBA, announced that it was devoting a section of the CBAO to feminist legal analysis. The section was described to CBAO members as providing 'an interdisciplinary forum for the cross-pollination of ideas between academics and practitioners to apply and extend the feminist legal analysis of law, and to advise the CBAO on the application of feminist analysis to legislation and submissions.'[32] The development and implementation of feminist policies was now, apparently, a goal of the CBAO.

These recent developments in Canadian law schools and the CBA point to a transformation in assumptions about, and approaches to, legal and constitutional analysis that have had a significant effect on constitutional reform and interpretation. No longer is the constitution considered to reflect a permanent order or as maintaining fixed constitutional forms. Rather it is a register of social pressures that must change and adapt to changing circumstances. The constitution is not a guide to politics so much as to be guided by politics. The implication is that as the constitution adapts to changing circumstances, so the rules and principles that apply to the circumstances must change with them. No longer a series of neutral rules for the resolution and management of political disputes, the constitution has become, in many important respects, a forum for the implementation of partisan programs. Liberal constitutionalism has been displaced, in increasing measure, by programmatic liberalism, a conception of the constitution that views it as a vehicle for potentially unlimited reform. This was particularly evident during the Charlottetown negotiations, where the constitution finally resembled less a fundamental law than a panacea for a constellation of fashionable social and political problems.

Tocqueville admonished that those who live in democratic times do not easily appreciate the utility of forms. Democratic peoples are anxious peoples. They ordinarily aspire 'only to facile and immediate pleasures', throwing 'themselves impetuously toward the object of each of their desires, the least delays making them desperate'. Forms are important in democracies because they provide a wall of separation between the weak and the strong, the governed and the government. They protect against the immoderate and impassioned impulses of both majorities and minorities. Yet, despite the expediency of them, democratic peoples have less respect for forms than other peoples.[33] The challenge to democracies is to respect constitutional forms. Yet in Canada, under the auspices of our constitutional *cognoscenti*, many individuals and groups have become the anxious democrats Tocqueville described in *Democracy in America*. Seeking immediate political results, they eschew constitutional forms in favour of constitutional substance. Neither reason, nor objectivity, nor constitutional formalities can get in the way of the politically desirable results. The sequelae have been a debilitation of our constitutionalism and the de-legitimization of law.

The essays in this collection respond to these recent trends in Canadian constitutional politics. They are directed, in particular, at Canadian constitutional scholarship, a scholarship that has tended to regard the constitution more with an eye to utilitarian opportunism than with a view to constructing a reasoned, principled document and accompanying body of law that might serve as a guide to Canadian politics. For over one hundred years, the *British North America Act* and constitutional conventions served as a political compass for Canadian politics. It is difficult to discern what, if anything, has filled the void left by the recent period of constitutional disruption and change that has so affected our social and political life. The essays in this collection address this problem, as well as other issues, in an attempt to re-examine the assumptions and implications of our current constitutional state.

The essays are divided into three sections: Part I, 'Constitutional Reform', Part II, 'Constitutional Interpretation', and Part III, 'Constitutional Theory'.

PART I: CONSTITUTIONAL REFORM

The first essay in the collection, by Robert Martin, looks at a much disregarded question of constitutional reform: why was the *British North America Act* renamed the *Constitution Act* in 1982? This change in the name of our most fundamental constitutional document has gone virtually unnoticed in the burgeoning literature on the Canadian constitution. Yet it succinctly symbolizes the loss of our collective identity. British North America not only represented, negatively, the expression of colonial, settler origins, an outpost of the British Empire. It spoke, positively, of our uniqueness in North America, our emphasis on a more collective good and public order, one distinct from the celebration of individual freedom that forms the ideological cement of American civilization.

In 1982, Martin contends, there was no public voice raised in opposition to the loss of British North America because Canadians no longer understood what that meant. The idea that had provided a purpose and justification for the Canadian state had evaporated. In its place, it was perhaps only natural that we should adopt, on the one hand, that historically and ideologically most American of constitutional documents, the Charter of Rights and Freedoms, and, on the other hand, multiculturalism, a policy that announced the end of any unifying idea or culture in Canada and the adoption of moral and intellectual relativism as our political credo. The Preamble to the failed Charlottetown Accord, the 'Canada Clause', recognized that we were a country in need of a new national purpose. But the statement of 'fundamental values' that was contained in that clause was little more than a pastiche of well-intentioned banalities, affirming that Canada was a country mired in a deep intellectual crisis. Recently, Martin suggests, Canadians have approached constitutional reform in the same way that multiculturalism approaches culture: not unlike going to a supermarket where we are offered an unlimited number of possibilities, filling our constitutional cart with an incoherent array of different products. It would be unwise to want to return to British North America, but in the wake of the recent disconcerting, dyspeptic attempts at constitutional reform, we should at least be cognizant of what we have lost.

In his essay on Pierre Trudeau's moral vision, H.D. Forbes again visits the theme of multiculturalism, this time from the vantage of Trudeau's three great legacies to Canada: official bilingualism, multiculturalism, and the Charter. Forbes argues that Trudeau conceived multiculturalism as an extension of the animating principle of official bilingualism. In the same way that official bilingualism used government to protect French and English, avoiding the immoderate and retrograde idea of national sovereignty, multiculturalism would use government to protect the national qualities of groups, recognizing and accommodating cultural and ethnic differences without making these differences the architectonic principle of political order.

Forbes points out that Trudeau saved his most vehement opposition for nationalism. Nationalism for Trudeau was a political creed that was impractical: there is no objective standard of nationality. It was undesirable: more and more members of different ethnic groups are living on common territory. Quebec nationalism became a threat to Canada, and Trudeau's response was bilingualism and an entrenched bill of rights. According to Forbes, bilingualism was intended to mollify the tensions between the English and the French by establishing individual rights that were national in scope and unrelated to territory. Trudeau viewed the 'separatist' approach to the problems of language and culture as unprincipled, if not antediluvian. Separatism would create two linguistic ghettos, foster bigotry, and put off Canada's inevitable day of reckoning. Fundamental rights should not depend on where one lived, nor should they depend on the will of the majority. Ethnic accommodation, an extension of the tolerance of English and French throughout Canada, would best be served by well-educated lawyers and judges, men and women who understood and sympathized with the constitutional experiment being conducted. Such an élite would be better guardians of rights than those small-time lawyers, farmers, businessmen, and other politicians who, in a system of parliamentary supremacy, could all too readily translate majority opinion into laws and policies.

Trudeau's vision, much derided and even now difficult to spell out, was a moral vision. It was not merely an economic plan aimed at material welfare; rather, it incited Canadians to stop thinking of their country as entirely their own, to take seriously, perhaps as no other country had, the injunction 'love thy neighbour'. In an increasingly integrated global village, at a time of intensifying national tensions and 'ethnic cleansing', Canadians had the opportunity to become the apogee of the modern political world, a beacon of tolerance, universality, and diversity. They should not squander the moment. The guiding light for Trudeau's vision was a simple moral imperative: that those who overcome indignation are happier than those who let it rule their lives. Forbes maintains that, however the experiment Trudeau began turns out, there is little doubt it has furthered mankind's political knowledge and benefited humanity.

Christopher Manfredi's essay assesses Trudeau's legacy in a significantly different light. Defending Canada's rejection of the Charlottetown Accord, Manfredi argues that the Accord represented the apex of a theory and practice in Canadian constitutionalism that, for almost a generation, had looked to constitutional reform as the means of resolving the underlying political conflicts in Canada. The solution to the problems of social justice and national unity, liberty and equality have been portrayed by Canadian intellectual and political élites as just a 'Canada clause' away. Such a view of constitutional politics betrays a fundamental misunderstanding about the utility and function of a constitution. A constitution provides an institutional framework of formal rules for regulating political disputes. It may shift the institutional focus for settling such disputes but it cannot eliminate them.

The attempt to eliminate political disputes through the mechanism of constitutional reform is, in fact, profoundly illiberal. Just as the Charter was designed in part to suppress the centrifugal forces at work in Canada, proponents of the Charlottetown Accord's 'Canada clause' and 'social and economic union' argued that they would help define Canada's elusive national identity. But, Manfredi observes, 'the quest for Canadian identity is just as pointless as the quest for Canadian literature. . . . A Canadian identity cannot be captured at a particular moment and imposed through an act of constitutional will; at best, the constitution can supply the political mechanisms for the gradual development of identity.' To suggest, as proponents of the 'social charter' did, that it would merely constitutionalize a national consensus with respect to universal social programs concealed the fact that if such a consensus actually existed there would be little need to protect it constitutionally. In truth, the proposal for a social charter was a disingenuous attempt to insulate contentious social policy from further legislative scrutiny by enshrining it in the constitution. The unpalatable nature of the vision of Canadian identity embodied in the Charlottetown Accord perhaps explains its almost categorical rejection throughout Canada.

In a sense, the Charlottetown Accord was the necessary outgrowth of the legacy of the Charter. The constitutionalizing of policy under the guise of protecting political rights, begun by the Trudeau government, was extended, in the Charlottetown Accord, to the ubiquitous matters of economic and social policy. The groups that the Charter had endowed with constitutional status demanded greater and greater access to negotiations, eventually insisting on guardianship over the substance of constitutional reform.

Manfredi maintains that the pre- and post-Charter attempts at constitutionally resolving such issues as national unity, social welfare, and economic policy show that constitutional reform is not likely going to settle such problems or end deliberations about the common good. In addition, the attempt made by advocates of the social charter to constitutionalize national standards reveals a fundamental misconception about the values of federalism, representative democracy, and separation of powers in a liberal regime. Advocates of the social charter treated the provinces as mere administrative units of the national government. For the Ontario NDP, which had originally proposed the charter, as well as for the other governments endorsing it, the charter was both a means of ensuring that the provinces could keep social policy promises they could no longer afford and an expedient by which popular opposition to such policy could be permanently overcome. Paradoxically, pre- and post-Charter politics manifests elements of illiberal politics. If constitutional progress is to be achieved in Canada, Manfredi maintains, Canadians are going to have to rediscover the virtues of a limited constitution, as well as abandon the anachronistic notion that Canada was and continues to be a compact between two, perhaps now three, founding nations.

PART II: CONSTITUTIONAL INTERPRETATION

If the Charter has served to significantly determine the process and substance of the latest rounds of constitutional negotiations, its effects on Canadian politics have not been limited to constitutional reform. Perhaps its most enduring influence has been achieved through litigation. The seven essays in the second part of the book examine the general and specific effects of Charter litigation, as well as the ways in which the Charter and related developments in Canadian public policy have altered the liberal democratic equation in Canada, the balance between rights and equality or between the limits of government action, on the one hand, and the prerogative of constitutionally elected majorities to rule, on the other. The final essay proposes a solution to the problem of judicial supremacy that the Charter has created.

In the first essay of part II, Rainer Knopff and F.L. Morton argue that, contrary to original promises from governments and commentators, the Charter has developed as neither a democratic nor a liberal constitutional document. Rather, it has engendered a type of legalized politics that bypasses democratic processes in favour of a coalition of social movements Knopff and Morton refer to as the 'Court Party'. The Court Party consists of four principal, overlapping constituencies: (1) national unity advocates—those who view the Charter as a centralizing counterpoise to the centrifugal forces of regionalism and provincialism; (2) Charter Canadians—groups that seek and acquire constitutional recognition, crystallizing around non-terri-torial identities such as sex, language, ethnicity, and disability; (3) social engineers—those who believe that the evils of the world are caused by defec-tive, and hence corrigible, social institutions rather than by human nature; and (4) post-materialists—individuals and groups that constitute the social and institutional nexus of the Court Party.

Socially, the members of the Court Party are drawn from sectors of the economy that are both affluent and highly educated. They are neither poor nor working-class but form a significant part of what has been called the 'knowledge industry', the locus of power in modern technological society. Institutionally, the Court Party achieves its postmaterialist program, not by relying on traditional representative bodies or popular elections, but (as its name implies) by depending on the courts. Although its advocates often use democratic rhetoric to support their causes, the Court Party is profoundly anti-democratic, anti-majoritarian.

Unlike traditional interest groups, the Court Party tends to advocate not less, but more, government intervention in the form of increased state ser-vices, benefits, or regulations. Since the new coalition of Charter litigants understands the state, not as the creation of a pre-existing society, but rather society as the creation of a pre-established state, the task of the Court Party becomes the potentially unlimited one of curing the interminable evils of society through state-sponsored reconstructive social engineering. The judiciary, an institution that emphasizes the articulated rationality of intel-lectuals, proves to be the ideal tool for rebuilding society from the top down. The Court Party seeks then to transform the traditional function of the judi-ciary as a check on government by inviting the courts to amplify remedial state action.

When the novel elements characteristic of the Court Party are combined with the judicial practices that have emerged under the Charter, the result is a symbiotic relationship in which the Charter gives impetus and legitimacy to the politics of postmaterialism, while the Court Party works to make the Charter a force in the mainstream of the Canadian political process. The

Supreme Court has responded to the activist invocations of the Court Party by casting off its old adjudicatory role, promulgating standards for individual litigants, and adopting a new role as the oracle on the constitution, issuing broad declarations of constitutional policy and creating standards for the whole of society.

The new politics of post-materialism, Knopff and Morton point out, is a politics of reform that demands obedience. Willing to put off democracy today for the sake of achieving it more perfectly tomorrow, the post-materialist ethic is a guardian ethic that requires faith in a new vanguard of guardians. To the extent Canadians do not agree with the advocacy of the guardians, the guardians have had to implement their policies by other means. Using the Charter as the vehicle for doing so, they have rendered it, not the friend, but the foe, of liberal constitutionalism.

Bradley Watson describes the Charter, in similar terms, as a document reflecting the crisis of the liberal imagination. Intended to unify Canada, both in symbolic and legal terms, as well as to guarantee fundamental rights and freedoms, the Charter has instead served to transfer power to a small coterie of liberal academics, lawyers, and judges who view it as a convenient means through which to realize the new politics of the self. It is commonly understood that the philosophy of liberalism is an individualist, rights-oriented philosophy. 'But what is not commonly understood,' Watson remarks, 'is the manner in which early modern liberalism has degenerated into late-twentieth-century self-expressive individualism, and the influence of this latter incarnation on political and legal thought.' The ideological framework that judges work with, provided to them by the law schools, is that law is higher than politics and the individual higher than the collectivity, free to create himself as he sees fit, without government interference. Within this framework, it becomes imperative to find the best means by which to secure the individual's freedom to define what he is, independently of the wishes of the majority. The language of rights turns out to be ideal for carrying out the individual's expanding claims, and the judiciary turns out to be the most expedient institution to restrain, if not ignore, the wishes of the majority.

But in all of this, Watson objects, the people of Canada are not well served. The Charter has evolved, not as a shield against government, but as a weapon used by interest groups to hold Canadian legislative bodies hostage to policies they could not achieve through the usual give and take of politics. Moreover, when self-expressive liberalism, which allows of no natural limits on individual self-creation, is combined with judicialized Charter politics, where the judiciary is provided with unprecedented power, the result is a revisionist jurisprudence. Judges can give constitutional provisions whatever meaning they please, hardening current intellectual fashions into constitutional policy for generations to come. Under the influence of the Charter and self-expressive liberalism, Canadian courts are destined to be activist and non-interpretivist, creating law that represents their own reading of social development and needs, while attenuating the fundamental principle of free government, the consent of the governed. Watson is adamant: the Charter has failed Canadians, displacing the forum in which conflicting interests and rights were traditionally balanced. Moral and political issues have been transformed into thin, inflexible legal issues. If Canadians are not to lose the Canada on which the Charter was imposed, they will have to oppose it more aggressively than they have done so far.

Since the proclamation of the Charter, the language of rights has become central to political discourse in Canada. This is understandable since Charter claims must be framed in the language of rights. But when we speak of rights, and particularly of constitutional rights, what exactly do we mean?

Karen Selick addresses this question, distinguishing between negative and positive rights under the Charter. Negative rights are rights to non-interference from others. Positive rights are entitlements, rights requiring others to provide advantages or material benefits to the rights claimant. Although both negative and positive rights impose obligations on others, there are differences between them. First, negative rights do not depend on economic or technological conditions for their fulfilment; positive rights do. Negative rights can be fulfilled at any time and place. Positive rights require an advanced stage of economic and technological development for their fulfilment. Second, negative rights, unlike positive rights, only require an act of will on the part of others. Positive rights require something more, namely, a positive commitment of some advantage or some object to the beneficiary. Finally, and most important, negative rights can co-exist without conflicting with the rights of others; positive rights cannot. Positive rights necessarily involve a conflict between individual rights since they require something to be taken from one person and given to another. Positive rights imply that everyone does not have the same rights. They are inegalitarian. Negative rights are not. Only negative rights, Selick maintains, are rights properly understood.

Selick highlights how the Charter contains a mixture of negative and positive rights, as well as how the judiciary has failed to apply rights theory in a consistent or principled fashion. Section 7, for instance, provides 'the right to life, liberty and security of the person'. Unlike the fifth and fourteenth amendments of the American Constitution, however, section 7 also provides that no one may be 'deprived of the right to life, liberty and security of the person except in accordance with the principles of fundamental justice.' Selick questions whether this means that the right to life is both a negative right as well as a positive right, the right not to be killed as well as the right to be provided with the material means to sustain one's life. The Supreme Court came close to upholding this latter interpretation in *Finlay v. Canada* (1993),[34] narrowly defeating a previously successful claim by a Manitoba welfare recipient that a small reduction in his welfare payments, made by the Manitoba government as compensation for an earlier overpayment, was a denial of his section 7 right to life, liberty and security of the person.

Selick points out further problems with sections 1, 6, 23, 27, 33 and 36 of the Charter. She is also critical of the absence of any property rights in the Charter, an indication, she suggests, of the strength of the environmentalist and feminist lobbies opposed to such rights.

In Selick's estimate, the most flagrantly contradictory provision of the Charter is section 15, the principal equality rights section. Section 15, in her opinion, guarantees equal treatment in subsection (1) and then provides for its denial in subsection (2), permitting special treatment to special groups. Section 15 has been rendered a 'gigantic affirmative action program'. '[N]ot only are the disadvantaged entitled to better-than-equal treatment under subsection 15(2), but they are also the only ones who are entitled to invoke the guarantee of equal treatment under subsection 15(1).'

There is room, in Selick's view, for constitutional reform, and she advances proposals in this regard. She concedes, however, that given the present intellectual climate, the same one that produced the offending texts of the Charter, the prospects for such reform are slim. Nothing short of a philosophical revolution could create the conditions required for change.

Anthony Peacock joins issue with Selick, advancing three propositions related to the problem of equality and equal rights. First, the moral vision animating equality rights initiatives such as section 15, as judicially construed, affirmative action, and human rights policy, may be described as a 'technology of equality' since it comports with many elements we can identify with technology. Second, since the problem of equality, or what we mean by 'political' equality or 'social' equality, and the proper role or powers of government in providing for equality, invites speculation on the meaning of rights, we must assume the existence of a standard beyond mere opinion that serves to arbitrate our questions concerning legitimate and illegitimate rights, moral and immoral visions of equality. If we are not to render the language of rights meaningless, giving them whatever meaning is convenient, we must assume the existence of natural rights. Third, the content of rights issues from their form. Rights have moral consequences, and we can choose better or worse regimes of rights. Peacock addresses this latter issue in the context of Tocqueville's ostensible distinction between moral and immoral rights, weak and strong visions of equality. He argues that Tocqueville illustrates how modern liberal democracies are prone to making society over in the image of an equality that always remains just beyond the present reality.

Section 15 jurisprudence, affirmative action, and human rights policy are exemplary of this trend, predicated as they are on the assumptions of modern social science that there are no natural rights and no natural limitations to human perfection. If there are no natural limitations to human perfection, there can be no limits to the modification of society in the name of equality. All social and political problems are conceived to originate in the 'system'. The object of political and legal reform is to eliminate more and more 'systemic barriers'. But where does such reform end? Does it have any limits? Tocqueville emphasized that the endless pursuit of greater equality requires an ever distending marriage of society to the state and the concomitant elimination of private life and self-government. This turns out to be of little significance to the advocates of the systemic model of politics because, according to them, there is no real private life and no real freedom. Individuals, including their thought, are the products of their environment. At the same time that the advocates of the systemic model tell us that individuals are the products of their environment, the post-modernists and deconstructionists, their intellectual acolytes, tell us that thought is the instrument of prejudice and control, the subjugated victim of power.

On this reading, rights must be defined in relation to the groups to which individuals belong. But when the existence of rights depends on the more or less imperceptible causes of social circumstance, social differences, and group affinities, is the meaning of rights not lost? Peacock concludes that the new vision of equality that animates section 15 jurisprudence, affirmative action, and human rights policy, ostensibly aimed at eliminating discrimination and disadvantage, proves to be strangely undiscriminating.

One of the most useful expedients for carrying out the Supreme Court's new function as the oracular authority on the constitution has been its use of evidence, particularly 'legislative fact' evidence. Examining the Supreme Court's use of evidence in Charter cases, John Pepall observes that evidence is most commonly used by the Court in section 1 litigation. Pepall shows how the use of evidence to determine the reasonableness of the work of legislatures has been both erratic and disingenuous. It served both to insulate the Court from criticism of the blatant imposition of its opinions on legislative bodies, as well as to preserve the Court's power of having the final say on political issues arising under the Charter.

In a typical civil or criminal case, courts deal with adjudicative facts, facts that exist between the parties: who did what to whom, where and when. In Charter cases, which involve legislative fact evidence, the Court is involved, not with truth between the parties, but with truth in general, with speculation on the wisdom of legislation. The rules of evidence, as well as the adversarial process, Pepall contends, are ill-suited to assessing the wisdom of the work of legislatures. The result has been a confused jurisprudence: masses of documents are heaped on the judiciary without controversy, the credibility of reports and studies substantiating or criticizing broad matters of policy cannot be tested, legal rules that provide no precise guidelines on when legal requirements have been met are promulgated, and the rule of law is undermined. 'In Charter cases judges appear to invoke evidence or pass it by depending on how it suits their arguments. It is often difficult to determine from the Court's logorrhoeic reasons exactly what evidence they considered and what they made of it.' If anything, the Supreme Court's use of evidence in

Charter litigation, particularly section 1 cases, has illustrated the incapacity of the Court to adequately assess questions of broad social and legislative policy. Rather than recognizing its limitations and placing restrictions on the use of evidence as well as on the extent of its scrutiny, the Supreme Court, Pepall observes, has chosen to enhance its political power by calling for, and ostensibly relying on, dubious political facts, overstepping its competence and perhaps its authority.

If the courts are unable to assess the wisdom of legislation and social policy, perhaps a corollary of this limitation is that they are unable to calculate the consequences of their decisions. Investigating the effects of *R. v. Stinchcombe* (1991),[35] the leading Canadian case on Crown disclosure and arguably the most important criminal law decision since the proclamation of the Charter, Gerald Owen observes how the Supreme Court's decision reveals interesting, if not peculiar, symptoms of the times. One such symptom has been the development of a jurisprudence of photocopying. Obliged to comply with *Stinchcombe*'s broad demands for disclosure, the courts in poorer provinces have had to develop rules concerning the rights of defendants to photocopy Crown productions. Ironically, in some smaller jurisdictions where written policies have displaced previous disclosure practices based on trust between counsel, the effect of *Stinchcombe* has been to tighten up, not broaden, the release of Crown information.

Owen describes *Stinchcombe* as an example of one branch of government committing another branch to significant expense and labour, compelling the police to reduce more and more activities to writing, and constraining prosecutors, as well as defence counsel, in the conduct of their investigations and litigation strategies. *Stinchcombe* reflects a broad trend in social and political policy, where drama and personal contact are reduced to information, documentation, and abstraction. The Charter itself is an aspect of this rationalistic movement, embodying an attempt to convert principles into abstract written formulas. Although *Stinchcombe* may help defendants to obtain disclosure, if it is deemed that broad disclosure obviates the necessity for preliminary inquiries, as Chief Justice Antonio Lamer has contended, defendants may learn the particulars of the case they have to meet, but they will miss out on face-to-face confrontation with the prosecution and its witnesses. Accordingly, they may get to know the Crown's evidence but not the Crown's strategy, tactics, or arguments. Since the disclosure requirements under *Stinchcombe* are broad and much evidence that would have to be disclosed is beyond the scope of the prosecutors' knowledge—prosecutors not knowing what is relevant—defendants may have to lay bare their own strategies and arguments if they wish to obtain documents relevant to their case. *Stinchcombe* leaves Crowns discretion and has helped defendants in many respects but, Owen warns, it has not eliminated abuses of process nor is the Charter ever likely to do so.

The final essay in the second part of the book, by Scott Reid, investigates critiques of the Charter and recommends a popular solution to the problem of judicial supremacy that the Charter has occasioned. Charter sceptics, who argue that the policy-making powers the Charter has conferred on judges must be curtailed, often fail to suggest remedies that are practical. In an extensive analysis, Reid documents the strengths and weaknesses of judicial supremacy and then surveys the solutions that have been proposed to curb its excesses. The last category of solutions surveyed, those which would use section 33 of the Charter (the legislative override) to rein in the judiciary's new powers, tend to encounter one or both of two insurmountable obstacles. Either they lack legitimacy, the Canadian people being hostile to any legislative override of the rights laid out in the Charter. Or, in the case of proposals to amend the override in such a way as to make it more palatable to the electorate, the amending formula is impossibly complex.

Reid's solutions to these problems are twofold. First, invest the override power in an institution other than the legislative branch of government. Second, change section 33 through legislation rather than constitutional amendment. The first remedy could be implemented by giving the override power to the political body that enjoys more popular respect than the judiciary itself, namely, the people. The second remedy could be implemented by legislation providing for the exercise of section 33 only where authorized by a referendum on the law in question.

Reid suggests that if referenda respecting the laws in question were placed on ballots during federal and provincial elections—a not unmanageable proposition since there would be few referenda in any term—the electorate would have a number of years to assess the effects of judicial rulings. Such a hiatus between the rulings and their scrutiny by the public would enhance the wisdom of popular deliberation concerning the laws at issue. In addition, referenda might help apprise judges of local and national community standards, and would thus provide a barometer the judiciary could use in section 1 deliberations respecting what reasonable limits can be placed on rights in a free and democratic society.

To those who might argue that the democratic override would facilitate 'mob rule' and give a tyrannical majority the prerogative it needs to run roughshod over the rights of minorities, Reid responds that the contrary has proved to be the case in countries, such as Switzerland, that have used direct democracy. The 1992 constitutional referendum is an example of how a potentially explosive national crisis was defused through a national popular vote on the Charlottetown Accord. Likely to temper, not aggravate, majoritarian tyranny, the democratic override, although not a complete answer to the problem of judicial supremacy, would nevertheless eliminate the necessity of having to create new laws after unpopular decisions. It would also separate politicians from some of the most partisan political disputes during elections, thereby reducing the potential for demagoguery and dissipating the critical mass necessary for majoritarian tyranny.

PART III: CONSTITUTIONAL THEORY

The final three essays in the volume address problems of constitutional the-ory, how we should think about Canada's constitutional problems in the broader context of liberal democratic thought and how democratic thought itself has been reconstituted through the new orthodoxy in legal and social scientific research.

Barry Cooper's contribution begins with what he contends is the surely uncontestable fact that Canadians have, as yet, failed to establish a coherent constitutional regime. The problem with constitutional politics in Canada, Cooper argues, is not the 'external' or 'elemental' one of constitutional laws and procedures. Canadians have adequately constituted a government for themselves. Rather, the problem in Canada is an 'internal' or 'substantive' one. Canadians have failed to constitute themselves a people. Thus, the coun-try is not a constitutional regime in the full sense of the term.

Cooper examines approaches to modern constitutionalism and illustrates how they are unable to explain the constitutional quandary peculiar to Canada. The conventional emphasis of political science departments and fac-ulties of law is on matters of law and procedure—techniques of rule such as parliamentary government, federalism, elections, bills of rights, and so on. There is little emphasis on the substantive component of constitutionalism, the meaning or purpose of a regime illuminated through symbols, stories, rit-uals, and myths. Cooper refers to this as 'articulation' and 'representation', the process by which individuals are integrated into a coherent political unit. Society must be articulated down to the individual and become representa-tive of itself. But what evidence is there that this has happened in Canada? 'The chief impediment to constitutional development in Canada is not,' Cooper declares, 'the logical tensions within the constitution—as between individual and collective rights, for instance. Nor is it the historical tendency of Canadian governments to expand their purpose from the securing of citi-zens' rights to proscribing the manner of their exercise, a major consequence of which has been to transform independent and economically productive citizens into dependent pensioners.' The chief impediment to constitutional development in Canada is something more fundamental, something inherent in the institutions that have failed to integrate individual citizens and in the symbols that have failed to express that integration. Cooper asks: if Canada is indeed a constitutional regime, as politicians, academics, and members of the media have proclaimed, where is the expression of it beyond mere procedural or legal forms, where is its mythic evocation, the bond that keeps the mysti-cal body politic together?

The implications of Cooper's argument are fairly clear: if Canadians are to constitute themselves a people, they will require representatives who are capable of realizing the governing ideas of institutions that are found in political communities and that to date have been disregarded. There is no authority without representation and no representation without a governing idea in behalf of which authority is exercised. Representation precedes constitutional law: if constitutional formalities do not accommodate regional concerns, such as Western demands for reform of the Senate or Quebec's demands that its constitutional relationship to the rest of Canada be defined, the Canadian people will express themselves through alternative means, as was evidenced by the success of regionally based political parties during the 1993 federal election.

The emergence of an underground economy, widespread tax avoidance, rejection of traditional parties, and the consistent failure of constitutional reform packages, reflect the evisceration of Canada's formal and informal constitutional forms. If those who represent Canadians remain intransigent, concentrating on legal or constitutional bargaining rather than addressing the needs of articulate political communities, Cooper contends, not only will the minor components of rule in Canada, the political parties, but the major components of rule, Parliament and federalism, risk extinction.

Tom Darby and Peter Emberley examine the relationship of nature and convention under the Canadian constitution, observing that there are few, if any, theoretical guidelines to Canadian constitutional reform or interpretation. Nature, the traditional standard for political order, has been abandoned. Liberal constitutionalism, originally guided by theories of nature and recognizing a tension between the natural in men and the conventional, balancing the two in a political order that acknowledged limits to change, has been replaced by an unabashed conventionalism. This is the essence of the modern movement known as 'political correctness'.

Under liberal constitutionalism, nature was neither temporary nor arbitrary nor historical. This is no longer the case. Today, constitutional theory is dominated by the politics of 'language'. Human and political phenomena are seen as 'perspectives', 'discourses', or 'culture', as purely conventional and hence arbitrary, mere instruments of power. Political institutions and legal forms that are seen to be arbitrary cannot enjoy authority. This applies to constitutions. The demise of the modern liberal democratic constitution, the central feature of the nation-state, reflects the disintegration of those common or shared experiences that traditionally made up the authority of liberal constitutionalism. Darby and Emberley describe how the experience of order, which was safeguarded by the nation-state and which legitimated its practices and institutions—the free individual, limited government, the rule of law, an independent judiciary, equality of opportunity, inalienable rights, a politically independent bureaucracy—is being dissipated and with it the meaning of the practices and institutions associated with liberal democracy.

In place of these, the authors declare, a politics of resentment and a justice of pity have arisen. Political correctness targets the medium through which people engage and understand one another—language. By expurgating speech of hierarchies, opinions, judgments and the ambiguities of everyday experience, political correctness seeks to replace concrete, particular experiences with a smooth, homogenous system of communication. The new language, and the new constitutional theory that is predicated on it, attempt to alter the world by renaming it. But the new experiment is misconceived, and the proposals for reform, Darby and Emberley maintain, are moved by a spirit of revenge. With no tradition, with no transcendent view of an order of reality, in short, with no standards to guide the modern constitutional project, can the plans for social and political reform that are advocated by the new reformers, extravagantly exceeding the purposes of constitutions, amount to anything but intellectual fantasy? Darby and Emberley suggest not.

The threats to liberal constitutionalism posed by the recent trends in social and political thought are again taken up by Robert Martin in his essay investigating how the current orthodoxy in Canadian legal and social scientific research has affected constitutional debate, public policy, and our understanding of Canadian democracy.

Martin defines orthodoxy as a widely accepted body of thought that determines the limits of what and how we may think. Our orthodoxy consists of five central elements: relativism, the idea that there is no distinction between truth and falsity; subjectivity, the assumption that since there is no objective truth, what matters in intellectual inquiry is one's subjective feelings; victimology, the identification of victim status with a recognized victim group, which obviates the need to prove tangible victimization; politicization, the rendering of everything from work, to literature, to personal and family relations political, partisan, and hence susceptible to being polarized into hostile, irreconcilable camps, the consequence of which is the inhibition of rational discourse; and cynicism, the offspring of the other elements of orthodoxy, complementing them by depicting political institutions, principles, and beliefs as embodiments of oppression.

Martin examines the ways in which orthodoxy has been explicitly and implicitly applied to restrain discussion and analysis. The state and universities provide examples of the explicit application of orthodoxy. The state, for instance, often defines social truth by accepting the abstractions of orthodoxy without concrete proof or scrutiny and incorporating these into legislation. Universities, ironically vanguards of orthodoxy, contribute to the restriction of discussion and scholarship by placing formal limits on what may be said or written on campuses.

Perhaps most dangerous is the implicit application of orthodoxy to research and policy. Orthodoxy works to transform the object of research from the search for truth to establishing that one is on the right side of an issue. Martin surveys examples of legal and social scientific scholarship that bear the hallmarks of orthodoxy. Noticeably absent in such scholarship is evidence substantiating the claims made. 'Abstractions are turned into concrete reality and then acquire an intellectual status that removes them from the normal constraints of critical discourse.' Governments and professional organizations surreptitiously incorporate elements of orthodoxy into their platforms. Martin examines four reports in this regard: the CBA's Wilson Report (1993), the Jury Selection Report (1994), the Panel on Violence against Women (1993), and the Date Abuse Report (1993). All four reports, Martin maintains, are exemplary of orthodoxy. All are conceived in the spirit of orthodoxy, setting as their objectives goals that are prominent among its advocates. All use the language of orthodoxy, a language directed toward results. The Panel on Violence Against Women and the Date Abuse Report, for instance, defined 'violence' and 'abuse' so broadly as to make the conclusions of the reports virtually inevitable. The observations and recommendations of the reports also reflect orthodox methodology, relying more on the power of received opinion than on substantive proof.

Martin concludes that legal and social scientific research are important, not only to intellectual projects, but to Canadian constitutionalism and democracy. 'The way we view ourselves and our society, the way we set our public agenda, and the way we address the various items on that agenda depend very much on the research of intellectuals.' Corrupt research compromises our ability to address the legal, political, and constitutional challenges that we face. Ultimately, it may sterilize Canadian democracy.

NOTES

1 Alan C. Cairns, *Charter versus Federalism: The Dilemmas of Constitutional Reform* (Montreal and Kingston: McGill-Queen's University Press, 1992), 3–10.

2 C. Herman Pritchett, *The American Constitutional System* (Toronto: McGraw-Hill, 1976), 2.

3 Allan Bloom, 'Introduction,' in *Confronting the Constitution*, ed. Allan Bloom (Washington, D.C.: American Enterprise Institute, 1990), 1.

4 I refer to the constitution throughout in the singular, although the 'Constitution of Canada' is formally defined in section 52(2) of the *Constitution Act, 1982*, as follows:
s. 52(2) The Constitution of Canada includes
(a) the *Canada Act 1982*, including this Act;
(b) the Acts and orders referred to in the schedule; and
(c) any amendment to any Act or order referred to in paragraph (a) or (b).
For a discussion of the sources of constitutional law in Canada, see Peter W. Hogg, *Constitutional Law of Canada*, 3rd edn (Scarborough: Carswell, 1992), 3–26.

5 By 'materialism,' I mean the socialist or Marxist doctrine that the material conditions of society must be changed in such a way that wealth and power are more equitably distributed. By 'post-materialism' I mean those progressive movements that concentrate on non-material issues, such as more equality between the sexes, greater rights to minorities, a cleaner environment, and better education. Post-materialists assume a given level of prosperity and are much less concerned than materialists with economic redistribution. Nonetheless, like the materialists, they believe in a more collectivist approach to politics and tend to support greater government intervention into society and the private lives of individuals in the name of the common or public good.

6 See Harry V. Jaffa, *Crisis of the House Divided: An Interpretation of the Lincoln-Douglas Debates* (Chicago: University of Chicago Press, 1982), 10.

7 Catharine MacKinnon, *Toward a Feminist Theory of the State* (Cambridge: Harvard University Press, 1989), 162.

8 Sheila McIntyre, 'Backlash against Equality: The "Tyranny" of the "Politically Correct"', (1993) 38 *McGill L.J.* 1, at 30.

9 Ibid., 17.

10 Ibid., 29–30.

11 Ibid., 29.

12 Michael Mandel, *The Charter of Rights and the Legalization of Politics in Canada* (Toronto: Thomson Educational Publishing, 1989), 309.

13 Ibid., 3, emphasis in original.

14 Ibid., 43.

15 Ibid., 52.

16 Ibid., 57, emphasis in original.

17 Harry J. Glasbeek and Michael Mandel, 'The Legalization of Politics in Advanced Capitalism: The Canadian Charter of Rights and Freedoms', *Socialist Studies* 2 (1984): 84. For a critique of criminal law in corporate society, see Glasbeek, 'Why Corporate Deviance is Not Treated as a Crime: The Need to Make "Profits" a Dirty Word', 22 *Osgoode Hall L.J.* 393 (1984).

18 Allan Hutchinson and Andrew Petter, 'Private Rights/Public Wrongs: The Liberal Lie of the Charter', 38 *University of Toronto L.J.* 278 (1986). See also Petter, 'Immaculate Deception: The Charter's Hidden Agenda', 45 *The Advocate*, 861, and Hutchinson, 'Unions Have to Go Political after Letdown of the Charter', *Globe and Mail*, 16 April 1987.

19 Joel Bakan, 'Constitutional Interpretation and Social Change: You Can't Always Get What You Want (Nor What You Need)', 70 *Canadian Bar Rev.* 307 (1991), at 318.

20 Ibid., 318–19.

21 Joel Bakan and David Schneiderman, eds, *Social Justice and the Constitution* (Ottawa: Carleton University Press, 1992), 10.

22 See F.L. Morton and Rainer Knopff, 'The Supreme Court as Vanguard of the Intelligentsia: The Charter Movement as Postmaterialist Politics', in Janet Ajzenstat, ed., *Canadian Constitutionalism: 1791–1991* (Ottawa: Canadian Study of Parliament Group, 1992), 57.

23 In the essay referred to above, for instance, McIntyre describes the Morton and Knopff essay cited at note 22 (originally delivered at a conference in 1991), as 'mythology' ('Backlash against Equality', 12). Commenting on the difficulties of restructuring universities and their curriculum, McIntyre goes so far as to proclaim that it has been her 'experience' that 'a lot was expected by many moderates in return for their support [of educational reform]: the right to be accredited as non-sexist and non-racist—i.e. as a different breed from most men and most

whites, particularly those who publicly opposed reforms' (ibid., 20–1). Most men and most whites, particularly those who opposed the reforms McIntyre found salutary, are sexist and racist. In support of this extraordinary statement no evidence is cited other than 'experience'. That such a bald allegation could be made without substantiation is perhaps indicative of the authority that feminism enjoys among leading Canadian law journals.

24 According to the CBA, over $350,000 was spent on the Task Force on Gender Equality. Funding was provided by the CBA, the federal government, provincial law foundations, law firms, and individual contributors.

25 'Counterpoint', *Lawyers Weekly*, 30 Oct. 1992, 19.

26 Betcherman Lecture, 'Will Women Judges Really Make a Difference?'

27 *National* 3, no. 1 (Aug./Sept. 1993): 13.

28 Ibid.

29 Greg Lanning, letter to the editor, *National* 3, no. 2 (Nov./Dec. 1993): 9.

30 George F. Takach, 'Engendering Respect', interview with Cecilia Johnstone, *National* 3, no. 1 (Jan./Feb. 1994): 22.

31 Telephone conversation with Canadian Bar Association (Ottawa), 7 Sept. 1995.

32 Canadian Bar Association-Ontario, *Sections Membership Information*, 1993–4, 7.

33 Alexis de Tocqueville, *De la Démocratie en Amérique* (Paris: Garnier-Flammarion, 1981), vol. 2, 393. The translation is my own.

34 [1993] 1 S.C.R. 487.

35 [1991] 3 S.C.R. 326.

Part I

Constitutional Reform

1

A Lament for British North America

Robert Martin

When, on 26 October 1992, the Canadian people rejected the package of constitutional reforms known as the Charlottetown Accord, they may have created a historical watershed. They may have abandoned a three-decade-long national fascination with constitutional reform.[1] This was a most welcome development. It shifted public attention away from the grand abstractions of constitutional law to the mundane but concrete realities of the lives of Canadians. Such a shift was desperately needed. One can only wish, idly, that it had happened sooner, for considerable damage had already been done.

While the interminable quest for the perfect constitution distorted Canada's politics and public discourse, the most significant legal changes it spawned were the result of the enactment of the Canada Act 1982. In particular, the adoption of the Canadian Charter of Rights and Freedoms transformed our law, our politics, and our culture.[2]

I want to look at an almost unnoticed bit of constitutional reform. This was the renaming of our basic constitutional document, the British North America Act of 1867. I will set out in detail the change that was made and describe the near-universal lack of interest it elicited. My central purpose is to argue that, despite the vast attention that has been lavished on it, our constitution no longer fulfils an essential—perhaps the most essential—function of a constitution. It no longer sets out a unifying national idea. Our constitution gives scant intellectual or emotional direction in the maintenance of a peculiarly *Canadian* society.

The largest part of the chapter will be devoted to a discussion of why any of this does or should matter. I will argue that the idea of British North America once provided coherence for the Canadian state. My conclusion will be, not that we should return to British North America, but that we are a country without a recognized and accepted national idea and with little prospect of creating a fresh one.

THE CANADA ACT 1982

The Canadian constitution[3] is not a popular, not a people's, constitution. In its language and its structure, it is a lawyers' constitution. Nowhere is this more apparent than in the perversely complicated package of amendments known formally as the Canada Act 1982. This brief statute, enacted by the Parliament of the United Kingdom, has a Schedule 'A' attached to it—the Canada Act 1982 in French. Then it has a Schedule 'B'—the Constitution Act, 1982. In fact, there are two Schedules 'B'. One is the Constitution Act, 1982, in English; the other the same statute in French.

There is, in turn, a Schedule to the Constitution Act, 1982. The function of this Schedule is to give new names to a series of statutes. The first of these is the original British North America Act, 1867. It is given the title Constitution Act, 1867. Now each amendment to the British North America Act had been called a British North America Act, with the year of its passage forming part of its title. Thus, an amending statute passed in 1907 was called the British North America Act, 1907. These amending statutes are also retitled. Each is now to be called Constitution Act followed by the year of its enactment.[4] The amending statute already noted is to be styled the Constitution Act, 1907.

As of 17 April 1982, the day the Canada Act 1982 took effect, Canada ceased to be British North America.

Where did the idea of making this change come from? I have not been able to discover an answer to this question. I turned initially to two people who had been important in constitutional reform.

Barry L. Strayer, now a judge of the Federal Court of Canada, is generally regarded as having played the leading role in drafting the Canada Act 1982 and its appendices. He could not recall who originated the idea nor did he remember any discussion of it.[5]

We do know that the renaming of the British North America Act made its first official appearance in the Victoria Charter of 1971,[6] a comprehensive proposal by the Government of Canada for constitutional reform. Mark MacGuigan is also a judge of the Federal Court of Canada. In 1972, as a Member of Parliament, he co-chaired the Special Joint Committee of the Senate and House of Commons on the Constitution of Canada.[7] The Victoria Charter loomed large in the deliberations of the committee. Mr Justice MacGuigan could not recall any discussion of the question of abandoning the phrase British North America.[8] There is no specific reference to the issue in the final report of the committee.

I then turned to published sources. Once upon a time, Canadian legal literature was scanty and superficial. It is no longer scanty. There is now a particularly vast literature about the constitution and, even more particularly, about the Canada Act 1982. This literature addresses the Act's genesis, its adoption, its content and its implications. Now I cannot claim to have read all this literature, but I have read a lot of it, certainly as much as any rational human being could be expected to. I have come across only one reference to the renaming of the British North America Act. In the second edition of his treatise *Constitutional Law of Canada*, published in 1985, Peter W. Hogg observed of the new name, 'This change seems to me to smack of rewriting history.'[9] Apart from this incisive observation, none of the many commentators on our process of constitutional reform, so far as I can discover, has directly addressed the purpose or significance of our jettisoning of British North America.[10]

So why was the change made? My surmise is that it was an attempt to make the constitution appear 'more Canadian'.[11] The parliamentary committee of 1972 did allude to this general point. It opined in its report: 'The measure of the inadequacy of the British North America Act is that it does not serve Canadians fully as either a mirror of ourselves or as an inspirational ideal.'[12] The implicit suggestion is that the very phrase 'British North America' had become a relic. This suggestion is strengthened by the fact that the Schedule to the Constitution Act, 1982 which actually effected the change is given the title 'Modernization of the Constitution'. Presumably no self-respecting 'modern' constitution would dare call itself the British North America Act.

Was this the case? To answer this question we must do two things. We must attempt, first, to discover the meaning of British North America. Then we must assess whether this was an idea that could claim by 1982 to exert any force in Canada.

THE MEANING OF BRITISH NORTH AMERICA

The sense of being British North America once gave coherence to the Canadian state. It gave Canadians an understanding of why Canada existed. What was British North America? What was the content of the idea? Like all significant ideas, this one was made up of contradictory and inconsistent elements.

In part, British North America was a narrow expression of our colonial, settler origins.[13] The phrase bespoke the outpost-of-empire, 'Ready, Aye, Ready' sense of being a bit of the mother country which simply happened to be located across the Atlantic Ocean. This was a romantic, defensive understanding of the meaning of British North America. It was alienating to non-British Canadians, and it limited our ability to develop a sense of ourselves as an autonomous state. If this had been all that British North America meant, its jettisoning would, by 1982, have been long overdue.

But British North America also expressed another more positive and more inclusive notion of being Canadian. It was not so much a statement of our 'Britishness' as of our uniqueness. This had primarily to do with the shared understanding that we stood for a different way of doing things in North America. We were not, emphatically not, like our neighbours. And we knew why. Our society was not based on 'life, liberty and the pursuit of happiness'; we were not founded on the celebration of individual freedom. We had chosen, rather, 'peace, order and good government'. The individual was to be subordinated to the collective. Life was not simply to be about the acquisition of wealth by individuals. We would also have obligations towards each other.

These notions about the distinctiveness of British North America remained central throughout much of our history. George Grant, appropriately enough, summed this up in an introduction that he wrote for the 1970 edition of *Lament for a Nation*. 'Our hope lay in the belief that on the northern half of this continent we could build a community which had a stronger sense of the common good and of public order than was possible under the individualism of the American capitalist dream.'[14] The sense of having avoided the crass individualism of American life was also important to the way British North America understood itself. Enoch Padolsky noted how Frederick Philip Grove, in an influential essay written in 1929, described the United States as 'dominated by a god called "Standard of Living", ruled by a law "which bows before economic obesity", with goals of "sensual enjoyment and the so-called conquest of nature", and dominated by a "new . . . plutocracy for the enslavement of the mind and the spirit".'[15]

The idea that British North America was a 'community with a character and experience of its own'[16] had acquired form and some vigour by the middle of the nineteenth century. Canadians understood that while they were part of North America, they were, in important ways, different from Americans. They took pride in having avoided the excesses, the republican licentiousness, which they saw as characterizing the society of the United States. Chief amongst those excesses was slavery. British North America was, in its own eyes, a better and freer society.

It was understood that British North America was not 'British' in a narrow ethnic sense, but that it had two constituent elements—English-speaking Canada and French-speaking Canada. The two elements had voluntarily come together in a single state that expressed both their duality and their common determination not to be American. English-speaking Canadians were not necessarily English or British; they simply spoke English.

Our democracy was also rooted in the notion of British North America. Our conception of democracy was not the American one, which saw democracy as the reconciliation of an infinite variety of hostile and competing interests. In the Canadian conception the source of democratic government was the Crown. A special understanding of the place of the Crown was implicit in the idea of British North America. The Crown was to function as the instrument that ensured for the people the working of their democratic institutions. The Crown was also the guarantor of the French language and the distinctive culture of Quebec. Democracy was for us an organic expression of our unity.[17]

The idea of British North America self-evidently underlay the impetus towards Confederation.[18] It was a motivating factor in our expansion to the West.[19] And it would seem that by the end of the First World War the idea was firmly fixed in the Canadian psyche. Grant expressed this with his accustomed eloquence: 'Growing up in Ontario the generation of the 1920s took it for granted that they belonged to a nation. The character of the country was self-evident. To say it was British was not to deny it was North American. To be a Canadian was to be a unique species of North American.'[20]

Yet the extraordinary fact is that, insofar as I can determine, not one public voice was raised in opposition to the end of British North America.

Two people one might have expected to speak out were Eugene Forsey and Frank Scott. A long-time associate of his told me that Forsey was privately unhappy about the change but did not say anything because he concluded it would be futile to make a fuss.[21] Forsey was the author of an excellent primer on Canadian government and politics, *How Canadians Govern Themselves*.[22] In the first edition, published in 1979, he discussed the British North America Act and set out its basic structure.[23] For the 1982 second edition he referred to 'the British North America Act, 1867 (now renamed the Constitution Act, 1867)',[24] but made no comment on the change. As for Frank Scott, he did for a time act as an adviser to Pierre Trudeau during the process of constitutional change that led to the Canada Act 1982. A recent and full biography of Scott discusses this role, but makes no reference to Scott's having had any reservations about abandoning British North America.[25]

THE DECLINE OF BRITISH NORTH AMERICA

The simple and incontrovertible fact is that by 1982 British North America was an idea that no longer moved Canadians; indeed it seems it was an idea which was barely intelligible to Canadians. It is very difficult to document the gradual, but inexorable, demise of an idea. There are no mileposts to point to. One day Canada was British North America and the next it was not.

But some enlightenment can be gleaned by looking at the decline of another bit of terminology that was very much tied up with British North America. This is the word 'Dominion'.

The word is found, appropriately enough, in the original British North America Act. The Preamble speaks of 'One Dominion under the Crown', while section 3 provides for the creation of 'One Dominion under the Name of Canada'. Strictly speaking, the official name of the new country was, simply, 'Canada', but usage sanctioned 'Dominion of Canada'.[26]

The word 'Dominion' appeared in the titles of many national institutions. The national government was referred to as the 'Dominion government', especially in order to distinguish it from provincial governments. And Canada's national day was called 'Dominion Day'. Slowly the term began to disappear. In the late 1930s the government of Canada began to use 'Canada' instead of 'Dominion of Canada'. 'Dominion' was removed from the names of national institutions and gradually expunged from the statute book.[27] Both writers on constitutional law and our judges have long since abandoned 'Dominion' and now use the phrase 'federal government'.[28] And in 1982 'Dominion Day' was renamed 'Canada Day'.[29]

I presume that 'Dominion' was consigned to the same fate as 'British North America' for the same reason—it was thought to connote a colonial, less than fully independent status. Particularly in the case of 'Dominion' this seems odd, for there was a time when the phrase 'Dominion status' was a constitutional term of art used to signify an independent, self-governing Commonwealth state. This usage, in a formal sense, dates back to the Statute of Westminster of 1931.[30]

The decline in the fortunes of 'British North America' went hand in hand with the waning in the minds of Canadians of the sense of their country's uniqueness. In a recent article William Christian addressed the question why George Grant wrote *Lament for a Nation* when he did. Christian's answer was straightforward. It was that Grant had come to 'see clearly that the dream of sustaining in Canada any sort of alternative to American civilization was irrevocably extinguished'.[31] The blame, Grant saw clearly, lay with Canadians themselves and their 'having come to accept the attractiveness of modernity'.[32] Or, as, in slightly different fashion, another commentator on Grant put it: 'Canada has ceased to be a nation, not because its political existence has ended, but because its distinctive intention has ceased to be important.'[33]

For Grant the end of the Canadian dream came in 1963, when a Canadian government allowed the United States to place nuclear weapons on Canadian soil. Others say the dream died with the Ogdensburg Agreement of 1940 and Canada's acceptance of continental defence under US leadership.[34] The point, however, is not to quibble over the precise date at which one could state with certainty that both the reality and the hope of an independent Canada had ended, but simply to note the existence of a continuing and seemingly unstoppable process.

Since, by 1982, Canadians no longer understood the meaning of British North America, it probably made some sense to abolish it and, at the same time, bring our constitution into closer conformity with that of the United States.[35]

The end of British North America was also, as Peter Hogg seems to have been the only commentator to notice,[36] a milestone in the abolition, or rewriting, of our history. This has had profound effects in inducing Canadians to abandon the sense of their own uniqueness. The preferred style in universities and secondary schools is either to deny that Canada has a history or to persuade students that such history as we might have is something to be ashamed of, that our past is fundamentally flawed.[37] This perspective is starkly set out in a document called *Antiracism and Ethnocultural Equity in School Boards: Guidelines for Policy Development and Implementation* issued by the Ontario Ministry of Education in 1993: 'Much of the traditional curriculum focuses on the values, experiences, achievements and perspectives of white-European members of Canadian society and excludes or distorts those of other groups in Canada and throughout the world.'[38] The solution is obvious. School boards are required to 'develop or modify curriculum to reflect a culturally and racially diverse society'.[39] They are, in effect, directed to rewrite our past.

DOES IT MAKE ANY DIFFERENCE?

In order to answer the question whether it makes any difference, we must address an even more fundamental question. Why do states exist? The simple answer, looking at many contemporary states, is that state boundaries are an expression of ethnic or linguistic or cultural boundaries. France has the shape it does because it encompasses human beings who view themselves as French. Of course, not every person living within the boundaries of France regards himself or herself as French, nor does every such person live in France. But the fundamental raison d'être of the French state is that it is the home of the French people.

But Canada, obviously, is neither ethnically nor linguistically nor culturally homogeneous. How do such states continue to exist? States that are not ethnically homogeneous or which contain within their boundaries a number of discrete ethnic groups face profound difficulties. The disintegration of Yugoslavia and the apparently intractable ethnic warfare in Sri Lanka are but two examples amongst dozens that can be seen today in every part of the globe.

How then are multi-ethnic states to survive and even prosper? The answer is not easy to find, since there are in fact few examples of multi-ethnic states that have been successful over the long term. An obvious possibility is for one ethnic group to dominate and oppress all the others. This is not a prescription for long-term stability, as can be seen in the recent history of the former USSR and the Republic of South Africa. Another possibility is a series of alliances amongst the ostensible leaders of the various ethnic groups. In order to work, however, this approach generally demands the exclusion of the mass of the people from active participation in politics.

The question with which I began this section must be rephrased once again. How can a *democratic*, multi-ethnic state be organized? It is possible that the only such state that has succeeded is the United States. What is its secret? Obviously, generally high levels of economic development and prosperity have played their part. Nonetheless, I would argue that the success of the United States as a multi-ethnic democracy is very much a function of the power of the ideological notion that has lain at the heart of its constitution, its politics, and its culture. That notion is individual freedom. Individual freedom and the commitment to it of generations of Americans have created the ideological cement that has allowed the United States to continue as a democratic, multi-ethnic state. I make no argument either for or against individual freedom as an idea, nor do I express any opinion as to its goodness or essential meaning. My point is simply that the ideological raison d'être for the United States has been and continues to be individual freedom.

Why, then, is there a Canadian state? Why does Canada exist? Why should it continue? Canada is not ethnically homogeneous. There is no single Canadian language. The ethnic justification for the existence of a Canadian state is not available. Is there an idea that gives a foundation and a direction to the Canadian state?

The idea of British North America once provided a purpose and a justification for the Canadian state. That idea has now disappeared and no fresh idea that could take its place has appeared. And with no such unifying idea it is hard to imagine a future for the Canadian state, or at least for a multi-ethnic, democratic Canadian state. Eugene Forsey clearly understood both the power and the importance of the idea that gave coherence to the Canadian state. Referring specifically to the Crown, he said; 'Without it, there can be no Canada, at best, just a blurred, faint, unmeaning carbon copy of some other country; a thing without character and without honour.'[40]

But, it might be objected, other ideas have come along. What about 'multiculturalism'? Or what about the idea of individual rights as embodied in the Charter? It is difficult to take multiculturalism seriously as an idea. Multiculturalism was invented a quarter of a century ago as an expedient by a federal Liberal Party desperate to win votes in Toronto. As an idea to inform and unify a state it is laughably inadequate. Multiculturalism announces that Canada, or at least the formally English-speaking parts of it, has no culture. This is not much of an ideology.

What is described as multiculturalism is either trivial or impossible. If 'culture' is taken to denote nothing more than the obviously observable fact that different peoples dress differently, have different dances, and prefer different foods, then multiculturalism is trivial. If, however, 'culture' refers to fundamental ideas about being human and about how human beings should live, multiculturalism is impossible. Whichever way we use 'culture', it must be evident that multiculturalism is not an idea upon which a state can be founded.[41]

Multiculturalism does little more than affirm our commitment to moral and intellectual relativism. That is, it affirms that we stand for precisely nothing. This was made evident in the preamble to the failed Charlottetown Accord, the so-called 'Canada Clause'.[42] It is, of course, interesting that the would-be constitution makers saw a need for the statement of a national idea, but the result was so flaccid as to be utterly worthless for the purpose. The Canada Clause would have told Canadians and the world that we are firmly on the side of goodness and are swell people. The Canada Clause was precisely what one would expect in the constitution of the country that is the world leader in synchronized swimming.

Many people have argued that the Canadian Charter of Rights and Freedoms, which, it will be recalled, became part of our constitution at the same time as we ceased to be British North America, has supplied us with a new idea of what we stand for as a state. Now, to a considerable extent, at least outside Quebec, this is true. But that is the problem. The Charter is, culturally, historically, and ideologically, an American document. It exalts individual freedom and its protection through legally enforceable rights. The Charter's enthusiastic acceptance by Canadians bespeaks the degree to which we can now understand ourselves only through American ideas. It symbolizes our loss of any uniquely Canadian sense of ourselves. To the extent that the Charter does provide a unifying national idea, it is an idea that trumpets the abandonment of our autonomy and our uniqueness. I can only agree completely with what Seymour Martin Lipset, an American political scientist, wrote: 'Perhaps the most important step that Canada has taken to Americanize itself—far greater in its implications than the signing of the free trade treaty—has been the incorporation into its constitution of a bill of rights, the Charter of Rights and Freedoms.'[43]

The Charter has also played its part in encouraging us to forget our own history. Law students are unshakeably convinced of two things about the Canada that existed before the Charter. First, Canadians simply had no rights until we adopted the Charter and, second, until it got a constitutional guarantee of rights, Canada was just not a proper, respectable country.

There is no longer a Canadian idea that can give coherence to the Canadian state. There is, then, no obvious basis upon which Canada may survive as a multi-ethnic democracy. This assertion will probably be regarded as contentious in what is now more or less officially referred to, not as English-speaking Canada, but as 'the rest of Canada', but it would be seen as self-evidently true by most people in Quebec. A substantial number of Québécois now see no raison d'être for the current Canadian state. No amount of constitutional tinkering will change this.

The estrangement lies much deeper. British North America was, I have suggested, the union of two elements—English-speaking Canada and French-speaking Canada. But one element, English-speaking Canada, has largely disappeared. The reaction of the French-speaking element is to argue that there is nothing left to be united with, that with one partner dead there can no longer be a union.

Canada is not merely in a deep economic crisis. We are in an equally serious intellectual crisis. We are without a sense of why we exist.[44] This is overwhelmingly apparent in the ease with which we accepted the integration of our economy with that of the United States and the silence with which the continuing destruction of our cultural and political institutions is greeted.

CONCLUSION

I want to conclude where I began, with the Charlottetown Accord of 1992. That document manifests the two central themes of this essay—a people consciously abolishing their own history and, as a result, being left with a constitution that provides them with scant intellectual or emotional direction.

The period from mid-1990, when the Meech Lake Accord failed to be formally implemented, to the autumn of 1992, when voters rejected the Charlottetown Accord, was one of national obsession with constitutional reform. There were Parliamentary committees and legislative committees in most provinces. There were citizens' forums and a series of national conferences. There were task forces and study groups. There were articles and reports and incessant lectures on television and radio.

Throughout the process we appeared to have convinced ourselves that making a constitution was the same as going to the supermarket. We seemed to believe that nothing more was involved than choosing from an unlimited range of proffered possibilities. We acted like bedazzled consumers, filling our constitutional cart with an incoherent jumble of questionable products. The result, a result a majority of Canadians had the good sense to reject, would have been a constitution having no connection, no resonance whatsoever, with our history, our traditions, and our culture. Had the Charlottetown Accord been accepted we would have taken the final step in a process in which the elimination of British North America was a significant watershed.

It would be foolish to suggest that we return to British North America. And I would not wish for an instant to recommend new attempts at constitutional reform. It is enough to draw attention to what we have lost.

NOTES

I wish to thank Jack Granatstein, Robert Hawkins, George Kerr, and Rande Kostal for their comments on an earlier draft. This essay was the basis for the 1993 Eugene Forsey Memorial Lecture on the Constitution, delivered in Halifax on 27 November 1993.

1 The process can be said to have begun with a meeting of Attorneys-General held in Ottawa on 6 and 7 October 1960. See Anne F. Bayefsky, *Canada's Constitution Act, 1982 and Amendments: A Documentary History* (Toronto, 1989), vol. I, 1.

2 The literature on the Charter is voluminous and, by and large, credulous and uncritical. The worst book, in my opinion, is Ian Greene, *The Charter of Rights* (Toronto, 1989). The only ones worth reading are Michael Mandel, *The Charter of Rights and the Legalization of Politics in Canada*, 2nd edn (Toronto, 1994) and Rainer

Knopff and F.L. Morton, *Charter Politics* (Scarborough, 1992). For my own views, see 'The Charter and the Crisis in Canada', in David E. Smith, Peter MacKinnon, and John C. Courtney, *After Meech Lake: Lessons for the Future* (Saskatoon, 1991), 121.

3   For a discussion of what is meant by this phrase, see Peter W. Hogg, *Constitutional Law of Canada*, 3rd edn (Scarborough, 1992), 3–26.

4   This statement is not absolutely correct. A few of the statutes that had amended the British North America Act, 1867, were repealed and the British North America Act, 1949, was renamed the Newfoundland Act.

5   Telephone conversation with Mr Justice Strayer, 29 Mar. 1993.

6   For the text, see Bayefsky, *Canada's Constitution Act*, 214–22.

7   The text of the committee's report is in ibid., 224–311.

8   Telephone conversation with Mr Justice MacGuigan, 19 Apr. 1993.

9   Scarborough, 1985, 5. This observation has survived into the third edition of the book. See *Constitutional Law of Canada*, 8. Peter Hogg is originally from New Zealand.

10 I must confess that at the time I did not grasp the significance of what was being done. Indeed, I described the Schedule to the Constitution Act, 1982, as 'housekeeping provisions'. See 'Introduction', in *Socialist Studies* 2 (1984): 6.

11 Mr Justice Strayer used this phrase. See n. 5 above.

12 Bayefsky, *Canada's Constitution Act*, 230.

13 For a forceful elaboration of this point of view, see John Conway, 'Politics, Culture and the Writing of Constitutions' in Harvey L. Dyck and H. Peter Crosby, eds, *Empire and Nations: Essays in Honour of Frederic H. Soward* (Toronto, 1969), 3.

14 Ottawa, 1970, x. See the interesting discussion in H.D. Forbes, 'The Political Thought of George Grant', *Journal of Canadian Studies* 26, no. 3 (1991): 46.

15 'Grove's "Nationhood" and the European Immigrant' in *Journal of Canadian Studies* 22, no. 1 (1987): 41.

16 This phrase as well as the ideas in this paragraph come from Allan Smith, 'Old Ontario and the Emergence of a National Frame of Mind', in F.H. Armstrong, H.A. Stevenson, and J.D. Wilson, eds, *Aspects of Nineteenth Century Ontario: Essays Presented to James J. Talman* (Toronto, 1974), 194.

17 My understanding of British North America is, I confess, profoundly Tory. That is hardly surprising since British North America is, itself, a uniquely Tory idea. My understanding is drawn from the writings of George Grant, Eugene Forsey, and Frank Scott and much influenced by Charles Taylor. The unique role of the Crown is discussed in Eugene Forsey, *Freedom and Order* (Toronto, 1974), 21–72. For a different perspective on Canadian Toryism, see Peter J. Smith, 'The Ideological Origins of Canadian Confederation', *Canadian Journal of Political Science* 20, no. 1: (1987): 3 and 'Civic Humanism vs. Liberalism—Fitting the Loyalists In', *Journal of Canadian Studies* 26, no. 2 (1991): 25.

18 John A. Macdonald's speech of 6 February 1865 to the legislature of the Province of Canada in which he urged adoption of the proposals for Confederation is a

classic text for understanding the idea of British North America. He referred, in several places, to 'the best interests and present and future prosperity of British North America'. He spoke of 'people possessed of skill, education and experience in the ways of the New World' and 'ardent attachment for this, our common country'. He warned of 'the defects which time and events have shown to exist in the American Constitution' and urged his compatriots to choose instead 'British laws, British connection, and British freedom' as well as to ensure that 'the rights of minorities are safeguarded'. *Parliamentary Debates on the Subject of the Confederation of the British North American Provinces* (Quebec, 1865), 25–45.

19 See Doug Owram, *Promise of Eden: The Canadian Expansionist Movement and the Idea of the West, 1856–1900,* (Toronto, 1980).

20 *Lament for a Nation* (Toronto, 1965), 3.

21 Telephone conversation with Graham Eglington, 20 May 1993.

22 *How Canadians Govern Themselves*, 1st edn, Ottawa, 1979; 2nd edn, Ottawa, 1982.

23 Ibid., 1st edn, 10–12.

24 Ibid., 2nd edn, 9.

25 Sandra Djwa, *The Politics of the Imagination: A Life of F.R. Scott* (Toronto, 1987), 429–37. Scott believed that the B.N.A. Act implied, by its nature, a degree of subordination between Canada and the U.K. and that this should be remedied by what he called repatriation. He did warn, however, against 'repatriation' 'at any price'. See Frank R. Scott, *Essays on the Constitution: Aspects of Canadian Law and Politics* (Toronto, 1977), 402.

26 Although the phrase does appear in legislation. See, for example, sections 3 and 5 of the British North America Act, 1871.

27 As far as I can tell, the only statute that still uses the word is the Dominion Controverted Elections Act, R.S.C. 1985, c. C-28. Despite its title, the Act is indexed under 'C' in the current revision of the statutes.

28 See the interesting discussion in Hogg, *Constitutional Law of Canada*, 3rd edn, 104–5. Early editions of Bora Laskin's *Canadian Constitutional Law* used 'Dominion' without any evident shame or embarrassment. See, for example, 2nd edn (Toronto, 1960), 30–7. Scott was not enthusiastic about either the term or the status. See *Essays on the Constitution*, 157.

29 See Holidays Act, R.S.C. 1985, c. H-5, s. 2. There was considerable controversy surrounding the passage of the amendment to the Holidays Act, R.S.C. 1970, c. H-7, which effected the change. In the first place this was a private member's bill, one of the very few ever to find its way into law. In the second place, it appears there were only 13 members present in the House of Commons when the motion to read the bill for a third time was adopted. The quorum in the House of Commons is 20. (Constitution Act, 1867, s. 48.) Further, only a few minutes were devoted to consideration of the bill by the House. And, finally, there was a lengthy and acrimonious debate about the bill in the Senate, a debate in which some Senators tried, without success, to discover why a private member's bill was being pushed through Parliament with such haste, particularly when an earlier government bill to the same effect had been tabled. In the Senate, at least, there was a full debate over the desirability of making the change. A Senator who favoured 'Canada Day' observed, 'History is not a stagnant pool.' (Canada, *Debates of the*

Senate, First Session, Thirty-Second Parliament, vol. IV, 22 July 1982, p. 4668.) A different view of history was advanced by a Senator who wished to retain 'Dominion Day': 'I am saddened that it seems so easy for people to cast aside, and to allow others to cast aside, our glorious history.' (Ibid., 27 July 1982, p. 4685.)

30 See the discussion in S.A. deSmith, *The New Commonwealth and Its Constitutions* (London, 1964), 1–13.

31 'George Grant's Lament', *Queen's Quarterly* 100, no. 1 (1993): 206.

32 Ibid., 210.

33 H.D. Forbes, *Political Thought*. 50.

34 See J.L. Granatstein, *How Britain's Weakness Forced Canada into the Arms of the United States* (Toronto, 1989).

35 Some commentators contrived not to understand that this was happening. See, for example, D. Smiley, 'A Dangerous Deed: The Constitution Act, 1982' and R. Whitaker, 'Democracy and the Canadian Constitution', in Keith Banting and Richard Simeon, eds, *And No-one Cheered* (Toronto, 1982). Others, however, did understand. See Ronald I. Cheffins and Patricia A. Johnson, *The Revised Canadian Constitution: Politics as Law* (Toronto, 1986), 145–56.

36 See n. 9 above.

37 See my article, 'How I Lost My Father—Twice', *The Globe and Mail*, 11 Nov. 1991. In a very similar vein, see T. Dan Gardner, 'A Vanishing War,' *The Globe and Mail*, 3 May 1995. The most egregious manifestation yet of this fashion is Alvin Finkel and Margaret Conrad with Veronica Strong-Boag, *History of the Canadian Peoples*, 2 vols. (Mississauga, 1993).

38 Toronto, 1993, 13.

39 Ibid., 14.

40 Forsey, *Freedom and Order*, 49.

41 For a systematic critique of multiculturalism and an account of the dangers which it contains, see Neil Bissoondath, *Selling Illusions: The Cult of Multiculturalism in Canada* (Toronto, 1994).

42 The Canada Clause would have been added as part of a new section 2 of the Constitution Act, 1867. The following would have become some of our 'fundamental characteristics'.
e. Canadians are committed to racial and ethnic equality in a society that includes citizens from many lands who have contributed and continue to contribute, to the building of a strong Canada that reflects its cultural and racial diversity;
f. Canadians are committed to a respect for individual and collective human rights and freedoms of all people;
Consensus Report on the Constitution: Final Text, Charlottetown, 28 Aug. 1992, 1. First prize in the vacuity sweepstakes must go to the proposal put forward in 1992 by the Government of Ontario. Its suggested 'Canada Clause' would have advocated 'democratic participation by all Canadians, whatever their race, gender, religion, culture, or physical or mental disability; and concern for the well-being of all Canadians' as well as 'respect for the diversity of individuals, groups and communities'. Legislative Assembly, Select Committee on Ontario in Confederation, *Final Report*, Toronto, 1992, 10.

43 Seymour Martin Lipset, *Continental Divide: The Values and Institutions of the United States and Canada* (New York, 1992), 225.

44 This question is explored in two recent works: William Kaplan, ed., *Belonging: The Meaning and Future of Canadian Citizenship* (Montreal and Kingston, 1993) and Leslie A. Pal, *Interests of State: The Politics of Language, Multiculturalism, and Feminism in Canada* (Montreal and Kingston), 1993.

2

Trudeau's Moral Vision

H.D. Forbes

The universal and homogeneous state is the pinnacle of political striving.

George Grant, *Lament for a Nation*

Pierre Elliott Trudeau was surely one of the most thoughtful and articulate prime ministers Canada has ever had. He belongs to the small class of truly memorable Canadian leaders. He combined great practical achievements—as great as those of Laurier or Borden—with a more theoretical or philosophic cast of mind. It is surprising, then, to find him, in his recent *Memoirs*, showing so little interest in questions of a theoretical or philosophic character.[1] One might have expected him, in good health and with the leisure of retirement, to reflect on the meaning of what he did in office and to lay it before his readers in general terms, linking it to mankind's long tradition of thought about politics. What one finds, in fact, is an abundance of photographs and personal details but a poverty of general discussion. There is something very Canadian about such intellectual modesty (and such delight in being seen in the company of celebrities), but it is disappointing, and it invites this attempt to spell out the good implicit in the deeds he describes.

Reflection on Trudeau's career is inseparable for me from a certain nostalgia. I was in my early twenties when Trudeau stepped onto the national stage, and for me, he was the intellectual in politics. He had achieved high office without sacrificing his personal or intellectual independence. He offered a far more principled, intelligent, generous, and progressive response to the challenges of the time than did any of his rivals. He represented, for me, the real end of the Diefenbaker era. Wishful longing to return to an earlier time, or vague regrets about 'historical might-have-beens', may have no place in the life of a rational man, as Trudeau sometimes says, but in the interpretation of the past they should be given some weight. The realities of the present (and the past) are certainly a clue to the meaning of Trudeau's career, but the hopes that accompanied his rise to power are also important. Political leaders deal in dreams as well as realities.

Interpretation is a difficult art, though perhaps it deserves a larger place in political science than do the methods of the sciences proper. It aims to understand events, not by subsuming them under laws or principles of causation, but by clarifying the purposes or intentions they expressed. Purposes and intentions are of course always somewhat hidden; unconscious thoughts and motives are hidden even from introspection. The interpreter must try to find a meaningful pattern in a host of external details. An acceptable pattern must make sense as a whole and must fit the details. The task is like that of understanding a difficult text: starting from some assumption about the author's intentions, one examines its details, passing back and forth between parts and the whole and gradually refining one's preconceptions, as one pays closer and closer attention to what the author has actually said. The interpretation of politics is especially difficult because of the part that deliberate dissembling plays in it. If too much is taken at face value the result may be superficiality, but too much probing beneath the surface may reveal only the ingenuity (or paranoia) of the interpreter.

EARLY WRITINGS

Any interpretation of Trudeau's politics must begin from what he wrote between 1950 and 1965. He first revealed himself to the public through these writings, which became the foundation of his political career. Recognizing this, biographers and other writers have quite properly given them more attention than Trudeau does in his *Memoirs*. They have tended to follow the lead of Gérard Pelletier, who saw in them 'a genuine theory of politics—that is, a complete and coherent system of responses based on a clear conception of men and society', the result of 'an entire lifetime of study and meditation'.[2]

The issue here is not the value of Trudeau's contributions to political theory. There is no need to debate what is implied by his neglect of his own achievements in this realm. The issue is rather the completeness and explicitness of his 'system'. It is only a short step from Pelletier's view of Trudeau as a political theorist or philosopher to George Radwanski's view of him as a politician who operated 'not by instinct or improvisation, but by constant reference to an elaborate philosophical framework'.[3] If this were true, Trudeau's actions in the 1970s and 1980s could be understood by referring them back to the principles he elaborated in the 1950s and 1960s. But this rule of interpretation is in fact unhelpful where one might expect it to be the most use.

Consider for example the confusing twists and turns of Trudeau's economic policies in the mid-1970s. Some commentators say that Trudeau must be understood as a liberal: he put the rights of the individual above social or collective goals. Others hold that Trudeau was really a socialist: he believed that planning should replace the market, because social justice should take priority over individual rights. In practice, Trudeau seems to have been of two minds, flipping and flopping between liberalism and socialism. Can Trudeau's early writings be used to sort out the confusion? One might well expect that a system of political theory drawn up in the middle years of the twentieth century, after a lifetime of study and meditation, would deal with the broad question, long disputed, of liberalism versus socialism. Admittedly, even in the 1950s some writers were proclaiming the end of ideology or the end of history. Yet there remained a few true believers in the rival ideologies. But in Trudeau's writings, despite numerous indications of his sympathy for socialism, one cannot find any coherent discussion of the relevant issues.[4]

The absence of a theory about markets and planning, or about the rights of private property as against the claims of the state, or about classes and individuals, is part of a larger gap. Judging from his early writings, Trudeau is a liberal (or socialist) without any clear theory of rights of any kind. This is especially noteworthy since so much of his political practice before and after 1965 focused on the defence of rights. But what exactly are rights? Are they natural or man-made? Discovered or created? How can they be defined and defended? Do we know what they are independently of what the political authorities tell us, or do we have to wait until they speak before we can know what they are? (Do we perhaps have only such rights as they deign to give us?) Which authorities? How do nurses compare with engineers as authorities? Where do lawyers stand on the scale of relevant expertise? These are important, difficult questions, much discussed over the years. Trudeau's early writings, however, leave the impression that there is nothing controversial among men of good will about either the nature or the definition of rights. Rights exist; they are a good thing; the more the better.

The same is true, more or less, of 'democracy'. Trudeau evidently thought it was a good thing, like good government. Quebec apparently needed more of it. But more of what exactly? Why is more democracy better than less? Would it mean more majority rule or more minority rights? More popular participation in politics or more expertise among politicians?

Trudeau's silence about democracy is more surprising than his silence about rights. Regarding rights, perhaps all that can be said was said long ago. Questions about their nature and scope were hotly debated two or three centuries ago. Since then rights have had a much higher status in practical politics than in its theory. Today there is a lot of discussion of legal rights, but little of moral or natural rights, and Trudeau's silence is in no way remarkable. With respect to democracy, however, the situation is different. The 'psychology' and 'sociology' of modern democracy have been under intense scrutiny for more than a century. There is a vast recent literature on conformism and individualism, the apathy and ignorance of mass electorates, political parties, propaganda, false consciousness, interest groups, power élites, bureaucracy, the iron law of oligarchy, the role of the press or the media, voting cycles, systems of representation and methods of voting, and so on. The attacks on parliamentary democracy from both left and right have evoked thoughtful discussions of its fundamental principles as well as dogmatic defences. But there is only the faintest echo of all this in what Trudeau wrote between 1950 and 1965.

The topic on which Trudeau had the most to say in his early writings was clearly nationalism. In the background was the French-Canadian nationalism, leaning towards separatism, that flourished in the 1930s under the tutelage of Abbé Groulx. It appealed to a 'principle of nationalities' that had become important in European politics in the nineteenth century and that had been used in redrawing the map of the continent after the First World War. Just as Poland and Italy were nations that should be states, so was French Canada or Quebec, the nationalists said. Justice demanded that French Canadians be released from their bondage and allowed to take their rightful place in the fellowship of peoples. Trudeau always seems to have taken this argument seriously (as if it went to the root of his being), but he has never shown much sympathy for it. His most substantial contribution to the literature of Canadian politics, 'Quebec on the Eve of the Asbestos Strike' (his 90-page introduction to *La Grève de l'amiante*), mercilessly analyses the social context and intellectual affinities of this nationalism, concluding that it is essentially an escapism, compounded of weakness, nostalgia, and resentment.[5] Between the 1930s and the 1960s separatist nationalism seemed to change its ideological stripes, but perhaps not its spots. A little more than half of *Federalism and the French Canadians* consists of Trudeau's briefs and articles against the new separatist nationalism of the early 1960s. The book ends with the following declaration: 'Separatism a revolution? My eye. A counter-revolution; the national-socialist counter-revolution.'

Trudeau's broader objections to the principle of nationalities are similar to those of Lord Acton.[6] He condemns it as both impractical and undesirable. It is impractical because (1) there is no objective standard of nationality, no generally accepted way of determining which ethnic groups should count as nations, and because (2) the members of different ethnic groups are more and more living interspersed on common territories, so that it is less and less possible to draw any 'boundaries' between them. Any attempt to apply the principle of nationalities creates more problems than it solves. If Quebec can assert a right of self-determination, why not Westmount (or New Quebec)? Ethnically homogeneous states would be undesirable (even if they could be created without provoking severe conflicts) because they would put the natural or physical bonds of race or nationality above the ethical duties of citizenship, and because they would lack the protections for liberty and the incentives for progress that a diverse and divided population provides.[7] Nationalism is not only dangerous in practice, it is retrograde in principle. These objections, which Trudeau levelled at Quebec separatists, are the same that Lord Acton had used against Irish nationalists a century earlier.

Like Acton, Trudeau favours federalism as the best political framework for a diverse people. Federalism permits different institutions on different territories and can thus take into account some of the reasoning about ethnicity and politics that underlies the principle of nationalities:

> It is obviously impossible, as well as undesirable, to reach unanimity on all things. . . . The federal state . . . deliberately reduces the national consensus to the greatest common denominator between the various groups composing the nation. . . . When national consensus on all things is not desirable or cannot readily obtain, the area of consensus is reduced in order that consensus on some things be reached.[8]

Thus the French in Quebec can have one set of laws, which they prefer, while the English elsewhere can have another set, more to their taste. Policy making with minimal cultural or ethnic content can be put in the hands of the central government, while provincial governments can exercise jurisdiction over policies relating to cultural development. Quebec can thus provide itself with the institutions it needs to express its national characteristics without (it seems) provoking any bitter conflicts or violating any basic rights of others. But how can this be achieved in practice? Which rights are to be regarded as basic, for example, and how should a province be permitted to assert its cultural distinctiveness? Apart from endorsing 'balance' and 'efficiency', Trudeau says almost nothing about the division of powers in Canada or elsewhere.

The great difference between ethnically distinct provinces or states within a federal structure and sovereign nation-states is, of course, the location of sovereignty. In the former case, 'coercive authority over the entire territory remains a monopoly of the (central) state.'[9] There is no comparable general coercive authority in the world of nation-states. Would mankind be better off if there were such an authority? Many in this century have thought so. In the 1940s and 1950s, in particular, there was a good deal of discussion of 'union now' and 'world peace through world law'. From time to time in his early writings, Trudeau seems to endorse world federalism, but he gives scarcely any attention (no more than Acton did) to the complex arguments for and against imperialism and a world state.

THOUGHT AND ACTION

Many people who write about politics, like those who practise it by holding office, downplay the importance of 'ideas'. The abstruse reasoning of political theorists they think can be safely ignored. Only simple, widely shared ideas can have any influence on democratic politics.[10] Of course, some *scientific*

theories constructed to account for observations and to predict future observations—for example, the theories of Einstein or Keynes—sometimes have
an impact. But hot air about 'values' has none. With regard to 'themes' like
'the absolute value of the individual' or 'the supremacy of rationality', the only
important thing is not to shock the bourgeois.[11] Trudeau no more became a
politician by immersing himself in the study of political theory or political
science than Seinfeld learned his trade by reading scientific treatises on
humour. Political leadership has more to do with talent and inspiration than
with 'logic' (that is, explicit reasoning about theories and ideals).

This view raises difficult questions about the relations between theory and
practice generally, not just in contemporary democratic politics. With regard
to Trudeau specifically, it raises interesting questions about the sources of his
electoral appeal and his authority among his colleagues. For example, how
much weight should be put on the sexual revolution of the 1960s and his
sexual mystique?

Against this background, it would be easy to misunderstand the point of
the previous section. I have not been arguing that Trudeau's *ideas* are irrelevant, but only that his writings have limited value for determining what his
ideas were. To say that Trudeau did not first work out a set of principles (in
theory) and then apply them (in practice) is not to say that he lacked principles altogether. Nor is it to say that his early writings shed no light on the
principles implicit in his practice. They show, for example, some of his reasons for thinking that bilingualism and an entrenched bill of rights would be
the best remedies for Canada's constitutional ills—a position he was defending before he decided to seek election to Parliament as a Liberal. They reveal,
more generally, that he regarded nationalism as more interesting and important than socialism—an insight that put him far ahead of most of the theory
class. Finally, they contain some references to 'polyethnic pluralism' that, I
shall argue below, are an important clue to his political thought. But to
understand this thought, one must look mainly at his practice, especially with
respect to constitutional questions. With respect to the economy, despite his
tendency to lean left, I would argue that he was mostly improvising, preach-
ing the market one day and controls the next, as economic circumstances
changed, and with them, the winds of public opinion. The same may be true
of foreign policy.[12] But with respect to the constitution, there seems to be a
theory implicit in his practice that is worth making explicit, for contemplation by theorists.

THE CHARTER

All agree that Trudeau's greatest achievement was constitutional reform. He
writes about it with justifiable pride in his *Memoirs*. 'I gave Quebec, and all
the rest of Canada, a new made-in-Canada constitution, with a new amending formula and a new charter of rights.'[13] For years he had fought for the

changes he was eventually able to make. The last stages of negotiation had required some very hard bargaining indeed to overcome the resistance among the provincial politicians to his 'people's package', but in the end, 'a national constituency had been created in favour of the charter, and that was as it should be.'[14] Poets and writers now have a solution to the old problem of the Canadian identity. 'With the charter in place, we can now say that Canada is a society where all people are equal and where they share some fundamental values based upon freedom.'[15]

The Charter is in most respects like any bill of rights. It declares that there are certain basic rights of citizens that the courts can uphold against legislative or administrative encroachments. It gives Canada a modern 'separation of powers' like that pioneered by the United States. It thus 'legalizes' politics: it gives lawyers and judges a larger role in the political process. In principle, they no longer just interpret and apply the laws passed by Parliament and the provincial legislatures: they also sit in judgement over them. It changes Canada's 'political culture' by encouraging talk about 'rights' and 'the constitution' and discouraging appeals to 'majority opinion'. Its purpose is undoubtedly to check and limit the 'populism' of democracy. It reduces the importance of popular participation in electoral and legislative politics, while elevating that of litigation and 'court challenges'.

Several important features distinguish Trudeau's Charter from other bills of rights, most notably, section 33, which preserves the form and some of the substance of parliamentary supremacy. The ingenuity shown in drafting 'this mealy-mouthed "notwithstanding" clause' was apparently the key to the acceptance of the Charter by seven of the infamous 'Gang of Eight'.[16] Among the Charter's other distinctive features, perhaps the most important are its provisions respecting official languages. Sections 16–23 'constitutionalize' the language policies Trudeau adopted in 1969 (of which more below). The resulting 'language rights' are not among those traditionally seen as 'basic rights that cannot be taken away by any government', nor do they lend themselves to illustrating the idea that 'all people are equal'.[17] The total silence of the Charter about property rights—which have traditionally been counted among the most important individual rights needing protection from government—is another interesting feature.[18] The most modern part of the Charter is section 15, which protects 'equality rights'. Section 15(1) flatly prohibits 'discrimination', especially 'discrimination based on race, national or ethnic origin, colour, religion, sex, age or mental or physical disability'. Section 15(2) permits discrimination on these prohibited grounds provided its purpose is to ameliorate the condition of otherwise 'disadvantaged' individuals or groups. Section 1 declares that the 'rights and freedoms' of Canadians, basic or otherwise, are in principle subordinate to the laws and policies needed 'in a free and democratic society'. This section makes explicit what was implicit in Trudeau's silence about rights noted earlier: the concept of 'rights' is a philosophical nullity. In developing a jurisprudence of rights, judges should not squint at rights, but rather focus on the requirements of freedom and democracy. Section 27 advises them to exercise their discretion in such a way as to preserve and enhance 'the multicultural heritage of Canadians'.

The important question for present purposes is not how the Charter has in fact been used so far, but rather how Trudeau intended it to be used. Clearly it shifts power from elected politicians to top-flight lawyers, law professors, and judges. It instructs them to consider a wider range of complaints and to try to resolve them by balancing various traditional rights against the need to create a truly free and democratic society. In particular, it instructs them to do what they can to elevate the status of 'identifiable' groups (the groups on the 'disadvantaged' side of the prohibited distinctions having to do with race, national or ethnic origin, and so on). The Charter thus helps to clarify and impose a new definition of Canada, unlike any imagined by those poets and writers like Blair Fraser who 50 years ago went on 'the search for identity'. In principle, Canada is now a country where individuals from a wide range of backgrounds meet and mingle on a footing of equality supervised by the judiciary.

OFFICIAL BILINGUALISM

Trudeau's second great achievement was official bilingualism. Something like the Official Languages Act of 1969 was obviously needed when he became Prime Minister, but the opposition to it was formidable. The need had been made clear by the rapid growth of separatist nationalism after 1959. If something was not done to alter the status of French in Canada, it seemed clear that the separatists would soon have the support of most Quebeckers. The need was made clearer still, and an expectation of reform was nourished, by the appointment of the Royal Commission on Bilingualism and Biculturalism in 1963. Its research showed how meagre in practice were the language rights guaranteed by the British North America Act of 1867. The commission's recommendations formed the basis for the Official Languages Act drawn up by Trudeau. The aim of the Act is simple enough to state and hard to oppose: English and French should have equal official status, so that francophone Canadians will generally be able to communicate in their own language with the federal government and its agencies. The details of the Act, being details, are also hard to oppose. But as Trudeau points out in his *Memoirs*, 'you don't overturn the habits of a lifetime without drawing some hostile fire.'[19]

During Trudeau's years in office, 'bilingualism' was the great symbol of the new conception of Canada he represented. The root of the immediate political problem was a question of status. The superiority of English to French, some thought, had been established long ago by Wolfe and Wellington and confirmed more recently by the inability of the French to stand up to the Germans. The linguistic difference was also, broadly speaking, a religious and political difference: English was Protestant, while French was Catholic. For many, Protestantism meant freedom, enlightenment, and progress, while Catholicism meant superstition, submission to authority, and stagnation. Official equality for the English and French languages meant treating those who had previously been regarded as naturally (or culturally) inferior, the French, as if they were equal. It meant abandoning the idea that the French in Canada would one day all be 'English'—free, rational, progressive, 'Protestant' individuals, more or less indistinguishable from the English-speaking majority. No longer could anglophones insist with a good conscience on speaking English to francophones (knowing that they were helping them to practise their English). Trudeau's new order was hard to oppose in principle (the English, after all, were in the habit of claiming equality as an *English* principle), and the real source of irritation could not be found in the details of the Official Languages Act. Its opponents were reduced to fulminating about vague conspiracies to 'force French down the throat of every farmer in western Canada'.[20]

The Act has had a great impact on Canadian life. Billions have been spent on bilingualism, and the look of the country has been changed, from its cereal boxes to its airports. The farmers in Alberta may not be speaking French, but more of the civil servants in Ottawa are. The Act has been an affirmative-action program for French Canadians in the federal civil service. The principle of equality it represents has had effects on education wherever parents think of careers in the civil service for their children and wherever they want to show their support for the principle of equality.[21] Party politics has been transformed. Since Joe Clark replaced Robert Stanfield, the leaders of all the major national parties have been more or less bilingual. Only the strength of the Reform Party suggests the importance of the continuing opposition to official bilingualism in English Canada.

The main question here is not whether Trudeau's policy has solved the problem it was meant to solve. It surely helped to ward off separation for the better part of a generation, but it seems not to have overcome the 'two solitudes'—the great barrier to friendly meeting and mingling created by the historic inequality between English and French. Perhaps no policy can quickly overcome rifts in society of this sort, or perhaps some other policy, stressing territory more than individual rights, might have worked better. But the question here has to do with the interpretation of Trudeau's intentions. What does the policy he promoted reveal about his understanding of the nature or purpose of Canada and the principles that should govern its political life?

Trudeau's policy stressed the right of the individual to receive services from the federal government in the official language of his or her choice.[22] It tried to resolve the conflict between English and French (and defeat separatism) by defining individual language rights that are in principle unrelated to territory. One's fundamental rights should not depend on where one lives. The whole 'separatist' approach to problems of language and culture should be rejected: Canada's problems cannot be solved by creating two linguistic ghettos, French in Quebec and English elsewhere, because that would just foster bigotry and put off the day of reckoning. A country like Canada can survive only if it can ensure that all its citizens feel at home everywhere on its territory.[23] The way to do this is to give them all equal rights and to provide effective guarantees for these rights, which are the same everywhere.

The individual rights in question here are clearly not 'natural rights' in the sense that, say, freedom of opinion or freedom of expression may be regarded as natural rights. The right to fill out one's income tax form and to buy a stamp in the official language of one's choice are not rights that individuals can easily be imagined exercising in the state of nature or worrying much about in the original position. They flow from a policy; the policy serves the end of *Canadian* unity; and it does not treat all languages equally. (If a Spanish-speaking immigrant to Canada were to assert a *natural* right to the language of his or her choice, it would presumably be a demand for laws, stamps, and other services in Spanish, not French or English.) If the rights in question have any source beyond the policy—any grounding better than the will of those in power—then it must be found in some theory about the rights of distinct national or cultural groups. As already noted, there is no such theory in Trudeau's writings about nationalism. (Would mankind benefit, as Mazzini argued, if Italian culture were allowed to blossom without Austrian supervision and pruning? Neither Acton nor Trudeau faces this question.) Trudeau says nothing relevant about the rights of conquerors or of founding peoples or of superior cultures (like those of Shakespeare and Molière, or Mozart and Verdi, and so on), nor even about diversity itself. He stresses the threat of nationalism to individual rights, not the derivation of these rights from nationalism.

MULTICULTURALISM

Bilingualism brought in its train, both practically and theoretically, multiculturalism, which is not generally regarded as one of Trudeau's great achievements. In fact, he does not even mention it in his *Memoirs*, despite its being an integral part of his constitutional politics.[24]

As already explained, 'bilingualism' had to do with a problem of the relative status of English and French: were they really to be equal in status (as one reading of the British North America Act required), or was French to be gradually lowered and English raised (as another reading suggested)? 'English' and 'French' here refer to nationalities as well as languages. Were the two nationalities to be equal as 'founding races' or was one to be superior to the other? Having opted for equality ('bilingualism'), the government could not very well avoid the question of the status of the other nationalities in Canada. For example, what about the Scots? Were the cousins and descendants of John Strachan, William Lyon Mackenzie, and John A. Macdonald to meet the English and the French on a footing of equality or were they to be treated as inferiors? The question was put on the political agenda by the title and terms of reference of the Royal Commission on Bilingualism and Biculturalism. This commission produced a clearly focused and politically important demand for 'multiculturalism'.

In 1970 the commission published Volume 4 of its *Report*, entitled 'The Cultural Contributions of the Other Ethnic Groups'. Some response was required from the federal government. In October 1971, Trudeau declared in the House of Commons that 'although there are two official languages, there is no official culture, nor does any ethnic group take precedence over any other.' The government had to have a common cultural policy for all Canadians, he said, but it had to be one that recognized their equality, while helping to break down discriminatory attitudes and cultural jealousies. 'A policy of multiculturalism within a bilingual framework commends itself to the government as the most suitable means of assuring the cultural freedom of Canadians.'[25]

From the beginning there has been a strong tendency among many Canadians to deride Trudeau's policy of multiculturalism. It has clearly been too much for some and too little for others. Indeed, there seems to be a disparity between Trudeau's rather grandiose declarations ('cultural pluralism is the very essence of Canadian identity' and 'every ethnic group has the right to preserve and develop its own culture and values within the Canadian context') and the very modest subsidies he was prepared to provide for the cultural activities of 'the other ethnic groups'. His policy could be dismissed as a 'sop to ethnics'—merely a cheap attempt to buy their votes. Central and eastern Europeans, in particular, who had been the most offended by the B and B Commission, with its talk of 'two founding races' and its emphasis on French Canadians, were not mollified. They were alienated by Trudeau's efforts at *rapprochement* with the Soviet Union (unlike the staunch anti-communism of John Diefenbaker); they disliked Trudeau's language policies; and they dismissed 'his efforts at multiculturalism as halfhearted and insincere'.[26] Those who wanted a meatier multiculturalism (for example, recognition of Ukrainian as an official language) could thus join with those who dreaded the prospect in nervously laughing Trudeau's modest proposals out of court.

All would now agree, however, that multiculturalism (whatever it may mean) has become an important part of the Canadian identity.[27] At the very least, Trudeau's statement popularized a neologism and changed Canada's 'symbolic politics'. It raised 'diversity' even higher in Canada's pantheon of values. Canadians today are even more inclined than they were a generation ago to find Canada's unity in its respect for diversity. Like Northrop Frye, they tend to oppose real unity (in diversity) to mere uniformity. 'Uniformity, where everyone "belongs", uses the same clichés, thinks alike and behaves alike, produces a society which seems comfortable at first but is totally lacking in human dignity. Real unity tolerates dissent and rejoices in variety of outlook and tradition, recognizes that it is man's destiny to unite and not divide . . . Unity, so understood, is the extra dimension that raises the sense of belonging into genuine human life.'[28]

Now a city or country populated by intellectual or genetic clones of one individual, however eminent, might trumpet its devotion to diversity, but it would lack the raw materials, so to speak, for a truly diverse society. For that, people of different ethnic or cultural backgrounds are needed. The supply of them, in a country like Canada, is mainly regulated by immigration policy. An important change in that policy took place in the 1960s, just before Trudeau became Prime Minister. In 1966 and 1967 his friend and mentor, Jean Marchand, made changes in the immigration regulations and administrative practices of the Department of Manpower and Immigration that greatly diversified the flow of immigrants into Canada.[29] Most immigrants now come from 'non-traditional sources', in other words, from Asia, Africa, and the Caribbean. The results are now clearly visible in cities like Toronto, Montreal, and Vancouver. Trudeau's greatest contribution to the building of a truly multicultural Canada (and not just a more Ukrainian one) may have been the support he gave this policy, in action if not in words. But the statement he made in 1971, defining Canada as a multicultural country, helped to ward off criticism from others. Immigration, always a difficult topic to discuss in a country like Canada, became one that intelligent and responsible people of good will avoided altogether, except to repeat a few clichés about the value of diversity.

A second important effect of Trudeau's official multiculturalism was to increase acceptance of the idea that government action is needed to overcome 'cultural barriers' to the full participation of some cultural groups in Canadian society:

> A policy of multiculturalism within a bilingual framework is basically the conscious support of individual freedom of choice. We are free to be ourselves. But this cannot be left to chance. It must be fostered and pursued actively. If freedom of choice is in danger for some ethnic groups, it is in danger for all. It is the policy of this government to eliminate any such danger and to 'safeguard' this freedom.[30]

The policy recognized, in effect, that the liberal idea of individual rights and a limited state was no more satisfactory for 'culture' than it was for 'language'.[31] Peaceful diversity requires a more active role for the state in society.

One purpose of the Official Languages Act was to counter the 'social' pressures to learn English associated with a linguistic regime of *laissez-faire, laissez-passer*. Unless the federal government could reduce and regulate these pressures in a satisfactory way, the French in Quebec would naturally seek independence, and Canada would be involved in a potentially nasty political divorce.[32] Similarly, 'culture' has an unavoidable public dimension, and the private or social pressures for cultural assimilation can be at least as great as those for linguistic assimilation.[33] As with language, so with culture: the process of assimilation tends to be associated with arrogance on one side and resentment on the other—emotions that are sometimes expressed in nasty political forms (ethnic chauvinism, xenophobia, bigotry, prejudice, discrimination, alienation, lawlessness, terrorism, and so on). If Canadians of many different ethnic backgrounds were to meet and mingle peacefully on a footing of equality, Canadian governments would have to make deliberate efforts to ensure that all relevant cultures received proper official recognition and that the process of assimilation (better called 'integration') did not leave any of them feeling demeaned and degraded. They would have to ensure that the institutions of society were truly 'representative'. They would have to teach tolerance more actively, monitor tensions, and be prepared to nip any serious conflicts in the bud.[34] In short, they would have to have some multicultural *policies*. Trudeau's statement was the formal, official recognition of this new need.

Trudeau's statement and his policy do not deserve the derision they have received, nor should he have kept silent about them in his *Memoirs*. They were not just a short-sighted bit of electoral politicking, an unsuccessful attempt to win the West for the Liberals. They did far more than sprinkle a few million dollars on folk dancers in church basements. They clarified the Canadian identity, provided a framework or foundation for a new immigration policy, and marked an important step in developing a new technology of tolerance. There was nothing obviously fanciful or extravagant in Trudeau's vision of a multicultural society. He never advocated absolute equality of status for absolutely all cultures (such as medicare billing numbers for witch doctors). His policy had to do with 'culture'—food, clothing, gods, puppets, dancing, and so on—not 'technology', where there is a real better and worse. Strict equality even of 'cultures' was less important than finding something to celebrate in each. With respect to individual rights and limited government, his policy rested on the same foundations as the Official Languages Act. It had deep roots, not just in Canadian politics, but in the English and other political traditions.

PLURALISM AND TOLERANCE

Interpretation is like connecting unnumbered dots to form a picture. Since there are no numbers, there is no definitely right or wrong picture, but some are better than others—some may be more pleasing or useful, while others may connect all the dots in a more natural way. Interpretation always risks creating patterns where none really exist—like seeing rabbits or elephants in clouds. In the case of Trudeau, however, there does seem to be a pattern to his politics. He had a vision, at least in the sense of an overall goal or a notion of what he wanted to achieve. But it is not one well described by standard terms like conservatism, liberalism, socialism, or nationalism.[35]

Trudeau expressed his goal best, I think, in 'La Nouvelle Trahison des clercs', the most important of the articles he wrote for *Cité libre* objecting to the new separatist nationalism of the early 1960s.[36] His objection, he explained, was not to the existence of nations, but to the idea that they should necessarily be sovereign. He opposed the principle of nationalities because he cared about the future of his own people, 'la nation canadienne-française'. Like other nations, it was the repository of certain important values (a cultural heritage, common traditions, and so on), but these must ultimately be transcended in the direction of a more intelligent and civilized life for all. 'The history of civilization is a chronicle of the subordination of tribal "nationalism" to wider interests.'[37] French Canadians must not confine themselves to a historical backwater. Their nation will eventually disappear, and Canada itself will not endure forever, but for the immediate future, it is important that Quebec remain a part of Canada, for Canadian federalism provides an admirable framework for preserving, elevating, and amplifying the national life of French Canadians. Their aim should be to make Canada as a whole neither English nor French, but a truly pluralist and polyethnic state:

> The die is cast in Canada: there are two main ethnic and linguistic groups; each is too strong and too deeply rooted in the past, too firmly bound to a mother-culture, to be able to engulf the other. But if the two will collaborate at the hub of a truly pluralistic state, Canada could become the envied seat of a form of federalism that belongs to tomorrow's world. Better than the American melting-pot, Canada could offer an example to all those new Asian and African states . . . who must discover how to govern their polyethnic populations with proper regard for justice and liberty. What better reason for cold-shouldering the lure of annexation to the United States? Canadian federalism is an experiment of major proportions; it could become a brilliant prototype for the moulding of tomorrow's civilization.[38]

Neither language group can crush the other, but both could lose by default, if they were to retreat into narrow nationalistic shells, there to die of spiritual asphyxiation. Rather than being parties to a new escapism, the leaders of opinion in Quebec should pin their hopes on the triumph of humanity. 'Victory is promised to the nation that rejects its nationalistic obsessions and, with the full support of its members, applies all the powers at its command to the pursuit of the most far-reaching and human ideal.'[39]

Trudeau's appeal to French-Canadian national feeling was also an appeal to that of English-speaking Canadians.[40] Their cooperation was obviously needed to build a new Canada. Canada would not become the 'brilliant prototype' ('outil génial') Trudeau had in mind if French and English could not overcome their longstanding mutual suspicion and animosity. If the country were to descend into civil war and ethnic cleansing, as some other experiments in multinational federalism have, it might still provide an example for the rest of the world, but not one to envy or imitate.

Trudeau thought that constitutionally entrenched official bilingualism was the key to putting French-English relations on a new footing. An official recognition of the absolute equality of the two languages would overcome the taint of inequality associated with the narrow provisions of the BNA Act. It would make language a matter of individual rights, reducing the pressures on French Canadians to assimilate, while detaching the protection of the French language from the powers of the Quebec government. Thus it would be a big step towards defining a truly *political* nationality for Canada as a whole, one acceptable in principle to all its constituent nationalities.

Bilingualism implied biculturalism, however, so it was not an acceptable stopping point. It could never satisfy the roughly one-third of Canadians in 1969 who thought of themselves as neither English nor French. And it would be unacceptable more fundamentally to all idealistic Canadians, present and future, willing to rise to the challenge of polyethnic pluralism. A 'two-nations' Canada would be at best a simplified Switzerland, peaceful but boring. With sparsely settled 'cantons' bigger than France and Germany, it might show distant observers that good fences—huge rivers, towering mountains, trackless wastes—make good neighbours, but it would be of little interest to those Asians and Africans needing to learn the arts of modern government. Their crowded countries better illustrated the 'global village' of tomorrow. The challenge was to discover a way for very different peoples to live together peacefully in close proximity, despite their differences. They had to be able to hold on to their identities, while intermarrying and generally remaining open to the values of others. New structures had to be developed for protecting the national qualities of groups like the French Canadians without regressing to the ridiculous and retrograde idea of national sovereignty. Canadians had to accept the challenge that Americans were then facing, of integrating not just different European nationalities, but different races and very different religions, without 'melting' them all down to a low common denominator. In a word, Canada had to become not just bilingual or bicultural, but multicultural.

Past experience suggested that such an experiment in ethnic accommodation could best be conducted within a political framework that gave considerable power to well-educated lawyers and judges.[41] In a system of parliamentary supremacy, elected politicians (small-time lawyers, farmers, insurance salesmen, and so on) can too easily and quickly translate majority opinion into laws and policies. More protection is needed for minority rights. Ultimate power should be in the hands of men and women who truly understand and sympathize with the experiment being conducted. A multicultural country is one that needs a good charter of rights and freedoms. No one can say now what eminent lawyers may eventually make of phrases like 'a free and democratic society' or 'the multicultural heritage of Canadians', in the infinite stretch of future time (as Canada and French Canadians are disappearing), but for the future that concerns us here and now, they are sufficiently clear.

None of the standard terms—conservatism, liberalism, socialism, and nationalism—properly sums up Trudeau's 'vision'. One might see it simply as the product of an abstract moralism, but the best one-word description, I would argue, is 'pluralism'. This word has the advantage, among others, of linking an important cluster of dots—the legislation Trudeau introduced as Justice Minister in 1967—with the larger picture.

In 1967 Trudeau defended the changes in divorce law and the Criminal Code that Pearson had asked him to present, by distinguishing between sin and crime. He repeats himself in his *Memoirs*:

> What is considered sinful in one of the great religions to which citizens belong isn't necessarily sinful in the others. Criminal law therefore cannot be based on the notion of sin; it is crimes that it must define. But I also had to make it understood that in decriminalizing a given action, the law was in no way challenging the moral beliefs of any given religion.[42]

It was not clear at the time, nor is it clear from what Trudeau says now in his *Memoirs*, how the sin-crime distinction applies to divorce, homosexuality, and abortion.[43] But it was obvious at the time that many Canadians, including Trudeau, believed that Canada would be a freer and more just society if more sexual activities were officially regarded as matters of individual choice. Individuals should not be regarded as criminals just because they are out of step sexually with most of their compatriots. The state should not try so hard to confine the most popular sexual activity to marriage, and it should adopt a more relaxed attitude towards the most important consequence of that activity, pregnancy, by allowing its control to begin after conception. In short, Trudeau was, by the standards of the time, a pluralist sexually as well as ethnically, and it is reasonable for interpreters to make a connection, as the term 'pluralism' does, between sex and ethnicity.[44]

'Tolerance' is another important and revealing term, one that Trudeau himself sometimes invokes, as a general principle or value beyond legal or conventional rights, to justify his various reforms. Thus in his *Memoirs* he reproaches Robert Bourassa for passing Bill 22 in 1974, which made French the 'official language of Quebec', because it 'hurt our efforts to build a more tolerant Canada'.[45] A good or just society, in Trudeau's view, should tolerate many different customs and values. It should cultivate a plurality of opinions, tastes, and ways of life (or at least 'lifestyles') by the 'neutrality' of its laws and symbols and the protection it provides for relevant individual rights. Such a society should not simply express the opinions or uphold the norms of 'the majority', nor should it refrain from intervening in society to protect 'the minority', since diversity can be as effectively destroyed or repressed by private discrimination as by official disapproval.

'Tolerance' is worth pondering because it has a long history in liberal political thought and because its meaning is notoriously slippery. For example, one can say that Canada tolerated French before 1969, just as Quebec has tolerated English since 1974. Yet there is also a point in saying that Canada became more tolerant of French, and Quebec less tolerant of English, while Trudeau was Prime Minister. Tolerance sometimes refers to changes in the relative status of different groups: a tolerant society is one that raises the status of individuals or groups previously held in lower esteem. An intolerant one does the opposite. So, did Robert Bourassa increase tolerance in Canada (by raising the status of French, as Trudeau was doing) or did he reduce it (by lowering the status of English)? The difficulty is obviously that one person's elevation sometimes requires another's demotion, so there may be a certain deception in claiming to increase tolerance generally ('to build a more tolerant Canada'). In practice, any policy of affirming individual rights (derived from the rights that particular groups have to public recognition) may have negative effects on the status of other individuals or groups. For example, a policy of official bilingualism tends to elevate the status of those, like Trudeau, who are 'naturally' bilingual (having grown up in Montreal, the son of Charles Trudeau and Grace Elliott). Unilingual individuals, by contrast, see their opportunities shrink and their status in society drop. More generally, a policy of recognizing and cultivating diversity increases the value of 'tolerant' attitudes or traits of character. It puts a premium on the ability to cope gracefully with diversity. It lowers the status of those who meet difference with stiff, awkward, or embarrassed silence, or worse, with angry, intolerant condemnation. They suffer from greater intolerance than before.

CONCLUSIONS

Bilingualism, multiculturalism, and the Charter are Trudeau's great legacy to Canadians. Many other important things have been neglected in this brief survey of his achievements, some because they were not really achievements, others because they were not really his.[46] Trudeau has always liked to talk about the injustice of economic inequality, and when he came to power, it seems that he wanted to do what he could to equalize opportunities, but he had a realistic appreciation of the difficulties, and in the end, he had achieved little. Economic reform had clearly not been his top priority. He promoted the growth of the welfare state, completing the work of his predecessors, but the most important economic problems he faced, such as stagflation, were unprecedented, and his main economic policies bear the mark of improvisation. Bilingualism, multiculturalism, and the Charter, by contrast, seem to express a clearer and more personal vision. With them, Trudeau put his own stamp on the country.

He did so without working out a detailed plan, before he became Prime Minister, of what he would do once he held that office. It would surely have seemed to him a waste of time. His vision cannot be spelled out fully even now. Politics is largely a matter of improvisation. It defies detailed prediction. Trudeau seems to have recognized the importance of Fortuna before 1968, but if not, he was surely aware of it after that magic year. And he seems to have known from the beginning that he was recommending an *experiment*, the details of which would have to be worked out as it progressed.[47] Like any experiment, its outcome would be somewhat unpredictable. One might entertain reasonable hopes (most experiments in natural science and technology have reasonably predictable outcomes), but the important thing was for a changing Canada to change in the right way, moving away from an unappealing 'dualism' towards universal values, that is to say, a more open, civilized, and tolerant way of life for all.

Trudeau's vision was a *moral* vision because it involved more than just good economic planning to increase the material wealth of Canadians. In fact, it demanded that they make some material and other sacrifices. It appealed to their moral sense, challenging them to rise above their irrational fears and traditional prejudices in order to do something important for mankind. Abstract morality, one can say, means not making favourable exceptions for oneself. Trudeau taught Canadians to stop thinking of their country as simply their own. They should follow the real underlying principles of the morality they professed and learn to 'love their neighbours' in a modern, universal sense. The pluralism he promoted meant putting universal moral values above political caution, conventional morality, and the narrow self-interest of 'the majority'.[48] Groups used to occupying centre stage would have to make room for others. In particular, 'the English Canadians, with their own nationalism, will have to retire gracefully to their proper place, consenting to modify their own precious image of what Canada should be.'[49] This retirement would involve territory and political traditions as well as symbols like the flag and the monarchy. A truly tolerant Canada would be one that opened its vast territory and shared its abundant natural resources with newcomers from every land. A big, boring 'Swiss' Canada might provide a comfortable home for 25 million or so like-minded European Canadians, with lots of lakes and open spaces for all, and a few dull cities with good restaurants, but it would do nothing for human dignity. A Canada moving towards a real polyethnic pluralism would have to share more widely and accept a little more crowding, turmoil, and judicial (and quasi-judicial) supervision. Canadians would have to discover new ways of ferreting out and punishing 'hate' without seeming to compromise their deep devotion to diversity of opinions and behaviour or their liberal principles of individual rights. They would have to learn to care and share universally, as true morality demands, and not just *en famille*, as comes more naturally.

Trudeau's vision was a moral vision, finally, because it demanded a special kind of self-sacrifice, connected with its being, at least on the surface, an experiment. If successful, all Canadians will of course benefit more or less. Those who designed and conducted the experiment will enjoy everlasting fame as benefactors of mankind. But if the experiment fails to produce a model for imitation, the reputations of some leaders may suffer, and so will the country. The real beneficiaries will be people living elsewhere. Doctors who test new drugs on themselves put the interests of their patients ahead of their own immediate interests. Similarly, Trudeau called upon Canadians to embark on a noble experiment for the sake of increasing mankind's political knowledge. Humanity stands to gain from Trudeau's experiment with Canada, no matter how it turns out.

NOTES

1 Pierre Elliott Trudeau, *Memoirs* (Toronto: McClelland and Stewart, 1993).

2 Gérard Pelletier, 'Preface', in Pierre Elliott Trudeau, *Federalism and the French Canadians* (Toronto: Macmillan, 1968), xvi. Cf. Trudeau, *Memoirs*, 47.

3 George Radwanski, *Trudeau* (Toronto: Macmillan, 1978), 119.

4 Jacques Hébert and Pierre Elliott Trudeau, *Two Innocents in Red China*, trans. I.M. Owen (Toronto: Oxford, 1968) deserves more attention in this connection than Pierre Elliott Trudeau, 'Economic Rights,' *McGill Law Journal* 8 (1962): 121–5. The article makes clear only that Trudeau was then willing to put utilitarian economic objectives (full employment, social welfare, and income redistribution) above the protection of 'civil rights' or 'civil liberties'.

5 'Comment ne pas voir, ayant passé à travers la broussaille de ce chapitre, que pendant la première moitié du XXe siècle, le progrès matériel dans le Québec ne s'est opéré qu'à notre corps et à notre esprit défendant?' *La Grève de l'amiante*, ed. Pierre Elliott Trudeau (Montreal: Jour, 1956), 87.

6 See John Emerich Edward Dahlberg Acton, 'Nationality' (1862), in *Essays on Freedom and Power*, ed. Gertrude Himmelfarb (London: Thames and Hudson, 1956).

7 Trudeau, *Federalism*, 4, 29, 169.

8 Trudeau, *Federalism*, 191. See also 33–6, 154, 177–8, 180, and 198.

9 *Federalism*, 191.

10 Electoral politics, in particular, is often said to be a matter of 'leadership images' and 'charisma' rather than 'issues'. Some *little* issues may play a role, but only the kind that Trudeau called 'goodies', not competing 'visions'. Cf. Harold D. Clarke, Jane Jenson, Lawrence LeDuc, and Jon H. Pammett, *Political Choice in Canada* (Toronto: McGraw-Hill Ryerson, 1979) and idem., *Absent Mandate: The Politics of Discontent in Canada* (Toronto: Gage, 1984).

11 Cf. Radwanski, *Trudeau*, 120.

12 See *Memoirs*, 202 and 224. Cf. J.L. Granatstein and Robert Bothwell, *Pirouette: Pierre Trudeau and Canadian Foreign Policy* (Toronto: University of Toronto Press, 1990), xiii.

13 *Memoirs*, 283, also 329.

14 *Memoirs*, 322.

15 *Memoirs*, 323.

16 *Memoirs*, 323.

17 Cf. *Memoirs*, 323.

18 Cf. Pierre Elliott Trudeau, *The Constitution and the People of Canada* (Ottawa: Government of Canada, 1969), 52.

19 *Memoirs*, 126.

20 *Memoirs*, 127.

21 'Tens of thousands of anglophones have gathered together under the banner of Canadian Parents for French, voting, as it were, with their children's feet.' *Memoirs*, 128.

22 For some typical statements, see Pierre Elliott Trudeau, 'The Values of a Just Society', in *Towards a Just Society: The Trudeau Years*, ed. Thomas S. Axworthy and Pierre Elliott Trudeau (Toronto: Viking, 1990), 363–4 and 368.

23 *Federalism*, 161–7, 188–90, 193, and 198–201.

24 Cf. Donald Johnston, ed., *With a Bang, Not a Whimper: Pierre Trudeau Speaks Out* (Toronto: Stoddart, 1988), passim.

25 House of Commons, *Debates* 1971 (8 October) VIII, 8545–6.

26 Howard Palmer, *Ethnicity and Politics in Canada since Confederation* (Ottawa: Canadian Historical Association, 1991), 22.

27 The evidence for this is not just section 27 of the Constitution Act of 1982, but the recent multiculturalism Acts and the changes in curricula and general political rhetoric that are all around us.

28 Northrop Frye, quoted in Government of Canada, *A National Understanding: The Official Languages of Canada* (Ottawa: Supply and Services Canada, 1977), 5.

29 See Freda Hawkins, *Canada and Immigration* (Montreal and Kingston: McGill-Queen's University Press, 1972). The shift to a system of controls that does not discriminate on grounds of race, national or ethnic origin, colour, religion, or sex began under the direction of John Diefenbaker and was completed by the passage of a new Immigration Act in 1976.

30 *Debates*, 8546.

31 I am using 'liberal' here as a kind of shorthand to refer to certain familiar institutions and principles that arose in the seventeenth century against a background of violent religious conflict. The 'liberal' solution to this conflict was 'toleration' and the 'separation of Church and State'. All citizens should have the same rights, regardless of their religious affiliations, and the state should cease to have a confessional character. The public sphere should be religiously neutral; religion should become a matter of 'private' practice and belief. More broadly, the jurisdiction of the state, since it is that of compulsion, should be as small as possible, while that of society, the realm of freedom, should be as large as possible. There are obvious affinities between liberalism in this sense and the more familiar economic liberalism of the eighteenth and nineteenth centuries. That there can be more than one sensible definition of a widely used term like 'liberalism' should go without saying.

32 Cf. Government of Canada, *A National Understanding*, 18.

33 The state cannot help favouring or disfavouring particular cultures. The conflicts between cultures cannot be resolved, generally speaking, by 'toleration' and 'neutrality'. Just as the state has to publish its laws in some language (or languages), it has to put some 'cultural' content into them. This is not to say that governments cannot remain neutral between, say, an 'English' taste for beer and a 'French' preference for wine, though even in this case there is a problem of how to apply the taxes in a non-discriminatory way (by volume, alcohol content, pre-tax price, etc.). Needless to say, there is a certain cultural content in the higher taxes on wine than on Perrier.

34 In January 1965 the Minister of Justice, Guy Favreau, appointed a special committee to study the problem of 'hate propaganda' in Canada and to make recommendations. Trudeau was a member of this committee and joined its other

members in seeing a 'clear and present danger' (in the possibility that 'in times of social stress' individuals and groups promoting hate 'could mushroom into a real and monstrous threat to our way of life') and in recommending, therefore, that the Criminal Code be amended to make 'every one who by communicating statements, willfully promotes hatred or contempt against any identifiable group' guilty of an indictable offence and liable to imprisonment for two years. See *Report to the Minister of Justice on the Special Committee on Hate Propaganda in Canada* (Ottawa: Queen's Printer, 1966), especially 24–5 and 59–71. Among the amendments to the Criminal Code passed in 1969 were new sections dealing with hate propaganda. In 1977 the Canadian Human Rights Act was passed, establishing the Canadian Human Rights Commission. On the fundamental importance of individual rights, especially the right to unfettered freedom of speech, see Pierre Elliott Trudeau, *Approaches to Politics*, trans. I.M. Owen (Toronto: Oxford University Press, 1970), 80–1, and 'Values of a Just Society', 363–4.

35 For arguments in favour of each of these descriptions, see Ed Broadbent, *The Liberal Rip-Off: Trudeauism vs. The Politics of Equality* (Toronto: New Press, 1970); William Christian and Colin Campbell, *Political Parties and Ideologies in Canada*, 3rd edn (Toronto: McGraw-Hill Ryerson, 1990); Philip C. Bom, *Trudeau's Canada: Truth and Consequences* (St Catharines: Guardian, 1977); William D. Gairdner, *The Trouble with Canada: A Citizen Speaks Out* (Toronto: Stoddart, 1990); and Larry Zolf, *Just Watch Me: Remembering Pierre Trudeau* (Toronto: Lorimer, 1984). For 'intellectual liberalism', 'Pan-Canadianism', and 'civic rationalism', see James Laxer and Robert Laxer, *The Liberal Idea of Canada: Pierre Trudeau and the Question of Canada's Survival* (Toronto: Lorimer, 1977); Douglas V. Verney, *Three Civilizations, Two Cultures, One State: Canada's Political Traditions* (Durham: Duke University Press, 1986); and Kevin J. Christiano, 'Federalism as a Canadian National Ideal: The Civic Rationalism of Pierre Elliott Trudeau', *Dalhousie Review* 69 (1989), 248–69.

36 See *Federalism*, 151–81.

37 *Federalism*, 156 and 177. The history of civilization is also, it seems, a chronicle of the subordination of false authorities to the will of the people. The tribal shamans and witch doctors lose their power as the people, progressively enlightened, recognize the limited and purely secular justification for political authority, which cannot (or at least it should not) impose itself, but must court the favour of the people, as in a modern democracy. See Trudeau, *Approaches*. Finally, 'for humanity, progress is the slow journey towards personal freedom.' *Federalism*, 209. In short, history is on the side of peace, democracy, and freedom.

38 *Federalism*, 178–9. *Traduttore, traditore*. I can do no better than Patricia Claxton, whose version presumably had Trudeau's approval, but the French original of this passage is worth reading. See also Pierre Elliott Trudeau et al., 'An Appeal for Realism in Politics,' *Canadian Forum*, May 1964, 33, and Pierre Elliott Trudeau, *Conversation with Canadians* (Toronto: University of Toronto Press, 1972), 6, 14–15, 22, 32–6, 191, 195, 197, 204, and 209.

39 *Federalism*, p. 180. On the connection between this ideal and world government, see 4, 158, 169–70, 195–6, and 202.

40 Trudeau's reputation as an anti-nationalist has tended to hide his appeals to national feeling. In his lengthy discussion of nationalism as a sentiment (the 'gum', 'glue', or 'tool' of national emotion), he never says that political craftsmen should refrain from using it in their construction projects. *Federalism*, 188–96. See

also Pierre Elliott Trudeau, 'À propos de "domination économique"', *Cité libre* 20 (May 1958), 7–18.

41   Trudeau's rise to power in Canada coincided with the growth of the modern civil rights movement in the United States, which had started with *Brown v. Board of Education* in 1954. For some vague but relevant remarks about the American experience with judicial review, see Pierre Elliott Trudeau, 'Les Droits de l'homme et la Suprématie parlementaire', in *Human Rights, Federalism, and Minorities*, ed. Allan Gotlieb (Toronto: Canadian Institute of International Affairs, 1970), 12. For the crucial comparison with Britain, see *Memoirs*, 308. To say that lawyers and judges deserve more power is not of course to say that they are *infallible*. In the famous *Patriation Reference*, for example, Canada's most eminent judges seem to have been unable to think straight about a simple legal question. See Pierre Elliott Trudeau, *Fatal Tilt: Speaking Out about Sovereignty* (Toronto: Harper Collins, 1991).

42   *Memoirs*, 83.

43   Trudeau's exceedingly brief remarks on these matters in his *Memoirs* are a very good illustration of his tendency to avoid general discussion. His sin-crime distinction seems to be a version of the liberal public-private or state-society distinction, and it seems to beg the question. All the relevant activities can have serious effects on others (unlike, say, solitary masturbation). The idea that the laws regulating them can be changed without affecting 'moral beliefs' is one that it would be interesting to hear Trudeau explain in detail, particularly with the benefit of hindsight. The suggestion that Catholics, Protestants, and Jews had been quarrelling for centuries about sodomy, bestiality, and abortion is one of those *canards* that Trudeau might have been expected to scorn as *une connerie*.

44   Cf. Jacques Hébert, 'Legislating for Freedom', in *Towards a Just Society*, 131–47.

45   *Memoirs*, 235. See also Trudeau, 'Values of a Just Society', 364–8.

46   Some argue that our present public debt is largely a legacy of Trudeau's years in power, but I have not heard anyone argue that the changes in government programs and public finance responsible for it were among his *achievements*. On the specifics of economic policy, Trudeau is inclined to share the credit widely. Thus finance department officials apparently promoted wage and price controls in the mid-1970s, against Trudeau's opposition. The National Energy Policy of the early 1980s was the work of many hands, but mainly those of Marc Lalonde. Allan MacEachen gets credit for the attempt to close tax loopholes in the 1981 budget. *Memoirs*, 192–6, 291, and 296.

47   He was presumably not so naïve, however, as to think that 'the Canadian experience' had somehow inoculated Canadians against the racism that was on display at the time in the United States and the United Kingdom. It is reasonable to suppose that anyone as intelligent and farseeing as Trudeau would anticipate that the immigration reforms of the early 1960s might eventually produce a serious practical problem of racism. When he writes that culturally homogeneous states, organized on the basis of ethnic attributes, 'inevitably become chauvinistic and intolerant', he is presumably not so unsophisticated as to mix up a tautology with an empirical proposition. *Federalism*, 4, and 'Values of a Just Society', 366–7.

48   One need not exaggerate the self-sacrifice demanded in order to recognize that some sacrifice was involved. The immigration policy Trudeau supported, for example, tended to lower the price of labour and raise the price of urban land,

which undoubtedly took some of the sting out of the sacrifice demanded from the employers of labour and the owners of urban land.

49 *Federalism*, 178. Again, the element of self-sacrifice should not be exaggerated. In a modern society, a person's 'status rewards' may depend as much on his country's reputation abroad as on its domestic arrangements. Even English Canadians, when travelling abroad and talking politics with knowledgeable foreigners (around the pool in Florida or at a conference in Italy), could bask in the glow of their truly multicultural society, which others were envying and trying to imitate.

3

On the Virtues of a Limited Constitution: Why Canadians Were Right to Reject the Charlottetown Accord

Christopher P. Manfredi

Since the mid-1960s, the theory and practice of Canadian constitutionalism have been dominated by the idea that constitutional reform holds the key to solving the various conflicts underlying political life in this country. Driven first by the 'threat' of Quebec nationalism and more recently by challenges to the hegemony of the welfare state, important segments of Canada's intellectual and political élite have become increasingly convinced that equality, liberty, social justice, and national unity are simply a few constitutional amendments away. Underlying this conviction is a conception of constitutionalism that is both overly optimistic and, in the final analysis, potentially destructive of liberal constitutional government itself. According to this profoundly anti-liberal conception of constitutionalism, the purpose of constitutions is to depoliticize public disagreement about important, and often divisive, matters.[1]

The reality, however, is that constitutions have a much more limited utility: they provide the institutional framework of formal rules according to which social and political conflicts are resolved.[2] Constitutions set the rules that establish decision-making bodies, the procedures that govern their operation, and the boundaries that define the scope of their legitimate decision-making authority. To be sure, these rules often include declarations of substantive rights, but it would be wrong to believe that constitutions can eliminate conflict by 'guaranteeing' those rights. At most, constitutions can shift the institutional focus for resolving political conflicts about those rights from electoral to judicial bodies.[3] The result is not the depoliticization of conflict, but the development of a new form of constitutional politics that satisfies special interests by granting them preferred constitutional status and by providing a new set of constitutional rules that might be manipulated to advance their policy agendas. Nowhere was this understanding of constitutional government more apparent than in the 'Canada Clause' and the 'Social and Economic Union' provisions of the Charlottetown Accord.

The purpose of this chapter is to document the rise of this form of constitutional politics and to show how it reached its apex in the framing of the Charlottetown Accord. I argue that political progress in Canada depends on rediscovering the virtues of a limited constitution based on the liberal democratic principles of universal citizenship and formal equality protected by procedural justice. To make this argument is to advance the radical proposition that we should abandon the anachronistic notion that Canada was, is, and must remain a compact between founding nations or cultures (now numbering three instead of the traditional two). Finally, the argument implicitly questions the wisdom of maintaining the peculiar institutions of a constitutional order based on this anachronism.

THE ASCENDANCY OF THE CONSTITUTION

For almost 30 years, Canada has been preoccupied by what Peter Russell, one of our most astute constitutional scholars and analysts, calls mega-constitutional change.[4] The constitutional amendments proposed during this period have involved more than merely marginal adjustments to meet modern conditions (although such changes have also been on the constitutional agenda): they have included proposals for comprehensive adjustments to the very principles underlying the Canadian regime. As Russell points out, mega-constitutional change in any regime is generally infrequent and of relatively short duration. For example, the last period of mega-constitutional politics in the United States—where the principles of the regime were at stake—was the Civil War and Reconstruction period. What makes Canada unique is the unrivalled intensity and duration of its most recent period of mega-constitutional politics. Indeed, on no fewer than four occasions since 1968, Canadian governments and other institutionalized social and political actors have engaged in highly visible, emotionally intense, and largely unsuccessful bargaining over formal constitutional amendments.

In its most recent manifestation, this mega-constitutional debate has coalesced around two competing principles. One principle is that Canada is a compact of founding peoples—originally two in number (English and French), but now generally recognized as also including aboriginal peoples. This principle has dominated Canadian constitutionalism, and it provides the rationale for Quebec's demand to be recognized as distinctive within the constitutional order because of its status as the home of one of the founding peoples. The second principle, which has gained momentum since 1982, is that Canada is a political regime founded on the principle of equal and universal rights of citizenship. This principle provides the rationale for demands that each of the country's political units be granted equal power and status, since each is equally the home of Canadian citizens. The tension between these two principles during the past three decades of mega-constitutional politics has made constitutional reform extraordinarily difficult.

Whether driven by one or the other of these fundamental principles, the proponents of constitutional reform have been united by a common quest for political sovereignty and national unity. One part of this quest has been for a domestic amending formula. Such a formula is important because the process of amending a nation's constitution defines the nature of sovereignty in that nation, while simultaneously revealing the character of the union created by the constitution.[5] The second part of this quest has been for the entrenchment of individual rights. This has an important effect on sovereignty, since it shifts sovereignty from Parliament and the provincial legislatures toward citizens, who are now capable of asserting their rights through litigation. Similarly, the entrenchment of rights promotes unity by shifting political discussion away from regional conflicts toward universal questions about rights and by enhancing the power of a nationally controlled political institution (the Supreme Court of Canada).[6] The constitutional vision contained in this approach is that of a nation of rights-bearing citizens whose principal allegiance is to the central government.

These principles and goals have had an important place in constitutional reform since 1968, when the then Justice Minister, Pierre Trudeau, tabled a policy paper entitled 'A Canadian Charter of Human Rights'.[7] Three years later the provincial premiers and Prime Minister Trudeau reached an agreement at a meeting in Victoria to patriate the constitution in a way that addressed the concern about both the amending formula and the entrenchment of rights. The Victoria agreement would have required amendments to be approved by the House of Commons, the legislatures of any province containing more than 25 per cent of the population, two Atlantic provinces, and two Western provinces containing 50 per cent of the Western population. In keeping with the two-founding-nations theory, this formula effectively gave both Quebec and Ontario a veto in the constitutional amendment process. In addition, the Victoria accord contained a limited charter of rights that protected language rights and democratic rights, such as the right to vote. The entire agreement ultimately failed, however, because of important objections raised later by Quebec and Alberta. In Quebec, Premier Robert Bourassa returned from Victoria to opposition from his cabinet, which attacked the accord for not providing Quebec with sufficient guarantees of cultural sovereignty. The reason for Alberta's opposition was a change in government, with newly elected Premier Peter Lougheed objecting to the veto over future constitutional amendments granted to Quebec and Ontario.

The failure of the Victoria plan pushed constitutional reform off centre stage until 1976, when the election of a separatist government in Quebec provoked additional demands for constitutional renewal. In 1978 the federal government under Pierre Trudeau responded to this pressure to resolve 'the crisis threatening the stability, unity, and prosperity of the country' by introducing Bill C–60, which contained a proposed Constitution of Canada Act and a charter of rights.[8] Although this charter would not have had constitutional status immediately, the federal government saw it as a first step toward overcoming provincial opposition to the constitutional entrenchment of rights and freedoms. This reform effort temporarily stalled in 1979, when the Progressive Conservative Party under the leadership of Joe Clark defeated Trudeau's Liberal Party in a national election. Trudeau returned to power in 1980, however, in time to lead the campaign against Quebec's referendum on sovereignty-association. During this campaign, Trudeau again promised Quebeckers and Canadians a renewed federalism. After winning the referendum, Trudeau took the first step toward keeping this promise in September 1980, when he presented a package of constitutional reforms, including patriation and a charter of rights, to a First Ministers' conference.

The vision of renewed federalism contained in this package proved almost universally unpopular. Failing to secure broad provincial acceptance of his plan for constitutional renewal, Trudeau announced that the federal government would proceed unilaterally toward implementation. This provoked the hostility of eight provinces, which took political and legal steps to block the plan. After acrimonious negotiations, punctuated by hearings before a special joint parliamentary committee and a crucial Supreme Court decision, the governments of Canada and nine provinces agreed in November 1981 to patriate the constitution and include within it a domestic amending formula and an entrenched Charter of Rights and Freedoms.[9] The product of this agreement, which Quebec refused to accept, was the Constitution Act, 1982.

The amending formula contained in the Constitution Act provided a general procedure for amending the constitution, as well as two special procedures. The general procedure, which applies to most matters, requires that amendments be approved by the Senate, the House of Commons, and two-thirds of the provinces that contain at least 50 per cent of the population. Under one of the special procedures, some matters (for example, the composition of the Supreme Court) must receive the unanimous consent of the federal and provincial governments. The second special procedure applies to amendments that affect linguistic matters within a province or the boundaries between two provinces. In these cases, only the federal government and the affected provinces must ratify the amendment. These amending procedures clearly envision the federal and provincial governments as the key players in constitutional modification, but they are less clear about the status of the provinces in relation to each other. In particular, the general amending formula gave greater weight in the process to the more populous provinces. This contrasts sharply with the US amending formula, in which all the states are equally weighted with respect to constitutional ratification.

In addition to these amendment provisions, the first thirty-four sections of the Act contain the Charter of Rights and Freedoms, which governs fundamental freedoms, democratic rights, mobility rights, legal rights, equality rights, language rights, and minority language education rights. The Charter also contains several interpretive clauses, as well as an enforcement provision (section 24), which sets forth a qualified exclusionary rule and permits courts 'of competent jurisdiction' to remedy infringements of rights in any way they consider 'appropriate and just in the circumstances'. Section 52(1) of the Act further provides that '[t]he Constitution of Canada is the supreme law of Canada, and any law that is inconsistent with the provisions of the Constitution is, to the extent of the inconsistency, of no force or effect.' As a whole, section 24 of the Charter and section 52(1) of the 1982 Constitution Act establish a regime of constitutional supremacy enforced by judicial review.

This regime is moderated somewhat, however, by section 33 of the Charter, which provides that both Parliament and the provincial legislatures may expressly declare that legislation shall operate 'notwithstanding' the Charter's constitutional protection of fundamental freedoms, legal rights and equality rights. Section 33 is controversial for two reasons. First, by granting legislative bodies the power to override the Charter through ordinary legislation, it appears to contradict the principle of constitutional supremacy. Second, section 33 was largely the product of short-term political trade-offs, and its inclusion in the Charter has been described as a 'classic example of raw bargaining'.[10] The circumstances under which it was used by the governments of both Quebec and Saskatchewan have not reduced the controversy surrounding the 'notwithstanding clause'.[11]

The strong opposition to any use of the notwithstanding clause to override an interpretation and application of Charter rights by the courts is also, however, the product of a historical accident and three misunderstandings. The historical accident is that Canadians saw a use of section 33 (by Quebec) that they found objectionable before the Supreme Court rendered an unpopular Charter decision.[12] One of the misunderstandings concerns the constitutional role of legislatures and courts in liberal constitutional theory. There is nothing in that theory that assigns the task of constitutional interpretation exclusively to courts. The second misunderstanding is the mistaken impression that the legislative process is characterized by the haphazard adoption of measures motivated by majority tyranny. Finally, opposition to section 33 is fuelled by a basic misunderstanding of the nature of Charter adjudication. As I have argued elsewhere, Charter cases only rarely resolve disputes about fundamental rights, and almost never resolve disputes about fundamental moral principles. In most cases, the dispute boils down to a conflict about the policy consequences of competing principles.[13]

The constitutional order created in 1982 remained undisturbed until

1985, when a newly elected government in Quebec presented five conditions that had to be met in order to secure the province's agreement to the 1982 document. These conditions included recognition of Quebec as a distinct society, greater power for the province in immigration matters, a voice in selecting Quebec justices for the Supreme Court, the ability to opt out (with compensation) of federal spending programs in areas of provincial jurisdiction, and recovery of the veto power over constitutional amendment that the province had traditionally asserted. This list found a receptive audience in a recently elected federal government that contained a large Quebec caucus. The result was two years of negotiation that produced the Meech Lake Accord of June 1987.[14]

The Accord addressed each of Quebec's conditions, but it was also influenced by the emerging principle of provincial equality. In effect, this principle prevented the federal government from granting new powers to Quebec without also offering those same powers to other provinces. Consequently, every province acquired new powers over immigration and the appointment of Supreme Court justices. Moreover, since Quebec's power over amendments to the constitution could not be enhanced without similarly enhancing that of the other provinces, the list of amendments requiring unanimous consent expanded. The 1987 Accord also contained a 'satisfaction guaranteed or your money back' clause that would have allowed provinces to receive compensation for opting out of amendments that transfer legislative power from the provincial to federal governments in any field of jurisdiction.[15]

The ratification of the 1987 agreement proceeded smoothly until 15 December 1988, when the Supreme Court struck down some provisions of Quebec's Charter of the French Language for violating the Canadian Charter of Rights and Freedoms. Three days after the decision, Quebec Premier Robert Bourassa announced his intention to enact new language legislation (Bill 178) that would be insulated from judicial review by a notwithstanding clause. Hostility towards Bourassa's decision to override the Supreme Court and invoke section 33 was immediate among Quebec's anglophone minority and in the rest of Canada. Indeed, Manitoba Premier Gary Filmon retaliated by withdrawing a resolution to ratify the Meech Lake constitutional accord from consideration by his province's legislature. New Brunswick's failure to ratify and Newfoundland's decision to revoke its earlier ratification put the Accord in even deeper political trouble.

The demise of the Meech Lake Accord after December 1988 reveals the difficulty of reconciling the traditional principles of Canadian constitutionalism with the new principles embedded in the Charter. This difficulty applies to both the process and the substance of constitutional reform. The Meech Lake agreement was the result of the same traditional approach to constitutional change that had produced the 1981 agreement: a (relatively) private round of negotiations among first ministers. However, as Alan Cairns has pointed out, the Charter radically transformed the terrain of constitutional

discourse between 1981 and 1987.[16] In providing special constitutional protection for various groups (all numerical minorities, except women), the
Charter conferred explicit constitutional status on those groups; and they
demanded the right to be heard in the process of constitutional change. Consequently, no proposal for constitutional reform that did not explicitly solicit
their contribution could enjoy full legitimacy. These groups not only claimed
access to the process, but also guardianship over the substance of constitutional change. Thus, their resistance to the Meech Lake Accord rose substantially as arguments mounted that the Accord's 'distinct society' clause might
weaken the Charter's force in Quebec. The enactment of Bill 178 appeared to
confirm this fear, and the agreement lost most of whatever legitimacy it had
enjoyed outside of Quebec.

This episode in Canadian constitutional development is also very revealing
about the way in which the Charter has come to be viewed by those groups
with a direct stake in it. In their view, the Charter is not simply one part of the
'supreme law of Canada': it is the supreme law itself; and any government
action, including formal constitutional amendment, that threatens to weaken
the Charter is considered constitutionally—not simply politically—illegitimate. The stakes of the game are raised considerably when the competition
among interest groups moves from the parliamentary to the constitutional
arena, and this explains the strong incentive that groups have to safeguard
their constitutional positions.

The federal government recognized this new aspect of constitutional politics in its post-Meech Lake proposals for constitutional reform.[17] First, the
government proposed to define the nature of Quebec's distinct society more
clearly and, more important, to place the new distinct society clause within
the Charter itself. This would have transformed the clause from an overarch-
ing constitutional principle superior to the Charter—as critics argued was
the case in the Meech Lake Accord—into merely one interpretive clause
among several others. Second, the government proposed to amend section 33
of the Charter to provide that legislative overrides could only be invoked with
the approval of 66 per cent of the Members of Parliament or provincial legislatures. The obvious aim of this proposal was to make the 'notwithstanding
clause' more difficult to enact. Both of these proposals sought to assuage the
concern that the Charter might be weakened by constitutional reform.

The desire to constitutionalize policy matters covered by political rights,
which underlies the pre-eminence now enjoyed by the Charter in constitutional debates, was then extended to economic and social policy. Although the
enforcement of the Charter's fundamental freedoms, legal rights, and equality rights has an obvious influence on economic and social policy, the proposal to entrench a charter of social and economic rights in the constitution
was intended to make this more explicit and to ensure that the constitutional
development of these policies took a particular direction. This proposal first
took concrete form in September 1991 at the initiative of the NDP govern-

ment of Ontario. Responding partly to the federal government's proposal to entrench traditional property rights,[18] and partly to concern about the fate of disadvantaged social and economic groups under ordinary Charter litigation, the Ontario government urged the adoption of a social charter 'that would entrench our commitment to social justice more explicitly, and would make governments more accountable, either in the courts or some other adjudicative body, for the obligations raised by that commitment'.[19] This proposal generated extensive debate about the desirability of entrenching such rights, the nature of the rights themselves, and the mechanism for enforcing constitutionally entrenched social and economic rights. These debates and the constitutional proposals they generated are discussed in the next section of the chapter.

There is an important parallel between some of the principal arguments marshalled in support of a social charter and the reasons for the Trudeau government's push for the Charter of Rights and Freedoms. Just as the 1982 Charter was designed in part to counteract the centrifugal forces at work in Canada, many proponents of a social charter believed it would help to shape the still elusive Canadian national identity. Thus, the government of Ontario argued that the constitutional entrenchment of social rights would protect the 'institutions of social policy' through which our common identity is now expressed.[20] The difficulty with this argument is that, while a social charter might express a set of objectives with which all Canadians can agree, that is perhaps the easiest task in politics. Real conflict emerges when the discussion turns to setting priorities among these goals and to designing specific means for achieving them. As the history of constitutional reform from 1971 to the early 1990s suggests, Canadians have increasingly come to expect more from their constitution than the document can deliver. As I will argue later in this chapter, we might be better off rediscovering the value of constitutional parsimony.

THE CHARLOTTETOWN FOLLY

Constitutional parsimony, however, is precisely not what Canada's leaders produced for the voters' consideration in the autumn of 1992. Both the *Consensus Report on the Constitution* issued by the provincial First Ministers and the territorial and aboriginal leaders in August of 1992 and the draft legal text cobbled together a mere 17 days before the national referendum on the Charlottetown Accord were massive documents that attempted to resolve every constitutional grievance ever expressed by any government or interest group. Given the process that produced the Accord, this outcome was perhaps inevitable.

The political fallout from the failure of Meech Lake was twofold. First, Quebec refused to participate in any constitutional negotiations until Canada was prepared to present a final settlement. Both the provincial government and the Quebec Liberal Party created constitutional commissions (the Bélanger-Campeau Commission and the Allaire Commission respectively), each of which advocated greater decentralization of political power. In addition, Quebec enacted legislation requiring a referendum on either sovereignty or a new constitutional package before the end of October 1992, effectively establishing a deadline for revised proposals. Second, the failure of Meech Lake generated demands for a more participatory constitutional process. At the provincial level, this demand led Alberta and British Columbia to enact legislation requiring referenda before legislative approval could be given to any constitutional accord. With at least three provinces requiring referenda, it became inevitable that constitutional drafting would be influenced by considerations drawn from the electoral politics peculiar to that process.

The federal government took the demands for citizen participation particularly seriously. At the outset of the post-Meech process, it established two separate bodies: the Beaudoin-Edwards Commission, which examined the amending formula; and the Citizens' Forum on the Constitution, which collected citizens' opinions on the broad subject of constitutional reform. On the one hand, the Beaudoin-Edwards Commission advocated a 'forward to the past' strategy by calling for a return to the amending formula agreed to at Victoria in 1971. On the other hand, it embraced the new participatory ethic by recommending the institutionalization of constitutional referenda and the creation of a constituent assembly. The Citizens' Forum, chaired by Keith Spicer, used an entirely new approach: constitution-making by toll-free number. Canadians were invited to call and offer their suggestions for constitutional reform, an opportunity taken by approximately 400,000 people. Unfortunately, the gist of their comments was that too much time was being wasted on the constitution that might be better spent on economic and environmental issues.

In the midst of gathering all these opinions, the federal government issued its own proposals for constitutional reform in September 1991. The proposals contained 28 separate recommendations and dealt with eight principal subjects: the nature of Canada, Quebec as a distinct society, changes to the Charter, aboriginal self-government, Senate reform, the Supreme Court, economic union, and the division of powers. The task of gathering public reaction to the proposals was delegated to a third committee ultimately chaired by the constitutionally ubiquitous Gérard Beaudoin and the Progressive Conservative MP Dorothy Dobbie. This committee was almost a complete disaster from the outset, experiencing logistical difficulties and a complete absence of public interest. Consequently, the committee was reconstituted and supplemented by five constitutional conferences in Halifax, Montreal, Toronto, Calgary, and Vancouver. The committee then met for two weeks in closed-door session to produce a 125-page report recommending changes to all of the federal proposals. The final step in the process was a meeting of First Ministers during July and August of 1992. Although Quebec did not attend any of the July meetings, it was present at the final two sets of meetings in Ottawa (August 18–22) and Charlottetown (August 27–28).

The substance of the Accord agreed to in Charlottetown attempted to deal with six separate issues, namely, unity and diversity, social and economic union, institutional reform of both the Senate and House of Commons, the division of powers, aboriginal self-government, and the constitutional amendment process. Without diminishing the importance of the last four of these issues, it is arguably in the Canada Clause (promoting unity and diversity) and the provisions for economic and social union that one finds the clearest evidence of our recent penchant to seek final constitutional solutions to indeterminate political questions. Implicit in these two parts of the Charlottetown Accord was the belief that, with a few constitutional phrases, Canadians could:

(1) achieve unity while recognizing and celebrating diversity.
(2) promote economic efficiency and national markets while ensuring social justice through national standards for the provision of welfare.
(3) achieve all of this without undermining the Charter's privileged position in our constitutional order.

To achieve all of this goals simultaneously would be extraordinarily difficult, and Canadians were properly suspicious of a proposal that purported to do so.

THE CANADA CLAUSE

In its February 1992 report, the Beaudoin-Dobbie Committee asserted that it was vitally important that the constitution contain a statement of Canadian identity and values that was both 'memorable and inclusive'. According to the committee, this was necessary to ensure that the constitution, which had 'allowed us to achieve a degree of harmony and prosperity that is the envy of the modern world', would continue 'to respond to the fundamental needs and aspirations of all Canadians'.[21] The committee recommended that this objective be accomplished through the inclusion of a 'poetic' preamble and a more legalistic Canada Clause. The preamble suggested by the committee was the embarrassingly sentimental product of the collective talents of the Writers Union of Canada ('We are the people of Canada, drawn from the four winds of the earth, a privileged people, citizens of a sovereign state'), and it mercifully disappeared from the Charlottetown Accord.[22] The Canada Clause proposal, however, survived the report.

In its final legal form, the Canada Clause would have amended the Constitution Act, 1867 to require that the constitution generally, and the charter in particular, be interpreted consistently with eight fundamental characteristics of Canada. These characteristics were described in the following terms:

(a) Canada is a democracy committed to a parliamentary and federal system of government and to the rule of law;

(b) the Aboriginal peoples of Canada, being the first peoples to govern this land, have the right to promote their languages, cultures and traditions and to ensure the integrity of their societies, and their governments constitute one of the three orders of government in Canada;

(c) Quebec constitutes within Canada a distinct society, which includes a French-speaking majority, a unique culture and a civil law tradition;

(d) Canadians and their governments are committed to the vitality and development of official language minority communities throughout Canada;

(e) Canadians are committed to racial and ethnic equality in a society that includes citizens from many lands who have contributed, and continue to contribute, to the building of a strong Canada that reflects its cultural and racial diversity;

(f) Canadians are committed to a respect for individual and collective human rights and freedoms of all people;

(g) Canadians are committed to the equality of female and male persons; and

(h) Canadians confirm the principle of the equality of the provinces at the same time as recognizing their diverse characteristics.

Finally, the Canada Clause affirmed the 'role of the legislature and Government of Quebec to preserve and promote the distinct society of Quebec'.

The authors of the Charlottetown Accord and its legal text designed the Canada Clause to serve both symbolic and operational functions. As a symbolic statement of platitudes about the nature of Canada, the clause was relatively harmless, merely suggesting that Canada is all things to all people. As a functional statement about how the constitution and the Charter should be interpreted, however, the clause was much more significant. To understand this significance, one must recognize that post-charter constitutional politics has become a struggle to acquire constitutional resources, maximize their value, and mobilize them to redistribute political power. Constitutional politics is thus best understood as a competitive game of institutional design in which the principal goal is to establish or modify the framework of formal procedural and substantive rules in a manner that favours one set of policies rather than another. Constitutional reform is an especially powerful form of institutional design because constitutional rules have a broad effect on the lower-level rules according to which other institutions operate. The Charter creates a particular arena for institutional design through constitutional politics in which first-order rules (the rights and freedoms actually enumerated in the document) are manipulated to generate and modify more policy-relevant second-order rules (the judicial interpretation and application of first-order rules). The result is that first-order rules are no longer evaluated on their own merits, but according to what they might contribute to various litigation strategies.

In the post-Charter world, therefore, the constitution no longer serves the quintessentially liberal purpose of prescribing, 'in advance, a fixed sphere of permitted and prohibited state action'.[23] Rather, constitutional rules have become political resources that state-based actors distribute, and for which society-based actors compete in order to serve their broader policy objectives. The value of these resources depends, however, on the generality of the language in which the rule is expressed and on the existence and nature of rules of interpretation. This explains the battle over the Canada Clause: each of the groups involved wanted a set of interpretive rules that would further entrench its preferences in the constitution while ensuring that the clause did not reduce the value of the constitutional resources it already possessed in the form of Charter rights. It also explains the sudden interest in a constitutional declaration of social and economic rights.

THE ECONOMIC AND SOCIAL UNION

Economic issues had a central place in the federal government's development of its constitutional proposals in 1991. Initially, the federal government's principal concerns were to constitutionalize property rights and strengthen the economic union among the provinces. The government addressed the first concern by proposing a straightforward amendment to the Charter of Rights and Freedoms that would have given constitutional protection to property rights. The second concern generated 15 separate proposals, of which the most important were for a Canadian common market and federal management of the economic union.[24] The common market proposal consisted of an amendment to section 121 of the Constitution Act, 1867, to declare that 'Canada is an economic union within which persons, goods, services and capital may move freely without barriers or restrictions based on provincial or territorial boundaries.' The proposed amendment would have prohibited the federal and provincial governments from contravening the principle of economic union by either law or practice. The second proposal consisted of an amendment to section 91 of the Constitution Act, 1867, granting the federal Parliament exclusive power to 'make laws in relation to any matter that it declares to be for the efficient functioning of the economic union'.

The federal government's proposal to create a constitutionally protected 'economic union' provided the inspiration for what was, at least for Canada, perhaps the most novel component of the Charlottetown Accord. Shortly after the publication of these proposals, the Government of Ontario proposed that the constitution also include a 'social charter' that would act as a counterweight to the economic union proposals. In its final form, the Ontario proposal provided that the 'social charter should constitutionally entrench the positive obligations of governments to provide social programs and set national standards.' Ontario also proposed to amend the Constitution Act,

1982 to provide specific protection for health care, social services and welfare, primary and secondary education, and environmental protection. The proposal recognized, however, that scepticism was mounting about the desirability of asking the courts to interfere in policy questions of this sort; and it suggested that these constitutional obligations be enforced by an independent commission rather than by judicial bodies.

The Ontario proposal did not have much effect on the constitutional negotiations until the Montreal conference on the economic union, where it unexpectedly emerged as a counterbalance to the federal proposals for an economic union. The idea was subsequently picked up by the Beaudoin-Dobbie Committee, which added a 'social covenant' to the economic union amendments. The committee recommended that section 36 of the Constitution Act, 1982, be amended to underscore the federal and provincial commitment to providing comprehensive and universal public health care; reasonable access to housing, food and other basic necessities; high-quality public education at all levels; protection for collective bargaining; and a clean environment. These commitments, the committee suggested, should be monitored and promoted by an intergovernmental review agency.

Ironically, both the Ontario proposals and the version of the social covenant found in the Beaudoin-Dobbie report generated the greatest debate among the group most likely to support them: the Canadian left. Much of this debate is collected in a volume entitled *Social Justice and the Constitution: Perspectives on a Social Union for Canada*.[25] Reading the essays in this collection is a little bit like strolling through an intellectual museum, where each author (all but one of whom are lawyers or professors at leading Canadian law schools) examines the potential contribution of a social charter to the realization of a truly just society in which the class-based foundations of problems like poor health and environmental degradation are dissolved. Joel Bakan's discussion of health care policy is typical of the essays that are critical of the social charter idea. According to Bakan, Canada is 'a society of classes, intersected by gender and race inequalities, with a radically unequal distribution of wealth and income and correspondingly unequal levels of health in its people'. The objective of state policy, Bakan argues, should be to reduce 'health risks determined by class' by 'transforming social relations that determine who gets sick and who stays healthy'.[26] A social charter, Bakan concludes, will not push governments 'to break out of the reification of social services . . ., and to attack the causes of poverty and ill health with concrete social and economic policies aimed at reducing the unequal distribution of wealth and income'.[27] A classless society, it appears, is the panacea for most physical ailments.

Not all of the essays in the collection are as critical as Bakan's, however. Jennifer Nedelsky and Craig Scott, for example, offer a strong defence of the social charter idea, as well as a comprehensive alternative to both the Ontario and Beaudoin-Dobbie proposals. In their view, there are two obstacles to an effective charter of social rights: the traditional conception of rights as trumps, and the use of the courts as the principal institutional means for defining and enforcing rights. Consequently, their proposal for an alternative social charter was based on 'the notion of rights as sites of dialogues, metaphorical forums in which members of society converse about different claims regarding basic values and relationships'.[28] However, Nedelsky and Scott do not explain why a separate social charter, containing distinctive institutional mechanisms, is necessary for the type of conversation they desire. More precisely, they do not explain why the current conversation on these issues, which, in fact, does occur in existing legislative bodies, is inadequate. It is possible, however, to understand their dissatisfaction with the current dialogue about these matters by examining the political goal of the social charter's advocates.

The conventional explanation for the emergence of the social-charter proposal points to three overlapping political goals among the proposal's proponents. The first of these goals was the desire, mentioned above, to provide a counterweight to the federal government's proposal to entrench property rights in the constitution and to strengthen the economic union by reducing the capacity of provincial governments to regulate their economies in a manner that impeded the free movement of goods, services, and capital among provinces. The second goal was to ensure that the vision of social justice that was embodied in existing social programs would not be undermined by the vicissitudes of democratic politics in a federal state. Finally, the proponents of the social charter sought to preserve and promote the common national identity supposedly embodied in the existing social programs. Each of these explanations is plausible, and indeed correct in some sense. However, other political purposes also motivated two of the social charter's strongest supporters: the Ontario provincial government and the federal New Democratic Party (NDP).

For Ontario, as well as other provinces, the social charter was important as a means of permitting the provincial governments to keep social policy promises that they could no longer afford. A social charter, in other words, would have imposed a constitutional obligation on the federal government to finance social programs administered by the provinces.[29] However enforced, this obligation would have allowed the provinces to continue to take the political credit for providing social programs without accepting the blame for the taxes or deficits necessary to pay for them. Ironically, this outcome held the potential for undermining national unity by exaggerating the beneficence of the provinces and the rapaciousness of the federal government. The threat to unity came from the possibility that individuals might identify themselves even more strongly with their province at the expense of their identification with the central government.

For the federal NDP, the benefits of the social charter would have come from the creation of an institutional mechanism through which it could more effectively pursue its national policies. The significance of this opportunity to establish an institutional alternative to Parliament for the formation of social policy was not lost on a political party that has finished no better than third in 18 consecutive national elections. Although the Charlottetown Accord did not specify the structure of this institution, the Nedelsky-Scott proposal on behalf of the National Anti-Poverty Organization envisioned the establishment of a social rights council and tribunal modelled after human rights tribunals.[30] Like human rights tribunals, these institutions were not designed to be disinterested participants in the process of defining and allocating social rights.[31] In fact, one of the qualifications for appointment to the council would be a 'commitment to the objectives of the Social Charter'. Similarly, one-third of the members of the tribunal would be appointed from 'non-governmental organizations representing vulnerable and disadvantaged groups', and the tribunal would 'be made accessible to members of disadvantaged groups and their representative organizations by all reasonable means, including the provision of necessary funding by appropriate governments'. The clear intent in these proposals was to create decision-making bodies that would be naturally inclined toward policies advocated by the NDP's constituency.

Why would a conservative federal government dedicated to continent-wide free trade and reduction of expenditures agree to include even a moderate social charter in the Charlottetown Accord? The answer to this question lies in the lessons of 1980-82. During the patriation debate, the federal government discovered that it could use the Charter of Rights and Freedoms to generate popular support for its constitutional position, which could then be mobilized against opposition by provincial governments to the plan. By drawing attention to the Charter, the federal government effectively accused its provincial adversaries of seeking to deny an important benefit to Canadians: constitutional protection of their fundamental rights to liberty and equality. The social charter had the potential to be used in a similar fashion, that is, to attack the opponents of any constitutional accord for wanting to deny social justice to Canadians. That the strategy failed says more about the skill with which it was implemented than about the social charter's capacity to insulate the constitutional agreement from certain types of criticism.

Whatever its political utility to various participants in constitutional politics, the social charter proposal was both unnecessary and pernicious. According to its advocates, the social charter would merely have given constitutional expression to a national consensus about the types of social programs that should be provided on a universal basis. The flaw in this argument, of course, is that, if a national consensus does indeed exist, then existing programs are not really in jeopardy. No one can seriously argue, for example, that Canada will revert to a US-style system of exclusively private health insurance, since there are too many incentives—for physicians, patients, and governments—to maintain the current system. The disagreements that do arise are about issues like the relative financial obligations of federal and provincial governments, expansion and contraction of services, the possibility of user fees, and so on. These are all policy matters for and against which reasonable arguments can be made without undermining the basic commitment to universal, public health insurance. What the social charter's proponents sought to protect was their particular vision of what constitutes proper social programs, not the national commitment to the existence of such programs. The existing institutional mechanisms, which give voice to political parties and interest groups that advocate more extensive social spending, and which provide incentives for governments to spend public funds, are sufficient to safeguard the essential elements of social programs. Indeed, it takes extraordinary political courage for a government to cut such programs in any meaningful way. One need only examine the expenditures of the federal government between 1984 and 1993 to confirm this.

Constitutional entrenchment, in other words, is unnecessary precisely in those cases where a deep national consensus exists. For example, although there is no explicit constitutional prohibition against slavery in Canada, no one would suggest that such a prohibition is necessary to prevent its being established. Furthermore, if the establishment of slavery were to become politically feasible in Canada, it would signal such a corruption of liberal democracy that we would face a crisis from which no constitution could save us. Similarly, there is no reason to entrench property rights in the constitution, since no politically serious movement exists to abolish the ownership of private property. There is, of course, extensive debate about the appropriate level and economic efficiency of public regulation of private property, but this is perfectly consistent with liberal principles.

While the social charter was unnecessary to protect the basic national consensus on social policy, it was a crucial component in achieving a more pernicious objective: the further erosion of federalism in Canada. The argument for national standards underlying the social charter proposal is, in essence, an argument against any type of federalism in which the provinces are more than simply administrative units of the national government. What the social charter's proponents failed to understand is that federalism is more than a convenient arrangement for the management of policies developed by a central government. Indeed, the value of federalism has been recognized, and celebrated, by commentators situated at both ends of the political spectrum.

The argument for federalism from the political right stresses the policy creativity it encourages, the efficiency generated by competition among governments, and the freedom that comes from allowing individuals to choose the public services for which they are willing to pay. On the left, federalism is celebrated for allowing the provinces to serve as experimental laboratories for progressive social policies, particularly in areas like health insurance and human rights. Moreover, federalism serves communitarian ends by devolving decision making to a more humane level of social interaction. Federalism contributes to democratic self-government by enhancing the representativeness of decision makers while simultaneously reducing the physical and psychological distance between rulers and ruled. In this way, federalism promotes both freedom and dignity in every sense of those terms. There is something very ironic—even contradictory—in arguing that the federal government should not manage an economic union because it might destroy diversity, while also arguing that a social charter is necessary to safeguard national standards for social programs.

The emphasis on economic and social-policy issues in the 1991 constitutional proposals and the final 1992 agreement reached in Charlottetown can be traced to the influence of the Charter on Canadian political thinking. Before the Charter, the only arenas for resolving conflicts among competing policy positions were the legislature and the executive. In the pre-Charter world, therefore, participants achieved victory by having their policies form the basis of legislation or executive action. The Charter, however, established a constitutional arena for resolving these conflicts and thereby encouraged policy competitors to raise their sights from legislating to constitutionalizing. Legislative and executive victories are no longer sufficient, since they can always be reversed by the courts. The struggle to incorporate particular economic and social policies in the constitution is due to this new recognition of the nature of policy competition.

THE VIRTUES OF A LIMITED CONSTITUTION

As I suggested at the outset, the most important lesson to draw from the framing and defeat of the Charlottetown Accord is that too much constitutionalism is just as dangerous to liberal regimes as is too little. The impulse underlying the vision of constitutionalism during the 'Canada Round' of negotiations that followed the defeat of the Meech Lake Accord was fear—fear of the uncertainty that comes from leaving open the definition of the common good, and fear of the ordinary deliberative process of politics as a means of defining that good. This fear, which is common among critics of liberalism, led the more sophisticated participants in the constitutional negotiations of 1991–2 to seek a final solution to disagreements about the good and to prevent the possibility of re-opening the question by constitutionalizing the solution they discovered. The irony, of course, is that constitutionalization does not necessarily end deliberation about the common good: it simply shifts the deliberations to another arena.

This constitutional impulse surfaced in both the Canada Clause and the proposals for a social and economic union. In the case of both sets of proposals, the architects of the Charlottetown Accord assumed that they knew the authoritative answer to the questions 'What is Canada?' and 'What policies are good for Canada?' More precisely, they assumed that prosperity and harmony require attachment to a common identity, which we can know and preserve only through the constitution. The reality, however, is that the quest for Canadian identity is just as pointless as the quest for Canadian literature.

Good literature, like good politics, seeks answers to universal questions about human existence; the characters and setting may be Canadian, but the problems are general. A Canadian identity cannot be captured at a particular moment and imposed through an act of constitutional will; at best, the constitution can supply the political mechanisms for the gradual development of identity.

In the final analysis, constitutions must be both limited and limiting. They must be limited in the sense that they give the widest possible latitude of operation to the deliberative process; they must be limiting in the sense that they provide a structural and institutional framework (which is not necessarily a framework of substantive rights) that constrains government power without enervating it. This reconciliation of energetic self-government with individual liberty is precisely what motivated the founders of liberal constitutionalism to propose a constitutional structure that divided legislative power federally, relied on representative (rather than direct) democracy, and separated the legislative, executive, and judicial power.[32] Contrary to the claims of its critics, liberal constitutions do not deny the possibility of moral growth; indeed, they provide for it by granting legislatures sufficient power to create new statutory rights, and by providing for an amendment process through which moral progress may be written into fundamental law. The essence of liberal constitutionalism is that rulers and citizens must be bound by the positive law of a constitution that embodies, however imperfectly, universal and eternal principles of moral justice. The task of rendering liberal constitutions more perfect belongs to the citizens who must live under them. This process of moral change is obviously slow and often produces results limited in their scope; but such is the quest for absolute moral principles in pluralist liberal democracies.

In constructing the Canada Clause and the provisions for social and economic union, the architects of Charlottetown, 1992, thought that they had captured the permanent and universal identity of Canada. Canadians ultimately rejected the accord, however, because the identity they saw embodied in it did not match their own self-image. That judgement, I would submit, was substantially correct.

NOTES

1 Stephen Holmes, *The Anatomy of Antiliberalism* (Cambridge, Mass.: Harvard University Press, 1993), 25.

2 George Tsebelis, *Nested Games: Rational Choice in Comparative Politics* (Berkeley, Calif.: University of California Press, 1990), 92–118.

3 No one has expressed this insight better than Peter Russell. See Peter H. Russell, 'The Political Purposes of the Canadian Charter of Rights and Freedoms', *Canadian Bar Review* 61 (1983): 1–33.

4 Peter Russell, *Constitutional Odyssey: Can Canadians Be a Sovereign People?* (Toronto: University of Toronto Press, 1992).

5 See Donald S. Lutz, *The Origins of American Constitutionalism* (Baton Rouge, La.: Louisiana State University Press, 1988), 81–95.

6 Russell, 'Political Purposes', 33.

7 The history of constitutional developments that follows is drawn extensively from Christopher P. Manfredi, *Judicial Power and the Charter: Canada and the Paradox of Liberal Constitutionalism* (Toronto: McClelland and Stewart, 1993), 12–14.

8 Government of Canada, *A Time for Action: Toward the Renewal of the Canadian Federation* (Ottawa, 1978), 8.

9 A history of these negotiations is contained in Roy Romanow, John Whyte, and Howard Leeson, *Canada Notwithstanding: The Making of the Constitution, 1976–1982* (Toronto: Carswell/Methuen, 1984).

10 Ibid., 211.

11 The details of how these two governments have used section 33 can be found in Manfredi, *Judicial Power and the Charter*, 200–2.

12 The first cases to generate significant public opposition were *Askov v. The Queen*, [1990] 2 S.C.R. 1199 and *Seaboyer v. The Queen*, [1991] 2 S.C.R. 577. The *Askov* decision concerned the right to be tried within a reasonable time, and the rule set by the Court resulted in thousands of stays of proceedings. The *Seaboyer* decision nullified the 'rape shield' provisions of the sexual assault law.

13 Manfredi, *Judicial Power and the Charter*, 210.

14 For a detailed history of this process, see Patrick Monahan, *Meech Lake: The Inside Story* (Toronto: University of Toronto Press, 1991).

15 The 1982 *Constitution Act* had limited this provision to language and culture.

16 Alan C. Cairns, 'Constitutional Minoritarianism in Canada', in Ronald L. Watts and Douglas M. Brown, eds, *Canada: The State of the Federation, 1990* (Kingston: Queen's University Institute of Intergovernmental Relations, 1990), 71–96.

17 Government of Canada, *Shaping Canada's Future Together: Proposals* (Ottawa: Supply and Services Canada, 1991).

18 Ibid., 3.

19 Will Kymlicka and Wayne J. Norman, 'The Social Charter Debate: Should Social Justice Be Constitutionalized?', *Network Analyses*, no. 2 (Jan. 1992): 2.

20 Government of Ontario, *A Canadian Social Charter: Making Our Shared Values Stronger* (Ministry of Intergovernmental Affairs, Sept. 1991): 1.

21 *Report of the Special Joint Committee on a Renewed Canada* (Ottawa: Supply and Services Canada, 1992), 21.

22 Ibid., 23. The second stanza of the 'poem' contained a more detailed description of the people of Canada:
        Trustees of a vast northern land,
        we celebrate its beauty and grandeur.
        Aboriginal peoples, immigrants,

> French-speaking, English-speaking,
> Canadians all,
> we honour our roots and value our
> diversity.

The recent activities of the Writers Union have been memorable, if not exactly inclusive. The Toronto feminist and social activist June Callwood was hounded out of the Union for allegedly 'racist' attitudes, and a Union conference was threatened with the loss of government funding for restricting attendance to 'writers of colour'. Pierre Berton has also been a target of the Union's ideological and attitudinal cleansing.

23 Richard S. Kay, 'Review of Christopher P. Manfredi, *Judicial Power and the Charter: Canada and the Paradox of Liberal Constitutionalism*', *American Review of Canadian Studies* 23 (Winter 1993): 626.

24 Government of Canada, *Shaping Canada's Future Together: Proposals* (Ottawa: Supply and Services Canada, 1991), 55–9. The other proposals were for harmonization of economic policies, reforms to the Bank of Canada to ensure that its first priority would be to achieve and preserve price stability; training; immigration; culture; broadcasting; residual powers; the federal declatory power; recognition of areas of exclusive provincial jurisdiction; legislative delegation; streamlining; the federal spending power, and the establishment of a Council of the Federation.

25 Joel Bakan and David Schneiderman, eds, *Social Justice and the Constitution: Perspectives on a Social Union for Canada* (Ottawa: Carleton University Press, 1992).

26 Joel Bakan, 'What's Wrong with Social Rights', in *Social Justice and the Constitution*, 91.

27 Ibid., 94.

28 Jennifer Nedelsky and Craig Scott, 'Constitutional Dialogue', in *Social Justice and the Constitution*, 62.

29 In the midst of the constitutional reform process, the Supreme Court ruled that the federal government may unilaterally alter its financial commitment to provincial and assistance programmes. The social-charter proposal was aimed partly at reversing this decision, which sanctioned federal action that wreaked havoc on provincial fiscal planning. A carefully worded amendment could have been drafted to prevent future federal decisions of this type, and probably would have found much support. Proponents of the social charter had more ambitious goals, however.

30 Bakan and Schneiderman, eds, *Social Justice and the Constitution*, 155–61.

31 Bias in human rights tribunals is discussed in Thomas Flanagan, Rainer Knopff, and Keith Archer, 'Selection Bias in Human Rights Tribunals: An Exploratory Study', *Canadian Public Administration* 31 (1988): 483–500.

32 Manfredi, *Judicial Power and the Charter*, 11.

Part II

Constitutional Interpretation

4

Canada's
Court Party

Rainer Knopff and F.L. Morton

This chapter discusses the rising prominence in Canadian public life of an institution and its partisans. The institution is the judiciary; its partisans constitute the 'Court Party'. Needless to say, the Court Party is not a party organized to compete for elected office, like the Liberals or the Reform Party. It looks more like a 'party' in the eighteenth-century meaning of that term—that is, a faction. This faction is an élite, though it purports to represent a broad base of interest groups and 'social movements'. What unites the Court Party's various elements is an interest in the judicialization of politics. It is rare, of course, to promote an institution for its own sake. Usually a movement or faction is attracted to an institution because it appears to offer the best prospects of furthering a particular political agenda. The Court Party is no exception.

To speak of the partisans of the judiciary may seem a little strange at first, but only because we have become accustomed to thinking of the courts as non-political bodies. With respect to other governmental institutions there is nothing at all remarkable in speaking of their partisans and of the resulting inter-institutional politics. The federal and provincial governments in Canada, for example, certainly have their respective partisans, and the politics of centralization versus provincial rights has been a perennial feature of Canadian public life. The same is true in other federal systems.

The executive and legislative branches of government also attract partisans in battles against each other. Violent rebellions broke out in nineteenth-century Canada over the question of whether to make the executive 'responsible' to the

legislature by requiring it to maintain the 'confidence' of a majority of legislators. Today the tables have turned and, worrying about the overly disciplined
parties and cabinet-dominated legislatures produced by 'responsible government', we wonder whether it might be better to stop treating every important
legislative vote as a test of 'confidence'. Similarly, in the United States, while it
was once possible to celebrate or lament an 'imperial' presidency,[1] observers
nowadays are more likely to debate the merits of an imperial Congress.[2]

The different political institutions in any regime attract partisans because
institutions are not neutral arenas in which substantive political battles are
fought. Institutions shape the political process in ways that enhance the
prospects of certain outcomes and diminish the prospects of others. Political
partisans will thus gravitate to the institutions most open to the policies they
prefer or most closed to those preferred by their opponents. Far from being
external to the substance of politics, institutions are often the very things at
stake in political struggles: 'politics is as much about institutions as it is constrained and channeled *by* them.'[3]

So, to repeat, the idea that institutions attract political partisans is commonplace with respect to all governmental institutions but the courts. The
idea of a court party seems outlandish only to the extent that courts are considered to be non-political institutions. But this view is declining. The courts
have never, in fact, been entirely non-political,[4] and there have even been
times in the past when their association with partisan factions has been
noticed and publicly remarked. As we shall see, Canada's current Court Party
has not been its only court party.

The dramatic explosion of policy making by the courts that accompanied
the advent of the Charter of Rights and Freedoms has once again made the
political significance of the courts readily apparent. Thus, an increasingly significant institutional battleground in Canada, as in other contemporary liberal democracies, especially those with entrenched constitutions, concerns
the balance of power between the judiciary and the more obviously political
branches of government. Institutional arguments in recent US history, for
example, have been as much about an 'imperial judiciary'[5] as about an 'imperial presidency'; most recently the argument is about whether the Supreme
Court has become more deferential to the executive and legislative branches,
and whether such a development should be welcomed or regretted.[6] The
same institutional struggle has become a prominent feature of Canadian
political life since the Charter of Rights and Freedoms was adopted in 1982.
Canada's Court Party is one of the armies that contests this newly prominent
battleground of Canadian politics.

COURT PARTY CONSTITUENCIES

Like the more familiar electoral parties, or political movements more generally, the Court Party is a coalition of several overlapping constituencies. We

have identified four such constituencies: (1) advocates of national unity (or 'unifiers'), (2) Charter Canadians, (3) social engineers, and (4) postmaterialists. A variety of overlapping interests and ideologies (as well as membership) lead these constituencies to join in promoting judicial power.

UNIFIERS

The 1982 Canadian Charter of Rights and Freedoms is clearly central to the increasing prominence of both judicial power and the extra-judicial partisans of that power. The Court Party is dominated by friends of the Charter, or Charterphiles. Among the strongest Charterphiles are those Canadians—concentrated in Ontario and Montreal—who believe that the Charter and the judicial power it promotes will help to solve Canada's national unity crisis. This wing of the Court Party is represented most prominently by former Prime Minister Pierre Trudeau, the 'father' of the Charter. From the beginning, Trudeau saw the Charter as much more than a rights-protecting document. Indeed, he saw it mainly as a 'counterweight' to the forces of decentralizing regionalism and provincialism. The Charter, he hoped, would lead Canadians to define themselves more in terms of rights they held in common and less in terms of geographical jurisdictions and communities that divided them.[7]

With respect to most of francophone Quebec, these hopes have been dashed. The Charter has actually intensified, rather than weakened, the nationalist projects for Quebec's disengagement from Canada. Because the Charter was constitutionally entrenched without Quebec's consent, it is held up in that province as evidence of English Canada's betrayal of its founding partner, and has fuelled, rather than doused, the fires of separatism.[8] Still, unifiers retain high hopes for the Charter's unifying potential, if not against the forces of Quebec separatism (at least in the short term), then at least against the forces of regional alienation in the rest of Canada.

In fact, even outside of Quebec, Canadians are as much divided by Charter rights as they are by regionalism. Charter rights are notoriously vague and ambiguous, and can thus occasion furious battles over their proper interpretation. Section 7 of the Charter, for example, protects the rights to 'life, liberty, and security of the person'. Does this section protect the 'life' of a human fetus or the 'liberty' of the mother to abort that fetus? The pro-life and pro-choice factions in the abortion controversy have engaged in prolonged and highly charged battles about this question.[9] Unifiers, however, prefer such 'cross-cutting cleavages' to the regional cleavages at the root of Canada's national unity crisis, and they like the Charter for its tendency to emphasize cross-cutting cleavages.[10] A person's views on abortion or employment equity, for example, have little to do with what province he or she lives in.

The Charter does not just engender battles about cross-cutting issues, of course; it also makes the courtroom the most prominent arena for conducting these battles. The courts now make substantive policy in areas that used to be the exclusive preserve of legislatures. But the legislative branch of govern-ment in Canada is federally divided while the judicial branch is not. The Canadian judiciary constitutes a single hierarchy, culminating in the Supreme Court, whose Charter interpretations are applicable across the country, regardless of federal jurisdiction. For example, such politically sensitive pol-icy issues as minority language education rights, which previously fell under provincial jurisdiction, are now decided to a considerable extent by the Supreme Court. The transfer of policy-making power from legislatures to courts, in other words, amounts to a centralization of policy-making power. For unifiers, who tend to fear excessive decentralization, this is a significant reason to 'join' the Court Party.

CHARTER CANADIANS

Alan Cairns coined the term Charter Canadians to describe those groups that sought and acquired constitutional status in the Charter of Rights and Free-doms or in closely related sections of the Constitution Act, 1982.[11] They did so in order to entrench policies they could not easily achieve through the leg-islative process. The list of original Charter Canadians, or Charter groups—those explicitly mentioned in the Constitution Act, 1982—comprises women (in sections 15 and 28); the multicultural community of racial, ethnic, and religious minorities (in sections 15 and 27); the mentally and physically dis-abled (in section 15); the elderly (in section 15); official language minorities (in sections 16–23); and aboriginals (in sections 25 and 35). Additional Char-ter groups, such as non-citizens[12] and homosexuals,[13] have since been added through the judicial interpretation of section 15.

Since it is the courts that 'enforce' Charter rights against reluctant and recalcitrant legislatures, the Charter groups have a vested interest in judicial power. Certainly these groups have actively used the Charter to lobby and lit-igate their various policy agendas. Indeed, many of these groups have acquired wholly new organizations designed mainly to exploit the new politi-cal opportunities afforded by the Charter. The archetypical example is the feminist Legal Education and Action Fund (LEAF). After having heavily influ-enced the wording of the equality rights sections (15 and 28) of the Charter in 1980–1, feminist groups then sought ways to take advantage of the broad wording. In 1984 the Canadian Advisory Council on the Status of Women published a study calling for the creation of a single, nation-wide 'legal action fund' to co-ordinate and pay for a policy of 'systematic litigation' of strategic 'test cases'.[14] The study reported that with the adoption of the Charter, 'we find ourselves at the opportune moment to stress litigation as a vehicle for social change.'[15] A year later LEAF was launched, and it has gone on to become the most frequent and most successful non-government intervener in Charter cases before the Supreme Court.[16]

What is true of LEAF is true of a rapidly growing list of organizations with a similar political genesis: the Charter Committee on Poverty Issues, the

Canadian Prisoners' Rights Network, the Equality Rights Committee of the Canadian Ethnocultural Council, and Equality for Gays and Lesbians Everywhere (EGALE), to name just a few.[17] These organizations are quite different from the individual litigant who employs constitutional arguments primarily as a means to obtain personal benefit, and for whom the broader policy consequences of a judicial opinion are thus a secondary by-product. For systematic litigation groups, the reverse is true: policy is the primary focus, and the individual case becomes just a convenient vehicle for pursuing the desired policy. To the extent that they are strongly oriented to litigation as a way of pursuing their desired policies, these groups are important components of the Court Party.

SOCIAL ENGINEERS

A third strand within the Court Party coalition—one that begins to illuminate the political agenda of the coalition—is captured by the term 'social engineer'. Social engineers take the view that the social evils of this world are caused, not by human nature, but by defective social institutions and systems. Cure the institutional ills, they believe, and natural human goodness will prevail. Such a cure, of course, implies comprehensive reconstruction of the defective social structures, that is, social engineering. For example, social engineers believe that crime has no natural causes, that it can be explained almost completely by such social factors as class inequality, and that it can be cured by social change.

Underlying the perspective of the social engineers is what Thomas Sowell calls the 'unconstrained' vision of human nature and society. This vision is best understood in relation to its opposite, the 'constrained' vision, which holds that there are inherent limits or 'constraints' on the human capacity to achieve social perfection. Social evil, in the constrained view, has natural causes, which can be checked and ameliorated, but not 'cured'.[18] Human nature, in other words, while not necessarily devoid of admirable social tendencies,[19] has its ineradicably asocial, even antisocial, side. Institutions can channel man's less admirable tendencies in more or less productive ways and can affect the relative balance between the good and bad sides of human nature, but no amount of social engineering can eradicate the latter. According to the unconstrained vision, by contrast, human beings are good by nature but corruptible by society. This view makes it possible to think society could be comprehensively re-engineered to end the corruption and make human goodness permanently victorious.

The unconstrained vision can lead to two quite different approaches to democracy: populism and democratic élitism. The populist approach arises when the corruption by society of natural human goodness is understood to affect only a nefarious élite, in which case the obvious answer is to promote increased democracy. The rule of the 'whole uncorrupted portion of the people'[20] can then be seen as an unmitigated good, bringing social and political life to a state of perfection. But, of course, the unconstrained vision does not in principle exclude the systemic corruption of the people as a whole. They too can be deformed by the social system. When this happens, democracy may still be the ultimate end—after the people have been returned to their natural purity—but it cannot be the immediate means. The achievement of true democracy will first require a period of purification through social reconstruction by a vanguard of purifiers. This is the route of major social engineering, and it necessarily involves democratic élitism.

Democratic élitism is the position that proponents of the unconstrained vision tend to be drawn toward today. Wishing to transform the formative 'system', they cannot entrust power to the people who have been formed by that system and who are likely simply to reproduce it. Thus the vanguard élite must temporarily exercise transformatory power—that is, it must engage in social engineering—which it can do only through institutions relatively unresponsive to the will of the corrupted many. In Canada there are only three plausible candidates: the Senate, the bureaucracy, and the courts. Inasmuch as the first two have little public legitimacy, only the courts are left.

POSTMATERIALISTS

To describe the Court Party coalition as composed of unifiers, Charter Canadians, and social engineers is accurate as far as it goes, but it misses the institutional and social nexus that nurtures the coalition. Historians and political analysts have long recognized that struggles between institutions are expressions of competing social forces. As James Mallory puts it, 'In a constitutional state with some degree of separation of powers, it may happen that a particular vested interest will capture control of one branch of the government but not another.'[21] Often newly emergent governmental institutions are strongly associated with rising social classes. Thus, the triumph of Parliament over the monarchy in the seventeenth century and the eclipse of the House of Lords by the House of Commons in the nineteenth century signalled the rising influence of first the landed aristocracy and subsequently the urban bourgeoisie. Similarly, Canada's struggles in the nineteenth century for responsible government saw the defeat of executive-ensconced social and economic élites (the 'Family Compact' in Upper Canada and the 'Château Clique' in Lower Canada) by democratic and, in the case of Lower Canada, nationalistic partisans of the legislature. The modern Court Party is also rooted in a 'new class': the so-called postmaterialist or postindustrial knowledge class.

Seymour Martin Lipset has observed that in post-war western democracies, the most dynamic agent of social change has been, not Marx's industrial proletariat, but a new 'oppositionist intelligentsia', drawn from and supported by the well-educated, more affluent strata of society.[22] Lipset and others have explained this change as a consequence of new and growing concerns with non-economic and social issues—'a clean environment, a better culture, equal status for women and minorities, the quality of education, international relations, greater democratization, and a more permissive morality, particularly as affecting familial and sexual issues'.[23] These new concerns are most prevalent outside the working classes. 'The reform elements concerned with postmaterialist or social issues largely derive their strength not from the workers and the less privileged, the social base of the Left in industrial society, but from segments of the well educated and affluent, students, academics, journalists, professionals and civil servants.'[24] These groups, each in its own way, are participants in the 'knowledge industry' that is a new locus of power in post-industrial democracies. 'Just as property was the foundation of élite power in industrial society, so knowledge (thus, a high level of education) is the vehicle of power in post-industrial politics of the administrative state.'[25]

Of course, it is as difficult today as it has always been for a 'knowledge class' to exercise power through majoritarian institutions (consider Plato's philosopher kings). This helps to explain why postmaterialism is attracted to the anti-majoritarian power of the courts. Unlike the progressive reformers of past generations who sought to transfer power from the 'few rich' to the 'many poor', the postmaterialist left finds itself in the minority and sees the majority as a problem. Inglehart has demonstrated that postmaterialist values are much more prominent among intellectual, bureaucratic, media, and political élites than among the general population. This fact, he argued, creates a 'tactical dilemma' for 'the Left in contemporary society':

> Postmaterialist forces have become powerful at the élite level; they demand major policy shifts in key areas, and they are far too influential among the militants and élites of Left parties to be ignored. But Postmaterialists are not equally strong at the mass level—which means that the parties of the Left are in danger of electoral defeat if they swing too far to the Postmaterialist side.[26]

As Mike Bygrave put it, 'the result is a seemingly insuperable problem for the left.'[27]

In fact, while Inglehart's 'tactical dilemma' does exist, Bygrave's 'insuperable problem' does not. The problem looms large only in so far as the postmaterialist left must compete in the majoritarian politics of elections and parliaments. To the extent that postmaterialists can move their policy agenda into the courts and the bureaucracy and pursue it through the rulings of sympathetic judges and administrators, the problem is minimized. Inglehart explicitly recognizes that postmaterialists are 'better equipped to attain their goals through bureaucratic institutions or the courts than through the electoral process'.[28] He points out that, whereas in the 1960s postmaterialism was symbolized by 'the student with a protest placard', it is now symbolized by 'the public interest lawyer, or the technocrat with an environmental impact statement'.[29] It is not surprising, then, that the rising power of the courts, as promoted by a Court Party, is the political project of the post-materialist 'new class' or 'knowledge class'.

THE ÉLITISM OF THE COURT PARTY

The postmaterialist knowledge class is, of course, an élite. And social engineers engage in democratic élitism. There is thus a symbiotic relationship between these two constituencies of the Court Party: social engineering necessarily involves the transformatory power of a vanguard élite, and that élite is drawn from the postmaterialist knowledge class. True, much of the social engineering proposed by this élite is said to serve the interests of 'disadvantaged' Charter-Canadian constituencies, but the rank and file of those constituencies must often undergo 'consciousness raising' before they understand their true interests. And for the 'false consciousness' of the rank and file to be overcome, they must be led by their vanguard, postmaterialist élite.[30] Similarly, the symbolic preoccupations of the unifiers seem most prominent among the same postmaterialist class. The Court Party, in short, is a party of élites. Indeed, it is an important manifestation of what Christopher Lasch calls the 'Revolt of the Élites'.[31]

The symbiosis of social engineering and the knowledge class should not surprise us. The post-materialist knowledge class is attracted to the unconstrained vision of the social engineer because that vision places a premium on the specialized knowledge of the intellectual. Again, this is best understood by comparison with the constrained vision, which emphasizes the dispersed and experiential knowledge of the citizenry at large.

Because the constrained vision views the knowledge of any one person as 'grossly inadequate for social decision-making', it conceives of socially relevant knowledge predominantly as '*experience*—transmitted socially in largely inarticulate forms, from prices which indicate costs, scarcities, and preferences, to traditions which evolve from the day-to-day experiences of millions in each generation, winnowing out in Darwinian competition what works from what does not work'.[32] Such mechanisms as prices and traditions make a complex society possible by co-ordinating 'knowledge from a tremendous range of contemporaries, as well as from the even more vast numbers of those from generations past'.[33] The social mechanisms of prices and traditions are much more powerful and effective agents of human progress than intellectual knowledge because they co-ordinate a much vaster body of social knowledge than any individual or intellectual élite could hope to possess.

For the unconstrained vision, by contrast, experience is 'vastly overrated' as compared to 'the general power of a cultivated mind', and the 'wisdom of the ages' is therefore seen 'as largely the illusions of the ignorant'.[34] In the words of William Godwin, 'the pretense of collective wisdom is the most palpable of all impostures.'[35] True wisdom, in this view, is to be found in the rationality, and individual judgement, of intellectual knowledge—that is, the knowledge of the instructed, cultivated élite. Thus, far from respecting the collective wisdom of the many, as embodied in such mechanisms as prices and traditions, the unconstrained vision emphasizes the role of the intellectual élite in

In other words the knowledge class doesn't believe in a reality that stubbornly escapes human control partly because it has 'seceded' from reality.

The masses, by contrast, have not seceded from reality because they have not been able to. For the farmer, the assembly worker, the homemaker, and the like, bedrock reality is palpable and inescapable. For Lasch this explains why the political instincts of the masses 'are demonstrably more conservative than those of their self-appointed spokesmen and would-be liberators'. The conservative instincts Lasch has in mind are largely those of Sowell's constrained vision. In particular, the masses 'have a more highly developed sense of limits than their betters. They understand, as their betters do not, that there are inherent limits on human control over the course of social development, over nature and the body, over the tragic elements in human life and history.'[39] When Ortega y Gasset wrote *The Revolt of the Masses*, he had in mind a mass man who 'looked forward to a future of "limitless possibilities" and "complete freedom".'[40] For Lasch, it is the knowledge élite, not the masses, that now hold this unconstrained vision of human possibility in western democracies, and it is thus now more accurate to speak of 'the revolt of the élites'. The Court Party is one manifestation of this revolt.

But why is it that these élites present themselves as the 'self-appointed spokesmen and would-be liberators' of disadvantaged groups (in Canada, the Charter groups)? How is it, in other words, that an obviously unequal élite comes to support the cause of equality? For the unconstrained vision, the answer is that the intellectual élite's power of reason—its defining virtue—will lead it to a reasoned support for justice. As Sowell points out, proponents of this vision often assume that intellectual élites are disinterested or are 'strangers to ambition'.[41] This might make sense under an older view of the 'disinterested' pursuit of knowledge, but it makes little sense from the postmodern perspective of intellectual activity as 'power-knowledge'. In this postmodern view, all knowledge is motivated by interests—except for an 'interest' in the universal 'truth', which allegedly doesn't exist—and it thus becomes unclear why anyone's reason would lead him to promote another's interest. We are thus compelled to wonder how the interests of the knowledge classes might be served by the egalitarian transformation of society.[42]

An obvious answer is that such transformation serves the power interests of the intellectual élite. Egalitarian social engineering does not give power to the many whose consciousness needs to be reconstructed, but to the vanguard élite that undertakes the reconstruction. True, the unconstrained vision sees this as *democratic* élitism—that is, as temporary élitism in the service of a more perfect future democracy—but it is worth noting that in even the most extreme attempts at social reconstruction (the Soviet experiment comes to mind), the goal, like a shimmering mirage in the distance, never seems to get any closer, and short of abandoning the reconstructive attempt, the 'transitional' period of democratic élitism turns out to be permanent. This is, of course, precisely what the constrained vision would predict—any attempt to reconstructing the unenlightened many. In other words, it flatters precisely the defining characteristic of the postmaterialist knowledge class.

It is not knowledge *per se* that is being flattered, of course, but knowledge as a prime lever of power. This connection between the knowledge and power of the postmaterialist class is further abetted by the model of knowledge that has gained prominence among that class. Post-materialism is associated with postmodernism, a central tenet of which is that knowledge does not stand apart from power, but in fact *is* power. The 'reality' we purport to understand does not exist independently of that understanding; on the contrary, reality is *constituted* or 'constructed' by our understanding of it. There is no knowledge independent of power; there is only 'power-knowledge'. It is power-knowledge that drives the 'social construction' or social engineering of reality by the knowledge class. The idea that there is no reality independent of human making reflects precisely the lack of limits or constraints that characterizes the unconstrained vision.

The combination of the unconstrained vision and the post-modern model of knowledge is attractive to the knowledge class, not only because it flatters its interests, but also because it is consistent with its life experience. Richard Herrnstein and Charles Murray have systematically described and analysed what others have also observed: the evolution of society's natural cognitive élite from a statistical aggregation into a true class, with its own life experience and distinct interests. They point out that until recently the best and the brightest were distributed throughout society, both geographically and occupationally. Nowadays, by contrast, a variety of sorting mechanisms—particularly the education system—separates them out and concentrates them in high-status, knowledge-based occupations and in the communities and networks of what one might call the 'internet society', where they meet mainly others like themselves.[36] One result, in Christopher Lasch's words, is that 'the thinking classes are fatally removed from the physical side of life':

> Their only relation to productive labor is that of consumers. They have no experience of making anything substantial or enduring. They live in a world of abstractions and images, a simulated world that consists of computerized models of reality—'hyperreality', as it has been called—as distinguished from the palpable, immediate, physical reality inhabited by ordinary men and women.[37]

This, according to Lasch, helps to explain 'their belief in the "social construction of" reality—the central dogma of post modernist thought'. Belief in this dogma

> reflects the experience of living in an artificial environment from which everything that resists human control (unavoidably, everything familiar and reassuring as well) has been rigorously excluded. Control has become their obsession. In their drive to insulate themselves against risk and contingency—against the unpredictable hazards that afflict human life—the thinking classes have seceded not just from the common world around them but from reality itself.[38]

achieve the impossible will not end unless those making the attempt recognize and concede its impossibility. A cynic might add that if attempting the impossible enhances one's power, one will be less likely to recognize or concede its impossibility. In this cynical view, the élite's egalitarian rhetoric turns out to be little more than a legitimating cover for its own unending (and unequal) power.[43] The power of the knowledge élite, of course, is best exercised through an institution that emphasizes the rationality of the intellectual. Again, the judiciary is a leading candidate.

THE COURT PARTY VS. TRADITIONAL JUDICIAL REVIEW

Not surprisingly, the Court Party is characterized not only by its interest in judicial power but also by its desire to use that power in non-traditional ways and for novel purposes; it thus rejects the traditional understanding of judicial review in almost all respects. According to this traditional understanding, judicial review of constitutionally entrenched rights could be said to have six primary elements. First, judicial review embodied a distrust of majoritarian democracy: it was understood as a way to protect individual rights and liberties, especially private property rights, against demagogues and misguided majority rule. Second, and closely related, it was premised on the classical liberal distinction between state (the public) and society and economy (the private), and was strongly portrayed as a defender of the latter against the former. Third, judicial review was inherently conservative or traditional, in the sense that it preferred and protected 'the ancient truths' against corruption by future majorities. Its purpose was to protect existing rights, not to create new ones. The corollary to this was that many important constitutional questions might never be addressed by the courts.[44] Fourth, constitutional rights were understood to be not just 'for' but also 'by' individuals. Rights claims were raised by individual litigants in the course of settling other legal disputes with the state. Among other things, this meant that the dispute came first, the constitutional issue second.[45] Fifth, judicial review was understood as an exercise of legal judgement not political will. This faith in judges as the paragons of impartial reason (as *lex loquens*), combined with their independence from both the people and the other organs of government, was the primary justification for vesting the power of enforcing constitutional norms in the judiciary. An element of this faith was that judges would never abuse the power of judicial review by injecting their own political preferences into the interpretation of the constitutional text.[46] Sixth, there has always been a nation-building or centralizing thrust implicit in judicial review.[47]

For Court-Party unifiers, the centralizing features of judicial review remain part of its attraction. The other features of traditional judicial review, however, have been largely rejected by Court Party activists. True, the anti-majoritarian inclinations of the post-materialist social engineers within the Court Party have something in common with the anti-majoritarianism that animated traditional judicial review. But the differences outweigh the similarities. The anti-majoritarianism of traditional judicial review was of a civil libertarian kind. It worried that misguided majorities might impel the state to do too much and looked to the courts to engage in 'negative activism', that is, to tell governments what they could *not* do. The anti-majoritarianism of the Court Party, by contrast, is inspired in part by the fear that democratic governments will do too little, and it looks to the courts to engage in 'positive activism', that is, to tell governments what they must do.

There has, in other words, been a role reversal. The generation of intellectuals who developed the welfare state—what Doug Owram called the 'government generation'[48]—saw judicial power as the friend of *laissez-faire* economics and the limited state, and thus as their enemy. And they were amply confirmed in this view by the actual practice of judicial review, which threw up seemingly endless roadblocks to the development of the welfare state in both Canada and the United States. As Mallory pointed out over a generation ago, in Canada 'the force that start[ed] our interpretive machinery in motion' in these cases was 'the reaction of a free economy against regulation'.[49] The same was true in the United States. The 'court parties' of that era, in other words, were the partisans of private property and *laissez-faire*, while their opponents, who controlled the legislatures, favoured the redistribution of private wealth and regulation.

In both countries, therefore, the government generation went to war against judicial power and eventually caused the courts to abandon their opposition to the welfare state. In the United States, the conflict between the Supreme Court and Franklin Roosevelt's 'New Deal' culminated in the court's capitulation in 1937. Corwin described this capitulation as nothing less than a 'constitutional revolution', because it marked the end in practice (if not in popular myth) of the American founders' ideal of guaranteeing 'limited government' through a written constitution. After the 1937 'Court Crisis', the American court publicly abdicated its traditional constitutional responsibilities (federalism, economic liberty, and property rights) and virtually disappeared from American politics for almost two decades—until its *School Desegregation Decision* in 1954.

In Canada an analogous if less dramatic conflict between the judiciary and the new welfare-state interventionism of the federal government also appeared to spell the end for a significant political role for the courts in the new welfare state. In particular, the Judicial Committee of the Privy Council, which had mounted the judicial opposition to the welfare state, was replaced by the Supreme Court as Canada's highest court of appeal, and political negotiation replaced judicial review as the preferred means of managing federal-provincial jurisdictional disputes.[50] The triumphant government generation in both countries, in short, was to a considerable extent an anti-court party. Its perspective lingered on in Canada into the 1960s, helping to swamp Diefenbaker's 1960 Bill of Rights and render it without effect.[51]

For the modern Court Party, by contrast, the tables have been turned and the judiciary appears as a potential ally and instrument of the active state, often against legislatures that refuse to extend state activism, or worse, have lost faith even in existing modes of state intervention and attempt to dismantle them. Thus, in contrast to the pre-Charter era, when the use of constitutional litigation by interest groups usually represented the efforts of members of society (individuals or corporations) to restrain the actions of the state,[52] many Charter groups litigate to try to force the expansion of state services, benefits, or regulation. This is clearly true of the numerous state-funded section 23 'minority language education rights' cases, such as the *Mahé* case from Alberta.[53] Expanding the state is also often the object of feminists and other 'equality seekers', who reject formal 'equality of opportunity' in the name of 'equality of results'. As Janine Brodie has written, most 'key feminist policy demands . . . call for more not less government and public spending.'[54] Constitutionally, this has led feminist legal scholars to reject a policy of 'non-discrimination' as inadequate.[55] Instead they have proposed sophisticated jurisprudential theories of 'disparate impact' and 'systemic discrimination' that invite judicial revision of legislative decision making.[56] This theory of systemic discrimination has been endorsed by other members of the section 15 club, and the Supreme Court accepted it in *Andrews*, its landmark section 15 ruling.[57] At a minimum this interpretation of section 15 challenges otherwise neutral government policies that disproportionately burden women and other 'disadvantaged' minorities. At a maximum it sanctions judicially ordered 'positive remedies' to achieve equal results. In the latter instance, Charter experts advocate the use of 'structural injunctions', a legal instrument, pioneered by American activists, by which the courts 'manage the reconstruction of a social institution' such as schools or prisons until they comply with constitutional standards. Failure to use such aggressive, state-extending remedies, says Helena Orton, former litigation director for LEAF, will render 'the guarantee of equality . . . deceitful and meaningless'.[58]

Such positive judicial activism was anomalous for traditional liberals because they thought government could infringe constitutional rights only through its positive actions—that is, by doing too much—not by failing to act and thus doing too little. For the Court Party, by contrast, a government's failure to act can be just as unconstitutional as its actions, and positive activism thus becomes a logical remedy. Traditional liberals might well wonder how such an approach to the Charter is possible. How, they might ask, can a document that, on its face, covers only the laws and policies of legislatures and governments[59] apply to the *absence* of law or policy? The answer given by Court Party theoreticians is that the decision not to impose law or policy is itself a legal or policy decision—that is, that non-law is also law, and thus subject to the Charter.

An example will help to clarify the point. Section 15 of the Charter explicitly prohibits only discrimination by 'laws'. From the traditional liberal perspective, this means that section 15 does not directly prohibit a private employer from refusing to hire, say, disabled employees. Moreover, although governments are free to address such private discrimination through statutory human rights codes, section 15 imposes no positive obligation to enact such legislation. Someone with this view might well believe that private discrimination against the disabled is wrong, and that legislation to prohibit it would be desirable, but would nevertheless deny that section 15's prohibition of public discrimination requires the state to legislate against private discrimination. If, by contrast, a government's decision not to enact such legislation is understood as legal permission for, even endorsement of, private discrimination, then we have a government policy that would be subject to section 15. As Dale Gibson has put it, 'If the term "law" in section 52(1) of the Charter were interpreted to include [such] permissive aspects of law as well as those which are prohibitory, the Charter would have a very wide range of operation.'[60] A very wide range indeed! Among other things, it would subject all government inaction—all public failures to right private wrongs—to judicial scrutiny under the Charter and would require positive action to remedy any unconstitutional inaction. In our example, it would require any government that had not legislated against private discrimination to do so.

The Court Party's conflating of state action and inaction involves a rejection of the traditional liberal ordering of state and society. In classical liberal theory the realm of social freedom precedes the state, which is based on consent. People consent to the establishment of the state, and thus to *some* limits by the state on their freedom, in order better to secure a remaining (and significant) realm of freedom. Thus, when a classical liberal uses the old adage 'whatever the law does not prohibit is permitted', he understands it as protecting an important residue of pre-political freedom, which does not owe its existence to the state. Court Party theoreticians understand the same adage very differently. They take it to mean that social freedom is permitted by the law and thus exists because of (as opposed to being better secured by) the state.[61] Instead of understanding the state as the creation of a pre-existing society, in other words, the Court Party sees society as the creation of the state. The social realm of private freedom is no longer understood as the residue of an original, pre-political freedom, the better protection of which constitutes the very raison d'être of the state, but as existing only because, and to the extent that, the state permits it. The state thus becomes responsible for the use and misuse of social freedom and can be forced to regulate the latter by constitutional standards.

As one might expect, the difference between the liberal and Court Party orderings of state and society is illuminated by Sowell's constrained and unconstrained visions. The classical liberal, looking at the world through constrained lenses, sees ineradicable human imperfection as the source of both the dissatisfaction with the pre-political state of freedom that underlies consent to government and the distrustful insistence on limiting and constraining that government. This perspective is most memorably captured by James Madison in *Federalist* 51:

> It may be a reflection on human nature that [checks and balances] should be necessary to control the abuses of government. But what is government itself but the greatest of all reflections on human nature? If men were angels, no government would be necessary. If angels were to govern men, neither external nor internal controls on government would be necessary. In framing a government which is to be administered by men over men, the great difficulty lies in this: you must first enable the government to control the governed; and in the next place oblige it to control itself.[62]

For the unconstrained vision, by contrast, human imperfection, and the wrongs (including the 'private' wrongs) it generates, being rooted not in nature but in social systems and structures, are ultimately curable through social engineering. Prejudice, crime, violence, and the like exist not because they are inevitable, but because their causes have been permitted to exist— permitted by the state. The democratic state, which could undertake the curative social engineering, drawing on the expertise of a vanguard knowledge élite, is thus responsible for the continued existence of such evils; but it is unlikely to take the necessary remedial actions to the extent that it remains responsive to the general corruption caused by its very failure to act. The way out of this vicious circle is through an alliance between the vanguard élite and the branch of government least responsive to the corrupted demos and most open to power-knowledge: the judiciary.

The Court Party is not always fully successful in striking and cementing the desired alliance, however. For example, the courts have insisted on maintaining a distinction between state and society, with the Charter applying only to the former.[63] Since this distinction is undermined by the doctrine that state inaction is essentially the same as state action, the courts have not fully accepted that doctrine. They have not, to be more precise, fully endorsed the view that public failures to redress private wrongs are necessarily subject to Charter scrutiny. The courts have gone part way in this direction, however, holding that *partial* action may be successfully challenged even if complete inaction is permissible. Thus, although a government doesn't have to legislate against private discrimination, if it chooses to do so, the legislation must extend to all the group traits protected against public discrimination by the Charter.[64] Having found that homosexuality was a prohibited ground of discrimination under section 15, for example, the Ontario Court of Appeal, in the case of *Haig and Birch*, concluded that the failure of the Canadian Human Rights Act to include sexual preference as a prohibited ground of discrimination was unconstitutional.[65]

Logically, of course, finding a partial action to be unconstitutional for not going far enough does not imply positive judicial activism if complete inaction is also permissible. Indeed, a perfectly logical response would be to invalidate the entire law, leaving it to the legislature to choose between the two constitutional alternatives: re-enacting a constitutionally comprehensive version of the law, or enacting no law at all. This is not what the Court Party has in mind, however. Understanding the 'staying power of a legal status quo',[66] such Court Party actors as LEAF argue that the courts should not dismantle desirable remedial legislation, thus establishing ground zero as the legal status quo, a status quo the government might well be tempted to leave in place. Judges 'should hesitate', LEAF advised the Supreme Court, 'to select a remedy that would leave the disadvantaged dependent on the actions of a majoritarian legislature to restore to them benefits' that have been struck down only because they are 'underinclusive'.[67] On the contrary, LEAF maintained, judges should not hesitate to read the unconstitutionally missing beneficiaries into the deficient legislation, thus placing the weight of the legal status quo at the interventionist end of the policy continuum. This is the ultimate in positive judicial activism, inasmuch as it allows the courts to bypass legislatures altogether and extend policies of state intervention directly, by rewriting legislation themselves. Here again, the Court Party perspective has met with only partial, but nevertheless significant success. The Supreme Court has accepted the legitimacy of reading in, but only when the missing beneficiaries are significantly fewer in number than those already included, thus making it safer to assume that the legislature would rather keep a slightly extended version of the legislation than abandon it altogether.[68] Homosexuals, it turns out, are a small enough group to qualify for reading into a list of legislative beneficiaries. Thus, in *Haig and Birch*, the Ontario Court of Appeal read sexual preference into the Canadian Human Rights Act.[69]

Clearly, cases such as *Haig and Birch* make it difficult to maintain the traditional picture of judicial review as a way of defending traditional rights, or as a conservative check on the tides of social change. Such reformist (as opposed to tradition-maintaining) tendencies of judicial power draw considerable sustenance from what is known as the 'non-interpretivist' approach to constitutional interpretation. Non-interpretivism emphasizes the need for constitutional flexibility and thus 'judicial updating' of constitutional principles to accommodate changing socio-economic conditions. Seeing the constitution as a 'living tree', whose contours must be shaped by judicial gardeners, non-interpretivism minimizes the importance of judicial fidelity to the constitutional text, its 'original understanding', or the 'framers' intent'.[70] Such a 'living tree' approach significantly enhances the ability of judges to act as agents of policy reform by giving them a free hand to 'discover' new meaning in broadly worded constitutional principles, establishing new rights if social need, as the appointed judges understand it, calls for them. Needless to say, the Court Party is a friend to non-interpretivism.

For newly created judicial standards to have widespread policy implications, moreover, they must apply well beyond the confines of the particular case before the court. Thus the Court Party has promoted and welcomed the Supreme Court's transformation from a traditional, British-style adjudicatory court to a court designed to solve social problems by issuing broad declarations of constitutional policy.[71] The Court now sees itself as the authoritative oracle of the constitution, empowered to develop its standards for society as a whole, rather than just for the litigants before it.[72] The establishment of constitutional policy now comes first, the concrete dispute second. Indeed, with the important exception of criminal cases involving legal rights, the individual litigant is vanishing in Charter litigation. Interest groups are increasingly the principal carrier of Charter litigation, if not as the litigant,[73] then as the financial backer[74] or intervener. Drawing on American experience of systematic litigation strategies, a new breed of Canadian interest groups have become adept at packaging their causes as cases and taking them to court.

The Supreme Court has facilitated interest-group litigation by adopting a new, open-door policy for non-government interveners. A rarity in the decade preceding the Charter, interest-group litigation has mushroomed since. By 1990, more than 100 interest-group interveners had participated in over half of all the Supreme Court's Charter cases.[75] The Court has also dramatically relaxed the doctrines of standing[76] and mootness,[77] making it easier for interest groups to bring their causes before the courts. Interest groups, which intervene to achieve goals that may be quite different from those of the immediate parties, have also benefited from the Court's willingness to address issues not actually raised by the factual situations of the parties.[78] The latter procedural changes are an index of the Court's willingness to issue broad declarations of constitutional policy even when there is no bona fide legal dispute before it that clearly implicates the policy questions it wishes to address. This is why disputes, the traditional stock in trade of courts, are now merely a sufficient and no longer a necessary condition for judicial intervention in public policy.

The effect of the Court's relaxing of the rules of evidence, relevance, standing, mootness, and intervener status, combined with the new sophistication of Canadian interest groups in using constitutional litigation as a political tactic, means that few major government policies are likely to escape a Charter challenge.[79] Judicial intervention in the policy-making process is no longer *ad hoc* and sporadic, dependent upon the fortuitous collision of individual interests and government policy; it has become more systematic and continuous.

It is an interest in such systematic, policy-oriented use of judicial power that lies at the heart of the Court Party. The Court Party does not, therefore, include such individual litigants as the criminally accused, who raise constitutional issues as part of their defence. Such persons certainly try to get the courts to change criminal justice policy, but primarily as a means to their main objective: going free. Changes in policy may be a by-product of their courtroom arguments, but such changes are not their main intention.

Nor does the Court Party include all interest groups that engage in systematic litigation. As we use the term, the Court Party excludes traditional civil libertarians and limited-state 'conservatives'. Unlike the individual liti-gant for whom the broader policy outcomes of judicial decisions are sec-ondary to the main object, civil libertarian and conservative interest groups, such as the National Citizens' Coalition, certainly engage in systematic, pol-icy-oriented litigation. Moreover, they often invite the courts to play an active role, but the kind of judicial activism they support serves as a tradi-tional and negative bulwark against the state, not as a way to defend or further develop the active state. The Court Party, in short, is defined both by its interest in the systematic use of judicial power and by the non-traditional pol-icy agenda to which it wants to harness that power.

Nor, finally, does the Court Party include all judges. As we have seen, the Supreme Court has accepted some, but definitely not all, Court-Party posi-tions. Indeed, the Court-Party agenda occasions significant and continuing disagreement among the members of that Court, as well as within the judi-ciary generally. Explaining why the Court Party is attracted to judicial power, as this chapter tries to do, is one thing. Determining the extent to which the Court Party has, to use Mallory's term, 'captured' the courts is quite another, and must be reserved to another occasion.[80]

CONCLUSION

Rival political interests or factions often gravitate to rival institutions or branches of government. This truism is a common point of departure for ana-lysts of the most obviously political institutions of government—the legisla-tive and executive branches, and the jurisdictional orders of federalism—and it has even been applied in past analyses of the judiciary. It has been argued, for example, that the dramatic assertion of judicial power at the birth of the modern welfare state reflected the interests and agenda of the economic élites that favoured relatively unregulated private enterprise. Making use of the courts enabled these interests to throw a veil of legalism over their agenda, of course, but political analysts rightly peered beneath the veil. The same scep-ticism should govern the analysis of the current outbreak of judicial power. Indeed, when prominent legal theory, drawing inspiration from post-mod-ernism, insists that law and the legal rationales of judges are little more than rationalizations of the power of particular interests, sceptical analysis of judi-cial power is especially appropriate. What interests and whose power is served by the newly reinvigorated judiciary? This should be the first question of analysis. If, to use our term, there was a 'court party' backing the Depression-era assertion of judicial power, chances are that a court party also underlies the current manifestation of that power. This chapter is part of our continu-ing attempt to describe Canada's modern Court Party.

We contend that Canada's modern Court Party, like its Depression-era predecessor—and as one might expect with any political faction attracted to an appointed institution—is a coalition of élites. The élites underlying the old and new court parties are quite different, however, with different agendas and thus different ways of using their favourite institution. The old court party was inspired by materialist élites who attempted to use the courts to resist the interventionist and redistributionism policies of elected governments. The postmaterialist knowledge class underlying the current Court Party, by contrast, wants to use the courts to further activist projects of social transformation, either in the service of national unity (by re-engineering political identities) or in the name of re-engineering the systemic or structural causes of evil in human relations. In sum, the old court party tried to block change, while the new Court Party is trying to lead change. What they share is their inability to win majority support for their policies through the normal electoral-legislative process, and thus their attraction to the courts as an alternative forum for political action.

NOTES

This chapter elaborates and refines arguments made in F.L. Morton and Rainer Knopff, 'The Supreme Court as the Vanguard of the Intelligentsia: The Charter Movement as Postmaterialist Politics', in Janet Ajzenstat, ed., *Canadian Constitutionalism: 1791–1991* (Ottawa: Canadian Study of Parliament Group, 1992), 57–80. Although the current chapter is substantially new, occasional passages of the earlier paper have been adapted to our present purpose. Permission to make use of this material is gratefully acknowledged. Both Rainer Knopff and F.L. Morton wish to acknowledge the assistance of the Social Sciences and Humanities Research Council (grant numbers 410–91–1396 and 410–92–0320 respectively). Among other things, this financial support allowed us to retain the very valuable research assistance of Michael Wagner.

1 Arthur M. Schlesinger, Jr, *The Imperial Presidency* (Toronto: Popular Library, 1974).

2 Allan Gotlieb, 'The Republican Rules of the Game', *Globe and Mail*, 1 January 1995.

3 Keith Archer, Roger Gibbins, Rainer Knopff, and Leslie A. Pal, *Parameters of Power: Canada's Political Institutions* (Toronto: Nelson, 1995), 507.

4 Peter H. Russell, 'The Effect of a Charter of Rights on the Policy-Making Role of Canadian Courts', *Canadian Public Administration* 25 (1982): 1–33.

5 Nathan Glazer, 'Towards an Imperial Judiciary', *Public Interest* 41 (Fall 1975): 104–23.

6 For two opposing views, see Gary L. McDowell, *Curbing the Courts: The Constitution and the Limits of Judicial Power* (Baton Rouge: Louisiana State University Press, 1988); and Herman Schwartz, *Packing the Courts: The Conservative Campaign to Rewrite the Constitution* (New York: Charles Scribner's Sons, 1988).

7 See Peter H. Russell, 'The Political Purposes of the Canadian Charter of Rights

and Freedoms', *Canadian Bar Review* (1983): 30–54; Rainer Knopff and F.L Morton, 'Nation-Building and the Canadian Charter of Rights and Freedoms', in Alan Cairns and Cynthia Williams, eds, *Constitutionalism, Citizenship, and Society in Canada* (Toronto: University of Toronto Press, 1985); Rainer Knopff and F.L. Morton, *Charter Politics* (Toronto: Nelson, 1992), chap. 4.

8 Guy LaForest, *Trudeau and the End of a Canadian Dream* (Montreal and Kingston: McGill-Queen's University Press, 1995).

9 See F.L. Morton, *Morgentaler v. Borowski: Abortion, The Charter, and the Courts* (Toronto: McClelland and Stewart, 1992).

10 Knopff and Morton, *Charter Politics*, chap. 4.

11 Alan Cairns, 'Citizens (Outsiders) and Governments (Insiders) in Constitution Making: The Case of Meech Lake', *Canadian Public Policy* 14 (1988): 121–45.

12 *Andrews* v. *Law Society of British Columbia*, [1989] 1 S.C.R. 143.

13 *Egan and Nesbitt v. The Queen* (Supreme Court of Canada, 25 May 1995), unreported.

14 M. Elizabeth Atcheson, Mary Eberts, and Beth Symes, *Women and Legal Action: Precedents, Resources and Strategies for the Future* (Ottawa: Canadian Advisory Council on the Status of Women, 1984), 163.

15 Ibid.

16 Ian Brodie, 'Interest Groups and the Charter of Rights and Freedoms: Interveners at the Supreme Court of Canada', MA thesis: University of Calgary, 1992; Lori Hausegger, 'The Effectiveness of Interest Group Litigation: An Assessment of LEAF's Participation in Supreme Court Cases', MA thesis, University of Calgary, 1994.

17 These are some of the groups that have received funding from the Court Challenges Program.

18 Cf. Rainer Knopff, *Human Rights and Social Technology: The New War on Discrimination* (Ottawa: Carleton University Press, 1989), esp. chaps. 1 and 8; Rainer Knopff, 'Rights, Power-Knowledge, and Social Technology', in Yusuf K. Umar, ed., *George Grant and the Future of Canada* (Calgary: University of Calgary Press, 1992), 59–73.

19 See James Q. Wilson, *The Moral Sense* (New York: Free Press, 1993).

20 Janet Ajzenstadt, *The Political Thought of Lord Durham* (Montreal and Kingston: McGill-Queen's University Press, 1988), 69.

21 J.R. Mallory, *Social Credit and the Federal Power in Canada* (Toronto: University of Toronto Press, 1954), 182, as quoted in Brodie, 'Interest Groups and the Charter', 67.

22 Seymour Martin Lipset, 'The Industrial Proletariat and the Intelligentsia in a Comparative Perspective', chap. 5 in his *Consensus and Conflict* (New Brunswick and Oxford: Transaction, 1985), 187.

23 Ibid., 196.

24 Ibid.

25 Ibid., 194.

26 Ronald Inglehart, *Culture Shift in Advanced Industrial Society* (Princeton: Princeton University Press, 1990), 325.

27 Mike Bygrave, 'Mind Your Language', *Guardian Weekly*, 26 May 1991, 22.

28 Inglehart, *Culture Shift*, 321.

29 Ibid., 331.

30 And the policies promoted by these élites often benefit mainly them. As Christopher Lasch argues, feminism's 'commitment to the two-career family' is of particular interest to the 'professional and managerial class', and largely explains the prominence of feminism in that class. Lasch, *The Revolt of the Élites and the Betrayal of Democracy* (New York: W.W. Norton, 1995), 33. Similarly, Thomas Sowell has gathered a wealth of international evidence showing how affirmative action programs usually benefit the already better-off segments of the disadvantaged groups in whose name they are undertaken. Sowell, *Preferential Policies: An International Perspective* (New York: William Morrow, 1990).

31 Lasch, *Revolt of the Élites*.

32 Thomas Sowell, *A Conflict of Visions* (New York: William Morrow, 1987), 40–1.

33 Ibid., 40.

34 Ibid., 43.

35 Quoted in ibid., 44.

36 Richard J. Herrnstein and Charles Murray, *The Bell Curve: Intelligence and Class Structure in American Life* (New York: Free Press, 1994), Part I.

37 Lasch, *Revolt of the Élites*, 20.

38 Ibid.

39 Ibid., 28.

40 Ibid., 26.

41 Sowell, *A Conflict of Visions*, 46, quoting Condorcet.

42 For further discussion see Knopff, 'Rights, Power-Knowledge, and Social Technology', 66–70.

43 Ibid., 70.

44 This is implicit in the very nature of a 'written' as opposed to an 'unwritten' or informal constitution. The practice of a written constitution and judicial review bespeaks a scepticism about future generations. Explicitly in the case of the American Constitution, and implicitly in most other instances, there is a sense that we, the present generation, know and respect what is just and right but that future generations are less likely to be so virtuous. The solution is to entrench constitutionally the standards of justice, making them difficult for future majorities either to alter (through formal amendment) or to ignore (by disobeying court decisions). Thus built into the traditional understanding of judicial review is an inherent conservatism, a preference for the 'old ways' and a distrust of the new.

45 See Knopff and Morton, *Charter Politics*, chap. 7, 'The Oracular Courtroom'.

46 This was a major theme in the first and most famous defence of judicial review, by Alexander Hamilton in *Federalist No. 78*.

47 In the United States, Alexander Hamilton proposed a national judiciary as the only alternative to armed force as a means of forcing the member states to fulfill their obligations toward the Union and one another. See *Federalist No. 15*. In Canada, many of the proponents *and opponents* of the first Supreme Court Act saw judicial review as a form of 'disallowance in disguise'. See Jennifer Smith, 'The Origins of Judicial Review in Canada', *Canadian Journal of Political Science* 16 (1983): 115. The critique of the Court as a covert agency of centralization is still very much alive. See André Bzdera, 'Comparative Analysis of Federal High Courts: A Political Theory of Judicial Review', *Canadian Journal of Political Science* 26 (1993): 1–29.

48 Doug Owram, *The Government Generation: Canadian Intellectuals and the State, 1900-1945* (Toronto: University of Toronto Press, 1986).

49 J.R. Mallory, 'The Courts and the Sovereignty of the Canadian Parliament', *Canadian Journal of Economics and Political Science* 10 (1944): 169.

50 See Paul Weiler, *In the Last Resort: A Critical Study of the Supreme Court of Canada* (Toronto: Carswell Methuen, 1974). See also J.A. Corry, *Law and Policy* (Toronto: Clark, Irwin, 1962), 62.

51 Alan Cairns, 'The Past and Future of the Canadian Administrative State', *University of Toronto Law Journal* 40 (1990): 319–61. So strong was the élites' belief in parliamentary supremacy that even when the Supreme Court was given the opportunity to enforce rights against the government—by the *1960 Bill of Rights*—it turned it down. Cf. J. Pigeon's dissent in *Drybones v. the Queen*, [1970] S.C.R. 282: 'In the traditional British system that is our own by virtue of the B.N.A. Act, the responsibility for updating the statutes in this changing world rests exclusively upon Parliament. If the Parliament of Canada intended to depart from that principle in enacting the Bill, one would expect to find clear language expressing that intention.' *Drybones* was the only pre-1982 case in which the 1960 Bill of Rights was used to invalidate a law, and Pigeon's dissent thus quickly became the *de facto* majority view. In 1975 in the first *Morgentaler* case, [1976] 1 S.C.R. 616, Chief Justice Laskin wrote what in effect was a funeral oration for the *Bill of Rights*: 'It cannot be forgotten that it is a statutory instrument, illustrative of Parliament's primacy within the limits of its assigned legislative authority, and this is a relative consideration in determining how far the language of the *Canadian Bill of Rights* should be taken in assessing the quality of federal enactments which are challenged under s.1(a).' Not even Laskin, the most activist member of the Court, was willing to accept Henry Morgentaler's invitation to follow *Roe v. Wade* and the reformist political role it implied for the courts.

52 See J.R. Mallory, *Social Credit and the Federal Power in Canada*, 30–2.

53 *Mahé* v. *Alberta*, [1990] 1 S.C.R. 342.

54 Brodie's examples include 'universal and affordable childcare, income security for single mothers and elderly women, the protection of women from male violence, affirmative action, and pay equity'. Janine Brodie, 'The Women's Movement outside Quebec: Shifting Relations with the Canadian State', in Kenneth McRoberts,

ed., *Beyond Quebec: Taking Stock of Canada* (Montreal and Kingston: McGill-Queen's University Press, 1995), 344.

55 See generally, Anne F. Bayefsky and Mary Eberts, eds, *Equality Rights and the Canadian Charter of Rights and Freedoms* (Toronto: Carswell, 1985).

56 See Rainer Knopff, 'What do Equality Rights Protect Canadians Against?' *Canadian Journal of Political Science* 20, no. 2 (1987): 265-86. This article illustrates that the primary effect of a jurisprudence of 'systemic discrimination' is an institutional transfer of policy-making authority to the courts and that the inconsistent application of the 'equal effects' principle discloses the ideological motivation of this transfer.

57 *Andrews v. Law Society of British Columbia*, [1989] 1 S.C.R. 143.

58 See 'Aggressive Challenges to Discrimination Urged', *The National* (Canadian Bar Association), Feb. 1989, 7.

59 Section 32 covers the 'application of the Charter'. It applies the Charter to 'the Parliament and government of Canada' and 'the legislature and government of each province'. Section 52 of the Constitution Act, 1982, says that 'any law that is inconsistent with the provisions of the Constitution is, to the extent of the inconsistency, of no force or effect.'

60 Dale Gibson, 'Distinguishing the Governors from the Governed: The meaning of "Government" under Section 32(1) of the Charter', *Manitoba Law Journal* 13, no. 4 (1983): 514.

61 Dale Gibson, 'The Charter of Rights and the Private Sector', *Manitoba Law Journal* 12 (1982): 218: '. . . every aspect of life falls within the law's embrace, in the sense that every act a person may commit is either prohibited or permitted by law. It has long been one of our most fundamental bulwarks of freedom that the law permits whatever it does not clearly proscribe. Viewed against this notion of the law's plentitude, it is possible to regard all private conduct as subject to law, and therefore to the Charter.'

62 Alexander Hamilton, James Madison, and John Jay, *The Federalist Papers*, Clinton Rossiter, ed. (New York: New American Library, 1961), 322.

63 *Dolphin Delivery Ltd. v. R.W.D.S.U., Local 580*, [1986] 2 S.C.R. 573. Also, *McKinney v. University of Guelph*, [1990] 2 S.C.R. 229.

64 *Blainey v. Ontario Hockey Association* (1986), 54 O.R. (2d) 177.

65 *Haig v. Canada*, 5 O.R. (3d) 245.

66 Thomas E. Flanagan, 'The Staying Power of the Status Quo: Collective Choice after Morgentaler', unpublished manuscript.

67 *Schacter v. Canada*, Factum of the Respondent/Intervenor, the Women's Legal Education and Action Fund, in the Supreme Court of Canada, File 21889, 29.

68 *Schacter v. Canada*, [1992] 2 S.C.R. 679.

69 *Haig v. Canada*, 5 O.R. (3d) 245.

70 The Court declared in its 1985 decision in *Reference re B.C. Motor Vehicle Act* that it would not be bound by 'the intent of the framers'.

71 See Carl and Ellen Baar, 'Diagnostic Adjudication in Appellate Courts: The Supreme Court of Canada and the Charter of Rights', *Osgoode Hall Law Journal* 27 (1989): 1–25.

72 See Knopff and Morton, *Charter Politics*, chap. 7.

73 Interest groups that have directly litigated Charter claims before the Supreme Court of Canada include the Quebec Association of Protestant Schools, Operation Dismantle, Société des Acadiens, Public Service Alliance of Canada, the Toronto Public School Board, BC Government Employees Union, and Committee for the Commonwealth of Canada. There are of course many more whose cases did not reach the Supreme Court.

74 For example, the Canadian Abortion Rights Action League (CARAL) covered most of the legal expenses incurred by Henry Morgentaler in his successful challenge to the abortion law. Campaign Life financially backed Joe Borowski's pro-life Charter case. The National Citizens' Coalition (NCC) financially backed the successful Charter challenge to restrictions on third-party ('PAC') election expenditures and also Merv Lavigne's unsuccessful challenge to labour union expenditures for political causes. The Canadian Council of Churches has sustained a continuous litigation campaign against the government's refugee-determination policies.

75 In politically charged cases involving abortion (*Daigle v. Tremblay* (1989)) and language rights (*Mahé v. Alberta* (1990)), the number of interest group interveners has reached as high as nine. These data come from Brodie, 'Interest Groups and the Charter'. This development parallels the American experience, where intervention by interest groups in constitutional cases has become the norm, not the exception. For example, *amici curiae* (the equivalent of interveners) were present in 53 per cent of the non-commercial cases before the US Supreme Court between 1970 and 1980, and in over two-thirds of the cases when criminal cases are also excluded. Karen O'Connor and Lee Epstein, 'Amicus Curiae Participation in US Supreme Court Litigation: An Appraisal of Hakman's "Folklore"', *Law and Society Review* 16 (1981–2): 311–18.

76 The doctrine of standing prevented people who objected to a law but were not directly affected by it from challenging it before the courts. This restriction on access partially protected the courts from constantly being forced into confrontations with Parliament by disgruntled losers in the political arena. The Supreme Court lost this protection in 1981, when it granted Joe Borowski standing to challenge Canada's abortion law despite the fact that he was not directly affected by it. *Minister of Justice v. Borowski*, [1981] 2 S.C.R. 575.

77 Justice Sopinka's opinion for a unanimous court in the second *Borowski* case, [1989] 1 S.C.R. 342, made it clear that mootness by itself is no longer an absolute barrier to hearing a case. Several other important Charter cases decided by the Court were also technically moot. Cf. *Skapinker v. Law Society of Upper Canada*, [1984] 1 S.C.R. 357; *Mercure v. Saskatchewan*, [1988] 1 S.C.R. 234; and *Andrews v. B.C. Law Society*, [1989] 1 S.C.R. 143.

78 In *Andrews* the Court responded more to issues raised by LEAF and other interveners-issues that did not address the immediate issue before the Court. In *R v. Edward Dewey Smith*, [1987] 1 S.C.R. 1045, the Court overturned a mandatory seven-year minimum sentence for importing illegal drugs, even though everyone agreed that Smith, the litigant, deserved at least seven years. For further discussion see Knopff and Morton, *Charter Politics*, chap. 7.

79 The fear voiced by Chief Justice Laskin in his dissent in the first Borowski case—that 'if standing is accorded to the appellant, other persons with an opposite point of view might seek to intervene and would be allowed to do so, the result would be to set up a battle between parties who do not have a direct interest [and] to wage it in a judicial arena'—has become the new reality.

80 This distinction was blurred in our earlier paper 'The Supreme Court as the Vanguard of the Intelligentsia'.

5

The Language of Rights and the Crisis of the Liberal Imagination

Bradley C.S. Watson

INTRODUCTION: A DISQUIETING LESSON

In 1787 Alexander Hamilton, one of the founders of the American regime, argued that a written enumeration of rights would pose a pressing and continuous danger to free government. He wrote in *The Federalist Papers* that the very existence of a bill of rights points to the reservation of certain rights not granted to the sovereign.[1] But, in the case of the United States, he argued, the people surrendered nothing and therefore any specific reservations were redundant.[2] But beyond redundancy, written bills of rights would teach subsequent generations precisely the wrong lessons: 'They would contain various exceptions to powers which are not granted; and, on this very account, would afford a colorable pretext to claim more than were granted. For why declare that things shall not be done which there is no power to do? Why, for instance, should it be said that the liberty of the press shall not be restrained, when no power is given by which restriction may be imposed?'[3]

On the practicalities of a written declaration of rights, using liberty of the press as an example, Hamilton asks,

> What is the liberty of the press? Who can give it any definition which would not leave the utmost latitude for evasion? I hold it to be impracticable; and from this I infer that its security, whatever fine declarations may be inserted in any constitution respecting it, must altogether depend on public opinion, and on the general spirit of the people and of the government.[4]

And so Hamilton reminds us that the usefulness of committing a right to paper varies in direct proportion to the meaningfulness with which that right can be specified in the abstract. Rights as general as freedom of the press, and of speech, do not have meanings that are reasonably precise, and committing them to paper will not serve to guarantee in a meaningful way the liberties of the people. The enumeration of such freedoms in a constitution, as we shall see, simply gives to the courts rather than to the two other branches of government or to the people the responsibility for engaging in the delicate balancing act required to give meaning to such freedoms. No one believes that, in the name of free speech, one has the right to yell 'fire' in a crowded movie theatre. The only relevant question is: who decides what is reasonable?

In his concluding remarks on the subject, Hamilton notes that the US Constitution itself is a bill of rights. Its overall scheme of separated powers, provisions for public security, and immunities and procedures bespeaks a concern for the rights of the people, even though the language utilized is not that of the abstract declarations that so many of us moderns, indeed, us Canadians, now think are somehow essential to our freedom. And yet, can anyone deny that, before the Charter of Rights and Freedoms, the British parliamentary tradition in Canada provided as firm a guarantee for the liberties of the people as virtually any system of government ever has? Or that its object, whatever its specific shortcomings, was anything other than protecting those liberties in the highest sense—in so far as they were compatible with peace, order, and good government?

Of course, the US Bill of Rights has long since been ratified (as the first 10 amendments to the US Constitution), as has the Canadian Charter of Rights and Freedoms. But, enlightened by the 200-year-old American debate, Canadians must now recognize that the Charter does not so much protect their liberties as threaten them. The meaning and political ramifications of the Charter are things that can no longer be left to the legal academy, which, unbeckoned, delivered the document to our doorstep. Politicians, political scientists, and citizens, if they wish to preserve the Canada on which the Charter was imposed, must take an active part in fighting for this Canada. It is a Canada that enjoyed the liberties made possible by a British parliamentary system. It is a Canada now under siege from interest groups that seek to constitutionalize political claims that they could not satisfy under the give and take of the political system. The Charter is their weapon; it is not our shield.

Hadley Arkes, in his insightful study *Beyond the Constitution*,[5] elaborates the type of reasoning that emanates from a bill of rights. 'The metaphor of the contract would suggest . . . that the government and the people stood on the same plane, with two distinct interests of comparable dignity. But that notion would be wholly out of keeping with the character of a republic or a popular government, in which authority emanated from the people, not from the government, and in which the government stood, in relation to the people, as an agent in relation to its sovereign.'[6] A further presumption implicit in this metaphor is that those things *not* mentioned in the bill of rights are somehow less important than those things that are. As Arkes notes of the US experience, 'in spite of the avowals in the Ninth Amendment, we have seen, in a number of signal cases, the casual denial of freedom and the cavalier destruction of certain rights precisely because these freedoms and rights were not apparently mentioned in the Bill of Rights or its sequelae.'[7] For example, 'The right to practice a legitimate business cannot be reckoned as any less fundamental than the right to speak, and yet it is not a right which seems to excite the concern of our jurists or civil libertarians.'[8]

Indeed, one may say that the right to own and acquire property, with its attendant freedoms, was not specified in the US Bill of Rights, not because it was not considered a right, or a 'fundamental' right, as is free speech. Rather, it was implicit in the very nature of a free society as understood by the founders of the United States, and its specification in the abstract would not privilege it in any meaningful way. What of the zoning, taxation, and licensing laws that every day affect this right? The manner in which such a right is *realized* (assuming, with the founders, that it exists by nature) is clearly a matter of convention or positive law. And so it is with freedom of speech and of the press and so forth. To say that rights are claimed 'under' or 'through' a written bill of rights is to adopt the language of legal positivism[9]—which even ordinary citizens in the United States and increasingly in Canada are wont to do—and thereby to deny the very possibility that our rights as human beings may be natural.

The dangerous lessons of a bill of rights on this score have been well learned by an American high priest of liberal legalism—Professor Laurence H. Tribe of the Harvard Law School. In Tribe's view, the US Supreme Court's interpretation of the right to an abortion as a 'fundamental' right based on the 'right to privacy' (itself a judicial invention, since these words do not appear in the US Constitution) is proper in so far as, by deeming it fundamental, the court requires a high level of judicial scrutiny before the right can be violated:

> If women were held not to have a fundamental liberty interest in control over their own bodies simply because that right is not expressly stated in the Constitution, not only could abortion be *prohibited*, but abortion as well as sterilization could be *mandated* by the state. If a person had no specially protected 'liberty' interest in privacy or in decisions about reproduction, the state could make a rational decision, for reasons of population control or eugenics, for example, to require abortions in certain circumstances. . . . The courts would be unable to interfere in the name of the Constitution.[10]

This reasoning is specious, but is entirely in keeping with the notion that 'real' rights are found in the written constitution, by a court of law (even if it has to go *beyond* what is enumerated to find them). And, once a real right is found, the people, acting through their elected representatives who use their best judgment to decide what reasonableness under the circumstances requires, may be ignored. The government, acting through the judicial branch, has taken away from the people those powers that the people believed they had. In so far as a court may now read non-enumerated clauses into a constitution to 'protect' rights, modern judicial reasoning has provided an even greater latitude for 'colorable pretexts' to be used to deny the people their traditional political freedoms. As Arkes notes,

> Anyone who contemplates the mind and sensibility reflected in the opinion of the Supreme Court in *Roe v. Wade* . . . may grasp the dangers that the Federalists saw in a Bill of Rights. . . . The teaching of the Bill of Rights threatened to affect the citizens of this republic with a brittle, almost childish literalism. It would misinstruct them about the grounds of their rights and the breadth of those freedoms that were protected under the Constitution. It would produce, in later generations, lawyers and judges who no longer knew how to deliberate about questions of justice.[11]

One might add that professors of law would suffer from the same debilitation. Tribe, for example, seems truly to believe that, in the absence of inventing a 'fundamental' constitutional right to privacy, forced abortion or even sterilization could readily be justified. But to order the sterilization of another human being is surely to treat that human being not as human but as a beast, and thereby to ignore the elementary natural equality on which all free government rests. The claims of legal positivism notwithstanding, free government, and deliberation over justice properly understood, ultimately rest on what human reason can tell us about the nature of things.

The issues of abortion and the personhood of fetuses are obviously inordinately complex, and it is not my intention to attempt to resolve them here. My point is rather that it stretches credulity to believe, as Professor Tribe apparently does, that there would be no legal or constitutional ground (assuming the constitution is not *simply* what judges say it is) to prevent *forced* sterilization or abortions if we did not deem voluntary abortions to be a 'fundamental' right.[12] The very use of the term 'fundamental' serves only to obscure, rather than clarify, the moral implications of a debate that really turns on the personhood of fetuses and how their rights, if personhood can be established, ought to be balanced against those of the mother.

In the view of Arkes, 'the principles of right and wrong, the principles of moral and legal judgment, existed antecedent to the Constitution.'[13] And I suggest that these principles existed before the Canadian Charter of Rights and Freedoms, and the imposition of the Charter serves not only to obscure them, but to transfer the responsibility for arriving at and implementing them to the unelected, liberal élites who constitute the Canadian legal establishment.

TRANSFERS OF POWER AND JUDICIAL ACTIVISM

Given the opportunity, the courts will not hesitate to take up the reins of power. Courts are a product of our legal culture, which is dominated by the notion that politics is somehow a lesser phenomenon than law—that, as Tribe's view exemplifies, politics is the province of mere politicians, whereas courts take care of rights, which are somehow fundamental and with which other branches of government or the people are incapable of dealing.

As Knopff and Morton argue in *Charter Politics*, our view of legality is dominated by the 'oracular courtroom',[14] in which judges are held to be 'the best expositors of legal meaning because they are more likely to reason correctly from agreed-upon principles than are more politically responsive officials. . . . Judges, in short, are the best oracles of what the law actually requires.'[15] This view stands in contradistinction to the older adjudicative view, which held that the primary judicial responsibility was to settle disputes between specific parties. Under that view, other branches of government could for example posit, through argument and action, their interpretation of what adherence to the constitution required even if this interpretation was at odds with the judicial interpretation as expounded in the particular case. Without affecting the rights of the parties as adjudicated in the particular instance, the executive branch, for example, could act on its contrary view in other cases and in general. That is what Abraham Lincoln did in acting contrary to the principles of the US Supreme Court's ruling in the infamous *Dred Scott* decision, which held slaves to be property.[16]

But the view that other branches of government might assert themselves against oracular judges has been almost entirely overridden in Canada today. The oracular courtroom's power is reinforced, paradoxically, by the notwithstanding clause in section 33 of the Charter. As Knopff and Morton note,

> Section 33 of the Charter, to be sure, embodies a scepticism of judicial finality in matters of constitutional interpretation, but with the exception of Quebec (and, in one case, Saskatchewan), governments have been reluctant to use it to override judicial decisions. No doubt they do not want to be seen to be violating rights. But this perception itself attests to the strength of the oracular courtroom—it assumes that section 33 can be used only to override rights as defined by judges rather than to express an alternative interpretation of those rights. It assumes, in other words, that Charter rights are what the judges say they are. Interestingly, this legalistic view of the legislative override is supported by the very wording of section 33, which allows legislatures to enact statutes 'notwithstanding' specified sections of the Charter. This clearly suggests that the legislation will be allowed to stand despite its violation of Charter rights. It is surely eloquent testimony to the power of legalism that the Charter provision most obviously embodying nonlegalistic scepticism of judicial power was phrased in legalistic language.[17]

As I have argued, rights in fact may be realized through the myriad conventions of a regime, however those conventions are created—consciously or by traditional usage. This is not to deny that rights are in a decisive sense higher than the day-to-day whims of the *demos* or their leaders in so far as rights inhere in human beings by nature. However, their realization must rely on convention, taking into account competing claims of right. Their exercise must be reasonable, whether or not this limitation is specified in a written charter, and whether or not judges enjoy a privileged position in defining reasonableness.

However, reinforced by the late-twentieth-century stunted notion of legalism and judicial privilege, it is likely that courts in Canada will increasingly use the Charter as their mandate to effect social transformations that in previous eras would have been the exclusive responsibility of the people acting through Parliament or the provinces. This general attitude toward judging can be seen in the upper echelons of the Canadian judiciary. For example, former Canadian Chief Justice Brian Dickson, in denying that the Charter has itself decisively 'Americanized' Canadian law,[18] admits that it has 'formed part of a process that acquired momentum quite some time ago'.[19] In Dickson's view, this process has been structured by social reality independent of the Charter:

> As constitutional, economic, and social problems reveal themselves in Canada in sharp relief, the relative anonymity and tranquillity which have hitherto characterized the court and its operations seem to be vanishing. It now seems plain that in the resolution of those problems the Supreme Court of Canada . . . will be met with the need for prodigious judicial statecraft in the years immediately ahead.[20]

But while admitting his long-standing predisposition toward judicial statecraft, Dickson admits:

> There can be little doubt that the arrival of the new 'rights' oriented issues . . . has provided a dimension to our courts' responsibilities that is in some sense analogous to one seen in connection with the history of American courts. . . . Indeed, the Charter gives our courts a mandate and the power to strike down legislation on the ground that it violates rights or freedoms.[21]

Furthermore, in Dickson's glowing tribute to the retired Supreme Court Justice Bertha Wilson, he praises her sense that 'judges had to strive to come up with what she called the "best modern theory" that could be devised to justify the existence of the right in question. And in her view, this exercise required that judges continually reassess the scope of the right in light of new facts, in light of contemporary social theory and in light of the context in which the right was called into play.'[22] Justice Dickson goes on, strangely, to equate this judicial dabbling in 'contemporary social theory' with a democratic frame of reference and to view Justice Wilson's conception of the judge's role in society as relatively modest. Were a judge truly modest or democratic, surely he or she would leave social theorizing to the intellectuals who presumably are more capable of it, and political practice to elected legislatures that are responsible in a meaningful way to the people.

It would seem, if one takes no less a figure than Justice Dickson seriously, that all judicial politics, when aided by a written enumeration of rights that has a high and clear constitutional status, are likely to be activist. That is to say, judicial politics will be such that the courts will take more and more authority away from other branches of government in their attempt to bring definition to the enumeration of rights. Once this transition is underway, the obfuscation of political and moral principles that Hamilton pointed to during the founding period of the United States is brought into full relief; in fact it is increased because, under the sway of contemporary moral philosophy, judicial politics are destined not only to be activist, but *non-interpretivist* as well. And, when anchored in nothing but the judge's 'values', or at least the judge's reading of contemporary mores through the prism of his or her 'values', judicial opinions are peculiarly subject to any pedagogy that may be floating around. Judicial interpretations will accordingly tend toward the latest intellectual fad. Thus the concern with the dangerous lessons of a written enumeration of rights is perhaps more dangerous today than even Hamilton imagined.

PHILOSOPHY AND NON-INTERPRETIVISM

Why will judicial politics tend to be non-interpretivist rather than interpretivist? That is, why will judges not be inclined to make bona fide efforts to find the original intent of the constitution makers, and thus use a relatively apolitical mode of construction? Why will they instead substitute their own reading of societal development and needs when adjudicating constitutional matters? The deepest reasons for judicial non-interpretivism parallel the reasons for judicial activism. The reasons will be unsettling to those who favour government by the people and a judiciary limited to something approaching the interpretation of law rather than its creation.

I suggest that late-twentieth-century political and moral philosophy, which judges do not seem particularly capable of resisting (being products as they are of the legal academy), strongly promotes non-interpretivist judicial activism.[23] This is the political philosophy of liberalism which, properly understood, has its roots in early modern political thought. It is a commonplace that this philosophy is individualist and rights-oriented. But what is not commonly understood is the manner in which early modern liberalism has degenerated into late-twentieth-century self-expressive individualism, and the influence of this latter incarnation on political and legal thought. Contemporary liberalism, especially as preached in and by the legal academy, is no longer fully aware of the tradition it rejects. The same cannot be said of the progenitors of the liberal imagination.

We see for the first time in Thomas Hobbes, writing in the seventeenth century, the unabashed description of an atomized society. The classical tradition for Hobbes fails because it does not properly recognize the primacy, in the moral universe, of the individual's passions. With a simple, sweeping concept, Hobbes thereby undermines the old certainties, simultaneously topples the traditions of reason and revelation, and constructs the individual anew at the centre of the moral universe, divorced from all duties beyond those to himself. The divination of right, whether through reason or revelation, can no longer be a force strong enough to order the polity because it is always subordinate to the passions. As Hobbes writes in *Leviathan*, 'The final cause, end, or design of men (who naturally love liberty, and dominion over others) in the introduction of that restraint upon themselves, in which we see them live in Commonwealths, is the foresight of their own preservation. . . . For the laws of nature, as justice, equity, modesty, mercy, and, in sum, doing to others as we would be done to, of themselves, without the terror of some power . . . are contrary to our natural passions.'[24] The low, rather than the high, becomes the proper focus of government.

Modernity, from the very beginning, has thus been downward-looking; contrary to the Platonic or Aristotelian understanding of political things, it knows only horizontal, contractual limitations to human conduct. Modernity rarely recognizes even the possibility of vertical limitations, much less the possibility that it is the task of philosophy to discern these limitations and the task of politics to ensure, within the realm of the possible, that they are abided by.

If fear is the root of political order, duties are quickly subordinated to rights. This is the core of the Hobbesian revolution. It is an understanding of the individual that has permeated western thought from Thomas Hobbes to John Rawls, for the most elemental version of all rights doctrines is the right to self-preservation. In its later incarnations, however, the political doctrine of liberalism has diminished the role of the sovereign as protector in order to make room for the more distinctly modern notion of sovereign as provider. Virtue becomes nothing more than those individual qualities that do not interfere with the sovereign's role, properly understood. And liberalism, in its contemporary endeavour of liberation without constraint, can be seen to have limited imagination: individual and political virtue are lost sight of in the headlong rush to celebrate individuality *per se*.

In the thought of John Locke, we see for the first time economic man coming to the fore of politics. Locke consciously rejects the view of human nature known to the ancients and replaces it with man as economic animal. The right to property, in a broad sense, becomes inextricably linked with the right to self-preservation. He thus paves the way for the truly modern notion that man's ends are found in material, or economic, self-satisfaction, which partially underlies not only Rawls but a variety of anti-liberal philosophers.[25]

Locke de-radicalizes Hobbes in the sense that in Locke's doctrine of natural right the natural passions play second fiddle to man and that which he creates. Creativity and creature comfort surpass fear as those elements which define man's social impulse. In regard to the crucial attributes of individuality, however, it cannot be said that Locke differs from Hobbes. Each has a vision of man largely defined by his private interests and of necessity concerned with politics as a means to individual well-being.

Rousseau lays the final foundations for the modern project by expressing discomfort with what modernity, in Hobbes and Locke, has wrought. But he is at the same time unwilling to abandon the romantic attraction of the free individual as the centre of the moral universe. For Rousseau the individual ought to be boundlessly free, as long as we understand that true freedom is not as the radical individualists, whether they be of the Hobbesian or Lockean variety, would have it. He thus sets the stage for the complex twentieth-century theories of right that both glorify the individual and purport to have a social conscience.

According to Rousseau, most of the characteristics we observe in the individual, including the destructive passions, cannot be assumed to be natural. In fact, 'one could say that savages are not evil precisely because they do not know what it is to be good; for it is neither the growth of enlightenment nor the restraint of law, but the calm of passions and the ignorance of vice which prevent them from doing evil.'[26] Vice is more likely to be one of the ill effects of the unnatural socialization process. The individual in the state of nature, beyond his innate desire for self-preservation, is a purely sentimental being. The individual is subject to extraordinary transformation, progressive or regressive, because his nature does not admit of a fixedness in regard to certain of those qualities that the classical, and even early modern (in the form of Hobbes and Locke), political science had accepted as given. Only the circumstances under which government is held to be legitimate can be defined with specificity: man himself cannot.

As Leo Strauss has noted of modern revolutionary thought, which follows in the tradition of Rousseau, 'The revolutionists assumed, we may say, that the natural is always individual and that therefore the uniform is unnatural or conventional. The human individual was to be liberated or to liberate himself so that he could pursue not just his happiness but his own version of happiness.'[27]

In Rousseau, civil society as it exists has emerged not from conscious rational choice, but from the process of change that man is constantly undergoing as a result of happenstance leading to happenstance. Historical process thus comes completely to replace nature as that which defines the individual's rights and duties.

In the best possible political solution to the corruption of civil society, the individual, as supremely free, becomes his own legislator; to be anything else would mean bowing to the will of others. Only the interest of every individual in generalizing his rights becomes a universal. To legislate is to be free within the context of a civil order; to be free in this sense is to be as close to the state of nature, and hence of goodness, as it is possible for the individual to be. And freedom in the state of nature amounts to the complete lack of many of those characteristics that all older forms of philosophy had accepted as defining the individual.

The door is thus opened to the final chapters in the evolution of the concept of individuality: the German attempts to rationalize the sovereign individual and historicize the rational faculties of all individuals. And when this door is opened, the thin remnants of nature and natural right still clung to by Hobbes, Locke, and even Rousseau finally melt into air. The idea of the sovereign, supreme individual quickly degenerates into the modern and post-modern politics of the self. This degeneration manifests itself in the new, self-expressive individualism (or, one might say, self-expressive liberalism).

The apotheosis of this process is represented by Friedrich Nietzsche, who is central to late modern and post-modern political and legal thought. As Harvey C. Mansfield, Jr has noted,

> Essential to the idea of self-expression, and common to both Marx and Nietzsche, is the belief that the self is totally produced, not at all given or fixed. . . . Lacking definition, the self must assert itself . . . and in its self-assertion it has no reason to respect the self-assertion of others. Others would deserve respect if they had rights, but rights attach only to selves that can be defined. If the self has no fixity, no definition even in its potentiality, then the self can be only what it becomes by its act of assertion. Its 'right' is as much or as little as it can exercise; the distinction between a right and its exercise is overridden.[28]

It is in this philosophic climate that judges have come increasingly to believe in the Nietzschean, nihilistic expansion of the self, because it so dominates their breeding ground—the legal academy. Mansfield points out that John Rawls's *A Theory of Justice*—an exemplar of contemporary jurisprudential thought within the academy—is not satisfied with an early modern, liberal conception of right, but seeks to provide the conditions whereby the self can *exercise* its rights. And this theory 'is surely the most widely used justification, especially in the law schools, for overriding the constitutional distinction between rights and their exercise. Crowds of young lawyers appear before the judiciary and the executive branch to press claims in advance and in defiance of what the people have voted.'[29]

The means must be found to ensure that the modern self—however it may reinvent itself on an almost daily basis—is both free and able to define what it is. Rawls provides merely the most noted justification for these means—the judicial branch of government—to be employed, regardless of the democratically expressed wishes of the majority. This is the critical point at which philosophy and constitutionalized politics join issue: the language of rights is the right language to expand the claims of the self.

This self-expressive liberalism is now, in principle, as endemic to Canada as it is to the United States. Although its deepest origins, which I have sketched, are not well understood, particularly in the legal academy, its practical consequences have been fully grasped by those who would use the courts to accomplish what they cannot achieve through the give and take of politics. And these practical consequences were grasped by those who framed and implemented the Charter. Their philosophical vision—the soul's yearning that is at the heart of modernity—could be made real.

PHILOSOPHY, POLITICS, AND JUDGING IN CANADA

Thanks largely to the Charter, but also to the philosophy from which and into which the Charter was born, Canadian judges are more active than they have traditionally been. Their activism, in other words, is an activism that comes to light in the particularly pernicious atmosphere of late-twentieth-century self-expressive liberalism. It is therefore accurate to say that judicial activism itself is not, strictly speaking, the heart of the problem. It is now merely one of the primary vehicles by which the new moral philosophy insinuates itself into Canadian life. This is a reality with which the Canadian legal academy is congenitally incapable of dealing, so stunted is its philosophical horizon. This horizon generally extends no further than John Rawls, or perhaps Ronald Dworkin or Robert Nozick on a clear day. Traditional Canada and, perhaps more important, the tradition of western philosophy are anachronisms for historians and theologians to preach about; they are not to stand in the way of realizing the brave new world of Charter politics.

At its most straightforward, this world is captured by Justice Wilson's rulings in cases such as *Morgentaler, Smoling and Scott v. The Queen*,[30] in which she exalts individual autonomy and the right to unconstrained private choice as a means to dignity and self-worth. In the same case, Chief Justice Dickson relied on a breach of the Charter's section 7 guarantees of security of the person to strike down the impugned Criminal Code provision that sought to restrict abortion. He thus concealed the court's policy-making role 'by converting indeterminate substantive issues into procedural questions'.[31] This case therefore captures in a nutshell two phenomena I have spoken of. First, it illustrates the obsessive concern with the self that is at the heart of modern philosophy and that, despite its democratic veneer, actually prevents the people from acting in a political sense. Second, it shows how the Charter encourages a kind of spurious reasoning that is legal in the most technical sense of the term and that does not take proper account of moral-political argument in its fullest sense. These phenomena have already manifested themselves in myriad Charter cases, and one can safely predict that they will reinforce each other and continue to dominate much constitutional litigation. The peculiar trappings of our Charter, compared to the US Bill of Rights, will not save us from this. Despite the judicial meaning given in *R. v. Oakes*[32] to section 1's limitation of Charter protections in so far as they are subject to 'reasonable limits' that are 'demonstrably justified in a free and democratic society', it is nonetheless the case that, 'technical details aside, the general tenor of the Oakes test is perfectly consistent with the modern approach to judicial review in the United States, where "balancing" has become a principal mode of constitutional adjudication. . . . What makes balancing controversial is that its emphasis on interest balancing and cost-benefit analysis fits uncomfortably within any traditional conception of the judicial function.'[33]

So, in Canada, the potential for dangerous lessons to be taught by our own written enumeration of rights is at least as pronounced as in the United States. Given the hegemony of liberalism throughout Canadian academic, media, and governing circles, it is not surprising that the élite classes ignored, or were ignorant of, the Hamiltonian warning and in fact celebrated the entire constitutional package of 1982, of which the Charter was a central part. For Roy Romanow, the current premier of Saskatchewan, 'the Constitution Act of 1982 is a political triumph for compromise and accommodation. Building upon it, future generations of Canadians can strengthen the fabric of nationhood.'[34]

For the late W.R. Lederman of Queen's University Faculty of Law,

> the Charter has been a resounding success. . . . the only change I would like to see is the elimination of Charter section 33, the notorious override clause. Except for that the Charter should, for the most part, stand as it is and thereby provide some guidelines for reforms in other parts of the constitution yet to come. This is the first decade in Canada when we have faced a coming period of major constitutional change with such a Charter in place as superior constitutional law. Moreover, the authoritative interpretation of the Charter is in the hands of the judges of our long-standing single national superior court system.[35]

Yet Lederman paradoxically laments the fact that the 'problem of limiting what is to be considered "constitutional" . . . is very real. The limits have to be severe. You cannot constitutionalize the whole legal system. One cannot turn every legal issue into a specially entrenched Charter issue.'[36] Yet Lederman does not seem to recognize that this is precisely what the Charter, and the new politics of the self, encourage us to do.

It took a 'No' vote of the people on the Charlottetown Accord to put an effective end to the latest round of dangerous constitutional tinkering that would most certainly have constitutionalized ever more aspects of Canadian life. This vote signalled a stunning upset not only for the government, but for the rest of the élites that constitute the Canadian establishment and that would transform rule of law into rule by lawyers. The people might not have been able to express fully their dissatisfaction with the Charlottetown Accord, but they knew well enough what it represented in practical terms.

The final, ignominious defeat of the Accord sounded the death knell, not only for the latest short-sighted attempt at constitutional revision, but perhaps also for politics as usual in Canada. It certainly presaged the virtual elimination of Brian Mulroney's Progressive Conservative Party—for many years a strange admixture of conservative stalwarts led by a thoroughgoing liberal élite utterly devoid of vision or a substantive understanding of the kind of Canada they haphazardly stumbled toward. On the merits of the issue and on its implications for Canadian electoral politics, the defeat of Charlottetown bodes well for Canada in the short term. But it is, to say the least, an open question whether the people will have the vision necessary to sustain and further their victory over the powers that would move Canada ever closer to judicial government.

CONCLUSION

As Knopff and Morton have pointed out, law and politics in Canada have always been intertwined, but 'the degree and scope of legalized politics occasioned by the Charter far surpasses what we had become accustomed to under the constitutional law of federalism. In myriad ways, the Charter of Rights and Freedoms has truly transformed the Canadian political landscape since its enactment in 1982.'[37] This transformation goes beyond mere symbolism to full-fledged institutional change, forcing Canadians to conduct politics in the courtroom.[38] The Charter, in short, represents the continuation of politics by other means. They are means that tend to lead to new and decisive winners and losers, taking away the traditional strictures and informal compromises that were at the heart of the old Canada. The result is a political landscape increasingly desiccated by judicially enforced liberalism and post-modernism. Increasingly we can argue, and express our individual anguish, only in the courtroom and under the rubric of rights; concomitantly, we increasingly can engage only in legal, not moral or political, reasoning.

As it comes to dominate our intellects, the liberal imagination narrows our horizons. We can no longer, with George Grant, hold our arms outstretched in love toward the further shore.[39] What the US Supreme Court has usurped by way of legislative prerogative in 200 years, its Canadian counterpart has usurped, in principle at least, in only 13—notwithstanding the controversial notwithstanding clause and other supposed checks on an imperial judiciary. The Charter sought to define, in liberal rights terms, broad unifying values for Canadians and to undergird basic rights and freedoms. It has succeeded only in increasing the transfer of power to a small coterie of liberal academics, lawyers, and judges, which was at least an implicit purpose of the Charter and was a necessary project for its strongest proponents. For we need only witness the failure of the Charlottetown Accord to see the remnants of power still in the hands of the *demos*, and their residual capacity to check, even if for the wrong reasons, liberalism's empire.

NOTES

1 Alexander Hamilton, '*Federalist* 84', in Clinton Rossiter, ed., *The Federalist Papers* (New York: Mentor, 1961), 512.

2 Ibid., 513.

3 Ibid., 513–14.

4 Ibid., 514.

5 Hadley Arkes, *Beyond the Constitution* (Princeton, N.J.: Princeton University Press, 1990).

6 Ibid., 60.

7   Ibid., 61.

8   Ibid., 74.

9   Ibid., 81.

10 Laurence H. Tribe, *Abortion: The Clash of Absolutes* (New York: W.W. Norton, 1990), 111.

11 Arkes, *Beyond the Constitution*, 79.

12 I suggest that there would be clear ground for any right-thinking judge to declare such practices illegal or unconstitutional in so far as they reflect an understanding of nature incompatible with free government. But I do not believe we would need to rely on the courts to make such a judgment. It could well be left to the good sense of the people and their representatives, whose moral sense of such matters is unlikely to be much behind the judiciary's.

13 Ibid., 81.

14 Rainer Knopff and F.L. Morton, *Charter Politics* (Scarborough, Ont.: Nelson, 1992), 169–96.

15 Ibid., 169.

16 Ibid., 176–7.

17 Ibid., 179–80.

18 A proposition that is itself put into question by Christopher P. Manfredi in 'The Use of United States Decisions by the Supreme Court of Canada under the Charter of Rights and Freedoms', *Canadian Journal of Political Science* 23 (1990): 499–518. As Manfredi notes, 'With respect to constitutional interpretation, the Supreme Court has adopted the modern reinterpretation of John Marshall's call for a generous interpretation of constitutional language. . . . [this] leads to a form of judicial review in which constitutions are continuously amended through judicial construction of new rights and limitations on legislative and executive power. This theory has been especially apparent in the Court's legal rights decisions, which strongly identify "human dignity" as the core right protected by procedural restrictions on government action. . . . judicial supremacy of the type reflected in the American jurisprudence used by the post-Charter Court potentially denies Canadians their most basic freedom and right of self-governance.' Ibid., 517–18.

19 Brian Dickson, C.J.C. (ret.), 'Has the Charter "Americanized" Canada's Judiciary? A Summary and Analysis', 26 *U.B.C. Law Review* 195, at 198 (1992).

20 Dickson, paper presented to the Conference at Case Western Reserve University, Cleveland, Ohio, 20 October 1979, as quoted in Dickson, ibid., at 197.

21 Dickson, 'Has the Charter "Americanized" Canada's Judiciary?' 199.

22 Brian Dickson, C.J.C. (ret.), 'Madam Justice Wilson: Trailblazer for Justice', 15 *Dalhousie Law Journal* 1, at 17 (1992).

23 This is more obvious in the case of the United States than Canada, although the phenomenon exists in Canada as well. The United States was explicitly founded on, and dedicated to, principles that are grounded in natural, as opposed to positive, rights. The Charter, being itself a product of the late twentieth century, was not so dedicated, and Canadian judges cannot, strictly speaking, be said to be

acting in a non-interpretivist manner if they do not recognize such high princi-ples. However, as Manfredi has shown, even the simulacra of principle, or original intent, that are contained in the Charter have been largely ignored in the brief 13 years the Supreme Court has had to interpret it. See Christopher P. Manfredi, *Judicial Power and the Charter: Canada and the Paradox of Liberal Constitutionalism* (Toronto: McClelland and Stewart, 1993), esp. 52–62.

24 Thomas Hobbes, *Leviathan*, chap. 17.

25 Material satisfaction is often a dominant concern even of post-liberal 'group-rights' theorists who, as the groups they identify as oppressed become increas-ingly fragmented and numerous, move closer to Locke than they perhaps realize.

26 Jean-Jacques Rousseau, 'Second Discourse', in Roger D. Masters, trans., *The First and Second Discourses* (New York: St Martin's, 1964), 129–30.

27 Leo Strauss, *Natural Right and History* (Chicago: University of Chicago Press, 1953), 14.

28 Harvey C. Mansfield, Jr, *America's Constitutional Soul* (Baltimore: Johns Hopkins University Press, 1991), 199.

29 Ibid., 34.

30 *Morgentaler, Smoling and Scott v. The Queen*, [1988] 1 S.C.R. 30.

31 Manfredi, *Judicial Power and the Charter*, 118.

32 *R. v. Oakes*, [1986] 1 S.C.R. 103.

33 Manfredi, *Judicial Power and the Charter*, 61.

34 Roy Romanow, '"Reworking the Miracle": The Constitutional Accord of 1981', 8 *Queen's Law Journal* 98 (1983).

35 W.R. Lederman, 'Constitutional Reform: Charter Rights and Freedoms', in David E. Smith, Peter MacKinnon, John C. Courtney, eds, *After Meech Lake: Lessons for the Future* (Saskatoon: Fifth House Publishers, 1991), 117.

36 Ibid., 119.

37 Knopff and Morton, *Charter Politics*, 1.

38 Ibid., 3.

39 George Grant, *Lament for a Nation* (Ottawa: Carleton University Press, 1989), 97.

6

Rights and Wrongs
in the Canadian Charter

Karen Selick

The 1980s and 1990s have witnessed an explosion of attention to 'rights' in Canada. Interest groups of all sorts are demanding that their members be treated in certain ways by government, business, or other individuals. The claims of the various groups may be totally unrelated to each other; for example, one group may claim an entitlement to shelter for the homeless, while another group may claim an entitlement to express its political opinions during federal election campaigns. Sometimes the claims of different groups may be diametrically opposed to each other: fulfilling the claim of one group would necessitate denying the claim of another. Despite these incongruities of subject matter and logical contradictions, claimants all like to couch their demands in terms of 'rights'.

Perhaps the interest in rights was sparked by the enactment of the Canadian Charter of Rights and Freedoms in 1982. Canada had previously had similar legislation called the Bill of Rights, but the bill did not have the status of being part of our constitution. It was not the supreme law of the land. The Charter, as part of Pierre Trudeau's repatriated constitution, came into being with a hoopla that brought it forcefully to the attention of every newspaper reader and television viewer in the country.

Unfortunately, while the general concept of rights seems to have stuck in many minds and inspired many hearts, few of those so enkindled seem to have pursued the object of their inspiration in any intellectually rigorous way. With their personal visions of 'the good' flitting before their eyes like butterflies, they have tried to use the concept of rights like a net to capture the pretty prize; but in doing so, they have unwittingly torn gaping holes in the net and let escape what they were hoping to secure.

This essay will try to point out the conceptual gashes in the popular notions about rights and mend them back into seamless whole fabric again. It will explain how the confusion has arisen, some of the consequences it has had, and what a rational system of rights would actually look like. Finally, it will consider whether the Canadian Charter of Rights and Freedoms has helped Canadians to attain their rights, and how it might be improved.

CHARACTERISTICS OF RIGHTS

There can be no more powerful claim than one that is justifiably called a right. We reserve the term 'right' to describe our highest, strongest, most compelling and inviolable claims. We must recognize the necessity of reserving a term for claims of this kind, and not trivialize the word by using it to encompass claims of a different nature—claims that could more properly be described as privileges or prerogatives. It is therefore important to discover the distinguishing features of rights.

Over the past four centuries, Western liberal democracies have viewed rights primarily as protective mechanisms. A right is like an invisible wall keeping us safe from the interference of others. Our most revered rights—to life, liberty, freedom of speech, and so on—have traditionally been interpreted as an entitlement not to be interfered with by others. The right to life, for example, simply meant the right not to have one's life taken away—the right not to be killed—by others. It did not mean the right to require others to give one the means of sustenance.

More recently there has been a trend towards defining rights to include much more than non-interference. Many people have started to speak of rights to specific forms of wealth, such as food, shelter, health care, housing, education, and so on. We can speculate on why these claims have been couched in the language of rights: perhaps it is to impart a sense of the importance the speaker attaches to the claim, or perhaps to borrow the respect and dignity that has come to be attached to the concept of rights. However, claims of this kind are very different in nature from our traditional understanding of rights and can be distinguished in many ways. For our immediate purposes, claims of this kind will be referred to as 'positive rights', while traditional claims to non-interference will be called 'negative rights'.[1]

Positive and negative rights share one characteristic: it is impossible to claim either kind of right without simultaneously making an implicit statement about some other person's obligation. In the case of a positive right, the implicit obligation of others is to provide some advantage or some material object that is the subject of the rights claim. In the case of a negative right, the implicit obligation of others is to refrain from taking away or interfering with the subject matter of the rights claim. In either case, however, an obligation is implied.

One distinction between negative and positive rights is that the former can be fulfilled regardless of time, place, and technology, while the latter depend heavily upon the economic, environmental, and technological conditions in which the rights claimant finds himself. A right not to be interfered with was as capable of fulfilment in prehistoric times and in any corner of the globe as it is in Canada in the 1990s. A right to food, however, could not be fulfilled in Ireland during the potato blight. It could not be fulfilled in many places and times during droughts or floods or famines. It is only in this century that agricultural technology has made it possible even to contemplate a guarantee of universal food.

A second distinction is that the fulfilment of a negative right requires nothing more than an act of will on the part of other human beings. If each of us simply agrees that he or she will not kill other people, then everyone's right to life is assured. This is not the case with a positive right. No amount of mental discipline, good intentions, or will-power will fulfil a right to food.

The most important distinction, however, between positive and negative rights is that the negative rights of all individuals can co-exist without conflict, but the positive rights of any single individual will necessarily bring him into conflict with at least one other human being. For example, your right not to be killed does not conflict with my right not to be killed. Both rights can be fulfilled; there is no necessity for either of us to be killed. However, your right to food, if you have not produced it yourself or traded something for it, necessarily implies that the food must be taken away from somebody else who has produced it or traded something for it, which leads to the question: what about that person's right to food?

This feature of positive rights is disturbing because it implies that people do not all have the same rights. If certain people have a right to food, certain others must of necessity lack that type of right, because their food is about to be taken away from them. In fact, positive rights effectively give some people the right to violate the rights of others. This negates our most basic conceptions about rights; it contradicts the very meaning of the term. One of the two conflicting 'rights' cannot be a genuine right if we sanction its abrogation.

I conclude, therefore, that the kind of claim that I have hitherto been calling a positive right is really not deserving of the name 'right' at all. Only negative rights can be enforced and fulfilled in favour of all individuals without creating a logical contradiction.

THE NEGATIVE RIGHTS

What are the negative rights? The first one mentioned whenever anyone lists them is the right to life. This is not mere convention or accident. The rights are indeed hierarchical; each one derives logically from the one before and all of them ultimately derive from the first, the right to life. The right to life is axiomatic. Anyone who is unwilling to grant the existence of this right cannot logically grant any other rights either. The exercise of any other right presupposes that the person exercising it will remain alive long enough to complete his or her intended actions. What good would it do to uphold the right to freedom of speech, for example, if one were not willing to uphold the speaker's right not to be shot halfway through his or her speech? Dead people cannot exercise rights to liberty, property, freedom of speech, or anything else. People must first be guaranteed the right to continue their existence before any of the other rights have any meaning or purpose.

Enough said. Readers who disagree with this proposition will probably also disagree with the rest of this essay, but a fuller discussion of this issue is beyond the scope of this chapter and can be found in other philosophical works.

The right to life, as already mentioned, does not mean the right to be provided with the means of sustaining one's life (for example, food or shelter). It is just the right not to have one's life taken away—the right not to be killed. This should not be taken too literally, however; it is really a shorthand term encompassing a right to non-interference with one's body. It would be silly to propose, for example, that one could be tortured or maimed with impunity provided one were not actually tortured all the way to death. Thus the right to life includes the right not to be physically assaulted or damaged.

Although no one is entitled to demand that they be given the means of sustaining their lives, everyone must be entitled to seek out those means, or else the right to life would be meaningless. Only the individual is in any position to determine how best to secure, prolong, and enhance his or her own life, and generally only the individual has any significant interest in doing so. This leads to the proposition that people must be left free to conduct their lives in the manner they themselves select. They must be free of coercion by others, so long as they themselves do not exercise coercion against others. This is the right to liberty; without it, the right to life is eviscerated.

Many of the traditional rights that have been claimed in democratic societies have been really nothing more than subsets or particular instances of the right to liberty. The four 'fundamental freedoms' guaranteed by the Canadian Charter of Rights and Freedoms are a good example. These are:

(a) freedom of conscience and religion;
(b) freedom of thought, belief, opinion and expression, including freedom of the press and other media of communication;
(c) freedom of peaceful assembly; and
(d) freedom of association.[2]

The first pair of these are essentially the liberty to exercise one's mental faculties and to translate one's thoughts into words and action. Since human beings sustain their lives through purposeful, deliberate, rational action (unlike animals, who act largely on instinct), this right must necessarily be included in the right to liberty.

The second pair are essentially the rights of individuals to exercise their liberty in concert with others. It would be strange indeed if a person were permitted to do or say whatever he pleased, but only so long as he did it by himself. If two or more people wish to assemble or associate with others, they are each exercising their separate rights of liberty, not some new right that applies only to groups.

Similarly, the right to liberty also necessarily includes the right to contract with others: the right to enter into voluntary agreements for the exchange of services or goods, or for mutual efforts to be applied toward a common goal. It is easy to think of ways in which the securing of one's life may be facilitated by, or even depend upon, interacting with others, and it would be contradictory to concede rights to life and liberty which did not encompass this right.

There are two famous American formulations of the basic negative rights: the right to 'life, liberty and the pursuit of happiness' in Jefferson's Declaration of Independence, and the right 'not to be deprived of life, liberty and property' in the Constitution of the United States.[3] The right to the pursuit of happiness would again appear to be simply another particular instance of the right to liberty. However, the right not to be deprived of property is sufficiently distinct and important to be enumerated as a separate right.

At a very basic and mundane level, it is clear that we must have the right not to be deprived of property simply because we have to be able to feed ourselves in order to survive. We will leave aside for the moment the issue of how we can legitimately come to acquire ownership of necessities such as food. It would be silly to say we have the liberty to work, acquire money, purchase food, prepare it, put it on our forks and convey it to our waiting mouths, if we did not also have the right to insist that no one else could snatch the food off our forks the instant before we inserted them. Again, without the right to own and determine the disposition of that property (the food), the rights to life and liberty would be eviscerated.

In the natural course of exercising their rights to life and liberty, people accumulate property—even if in some cases it is nothing more than food and clothing. To deprive them of their property later is equivalent to retroactively depriving them of that portion of their lives that they spent in acquiring the property. The right not to be deprived of property is therefore a necessary derivative of the rights to life and liberty.

It is important to distinguish between the type of property rights being discussed here and the 'positive right' to food, clothing, shelter and so on discussed above. The negative form of property right is simply the right not to be deprived by coercion of property that has been legitimately acquired. It is not a right to be given property by threatening or employing coercion against others.

How is property legitimately acquired? Philosophers such as John Locke[4] have discussed theories of original appropriation—the bringing of previously unowned property into private ownership by the application of one's labour to the unowned resource. This theory forms a good philosophical basis for property rights, but is beyond the scope of this essay and has been discussed extensively in the philosophical and economic literature. For these purposes, it will be sufficient to say that property is acquired through voluntary transactions only—that is, by transactions that do not violate the rights of others to their life, liberty or property; for example, by transforming one article of property into a different form, by trading one piece of property for another, by trading labour for property, or by receiving freely given gifts.

THE SOURCE OF RIGHTS

There have been lots of theories promulgated by philosophers about the source of rights. Some, like Jefferson and Locke, have fallen back on a religious source. They say that rights have been granted to human beings by God. Others have justified the existence of rights by a contractarian approach: we have rights because of some sort of 'social contract' entered into by our distant ancestors. Still others claim that rights arise out of the nature of reality and the nature of man.[5]

Few, if any, philosophers are willing to take the position that the source of rights is the government, that is, that we have only those rights which the state chooses to enact into law. This position would be open to attack on several fronts. It would imply that rights can change with time or from one place to another. It would imply that some people could have different rights than others. In short, it would contradict the very definition of rights. It is therefore generally accepted that rights exist whether or not a government has enumerated and guaranteed them in an official constitutional document. Britain has no formal constitution comparable to the American Bill of Rights or the Canadian Charter of Rights and Freedoms, but has for centuries been a place where the rights to life, liberty, and property have (for the most part) been respected.

In fact, the primary (if not the sole) function of government is to enforce rights between its citizens. Government is a mechanism to prevent or redress individual violations of citizens' rights to their lives, liberty, and property. Governments apprehend and punish those who violate others' rights—murderers, kidnappers, and thieves.

All too often, however, the threat to individuals' rights arises not from other individuals but from the state itself. This has often been the factor motivating past generations to attempt to codify their rights in documents like the US Bill of Rights. Even a casual perusal makes it clear that it was written not with the purpose of making individuals understand their obligations not to interfere with each other, but of making governments understand that they too would be bound by such obligations.

Canada's Charter contains a backhanded recognition of the fact that it is not the source of citizens' rights. Section 26 provides: 'The guarantee in this

Charter of certain rights and freedoms shall not be construed as denying the existence of any other rights and freedoms that exist in Canada.' Logically, if there is the possibility that other rights and freedoms exist, then this document cannot be the source of all rights and freedoms in Canada. Unfortunately, as we shall see below, Canadian courts interpreting the Charter have tended to act as if any rights not specifically enumerated do not exist.

FLAWS IN THE CANADIAN CHARTER OF RIGHTS AND FREEDOMS

If the theory of rights set out above is correct, then the Canadian Charter of Rights and Freedoms has numerous flaws. Furthermore, the interpretation of the Charter by our courts has also departed significantly from a consistent or principled application of rights theory.

POSITIVE RIGHTS IN THE CHARTER

Some sections of the Charter are unobjectionable by themselves, in that they are simple guarantees of negative rights. For example, section 2 (quoted above) guarantees particular instances of the right to liberty—specifically, freedom of thought, expression, and association.

Section 7 of the Charter at first glance appears to be almost the archetypal statement of basic negative rights: 'Everyone has the right to life, liberty and security of the person and the right not to be deprived thereof except in accordance with the principles of fundamental justice.' On closer examination, however, this section is ambiguous. Why is the right not to be deprived of life, liberty, and security of the person contained in a separate phrase from the main rights themselves? Is the right to life something different from the right *not to be deprived of* life? Could this section have been drafted with the deliberate intention of leaving open the interpretation that the rights to life, liberty, and security of the person actually encompass the positive right to be given the material means of sustaining one's life or achieving financial security, as well as the traditional negative right not to be killed?

Contrast the guarantee contained in the US Bill of Rights. The Fifth Amendment provides: '[N]or shall any person be subject for the same offense to be twice put in jeopardy of life or limb; nor shall be compelled in any criminal case to be a witness against himself, nor be deprived of life, liberty or property, without due process of law.' There is no double mention here of the right to life.[6] All that is mentioned is the right *not to be deprived of life*—clearly a negative-rights formulation.

There is reason for concern that the Canadian formulation will lead to a positive-rights interpretation. Already, court battles have been fought over this.

In one case a Manitoba welfare recipient, Robert Finlay, had received welfare overpayments totalling about $1,000 as a result of administrative errors.

When the overpayments were discovered, provincial welfare authorities applied a standard procedure to recover the money. They began deducting a small percentage of Mr Finlay's benefits from his subsequent cheques—a process that reduced his welfare payments by between $6 and $8 per month over a period of several years. He took the matter to court, claiming that the Canada Assistance Plan, under which the federal government provides money to the provinces for welfare, requires each province to provide a minimum standard of benefits, equivalent to 'the basic requirements of the person in need'.

Mr Finlay won his case at the Federal Court of Appeal but lost at the Supreme Court of Canada March 1993.[7] However, the loss was a narrow one: five judges to four. The majority included Mr Justice John Major, who had only recently joined the Supreme Court and was the last Supreme Court appointee of Prime Minister Brian Mulroney. Mr Major had been offered the position only after three senior female judges had turned it down. One cannot help but wonder: would the Finlay decision have been the same if one of those other judges had been sitting on that case?

Even more disturbing is the possibility that the outcome of the case might have turned on Mr Finlay's physical appearance. *The Globe and Mail*'s report on the case notes:

> In this regard, Mr Finlay—who now receives $506.16 a month and lives in a subsidized apartment—may not have helped his case by sitting in the front row of the Supreme Court gallery when his case was heard. He is considerably overweight, and Judge Sopinka [who wrote the majority decision], after asking a reporter later whether that was indeed Mr Finlay, noted privately that he did not appear to be going without food.[8]

Other cases making arguments similar to Mr Finlay's and explicitly relying on section 7 of the Charter are still working their way through the courts. Their progress was temporarily hampered by the termination of the federal Court Challenges Program in 1992, which funded groups wishing to bring Charter challenges to court. However, the Chrétien government reinstated the program in late 1994, earmarking $2.75 million per year for it. Furthermore, the advocates of positive rights include numerous lawyers, some of whom are willing to donate their services. It is likely to be only a matter of time before one of these cases makes it before a Supreme Court panel that is composed differently from the court that heard the Finlay case. The ambiguity of section 7 of the Charter provides a golden opportunity for positive-rights activists to implement their agenda.

There are other sections of the Charter that contain the seeds of a positive-rights interpretation. Section 23, for example, deals with minority language educational rights. The first subsection provides:

23(1) Citizens of Canada
(a) whose first language learned and still understood is that of the English or French linguistic minority population of the province in which they reside, or

(b) who have received their primary school instruction in Canada in English or French and reside in a province where the language in which they received that instruction is the language of the English or French linguistic minority population of the province,

have the right to have their children receive primary and secondary school instruction in that language in that province.

It is possible to place a negative-rights interpretation on this section, construing it to mean simply that parents who wish to educate their children in a minority language will not be interfered with. Logically, however, the section must mean something more than that. If that were all it meant, why would it apply only to certain categories of parents, rather than to all parents? No, this section is clearly meant to be interpreted, not only as a negative right not to be interfered with, but as a positive entitlement to education in a particular language; that is, education that somebody else will have to provide.

Publicly funded education has such a long history in Canada that it is almost a sacrilege to suggest that governments have no business providing this service. This is one positive right that many people cannot imagine the absence of. However, like everything else, the production of educational services is just one of many possible competing uses of resources. The materials that go into building public schools could be used for building houses or factories instead—or for building private schools. The teachers who work in public schools could spend their time instead on an assembly line, producing shoes or clothing for their young charges—or teaching them in private schools.

The mere fact that some people choose to label education as a necessity does not change the fact that a guarantee of publicly funded education is essentially the imposition of a positive right. In Canada's cold climate, shoes are also a necessity, but they are provided cheaply and efficiently by the marketplace, without government coercing some people into paying for what is used by someone else.

Other back-door access for positive rights in the Charter is found in section 27, which requires the Charter to be interpreted 'in a manner consistent with the preservation and enhancement of the multicultural heritage of Canadians', and section 36, which commits Parliament to the principle of making equalization payments to provincial governments. These sections are the excuses for innumerable programs that involve violating the negative rights of some Canadians in order to guarantee positive rights to others.

AFFIRMATIVE ACTION PROGRAMS

'Affirmative action' is a concept with a relatively short history. It came into common usage only in the decade preceding Canada's adoption of the Charter of Rights but somehow found its way into the Charter, where it sits cheek by jowl with rights and freedoms that have been part of our law for centuries. Explicit affirmative action provisions are found in subsection 6(4) of the Charter (dealing with 'mobility rights' of Canadian citizens and residents) and in section 15, which contains the most prominent example.

Known as the 'Equality Rights' section of the charter, section 15 reads:

15(1) Every individual is equal before and under the law and has the right to
the equal protection and equal benefit of the law without discrimination
and, in particular, without discrimination based on race, national or ethnic
origin, colour, religion, sex, age, or mental or physical disability.

(2) Subsection (1) does not preclude any law, program or activity that has as
its object the amelioration of conditions of disadvantaged individuals or
groups including those that are disadvantaged because of race, national or
ethnic origin, colour, religion, sex, age or mental or physical disability.

It is hard to imagine two paragraphs of any law that more directly contradict each other than these two. The first paragraph calls for equal treatment
for all, while the second sanctions the granting of special privileges to a few.
In response to this contradiction, more than one commentator has quoted
George Orwell's famous words, 'All animals are equal, but some animals are
more equal than others.'[9]

If legislation were enacted giving privileges to members of some disadvantaged group (for example, the disabled), it would clearly violate the intention
of subsection (1), which calls for equal treatment of all individuals without
discrimination. Able-bodied people, however, could not complain about a
violation of their equality rights because of subsection (2). The question
arises: if the able-bodied are being treated less favourably by the law than the
disabled, doesn't that fact in itself move them over into the category of 'the
disadvantaged' and thereby make them eligible for at least equal, if not better,
treatment?

Similar questions could be asked about the eligibility of many groups for
subparagraph 15(2) treatment. When is a person sufficiently disadvantaged to
qualify for special treatment? When does he cease to qualify? Who is the
judge of how disadvantaged you need to be, or when the affirmative action
programs have been successful enough that you no longer qualify for them?

Many people might suppose, for example, that Jewish Canadians or Japanese Canadians are disadvantaged because they have historically suffered widespread, open, and legally sanctioned discrimination in this country. However,
by all of the usual standards of success, both groups appear to be over-advan-
taged, rather than disadvantaged. In both groups, average income is well
above the Canadian average. For both groups, representation among the pro-
fessions is disproportionately high. Jews especially are over-represented in the
legal profession, an occupation that connotes a high degree of power rather
than powerlessness. Would an affirmative action program for these two
groups pass muster?

Perhaps even more disturbing than the mere presence of the affirmative
action sections of the Charter is the way the courts have interpreted them. In
July 1993 a married couple, Elaine and Walter Schachtschneider, challenged
certain provisions of the Income Tax Act that denied them tax deductions for

certain child-care expenses.[10] If they had been unmarried, they would have been entitled to the deductions. They claimed that their equality rights guaranteed under subsection 15(1) of the Charter had been violated and that the law discriminated against them because of their marital status.

The Federal Court of Appeal, turning the intention of section 15 on its head, held that there were no grounds for complaint because married people were not 'socially, politically or historically disadvantaged in Canada'. According to this interpretation, it is not everyone who is entitled to freedom from discrimination under the law, but only those who are historically disadvantaged.

To put it another way: not only are the disadvantaged entitled to better-than-equal treatment under subsection 15(2), but they are also the only ones who are entitled to invoke the guarantee of equal treatment under subsection 15(1). This interpretation transforms section 15 itself into a gigantic affirmative action program.

Even before the *Schachtschneider* case, the affirmative action provisions of the Charter contradicted our basic definition of rights as something that apply equally to all individuals, regardless of their personal characteristics and regardless of time, place, technology, and so on.

THE 'NOTWITHSTANDING' LOOPHOLE

Another serious flaw in the Charter's treatment of rights is the famous (or infamous) 'notwithstanding clause' contained in section 33. That section provides:

> 33. (1) Parliament or the legislature of a province may expressly declare in an Act of Parliament or of the legislature, as the case may be, that the Act or a provision thereof shall operate notwithstanding a provision included in section 2 or sections 7 to 15 of this Charter.
>
> (2) An Act or a provision of an Act in respect of which a declaration made under this section is in effect shall have such operation as it would have but for the provision of this Charter referred to in the declaration.
>
> (3) A declaration made under subsection (1) shall cease to have effect five years after it comes into force or on such earlier date as may be specified in the declaration.
>
> (4) Parliament or a legislature of a province may re-enact a declaration made under subsection (1).
>
> (5) Subsection (3) applies in respect of a re-enactment made under subsection (4).

In plain English, this section allows any provincial legislature or the federal parliament to override any of the rights and freedoms guaranteed in the Charter simply by voting to do so and inserting a particular formula of words into the legislation. The override lasts for five years but can be renewed by another simple vote of the legislature or parliament. To say that this section is a loophole in the Charter is to give new meaning to the word 'understatement'. The loophole quite tidily swallows up the entire principle.

Legislatures operate by the mechanism of majority rule. Often, however, a majority government can be formed with far less than a majority of popular support. The Ontario NDP majority government that took power in the fall of 1990, for example, received only 38 per cent of the popular vote. Similarly, the majority Conservative government that took power in Ontario in June 1995 had received 45 per cent of the popular vote. Because of our system of electing representatives geographically by a plurality, the same thing will happen more and more often as the number of political parties grows.

In an election contested by four major political parties, it would theoretically be possible for just over 25 per cent of the voters to elect a majority government. With five major parties, just over 20 per cent could elect a majority. New parties have been proliferating in Canada in the 1990s, and results like these are not entirely far-fetched.

No matter how difficult it may be to eliminate Charter rights by amending the constitution, it will be child's play under section 33 to override them for five years at a time.

Friedrich A. Hayek, in his book *The Constitution of Liberty*,[11] discusses the distinctions between constitutional legislation and other, 'everyday' types of legislation. Constitutional entrenchment is supposed to establish the entrenched principles as enduring fundamentals of the society, not to be affected by momentary passions and interests. The built-in obstacles to amending a constitution are deliberate; they force society to slow down and give thorough contemplation to whether it would be wise to overthrow what was once intended to be an enduring, fundamental principle. Section 33 of our Charter tosses away this protection and permits the fleeting whims of small minorities to override the deliberate, considered, time-honoured principles of a free society. Ironically though, because of other flaws in the Charter, section 33 could prove to be a double-edged sword that might occasionally help preserve rights rather than violate them. For example, if our courts in future approve certain affirmative action programs in reliance on section 15 of the Charter, or recognize positive rights under a perverse interpretation of sections 2 or 7, subsequent parliaments or provincial legislatures could amend their legislation to avoid the application of the court's decision by invoking the 'notwithstanding' clause. In the proper political climate, two Charter flaws could cancel each other out, defanging both of them. Obviously, the better course would be not to rely on happy accidents of this kind, but to eliminate both of the problems at their source.

THE SECTION 1 LOOPHOLE

Perhaps the main flaw in the Charter as a document designed to protect rights is the existence of section 1. This section reads: 'The Canadian Charter of Rights and Freedoms guarantees the rights and freedoms set out in it subject only to such reasonable limits prescribed by law as can be demonstrably justified in a free and democratic society.'

The power that this section gives to judges is unprecedented. Despite all the pains the drafters of the Charter may have taken to enshrine and guarantee fundamental rights in the many sections that follow, each case will boil down in the end to the opinion of one or more judges as to what is demonstrably justified in a free and democratic society. All of those carefully crafted rights will be nothing more than guidelines. What will really matter is the political persuasion of the judge or judges who decide the case.

Liberal democracies have long recognized that an important doctrine in the protection of rights and freedoms is the separation of powers of the legislative, executive, and judicial branches of government. Just as a constitution is supposed to set out enduring principles that will override temporary majority passions, so the function of the judiciary must be to decide individual disputes, having regard to pre-established general rules.

To quote Hayek again: 'Rules must not be made with particular cases in mind, nor must particular cases be decided in the light of anything but the general rule.'[12] Section 1 gives judges not only the power but the positive obligation to determine, in the context of particular cases, the general rules that are to govern a free and democratic society. They are authorized not only to judge, but to make law. The separation between the legislative and judicial functions is merged. Section 1 therefore violates one of the primary safeguards of freedom.

Section 1 contains an ambiguity that will prove troublesome should anyone ever care to argue it before a court. The difficulty lies in the phrase 'a free and democratic society'. The drafters of this clause presumably thought there was a difference between the words 'free' and 'democratic', or else they would not have included both. Yet they must also have believed, as many people do, that there was some compatibility or necessary connection between freedom and democracy.

This, in fact, is debatable. 'Democracy' simply means 'government by the people'. Democracy can indeed be a means of obtaining or preserving freedom, but it can also be a means by which a majority of the people vote to oppress a minority. The most famous example of this is the democratic election of Adolf Hitler in Germany in 1934. Although Hitler was elected in accordance with democratic measures, his government represented the antithesis of freedom.

On the other hand, there have been situations in different parts of the world where the people have had a great deal of freedom without having any significant say in the composition of the government. Hong Kong is an example. For many years the people of Hong Kong have enjoyed one of the lowest tax rates in the world—surely one measure of freedom. As well, there is very little government interference in either the economy or in people's personal lives. Yet until 1985 the residents of Hong Kong had no right whatsoever to elect representatives to the governing body. Their government was appointed by Britain. Only since 1985 have residents of Hong Kong been able to hold seats on the Legislative Council at all, and then only a minority of seats.

So if freedom and democracy are not synonymous, and do not necessarily exist in a country at the same time, what will Canadian courts do under section 1 of our Charter when confronted with this contradiction? Again, it will probably depend on the personal opinions of the justices who happen to be on the court when a particular case is heard. Those who value freedom more than democracy will be much more likely to decide the case in a way that would guarantee the negative rights and strike down the positive rights contained in the remaining sections of the Charter. Those who value democracy more than freedom will be more inclined to validate any legislation enacted by a provincial or federal government.

It is even possible to interpret section 1 in a manner that makes it almost tautological. When the court is asked to strike down legislation that violates a Charter right or freedom, it is being asked to override the acts of a democratically elected body that has acted in accordance with democratic procedures. Since Canada has always seemed to be, in most people's minds, a free country, there is a presumption that people acting freely would elect only a government that would continue to preserve their freedoms. Thus the mere fact that the impugned legislation emanates from a free and democratic source tinges it with an aura of justifiability in a free and democratic society. If such legislation were not reasonably justified in a free and democratic society (the argument goes), how did it ever come to be enacted in one?

It is this kind of reasoning that must explain some of the recent decisions of the Supreme Court of Canada. In *Edwards Books and Art v. The Queen*,[13] for example, the issue was Sunday shopping. *The Retail Business Holidays Act* of Ontario prohibited retail stores from opening on Sundays, subject to certain exceptions. Several retailers challenged the legislation on the grounds that it violated their freedom of religion. Five of the seven Supreme Court justices who heard the case agreed that the legislation did indeed violate freedom of religion. However, the court held that the violation was justified under section 1 of the Charter.

Mr Justice Dickson, for example, argued that the purpose of the legislation was to provide a common pause day that would allow people to enjoy 'a family visit to an uncle or grandmother, the attendance of a parent at a child's sports tournament, a picnic, a swim, or a hike in the park on a summer day or a family expedition to a zoo, circus or exhibition'. He held that the Act was addressed to 'a pressing and substantial concern'. This populist rhetoric imparts the same sort of warm, comfortable glow as discussions of free and democratic societies.

In light of subsequent events in Ontario, one wonders whether the justices involved in the *Edwards* decision now blush with embarrassment when they consider their sentimental language. By 1992 Ontarians had made it clear in the public opinion polls that what they would most like to do on Sunday family excursions was visit their local shopping malls. The government announced that it would immediately stop enforcing the law and eventually amend the Act, which it finally did in 1993. Avuncular visits and hikes in the park had apparently ceased to be pressing concerns.

It is shocking that the court in the *Edwards* case was prepared to allow its opinion of how Canadians should spend their leisure time to override an enshrined Charter right. Even worse is the fact that the court's opinion was in fact a misunderstanding of public opinion and that Charter rights were so cavalierly set aside, perhaps because our top judges don't do much shopping themselves and can't imagine anyone else wanting to do so.

NO PROPERTY RIGHTS

Another flaw in the Charter is the omission of any reference to property rights. The issue was debated before the Charter was enacted, and a deliberate decision was made to exclude property rights. Every so often, the issue resurfaces: for example, when the Charlottetown Accord was being drawn up in the summer of 1992. The suggestion that property rights should be explicitly guaranteed in the Canadian constitution invariably meets with howls of anguish from various interest groups. Environmentalists argue, for example, that it would prevent government regulation of the environment. Women's groups argue that it could reverse the direction that family law has taken in recent years towards an equal distribution of spouses' assets upon the breakdown of marriage.

These criticisms are, in fact, accurate: property rights would indeed have many of the effects that the interest groups complain of. But this is just another way of saying that the existing environmental and family law legislation violates property rights. There is no logical inference here that the regulation and legislation advocated by the interest groups are in fact the best method of dealing with matters such as the environment or the standard of living among women. The historical record demonstrates that environmental conditions are vastly superior in countries such as Canada and the United States, where property rights have been largely respected, than in the former Soviet Union and East Germany, where they were virtually non-existent. Similarly, conditions for women have been vastly superior in the countries that respect property rights than in the eastern bloc.

Attempts have been made to read property rights into other sections of the Charter, and some progress was made in the early years in lower courts. However, more recent decisions of higher courts have made it very clear that in the present political climate, those high in the pecking order of the Canadian judiciary do not intend to use the Charter, and specifically the section 7 rights to life, liberty and security of the person, to protect property rights.

As this is being written, another case is working its way through the courts that may provide some hope for the resurrection of property rights in the

Canadian legal system, although not necessarily under the Charter. The case involves a group of Ontario landlords who were affected retroactively by amendments to provincial rent control legislation enacted in 1991 by the NDP government. Their argument is that the effect of the legislation was virtually to deprive them of the benefits of their property without compensation. In a recent interim decision of the Ontario Court (General Division), the judge refused the request of the Ontario government to throw the case out for failure to disclose a cause of action. Mr Justice Montgomery said:

> When the court is faced with the task of declaring rights as affected by a statute, it is presumed that property rights are not to be taken, extinguished or expropriated without the concomitant obligation of the government to effect and the right of the subject to receive compensation therefor, unless the statute excludes compensation by its clear and express terms.[14]

The repeated references in this decision to the expression 'taking' suggest that it may have been influenced by some recent US case law concerning property rights, which the reader can learn more about from the book by law professor Richard Epstein, *Takings: Private Property and the Power of Eminent Domain*.[15]

In the United States, of course, property rights are protected explicitly under the Fifth Amendment. No such protection appears in Canada's Charter of Rights, unless some future judge finds the courage to read it into the catch-all clause, section 26 (which, as readers will recall from above, says that the enumeration of certain specific rights does not deny the existence of others that existed in Canada before the Charter). It will be interesting to watch for the ultimate outcome of this case, which could be the weather vane of the Canadian property rights issue.

AN IMPORTANT INTERPRETATIVE PROBLEM

One of the most consistent positions that has developed in Charter jurisprudence is an extremely restrictive definition of the word 'liberty' in section 7 of the Charter. Here are some of the things that Canada's judges have said about this guaranteed right:

> Whatever the precise contours of 'liberty' in s. 7, I cannot accept that it extends to an unconstrained right to transact business whenever one wishes.[16]

> There is no Charter-protected right to freedom of contract.[17]

> Ontario courts have uniformly held that the rights protected by s. 7 of the Charter do not include a right to engage in a particular type of professional activity or regulated economic sector.[18]

> In this province the courts have consistently held that the expression 'liberty and security of the person' in s. 7 relates to a person's physical and mental integrity and one's control over these. It does not describe any right of a corporation or the purely economic interests of a natural person: nor does s. 7 guarantee the right to unrestrained business activity or to practise a particular profession or occupation.[19]

In other words, the trend in Charter law seems to be that the section 7 right to liberty is to be interpreted as nothing more than the right not to be locked up. It is hard to imagine why the notion of doing business when one wishes to or freely engaging in contracts with other voluntary participants is so repugnant to our judiciary. In any event, their restrictive definition ignores the fact that the right not to be arbitrarily detained or imprisoned already has its own separate Charter protection in section 9.

I have checked several reputable dictionaries and can find nothing to suggest that the definition of 'liberty' is so circumscribed. The cases that adopt such a restrictive definition do not provide a persuasive—or indeed, any—rationale for so limiting the ambit of this word. Indeed, if one follows the facts of each case through to their possible denouements, one might argue that even under the restrictive definition all of these cases involve an aspect of liberty—because in each case, there is always the threat of imprisonment lurking in the background if the litigants do not obey the judgment of the court or the legislation being upheld.

Ultimately, every act of the state or of the judiciary is backed up by the threat of imprisonment, even if this is not always self-evident at first glance. Yes, there are other ways of dealing with those who break the law or defy court orders; but if a defiant citizen chooses to ignore alternative disciplinary measures, the measure of last resort is always imprisonment. Those who do not pay their fines, those who disobey injunctions, those who fail to attend in court when summoned, all end up in jail. This threat of imprisonment automatically makes every law, commercial or otherwise, a peril to a citizen's right not to be locked up, and a hazard to liberty even in the restricted sense.

SUMMARY AND CONCLUSION

The text of the Charter itself has been a disappointment to many who hoped that it would usher in an era of respect for rights. Equally disappointing, however, has been the manner in which Canadian courts have interpreted the Charter. The textual problems could be remedied by several simple measures:

(1) Eliminate the sections that explicitly provide for positive rights or that could be interpreted to permit positive rights.
(2) Eliminate the sections endorsing affirmative action programs.
(3) Eliminate the 'notwithstanding' clause.
(4) Eliminate section 1, with its unprecedented judicial powers.
(5) Add a guarantee of property rights.

Even if this were done, however, we would still have to contend with the problem of judges who place perverse interpretations on plain language (those who adopt a restrictive definition of liberty, for example). The power of the judiciary to make and change law while ostensibly interpreting it should not be underestimated. The US Bill of Rights has avoided most of the flaws that I have suggested should be eliminated from the Canadian Charter; yet the laws, the social systems, and the economic conditions of the two countries are at least as similar as those of any other pair of countries that could be compared. For at least a century, US courts have not permitted a trifling piece of paper like the constitution to stand in the way of modern legislators' attempts to make the country over in ways that would have been repugnant to those who drafted the constitution.

In any event, the probability of amending the Charter in the manner I have suggested is infinitesimally small in today's intellectual climate. The same philosophy (or lack of it) that produced the current crop of judges is equally responsible for producing the offending text of the Charter. What is needed before any change will occur is nothing short of a philosophical revolution—a drastic change in the way people think about rights and the role of government. This essay is an attempt to help bring about that new way of thinking.

NOTES

1 Some of the discussion that follows concerning the characteristics of rights is based on ideas found in Walter E. Block, *The US Bishops and Their Critics* (Vancouver: Fraser Institute, 1986).

2 Section 2, Canadian Charter of Rights and Freedoms.

3 In the Fifth and Fourteenth Amendments.

4 John Locke, *Second Treatise of Government*.

5 This is the approach taken by philosopher Ayn Rand, for example.

6 Nor is there any double mention of the right to life in the Due Process Clause of the Fourteenth Amendment.

7 *Finlay v. Canada (Minister of Finance)*, [1993] 1 S.C.R. 1080.

8 'Anti-poverty Bodies Hit by Court Ruling', *Globe and Mail*, 26 March 1993.

9 George Orwell, *Animal Farm* (repr., Markham, Ont.: Penguin, 1985).

10 *Schachtschneider v. Canada* (1993), 105 D.L.R. (4th) 162.

11 Washington, DC: Regnery Gateway, 1972.

12 Ibid., 210.

13 (1986) 35 D.L.R. (4th) 1.

14 *A & L Investments Ltd. et al. v. The Queen in right of Ontario* (1993), 13 O.R. (3d) 799.

15 Cambridge, Mass.: Harvard University Press, 1985.

16 *Edwards Books and Art v. The Queen* (1986), 35 D.L.R. (4th) 1, at 54, per Dickson, Chief Justice of Canada.

17 *Arlington Crane Service v. Ontario (Ministry of Labour)* (1988), 67 O.R.(2d) 225, at 263, per Henry J.

18 *Biscotti v. Ontario Securities Commission* (1990), 72 D.L.R. (4th) 385, at 389, per Moldaver J.

19 *Haddock v. Ontario (Attorney General)* (1990), 70 D.L.R. (4th) 644, at 660–1, per Henry J.

7

Strange Brew: Tocqueville, Rights, and the Technology of Equality

Anthony A. Peacock

Over the last generation, Canadian politics has been persistently reshaped in the image of an equality that always remains just beyond the present reality. The elements of this development are familiar enough to students of Canadian politics: the growth and stabilization of a national welfare state, the introduction to all federal jurisdictions of human rights legislation, with consistently expanding grounds of discrimination, the constitutionalization of broad equality rights in the Charter of Rights and Freedoms, and the introduction of affirmative action programs in education and employment. This aggrandizement of equality rights measures has been accompanied by a transformation and expansion of the meaning of equality, an attempt to increase social and political uniformity by making potential equality actual. The goal of promoting formal equality of opportunity, as many legal and political commentators have observed, has been replaced, in large measure, by a demand for an equality of economic and social results. Political equality, or the right to equal treatment before the law and to equal entitlement to participation in government, has given way to social equality, or the putative right to special or differential treatment based upon the social or biological characteristics of politically identifiable groups. Partisans of both the left and the right have used this new concept of equality as it has suited their purposes.

In this chapter I examine this change in the meaning of equality with a view to advancing three propositions.

First, we can describe the new phenomenon as a 'technology of equality' because it comports with many elements we may associate with technology, elements seen in the development of affirmative action and human rights policy, as well as in section 15 Charter litigation.

Second, if we are not to commit the error of rendering the language of rights meaningless, of collapsing 'rights into values', as Rainer Knopff has put it, rendering them 'whatever we choose or will them to be',[1] then we must assume the existence of a standard beyond mere opinion or agreement that serves to distinguish legitimate from illegitimate rights, moral from immoral visions of equality. We must assume the existence of natural rights.

An examination of the three equality rights initiatives—affirmative action, human rights, and section 15—which is provided in the next section of this chapter, reveals that there persists in Canada widespread ambiguity about the meaning of rights and the meaning of equality. Almost every commentary on the Charter remarks how it has changed what we understand by rights and the language in which we think about Canadian constitutionalism. F.L. Morton, for instance, has observed that in Canada before 1982 we did not have what Mary Ann Glendon has referred to as 'rights talk'.[2] 'Rights talk provides a rhetorical sword and a legal shield to groups and individuals who find themselves the target of majoritarian malice or government oppression.'[3] In *Charter versus Federalism*, Alan Cairns substantially agrees with Morton: 'In a few short years, the Charter has generated a vast, qualitatively impressive discourse organized around rights', a 'citizen-state discourse [that] is a counter-discourse to the traditional language of federalism'[4] and one in which a ' "governments' constitution" contrasts with the "citizens' constitution" generated by the Charter.'[5]

Cairns is no doubt right that the Charter has created a national constitutional discourse different from the old discourse centred on federal-provincial relations, a discourse that elevates citizens' rights as the foci of constitutional discussion. But if we accept Harvey Mansfield's distinction, that '[c]itizens are busy with what they can do for themselves and others; victims are concerned with what has been done to them and with what they can get from others',[6] it is plausible to argue that the Charter has created, at least in so far as equality rights are concerned, not a citizens' constitution but a victims' constitution, a constitution concerned with ameliorating the condition of disadvantaged groups. Former Supreme Court Justice Bertha Wilson described section 15 in these terms: 'S. 15 is designed to protect those groups who suffer social, political and legal disadvantage in our society.'[7] Chief Justice Antonio Lamer has also described 'the overall purpose of section 15— namely, to remedy or prevent discrimination against groups subject to stereotyping, historical disadvantage and political and social prejudice in Canadian society'.[8]

The difficulty with this concept of equality is not only that it requires the courts to pick and choose between groups deserving special constitutional status, a requirement that may result in resentment among those groups not constitutionally recognized.[9] It is also difficult to establish, with any precision, the 'historical disadvantage' or 'social, political and legal disadvantage' of groups within society. This is particularly so in the restricted, adversarial context of constitutional litigation. Consequently, establishing section 15 violations may depend more on popular or fashionable opinion than on concrete proof, especially if success in such litigation depends on the identification of individual status with group status and the establishment of group disadvantage independently of the legal classification being challenged.[10] The consequences of such requirements, inviting groups to create the correct social images in order to enjoy the benefits doing so provides, are obvious enough and extend beyond the purview of constitutional litigation.

My third proposition then is that the content of rights issues from their form. The language of rights has moral consequences, and we can conceive better and worse regimes of rights. This is central to understanding the moral vision animating current equality rights language in Canada. The Charter and initiatives such as affirmative action and human rights legislation have not only changed the language of Canadian politics and Canada's institutional structure. They have changed, in some measure, Canada's civic character. This was Glendon's point in *Rights Talk*. The indiscriminate use of the language of rights had led to an almost narcissistic irresponsibility in American politics, dividing American society into irreconcilable, self-serving, insular groups.[11]

Can the same analysis be applied to Canada? I attempt this in the final section of this paper, examining Tocqueville's ostensible distinction between moral and immoral rights, weak and strong visions of equality. Tocqueville foresaw the obfuscation of language in modern liberal democracies that would lead to the adoption of legal positivism as the dominant ideology of rights talk, an ideology that denies the legitimacy or existence of natural rights. In addition, Tocqueville described, in unparalleled detail, the pathology of depending on government not merely for the protection of rights but for the exercise of rights. Human rights and section 15 litigation, as well as affirmative action policy, signal a change in Canada's constitutional form. Just how these initiatives have changed this form is investigated in this paper.

THE TECHNOLOGY OF EQUALITY

ELEMENTS

The new results-oriented or substantive vision of equality can be defined as a technology of equality for a variety of reasons.

First, it is based on the assumption that Canadian society can be rebuilt in compliance with the always expanding vision of equality. It is just a matter of tearing down the old structures and erecting new ones in order to make reality conform with the new vision.

Second, and a necessary condition of the first assumption, is the presupposition that we have the knowledge required to determine social change, to create the desired results. Whereas traditional liberal thought assumed that individuals were free and that the effects of their actions were unpredictable, the new vision assumes that human action is predictable, and thus controllable. The new vision of equality is predicated on the credo of modern social science, that human beings do not *act* freely or spontaneously but *behave* predictably. If we understand technology as a marriage of making (*techné*) to knowledge (*logos*), the new vision of equality is a technology because it seeks social change on the basis of an ostensible knowledge of human behaviour.[12]

Third, the new vision of equality has been, and continues to be, promulgated by what Harold Innis has referred to as 'knowledge monopolies', those persons who control the workings of particular technologies and who accumulate power and authority, eventually forming, in Neil Postman's words, 'a kind of conspiracy against those who have no access to the specialized knowledge made available by the technology'.[13] In Canada, this knowledge monopoly consists, for the most part, of a small group of legal academics, lawyers, policy analysts, and bureaucrats who provide expert evidence in human rights, employment equity, and constitutional litigation and who often appear before legislative bodies and law reform commissions to advise on legislative reform.[14]

The new vision of equality is based on a rhetoric of 'discrimination' and 'disadvantage' that depends on proof of historical wrongs to justify its forward-looking results. As Mansfield has argued respecting affirmative action, '*background* is the key to the argument.'[15] Even if it claims to provide remedies that are only temporary and that are repugnant because they must take into account things such as race, colour, sex, and national origin, affirmative action invariably relies on a heritage of discrimination for its justification.[16] Again, this is consistent with the principles of modern technology. Heidegger, for instance, defined technology as a way of revealing, a calling forth that determines what we understand by truth.[17] Technology sets upon the world, commands it to give its reasons, orders it, and rearranges it. Enframing nature, technology unifies it and homogenizes it, giving it a meaning it previously never had.[18]

Essential to transforming this meaning of the world is the imperative of controlling language. If technology is to control the way we think, it must control the medium through which we think. It must control language.[19] Jacques Ellul has made a similar observation, describing 'technological rationality' as using ' "discourse" in every operation'. 'Spontaneity and personal creativity' are excluded. Technological rationality reduces 'method to its logical dimension alone'; facts, forces and phenomena are boiled down to a 'schema of logic'.[20]

The new war on discrimination is fought in terms similar to Ellul's description of technological rationality and Heidegger's description of the necessity of enframing events as well as the meaning of language in a way that determines how we think. Advocates of the substantive view of equality present the past as irrational, as xenophobic, racist, chauvinistic. As human behaviour can be controlled, the purpose of historical analysis, among other things, is to illustrate how irrational interests and passions are not natural but the historical products of culture and politics. They are therefore contingent and correctable. Historical scholarship can help reveal the necessity and rationality of proposed constitutional and statutory reforms. Knowledge can be wedded to power. If we understand the technology of equality as liberation theory, then it must present a history from which it is necessary to be liberated. 'Discrimination', in this model, must be understood in its broadest sense, as something more than mere intentional acts, as designating social and political forces that can be overcome through the appropriate social and political changes, through education and law reform, for instance.

The fourth element of the technology of equality is then the necessity of commanding the language of politics, of framing the interpretation of social and political events in a rhetoric favourable to the results that are sought to be achieved. This requires re-examining history, providing the factual ammunition necessary to sustain the rhetoric of discrimination and disadvantage.

Finally, the technology of equality, like technology itself, is necessarily active, admitting of infinite perfection. Technology is not only 'in touch with the concrete' and 'meant to be applied': it 'tends to accelerate its growth and progression incessantly and, in theory, indefinitely'.[21] The final aspect of the technology of equality is its infinite perfectibility. Progress can know no limits, since this would arrest the dynamism necessary for incessant change.

APPLICATION

Affirmative action, human rights policy, and the judicial construction of section 15 of the Charter fit the technology of equality.

SUBSTANTIVE EQUALITY

First, all three initiatives invoke a substantive vision of equality. Affirmative action, in both education and employment, either embraces ameliorative preferences, such as pre-employment upgrading of skills or qualifications for designated beneficiaries that stop short of numerical targets, or it adopts numerical goals or quotas. In the former instance ('soft' affirmative action), equal results for different groups are promoted but not insisted upon. In the latter instance ('hard' affirmative action), equal results are insisted upon.[22] In both cases, the object is the same: substantive equality. The difference between the two kinds of affirmative action is the degree to which substantive equality is pursued.

Human rights legislation has also evolved into a substantive-equal-rights measure. This is manifest both in the proliferation of grounds of discrimination under human rights legislation and in the adoption of the 'adverse effects' model of discrimination in human rights jurisprudence and legislation.

Since the 1960s, when the first human rights codes were proclaimed in

Canada, the grounds for discrimination prohibited by the legislation have expanded from biological or fundamental social differences that define ethnic identity, to what Thomas Flanagan has referred to as the more amorphous 'life cycle' and 'life style' criteria.[23] Flanagan defined life-cycle criteria as prohibitions such as sex, marital status, family status, age, pregnancy, and physical and mental handicap. Life-style criteria included prohibitions such as sexual orientation, source of income, political beliefs, criminal record, and drug and alcohol dependence. Flanagan argued that prohibitions such as race, colour, ancestry, and national origin, traditional criteria he termed 'stigmata', afforded little or no reason for treating some individuals differently from others. Life-cycle and life-style criteria, on the other hand, often provided grounds upon which individuals could be justifiably differentiated. Life-style criteria are distinguishable from other criteria because they tend to be acquired voluntarily. So are some life-cycle criteria. Since these criteria involve an element of human agency, they possess a certain moral character that stigmata and certain life-cycle criteria do not. Accordingly, the impropriety of discrimination involving these criteria is not as clear as the impropriety involving other forms of discrimination, where individuals are distinguished by characteristics that they cannot control and that are irrelevant to most employment operations, tenancy arrangements, and other activities to which human rights legislation applies.[24]

Flanagan's division of discriminatory prohibitions does have its defects. The three-part division of grounds of discrimination is imprecise, and the distinction between legitimate and illegitimate discriminatory actions might be clarified.[25] Nonetheless, his analysis helps to clarify the quantitative and qualitative changes in human rights legislation that have occurred over the last generation. Categories of discrimination have grown from an original, restricted list focusing on direct or intentional discrimination to over 30 prohibited grounds throughout Canadian jurisdictions, most now addressing more subtle, 'systemic' forms of discrimination.

The trend away from a concern with direct discrimination to systemic or unintentional forms of discrimination was accented by two landmark decisions of the Supreme Court, released concurrently in December 1985, *Ontario Human Rights Commission v. Simpsons-Sears Ltd ('O'Malley')*[26] and *Bhinder v. Canadian National Railway Co.*[27] In these cases, the Supreme Court recognized the concept of adverse-effect discrimination, establishing the rule that in the absence of explicit provisions to the contrary, human rights legislation did not require proof of intentional discrimination. As Justice McIntyre, writing for the Court in *O'Malley*, explained:

> The accepted rules of construction are flexible enough to enable the Court to recognize in the construction of a human rights code the special nature and purpose of the enactment . . . and give to it an interpretation which will advance its broad purposes. . . . Legislation of this type is . . . not quite constitutional but certainly more than the ordinary. . . .[28]

Although there was no specific provision prohibiting adverse effect discrimination in the Ontario Human Rights Code, the legislation at issue (and no similar provision in the Canadian Human Rights Act at issue in *Bhinder*), Justice McIntyre determined that the 'main approach' to the legislation was 'not to punish the discriminator, but rather to provide relief for victims of discrimination'.[29] Proof of intent was no longer a necessary element of proof of a discriminatory practice. The result was that 'an employment rule honestly made for sound economic or business reasons, equally applicable to all to whom it is intended to apply, may yet be discriminatory if it affects a person or group of persons differently from others to whom it may apply.'[30]

The *O'Malley* and *Bhinder* decisions marked a watershed in human rights litigation, the Supreme Court recognizing for the first time adverse-effect discrimination and in doing so adopting substantive equality as the goal of human rights jurisprudence. But in what sense exactly did the adoption of the adverse-effects model of discrimination equate to the adoption of a substantive understanding of equality?

Human rights legislation originally had the aim of eliminating racism and the concomitant of racism, lack of respect for individual dignity—hence its early emphasis on racial and 'ethnic' criteria of discrimination. The emphasis today is ostensibly the same. 'Generally, human rights codes aim at the elimination of actions based on stereotypes. Individualized assessments are required rather than decisions based on stereotypes about groups.'[31] But the adverse effect concept of discrimination has consequences that extend beyond an individual complainant, since others who share in the relevant characteristic and who are similarly situated will tend to enjoy the same remedial benefits as the complainant in any single case.[32] Consequently, employers, educators, landlords, and others whose actions are covered by human rights legislation must accommodate an increasing number of group traits that may be adversely affected by otherwise neutral rules as the grounds of discrimination under human rights codes become increasingly refined. Potential respondents to human rights complaints will have to take into account a growing number of relevant differences between individuals and groups in order to ensure that all groups are treated the same as the statistical majority. Ironically, this may result in less, not more, individual treatment since it will require those exposed to human rights claims to consider fewer and fewer personal characteristics as discriminatory prohibitions proliferate.[33] Nonetheless, by drawing attention to ever more group traits that may be adversely affected by specific measures, the adverse-effect concept of equality promotes equality of group results. As Christopher Manfredi observes, by progressively applying a large and liberal 'rule of interpretation to human rights legislation', as the Supreme Court did in cases such as *O'Malley* and *Bhinder*, 'the Court significantly enhanced the discretionary power of human rights commissions to develop means for achieving the substantive equality of traditionally disadvantaged groups like religious minorities and women.'[34]

Finally, the judicial construction of section 15 of the Charter, following closely the judicial interpretation of human rights legislation, has also constitutionalized a substantive view of equality. In the most important section 15 decision to date, *Andrews v. Law Society of British Columbia* (1989),[35] Justice McIntyre identified the principal purpose of the section with the purpose of human rights legislation. Specifically, section 15 was intended to ameliorate the condition of disadvantaged groups by preventing future discriminatory actions against such groups and compensating them for past wrongs. Writing for the majority on this issue, McIntyre was careful to qualify that the section was not an abstract guarantee of social equality between groups or individuals in their private actions but was 'concerned with the application of the law',[36] with the actions of governments as opposed to the actions of private individuals. In addition, although section 15(1) provided redress to individuals affected by statutory distinctions or classifications falling within either the enumerated grounds of discrimination listed in section 15(1) or analogous grounds, complainants nonetheless had to prove more than mere differential treatment to be entitled to a remedy. The words 'without discrimination' that followed the four equal rights protections outlined in section 15(1)[37] were 'a form of qualifier' that limited the forbidden distinctions under the section to those which caused harm to the complainant, or which, in McIntyre's words, involved 'prejudice or disadvantage'.[38] 'The effect of the impugned distinction or classification on the complainant must be considered.'[39] Otherwise, all distinctions created by law and affecting an enumerated or analogous ground of discrimination under section 15 might contravene the section and cause such cases to proceed immediately to the issue of justification under section 1. This would constitute an unwarranted interpretation of section 15 and expose too much legislation to constitutional challenge, a prospect McIntyre did not endorse.

The result of *Andrews* and subsequent jurisprudence developing the *Andrews* themes has been to concentrate the courts' attention on systemic discrimination and what McIntyre referred to as 'discrete and insular minorities',[40] groups distinguished from the majority by their inability to advance their common causes through regular political channels. On its face, the *Andrews* decision, Joel Bakan observes, 'effectively refutes the idea that equality is achieved through facially neutral laws (formal equality), and suggests a willingness on the part of the court to look at how the law contributes to or detracts from the actual equality of actors.'[41] Since modern Canadian legislation is not inclined to explicitly discriminate against designated groups— indeed, any inclination in this direction would signify a serious political crisis—the Supreme Court will continue to be occupied, as it has been in most section 15 cases since *Andrews*, with evaluating the *unintended* consequences of policy and legislation on special interests claiming to be discrete and insular minorities. Canadian courts will continue to be involved, increasingly, in results-oriented jurisprudence, examining the propensity of legislation to advance individual autonomy and the equal treatment of legally recognized minority groups.[42]

KNOWLEDGE AND BEHAVIOUR

Perhaps the most important respect in which affirmative action, human rights, and section 15 jurisprudence fit the technology of equality is the assumption that we know how to assess and control individual and group behaviour. A necessary condition of substantive equality—of conceiving equality on the basis of group rights and proportional representation—is a general knowledge of the behaviour of groups. Affirmative action, for instance, is tenable only if spontaneous and unpredictable action can be made predictable and controllable, only if groups can be made homogeneous and such things as occupational affinities can be transformed by reconceiving role models and adopting other social reforms. Affirmative action presupposes a sociological knowledge that encompasses an understanding of the composition and dynamics of groups: why they behave the way they do, why they are dispersed throughout society and the economy the way they are, how they act and react with one another, how they may be more equitably redistributed. Without such knowledge, affirmative action would be deprived of its moral and political authority. How, one might ask, could preferential policies that give designated groups special opportunities be justified without the assumption that such differential treatment was warranted by the evidence and would produce the claimed effects?

In human rights legislation we see a similar development with respect to the presumption of knowledge necessary to control discriminatory behaviour. As the prohibitions against discrimination under human rights legislation have become increasingly refined and as the test for discrimination has evolved from one of invidious intent to one of adverse effects, so the prospective knowledge required to meet the terms of the legislation has had to become increasingly precise. Individual treatment necessitates the rejection of predictive categorizations or generalizations of any kind, even those that do not manifest irrational prejudice toward specific groups. As Dale Gibson remarks:

> Even stereotypes based on statistically valid generalizations (e.g., that there is a higher incidence of alcoholism among Canadian Indians than among the general Canadian population; that women are, on average, physically weaker than men; that older people tend to be less agile than younger people) may be fallacious when applied to any individual member of the groups identified. . . . Statistically sound stereotypes are the more dangerous ones, in fact, because they are more likely to be given wide credence, and to be acted upon when decisions are being made.[43]

If we examine, as examples, the cases of employers and landlords, however, it is difficult to avoid generalizations of some sort in hiring decisions or in rental agreements because everything about an individual applicant, even a relative, can never be known. Predictive categorizations, to some degree, are inevitable.

The same applies to most, if not all, cases involving human rights legislation as well as the equal treatment requirements of section 15 following *Andrews*. Since the future can never be known until it happens, every future-oriented decision is based on incomplete knowledge. Although decisions such as the hiring of an employee or the renting of an apartment to a tenant require prospective generalizations—how the employee will perform, how the renter will respect the landlord's property and the rights of neighbours—compliance with human rights legislation, as well as with section 15, requires particularized, retrospective decisions, decisions that can look back, after the primary decision maker has acted, upon a closed universe of information and determine whether the primary actor acted on the basis of relevant criteria.[44] As human rights legislation has progressively expanded and as the meaning of discrimination under the law has changed, the knowledge required to comply with the legislation, as well as the knowledge required to scrutinize those subject to it, has grown.

Ultimately, what is required by human rights legislation and equality rights review under the Charter is third parties—human rights commissions, boards of inquiry and courts—possessing the power to review the decisions of first parties, such as employers and legislators. Only in this way can the rationality of individual treatment be maintained.

LANGUAGE

Since such a power of review over the primary actors means, among other things, that those who review the decisions will not be the ones who have to live with the consequences of the decisions, and since this power has grown with the growth of equality rights initiatives, many Canadians have found the expanding power granted human rights officials and judges under the Charter unpalatable. This sentiment has been further aggravated by the inconsistent application of the adverse effects model of discrimination, a necessary consequence of a concept of discrimination that focuses on group rights and social consequences rather than on the intent, motivation or purposes of the individuals or political actors involved.[45] Since a potentially infinite number of groups may be adversely affected by any particular legislation or private practice, certain groups will have to be selected over others in the enforcement of equal rights under the adverse effects concept of discrimination. Such a process of selection may not only breed resentment but may appear partisan and ideological, rendering suspect the transfer of power to courts and quasi-judicial bodies charged with enforcing such an understanding of discrimination.[46]

Selling substantive equality to the Canadian public remains a difficult task. Although most Canadians support the idea of equal opportunity, the justice of equality of results is not as immediately apparent. As Knopff has observed, since the achievement of equality of results requires not only the elimination or mitigation of direct discrimination but the overcoming of group occupational affinities, patterns of socialization and group consciousness, phenomena not generally viewed as intrinsically blameworthy, affirmative action has had to rely on a definition of discrimination that applies to such distinct activities as the overt differential treatment of women by employers and the effects of the traditional family on the female application rates for specific jobs.[47] In order to cash in on the hostility Canadians tend to feel towards acts of direct discrimination, while concealing their disagreement with those opposed to equality of results, proponents of affirmative action have had to blur qualitatively different actions by transforming the meaning of discrimination.

This transformation of the meaning of discrimination is then the third way in which affirmative action, human rights policy, and section 15 jurisprudence fit the technology of equality. All three initiatives use a definition of discrimination consistent with the substantive view of equality. In all three cases, 'discrimination' applies to everything from intentional acts to systemic barriers to social trends. It is difficult to conceive how any of the initiatives could be maintained independently of such a broad understanding of discrimination. Quotas and goals, for instance, would be impossible to justify if the causes of under-representation between designated groups could not be attributed primarily, if not entirely, to discrimination. The adoption of the adverse effects model of discrimination in human rights and section 15 litigation is inconceivable without an antecedent change in the meaning of discrimination, one that eliminated the need to establish intention as an element of a discriminatory practice, concentrating instead on the consequences or adverse impact of otherwise neutral rules.[48] Affirmative action, human rights, and section 15 jurisprudence are exemplary equality rights initiatives, reflecting changes in policy and constitutional doctrine that have coincided with changes in the meaning of language.

Some qualification of this observation, however, is necessary in the case of affirmative action, since the policy may not be an antidote to discrimination. Gibson highlighted this in an essay in which he responded to a critique of affirmative action by Knopff. Knopff had asserted that affirmative action depended on a rhetoric of discrimination, that to remain tenable policy, affirmative action had to explain departures from the numerically proportionate distribution of groups in the workplace and elsewhere as being the result of societal or systemic discrimination, not factors unrelated to discrimination. If affirmative action did not make these broad assumptions, the moral and political bedrock of the initiative would be undermined.[49]

Gibson disagreed with this assessment, contending that such an interpretation of affirmative action failed to appreciate its true remedial nature. Affirmative action, Gibson argued, is a 'no-fault' policy that provides disadvantaged minorities a means of catching up to the more fortunate majority, *regardless* of who is responsible for the disadvantage. Discrimination is therefore irrelevant to the issue of entitlement to the benefits of affirmative action. Rather, the focus is on disadvantage. What does it matter whether the misfortune of a target group arises from discrimination or some other factor beyond the designated group's control? Does not the paramountcy of equality require that redress be provided regardless of who, if anyone, can be blamed for the group's misfortune?

It is precisely the inability to prove discrimination that makes affirmative action such an appealing remedy over and above the traditional safeguards to minority rights. Whereas anti-discrimination laws concentrate on individual cases and require a finding of liability on the part of the responding party to invoke a remedy, a process that can be inefficient and costly, affirmative action focuses on disadvantages that can be statistically proved to be suffered by certain groups, ameliorating the condition of collectivities regardless of the facts of any individual case. Affirmative action avoids the expense and ostentatious morality associated with prosecuting anti-discrimination cases while providing those unfortunate minorities with the employment opportunities and income they otherwise would not have.

Gibson invites us then to see affirmative action not as a policy 'aimed primarily at prejudice or discussion' but as 'a supplement to anti-discrimination laws which attempts to advance equality of opportunity by positive, *no-fault* means'.[50] The approach of affirmative action 'is analogous, in one sense, to workers' compensation, no-fault automobile insurance, disability insurance, and other schemes to assist victims of misfortune without regard to whether someone can be legally blamed for the misfortune. It is a remedy that focuses on need, rather than on causation.'[51] Critics, such as Knopff, are incorrect to attack affirmative action on the basis that it does not eliminate discrimination since the elimination of discrimination is not its object. To impugn affirmative action for the interpretive error committed by some of its advocates— that affirmative action is aimed at eliminating discrimination—avoids confronting the substantive merits of the policy. Those substantive merits are the spreading of the social costs of improving the condition of minorities throughout the whole of society. The real question is, do the costs of affirmative action outweigh its benefits? To which the answer is simple: as the costs to the majority can be spread over a much larger population, the inconvenience of affirmative action is nominal, whereas the benefits it provides to recipients are significant and direct. From a strictly utilitarian perspective, affirmative action is good policy. It has 'a greater *individualized* impact for good than for evil'.[52]

For its critics, affirmative action conflates equality of opportunity with equality of economic and social results. Critics argue that equality of opportunity is not tantamount to the equal distribution or equal sharing of wealth precisely because people do not pursue opportunities equally. To focus on results independently of the individual causes of those results—to focus on need rather than on causation, for instance, as Gibson suggests—may eviscerate the principle of equality and what we might call the tradition of 'just deserts', a tradition that is at the heart of opposition to affirmative action.

Affirmative action may also undermine the pride of its beneficiaries.[53]

Since the policy asserts that beneficiaries require remedial measures and special help to succeed, it implies that they are not as capable as others of achieving things on their own. Perhaps more categorically, affirmative action implies that the beneficiaries are inferior or less able than disadvantaged non-beneficiaries who overcome things without assistance. Affirmative action explains this difference not by acknowledging this discrepancy but by attributing those residual numerical inequalities that persist to discrimination or, if we accept Gibson's explanation, by giving certain individuals preference over others without determining who, if anyone, is responsible for individual disadvantage; that is, without determining fault. The consequences of such a policy are predictable: contempt for beneficiaries among the majority of non-beneficiaries who do not get the special status or special help the beneficiaries get as well as resentment among those, such as employers, who feel they have to pay the costs of misguided social policy.

Finally, to the extent affirmative action confers special benefits on specific individuals, it denies others the right to participate in the market and the experience of acquisition. As far as modern constitutional democracies are concerned, this right is most fundamental. Affirmative action focuses on group rights, as opposed to individual rights. Perhaps more accurately, it is essentially unconcerned with the rights of individuals except in so far as they belong to groups that advocates of affirmative action identify as disadvantaged or discriminated against. This means that there will be a vast number—indeed, perhaps the vast majority—of individuals for whom affirmative action will afford no protection. Affirmative action effectively denies these individuals rights to the extent it provides special groups with special treatment. It may then be a misnomer to compare affirmative action to workers' compensation, no-fault automobile insurance, or disability insurance, not only because such schemes require, for the most part, contributions from beneficiaries before they are entitled to benefits, but also because the benefits provided under such schemes are not tantamount to a corresponding deprivation of the rights of others.

EQUALITY, PROGRESS, AND NATURAL RIGHTS

Whether we define affirmative action as compensatory justice for past and present discrimination or as social welfare aimed at alleviating disadvantage, the authority for such a policy originates in a social condition that extends far beyond affirmative action or concerns for equitable employment. The desire to eliminate discrimination and the desire to eliminate disadvantage originate in equality since both seek a greater equality of condition. Raymond Aron has commented that the two broad ideals of equality that animate modern civilization are that of 'economic equality' based on the 'equality of needs', and that of 'equality of opportunity', or the protest 'against the transmission of socio-economic inequalities from one generation to another. Taken to an extreme, the first argument would justify a proportionality between revenue and needs, the second a perfect equality from point of departure, a social order so to speak strictly non-hereditary, deprived of all continuity.'[54] We recognize aspects of both these definitions of equality in the desire to eliminate disadvantage and the desire to eliminate discrimination. The defence of affirmative action in the name of eliminating disadvantage is invoked under the auspices of a policy that, to use Gibson's words, focuses not merely on opportunity but 'on need'. The defence of affirmative action in the name of eliminating discrimination is invoked under the auspices of a policy that promotes more equitable opportunities of employment. It appears that either way affirmative action is defined, it employs aspects of these two broad definitions of equality that Aron said consumed modern society. The problem is that the two definitions are not necessarily compatible: 'They constitute a sort of permanent critique of a social order that condemns itself because it invokes ideas that taken to their limit are contradictory and gives itself a goal that is probably unattainable.'[55]

By way of summary, affirmative action invites us then to contemplate what exactly equality means. Affirmative action is not limited to political equality since it concerns the ostensibly non-political activities of earning an income and maintaining a job. We might even say that affirmative action challenges the very idea of what we usually associate with political equality because it establishes rights on the basis of characteristics that differentiate individuals rather than on the basis of characteristics that identify them. It also conceives rights to the necessities of life, for example, the right to earn a livelihood or to pursue a career, as the very ends of government rather than as pre-political rights that no government or political power has the right to interfere with or violate.[56] Affirmative action reflects a specific conception of the content of political life and what government should be.

So do human rights and section 15 jurisprudence. As the grounds of discrimination under human rights legislation have proliferated, as the non-enumerated grounds of discrimination under section 15(1) remain open-ended, and as both of these initiatives have endorsed a systemic or adverse effects concept of discrimination, permitting certain forms of differential treatment in certain circumstances and not in others, an obvious question that must be addressed is: What constitutes a legitimate ground of discrimination? What are the limits to prohibited conduct in the name of equality? Is indiscriminateness to become a moral imperative because its opposite is deemed to be discrimination?[57]

Human rights legislation and section 15 jurisprudence, like affirmative action, invite us then to clarify what precisely we mean by equality or equal treatment and, by implication, what rights attach to individuals as holders of equal rights. The issue of natural rights arises. It arises because the question of equality involves a balancing of rights, the rights of the majority versus the rights of the minority, the rights of employers versus the rights of employees, and so on. We cannot leave the question at a determination of rights alone.

The question of the proper rank and order of rights or the question of priorities arises. If we are to answer such a question, we cannot consider the needs or desires of any particular individual or group to be decisive because the needs and desires of the various individuals and groups conflict; indeed, this conflict is the very precondition of the question of priorities. We have to look beyond the particular rights of the claimants and judge them in accordance with some standard or principle beyond the rights themselves.[58] Traditionally, this standard was natural right, the natural being distinguishable from the conventional or what changes over time. 'A human being is said to be natural', Leo Strauss wrote, 'if he is guided by nature rather than by convention, or by inherited opinion, or by tradition, to say nothing of mere whims.'[59] The natural then is distinguished from what changes over time or from those customs or traditions that change from society to society, culture to culture. Natural rights are distinguishable from conventional or positive rights by attaching to all people at all times. They therefore precede government. They are not created by government, even though government may legally recognize them.

Affirmative action, human rights legislation, and section 15 of the Charter provide for legal or positive rights, rights established through legal process or agreement. In this sense, they are distinguishable from natural rights if we understand by such rights, rights preceding government and arrived at through a process of introspective reasoning.

But the rights protected by affirmative action, human rights legislation, and section 15 are also distinguishable from natural rights in another way. To the extent that they establish rights on the basis of the groups to which individuals belong, they make rights dependent on group affiliation. No longer do rights attach to all individuals at all times. Rather, they attach to certain individuals at certain times. Rights thus become relative, dependent not only on convention or agreement, but also on circumstance, which may change.

The problem with such a meaning of rights is that if we accept rights as deriving from principle and as being unchanging, we cannot leave the determination of rights to circumstance, or even to convention or to preferences. The reason is not merely one of principle but the problem of responsibility. As Strauss emphasized:

> Once we realize that the principles of our actions are arbitrary or have no other support than our blind choice, we really do not believe in them any more. We cannot wholeheartedly act upon them any more. We cannot live any more as responsible beings. In order to live, we have to silence the easily silenced voice of reason, which tells us that our principles are in themselves as good or as bad as any other principles. The more we cultivate reason, the more we cultivate nihilism.[60]

Nihilism is the situation that obtains where anything goes and where speech is equivalent to silence because the value posited is as justifiable as its negation.[61] Substantive equality brings us closer to nihilism because it establishes rights, not on the basis of reason or principle, but on the basis of expediency or social utility. Rights become matters of circumstance or mere vehicles to the attainment of results, specifically, equal results. They become what we make of them, not reflecting widely accepted principles but the necessity of the case, changing according to what the political situation requires. When rights become tools of expediency, attaching to specific groups, their moral authority is undermined because they are perceived to be both contingent and partisan to particular, group-based claims—an ironic development perhaps given the history of the language of rights.[62] This then is one of the effects of substantive equality: rights are made relative, and moral and political ambivalence are facilitated.

But substantive equality does more. By progressively erasing the distinction between the private and public spheres presupposed by the distinction between society and the state, a distinction originally established by the doctrine of natural rights (the idea that there are certain inalienable spheres of private activity), substantive equality threatens the liberal democratic equation that defines liberal democracies such as Canada. Substantive equal rights measures, such as affirmative action, human rights legislation, and section 15 jurisprudence, pursue norms inconsistent with traditional liberal democratic thought. To the extent that they do, we cannot regard such initiatives as mere policy preferences, choices about how best to carry into effect a program of equality, given a fixed, constitutional regime. Rather, they represent a choice between regime types themselves.

In *Democracy in America*, Tocqueville admonished that equality taken to an extreme is the great paradox of liberal democracy because it eventually threatens the very liberty—originally expressed in the form of natural rights—it was conceived to protect. The 'desire for equality always becomes more insatiable as equality becomes greater.'[63] In the new world, the 'prodigious influence' of equality on the 'public spirit' spreads beyond political morality and the law to 'obtain no less of an empire over civil society than over government', modifying 'everything that it does not produce', the manners, habits, opinions, sentiments, behaviour, will, tastes, and instincts of individuals.[64]

In the final section of this paper, we will examine how affirmative action, human rights policy, and section 15 jurisprudence with a view to illustrating how all three emerge from a moral vision anticipated by Tocqueville in *Democracy in America*. That vision is defined by its elevation of substantive equality or social equality to a status of pre-eminence. Social equality is distinguished from political equality by its emphasis on the characteristics that distinguish individuals or that make them different and that the concept of social equality necessarily presumes. A concept of equality that focuses on such characteristics will differentiate between individuals as much as possible; it will differentiate between individuals on the basis of social or biological characteristics, characteristics that can be infinitely refined and differentiated.

Such differentiation constitutes the final element of the technology of equality, permitting infinite progress through the progressive refinement of distinctions between individuals and groups. The result of such differentiation has been a growing array of positive rights, the concomitant of which has been a demand for greater control over the outcomes of private and public decision making by a coterie of egalitarian guardians.[65]

TOCQUEVILLE AND THE PROBLEM OF TUTELARY DEMOCRACY

MORAL AND IMMORAL RIGHTS, WEAK AND STRONG VISIONS OF EQUALITY

The problem of guardian democracy was at the heart of Tocqueville's concern for the evisceration of rights in *Democracy in America*. 'After the general idea of virtue', Tocqueville wrote,

> I know of no more beautiful than that of rights. . . . The idea of rights is nothing other than the idea of virtue introduced to the political world. . . .
> . . . [Just as there] are no great men without virtue [so] without respect for rights there is no great people: one can almost say there is no society; for what is a union of rational and intelligent beings of which force is the only tie?[66]

For Tocqueville, rights define the limits of political power. Without them there is no society; or rather, there is no civil society because the use of force is potentially unlimited. Rights, however, also require a reciprocity of respect and benefit between individuals. Tocqueville spoke of political rights. Political rights require equal treatment. Modern democrats will not tolerate unequal or special treatment because it is contrary to the spirit of democracy and the natural equality of individuals.[67]

Although Tocqueville never spoke explicitly about the problem of natural right or of nihilism, he did speak about the 'natural liberties' to 'act alone' and to form associations,[68] the paternal 'rights of nature',[69] 'the sacred rights of property and of the family',[70] and the 'rights of each' that transcend all classes.[71] He spoke about the refined nature that the modern exegesis of equality would assume among those who would find in most forms of social and political distinction a cause of inequality demanding remedy, and he asked his contemporaries: 'Have you not discovered that mores are being altered, and that with them the moral notion of rights is being effaced?'[72]

We might determine from this that Tocqueville conceived a moral and an immoral vision of rights. Without pushing this distinction too far, we can at least say that he conceived political rights in distinction from other forms of rights and he anticipated that change in the lexicon of equality that speaks to the distinction between political equality and social equality. He contrasted, for instance, that 'depraved taste for equality that inclines the weak to want to attract to their level the strong, and that reduces men to prefer equality in servitude to inequality in liberty' with that 'manly and legitimate passion for equality that excited men to want to be all strong and esteemed . . . . [and that] tends to elevate the small to the rank of the great.'[73] He remarked elsewhere that modern democrats have a 'much more ardent and indeed more tenacious love for equality than for liberty';[74] if given the choice, democrats will 'seek equality in liberty, and, if they cannot obtain it, they will still seek it in slavery.'[75]

> It is not that the peoples whose social state is democratic naturally despise liberty; on the contrary, they have an instinctive taste for it. But liberty is not the principal and continued object of their desire; what they cherish with an eternal love, is equality; they throw themselves toward liberty by rapid impulse and sudden effort, and, if they miss their goal, they are resigned; but nothing could satisfy them without equality, and they would rather consent to perish than to lose it.[76]

Tocqueville conceived two visions of equality, one 'manly and legitimate', the other 'depraved'. One, we might say, leads to 'equality in liberty', the other to 'equality in slavery'. We also know that Tocqueville conceived of a 'moral notion of rights', and he warned us to be wise to the 'principle of social utility'[77] as well as to those who purported to be 'the supporter of good law, the upholder of the oppressed, and the founder of order'.[78] We are invited then to speculate whether that immoral notion of rights Tocqueville incites us to contrast with the moral notion of rights arises concurrently with the rise of social utility and those who purport to be the supporters of good law and the upholders of the oppressed. Did Tocqueville contemplate by the distinction between manly and legitimate equality and depraved equality that distinction between political equality and social equality—that distinction between a vision of equality that results in actual inequality and a vision of equality that eventually demands an equality of economic and social results?

Tocqueville warned that where equality in servitude was preferred to equality in liberty the social state would be not only a state of restricted liberty but a state of indolence and indifference. He reminded us that such a state was the particular mode of corruption to which democracies were prone. As equality spreads, the passion for a greater equality of condition will also spread.[79] Democracies, by their very nature, are inclined to an adulteration that transforms the principle of equality from something pursued for the sake of opportunity, allowing the inequality of natural endowments to flourish, to something pursued for the sake of equality itself, for the sake of achieving a simple numerical equality of economic and social result. Tocqueville referred to a 'famous sect' of 'our day' that 'proposes to concentrate all property in the hands of a central power which would then distribute it to all individuals according to merit. This would be one way to escape that complete and eternal equality that appears to threaten democratic societies.' But

> there is another simpler and less dangerous remedy, that is to accord privileges to no one, to give equal enlightenment and independence to all, and to leave each the task of making a place on his own. Natural inequality will soon make itself felt, and wealth will immediately pass to the side of the most capable.
>
> Democratic and free societies will therefore always include a multitude of opulent and comfortable people.[80]

Democratic and free societies will apparently avoid the accumulation of all property and the power to distribute it in the hands of a central authority. Accumulating all property in a central authority is more dangerous than a system of 'natural inequality', than a system that allows each to make a place in the world 'on his own', permitting wealth to 'pass to the side of the most capable'. But why? Why would such a regime be preferred to a regime in which a central authority redistributed property?

Tocqueville seemed to contemplate at least two answers. First, the problem of knowledge. To distribute property according to a central authority's conception of merit presupposes a knowledge that no central authority could ever possess. Consequently a greater patronage and abuse than would be produced under a system of 'natural inequality' will likely ensue. Second, the problem of forms and the rule of law. By redistributing property according to a central authority's conception of merit, the constitutional forms and the rule of law essential to democracy would be undermined.

We can illustrate the difficulties here by looking at affirmative action, a modern policy that seeks greater social equality through the redistribution of employment opportunities by a central authority.

AFFIRMATIVE ACTION AND THE PROBLEM OF KNOWLEDGE

As an employment policy, affirmative action aims at the redistribution of income by restricting job opportunities to specific, limited classes. It carries, as part of its rhetorical arsenal, the ethos of social utility, the idea, as Gibson expressed it, that the rights of certain individuals can be restricted in the name of the greater common good or utility. Tocqueville warned us to be on guard against the principle of social utility. We might guess that he did so because the principle of social utility presents a moral vision opposed to the tradition of just deserts where individuals are entitled, as a matter of right, to the fruits of their labour. Tocqueville acknowledged the power of accident and force in politics and economics. His advocacy of a system of unregulated economic conditions, or what we today might call the 'free market', did not mean that these conditions or the market would reward individuals according to merit. They do not. The market rewards individuals according to value, according to the worth of individual services and products to others. Those who believe they deserve more on the basis of merit or who think that equal results will necessarily follow from equal opportunities may then be disappointed under a system of 'natural inequality' or a free market.

This, however, does not imply the intervention of a central authority as a remedy to the problem. Quite the contrary. In democratic societies 'the legislature, it is true, no longer accords privileges, but nature does.'[81] Equal opportunity does not translate into equal results in democratic societies because people possess talents, desires, will, fortitude, and other attributes and characteristics unequally. The abuses that can occur with redistributionist policies such as affirmative action are greater than in a system of natural inequality because of the conventional inequalities that can result from programs based on dubious assumptions about what causes group behaviour. When the power of the state is wedded to such putative knowledge, the potential for abuse is greater than if market forces were left to their own because once such power and knowledge have been wedded, the check on state power, which private action affords, is dissipated.[82] There is no further court of appeal for those, such as the non-beneficiaries of affirmative action, whose rights are denied. Such a dilemma does not exist in a free market, where there are indeed significant disadvantages and differences between individuals, but where opportunities, by the very fact that the market is *free*, are not permanently closed.

This is not to say that Tocqueville's formulation of 'manly and legitimate' equality is inconsistent with the principles of a 'welfare state', at least to the extent that such a state attempts to promote *formal* equality of opportunity by assisting those few 'small' with aptitude to rise to the level of the 'great'. What it is inconsistent with is a state of affairs where opportunities for classes of individuals are restricted in the name of achieving a substantive equality of result—what appears to be the case with policies such as affirmative action. 'Natural inequality' is 'very great', and 'fortunes [will] become unequal from the moment when each makes use of all his faculties to enrich himself.'[83] The desire 'to elevate the small to the rank of the great', which Tocqueville identified with the 'manly and legitimate passion for equality', cannot be a desire to achieve substantive equality. Tocqueville did not suggest that the capacities for achievement were equally distributed and that those 'small' with limited capacities could consistently, if ever, achieve greatness. Natural inequalities are a part of the human condition and will never be eliminated. The elevating of the small to the rank of the great that Tocqueville identified with strong equality must then mean providing that formal equality of opportunity that allows the few with capacity to achieve greatness. On the other hand, that 'depraved taste for equality that inclines the weak to want to attract to their level the strong' must mean something like the taste for equality of results. Natural endowments being unequally distributed, equality of results can only be achieved by limiting the liberty that permits the talented to flourish and by dragging the talented down to the level of the mediocre.[84] Policies, such as affirmative action, that attempt to restrict the opportunities of the more talented in the name of the less talented and the promotion of greater opportunity, would appear to be a species of the depraved taste for equality.

AFFIRMATIVE ACTION AND THE PROBLEM OF CONSTITUTIONAL FORMS AND THE RULE OF LAW

Tocqueville's admonition regarding the dangers of social utility was consistent with his admonition regarding the dangers of undermining constitutional forms and the rule of law (the idea that law should be applied generally without particular exceptions). Constitutional forms and the rule of law are particularly important in democracies because impatience with forms and those rules that impede the march of equality is more prevalent in democracies than in other regimes.[85] Affirmative action, like other redistributionist policies, makes respect for forms and the rule of law difficult, if not impossible, because the distribution of opportunities is determined, not by general rules or market forces, but by the discretion or preferences of authorities who single out individuals or groups for differential treatment. Opportunities are distributed, not on the basis of fixed, uniformly applied rules, but unequally on the basis of contingent, and hence alterable, social status. Decisions regarding what individuals must do, where they are to work, and what they are to receive are not derived from general precepts applicable to all, but are guided by the particular aims and ostensible knowledge of a central planning authority. F.A. Hayek has observed that policies that seek greater distributive justice run the risk of undermining not only the rule of law, but the constitutional and economic order itself.[86] Tocqueville would agree. When individual rights are restricted in the name of the greater common good, a change in constitutional forms, as well as in private and public mores, should be expected:[87]

> It happens that, at [the] same time and among [the] same nations where men have conceived a natural scorn for the rights of individuals, the rights of society have been naturally extended and consolidated. This means that men become less attached to individual rights, at the moment where it would be most necessary to retain and defend the few that remain.[88]

By creating rights for certain groups, and not others, affirmative action denies individual rights and also deprives individuals of the opportunity for self-government, the opportunity to exercise rights on their own, in freedom. Tocqueville was particularly concerned with the dangers that equality posed to freedom, proclaiming at the end of *Democracy in America*: 'I have sought to expose in broad daylight the perils with which equality threatens human independence because I firmly believe that these perils are the most formidable and the least foreseen of all those that the future holds.'[89]

Freedom, on Tocqueville's reading, was always in tension with equality because the demands of equality were potentially infinite. Particularly concerned with maintaining political rights and the rights of property,[90] Tocqueville affirmed that the economic inequalities flowing from the differences in natural endowments, always at odds with the demands of an equality of condition, were nevertheless just. The right to property was natural or inalienable—'sacred' as Tocqueville put it. Contemplating a regime of natural rights similar to that defended by the founders of modern liberalism, where inequality was permitted as the natural consequence of a just political order, Tocqueville proposed that the loss of faith in such rights signified the victory of equality over freedom and the undermining of liberal constitutional and political order.

This theme has been repeated by many critics of modern political and economic theory. Marc Plattner, for instance, has written: '[The] loss of belief in the justice of a liberal economic order . . . is the ultimate consequence of the rejection of the doctrine of natural rights by the tradition of political economy.'[91] We might add that it is not just the tradition of political economy that has rejected the doctrine of natural rights. It is all of the social sciences. And the rejection of natural rights leads not only to the 'loss of belief in the justice of a liberal economic order'. It leads to the loss of belief in the justice of any liberal order whatsoever. The rejection of natural rights leads, as we suggested earlier, to nihilism.

POSITIVISM AND THE MANUFACTURE OF RIGHTS

In terms of the language of rights, the eradication of natural rights implies that anything goes; rights become empty vessels into which we can pour any meaning we wish, which perhaps explains how human rights legislation and section 15 jurisprudence could give rise to a broad, and potentially unlimited, scope of rights. Such a proliferation of rights, however, leads to confusion and, ultimately, to an undermining of the sanctity of rights.[92] The obfuscation of the meaning of rights and the subverting of the sacred quality of rights can be explained by Tocqueville's physiognomy of equality.

Tocqueville is famous for his remarks that the effacement of language and the concomitant domination of public opinion will be significant determinants of political and intellectual life in advanced democracies. In Tocqueville's America 'tradition is taken only as information';[93] the 'origin of words is as lost as that of men, and it causes [as much] confusion in language as it does in society.'[94] Democrats are forgetful not only of their heritage and of tradition but of language and the signification of words. Like society itself, words forever change. 'The perpetual movement that reigns in a democracy tends . . . to ceaselessly renew the face of language, like that of affairs.'[95] At the same time, it is not a question 'of knowing whether there exists an intellectual authority in democratic ages, but only where is it deposited and what is its extent'.[96] The authority is public opinion, and its extent is significant. 'Not only is common opinion the only guide that remains for individual reason among democratic peoples, but it has among these peoples a power infinitely greater than among any other.'[97] Taken together, the obfuscation of language and the dominance of public opinion means that 'among [democratic] peoples, it is the majority that makes the law in matters of language, just as in everything else.'[98]

In the context of the language of rights then, we can say at least three things. First, and most obviously, the meaning of rights in modern democracies will be determined by the majority. Second, since majority opinion changes, the meaning of rights will also change. Third, and perhaps least obviously, if the meaning of rights ceaselessly changes, there will likely be a propensity in modern democracies to deny that any opinion about rights could be any more comprehensive, accurate or knowledgeable than any other opinion. The very possibility of natural rights or the idea that we could possess knowledge of the proper rank and order of rights will be denied and replaced by an ideology of openness and its offspring, legal positivism.

Tocqueville suggested that rights cast adrift in a climate of openness will be determined by fashionable opinion. But how exactly?

For Tocqueville, rights were inextricably tied to liberty. Liberty contrasted with equality: sometimes liberty was compatible with equality; sometimes it was not. As far as thought was concerned, the great threat to liberty was the paralysis of the mind that equality tended to precipitate. Although intellectual authority would be different in modern democracies than in previous regimes, in particular the aristocracies of the *ancien régime* that Tocqueville compared to modern democracy, it would by no means be any less influential. On the contrary, it could quite conceivably become too great, eventually closing off thought altogether. 'I perceive', Tocqueville wrote, 'how, under the empire of certain laws, democracy could extend the intellectual liberty that the social democratic state favored, in such a way that after having broken all the barriers that had been imposed on it by classes and men, the human mind would narrowly enchain itself to the general will of the greatest number.'[99]

The problem of succumbing to the general will, or what we might call 'public opinion', has a number of causes. First, the isolation of individuals. Contrary to Marxist ideology, modern democracies tend to reduce, not increase, class barriers. The traditional bonds of class, family, community, habit, and wealth become levelled in modern democracies because the prerogatives of birth and fortune are destroyed.[100] The result is a society of anonymous, insular, lonely, abandoned, impotent individuals. Second, the removal of these traditional restraints also has the effect of removing from individuals both the time and interest necessary to acquire independent knowledge. If one were to look for 'a passion that is natural to men which the obscurity of their origin and the mediocrity of their fortune excited and limited' one would find 'none more appropriate than the taste for well-being'.[101] Democratic man is consumed with the pursuit of wealth, the poor because they do not have it, the rich because they fear to lose it. Since the pursuit of wealth in democracy is open to all individuals, the definitive trait of a democracy will be competition, not thought. Anything that takes time away from the industry of individuals will be avoided. The penchants of modern democrats can then be easily envisioned. They will reject authority and look to themselves for most answers. Or rather, because everyone is in a similar predicament, they will determine that all opinion is equal, and will find truth on the side of the greatest number.[102]

The equality of opinions that is endemic to modern democracies has important practical consequences. For instance, the best social order or political regime will be conceived to be the regime that protects this fundamental equality. We are familiar with a number of the elements of this ideal: freedom of speech, the development of cultural heterogeneity or the protection of a variety of cultural identities ('multiculturalism'), uninhibited religion, or the right of everyone to believe what he or she wants.

In political or legal terms, this freedom of opinion translates into a virtually uninhibited scope of rights. We can say, with equal legitimacy, that people have a right to work or that they have no right to work, that they have a right to welfare or that they have no right to welfare, that they have a right to educate their children in the school of their choice or that they have no right to educate their children in the school of their choice. Rights, in a word, are limited only by the limits of human ingenuity and by what people are willing to produce as rights through convention or through the positive law. It may even become a prejudice that the only rights that exist are those entrenched in written or conventional law. In other words, it may become a prejudice that rights have their origin in agreement or convention, not reason or nature.[103] What this means is that rights, as Tocqueville predicted, will eventually be determined by public opinion.

Professor Peter Hogg, one of Canada's leading authorities on constitutional law, provides a recent example of how this reasoning works. In 'On Being a Positivist: A Reply to Professor Vaughan', Professor Hogg argued that he did 'not believe in natural rights' because

> there is no generally agreed-upon list of 'natural' rights; there is no agreement on the source of those rights; there is no agreement on the reasoning process by which such rights might be derived; and there is no agreement on how such rights could be enforced, although there probably is agreement that such rights never have been enforced.[104]

Professor Hogg's point regarding the difficulty of agreeing on natural rights, on their source, the process by which they might be discovered, and how they might be enforced, is well taken. The difficulty of reaching agreement on these issues is not easily overcome. But does this imply that natural rights do not exist? The corollary to Professor Hogg's argument is that the only rights that exist are those that are established through agreement or, as Professor Hogg said in an earlier paper, 'rights are creatures of law.'[105]

There are a number of problems with this argument. First, if rights are creatures of law or agreement, then, among other things, they are not that secure, since law and agreement tend to change. We understand rights, however, to be specifically immune from the inauspicious attacks of majority consent or agreement—what Professor Hogg appeared to recognize as the legitimate source of authority.

Second, and perhaps more fundamentally, the positivist argument apparently disregards the source of the legitimacy of agreement itself, at least in so far as agreement is considered the legitimate basis of rights. The source of such legitimacy would seem to be the natural equality of individuals, the natural right of all to contract or to agree to legally binding contracts. Otherwise, how could positivism be any more legitimate a regime of rights than other regimes?

Third, to the extent that agreement is not arrived at by blind preference, it is determined by rational judgment, which necessarily presupposes the existence of a standard beyond mere opinion that allows us to determine better from worse judgment. As far as rights are concerned, as soon as we begin to argue about their content, about what is a legitimate versus what is an illegitimate right, a serious versus a spurious right, we necessarily presuppose the existence of a standard that allows us to arbitrate between legitimate and illegitimate rights. We necessarily presuppose something that is akin to natural or inalienable rights. Otherwise why argue the issue? The fact that Professor Hogg is prepared to contest the issue of rights would appear to be indication enough of the contradictory nature of the positivist platform. Professor Hogg criticized Professor Vaughan for suggesting that 'our judges . . . be better educated in natural law and . . . apply it in their decisions. In my view, this would pose a serious threat to democratic government because it would authorize judges to give legal force to values that had never been approved by any democratic process.'[106] Independently of the question whether judges should apply the natural law in their decisions, why need values be approved by the democratic process? How, on the positivist argument, can we prefer democratic government or the democratic process to other forms of government or processes? Are these not value judgments that require us to transcend the positive law, to go beyond positivism to defend democracy?

Perhaps Professor Hogg could respond that we live under a democratic regime and that this makes our preference for democratic government less arbitrary or illegitimate because we are merely affirming values already given in law. But this would seem to beg the question, and not only because it fails to answer how we distinguish legitimate from illegitimate laws. Our preference for democracy (and I suspect Professor Hogg's preference) derives not from the positive law, but from reason and our knowledge of what is preferable. We prefer democracy to other forms of government, such as aristocracy, timocracy, or tyranny, because it preserves individual rights and public order better than these other regimes, not to mention its respect for the equal consent of all. We prefer democracy, not because the positive law tells us so, but because reason and our better judgment tell us so.

If reason tells us that democracy is better than other types of government, is it not also reason that allows us to distinguish legitimate from illegitimate rights, that allows us to distinguish which rights take priority? Is reason, for instance, not the basis on which we can determine that the right to life is fundamental and that without it the other rights, such as freedom of conscience and religion (section 2(a) of the Charter), the right to vote (section 3 of the Charter) or the 'legal rights' (sections 7–14 of the Charter), would be impossible? And in two hundred or even five hundred years, will we not think this same fundamental distinction sound? Is our thought with respect to rights as time-bound as Professor Hogg suggests?[107]

Finally, with respect to the agreement or not on the existence of natural rights, we need look no further than the American Declaration of Independence, which not only contemplates the existence of natural or inalienable rights, but specifies their content. For some, the American Constitution is simply an extrapolation of the Declaration's natural rights, a document intended to secure these rights more firmly than any prior constitutional arrangements, in particular, the Articles of Confederation.[108]

Professor Vaughan suggested that 'Hogg is clearly in the mainstream of contemporary legal thinking; the law schools of this country are overwhelmingly positivistic.'[109] We might enlarge upon this comment and suggest that Professor Hogg, as well as Canadian law schools, are in the mainstream of contemporary democratic thought. The predominant assumption is that rights are determined by convention or agreement; the most compelling—perhaps sole—authority that is recognized is the will of the majority. Hence, in so far as law schools treat the issue of rights, they do so only within the limited scope of issues that are current within public opinion. Professor Hogg maintained that Blackstone's natural law teaching was anachronistic and that his upholding of the sanctity of property rights and his failure to appreciate the equality of franchise were out of tune with the present day.[110] Law schools offer courses on such topics as law and gender, the conflict between minorities and the state, and native rights. One would be hard pressed to find a single Canadian law school that offered a course on rights that examined texts pre-dating this century or even the last 30 years. This means something.

DEMOCRACY AND REDISTRIBUTIVE JUSTICE

Related to the democratic inclination to conceive rights as the offspring of agreement or convention is the propensity to conceive the vast majority of rights in economic terms. In a famous passage, Tocqueville declared: 'What I reproach about equality, is not that it leads men to the pursuit of prohibited pleasures but that it absorbs them entirely in the pursuit of permitted pleasures.'[111] Since commerce and the desire for acquisition are what consume modern democrats, it is obvious that the most ardent disputes will involve things such as equal access to employment, minimum levels of subsistence, welfare, medicare, pension benefits, child care subsidies, and the like. As we noted earlier, at the heart of such disputes is the desire for equality of conditions—indeed, 'the principal passion that agitates men in [democratic times] is the love of this equality.'[112] However 'conditions', in this sense, will usually mean economic conditions and disputes as to justice will usually boil down to questions concerning economic inequality or redistributive justice. Policies such as affirmative action are sustained by concepts such as redistributive justice.

The defence of redistributive justice, however, can only take place within the broader context of defending distributive justice *per se*. At some point we have to justify why government or the state has the right to interfere in the distribution of wealth. This is a necessary precondition for the advocacy that any form of redistributive justice is a good thing. If we accept that the pursuit of wealth is fundamental to modern liberal democracies, then part of what we conceive to be freedom—indeed the vast part of that concept for the vast majority of individuals—will be the right to retain the products of one's labour. As Hannah Arendt has remarked, 'it has become almost axiomatic even in political theory to understand by political freedom not a political phenomenon, but on the contrary, the more or less free range of non-political activities which a given body politic will permit and guarantee to those who constitute it.'[113] In the most comprehensive defence of the American Constitution ever written, James Madison defined 'the first object of government' as 'the protection of different and unequal faculties of acquiring property'.[114] If we accept that freedom or liberty is conceived by most modern individuals, including Canadians, as the right to pursue 'the more or less free range of non-political activities', and in particular the fruits of one's labour, then freedom will be consistent with a great inequality; the 'different and unequal faculties of acquiring property' will lead to the different and unequal distribution of wealth.

It is not improbable, in democracies, that this inequality may be viewed as morally improper. John Rawls, in *A Theory of Justice*, for instance, presents a comprehensive defence of the distributive platform that rejects this idea of justice.[115] 'Once we decide to look for a conception of justice that nullifies the accidents of natural endowment and the contingencies of social circumstance,' Rawls declares, we will arrive at a position that leaves 'aside those aspects of the social world that seem arbitrary from a moral point of view'.[116] The problem is that it is a serious question whether the accidents of natural endowment are indeed arbitrary from a moral point of view. Early contractarian thought considered such endowments to be pre-moral or pre-political rights that no government or society had the right to interfere with or violate. We might even say that morality and the very institutional structure of liberal democratic society are built most fundamentally upon such rights. Rawls, who works very much within the contractarian tradition, accepts many of its assumptions, in particular the idea that society is composed of rational, calculating and consenting individuals who accept as 'primary goods' those things that facilitate the development of comfortable well-being: the enhancement of income, wealth, self-respect, and other things.[117] Rawls, however, rejects the 'naturalistic fallacy' or the idea that we can derive moral principles from ideas about human nature. The question of equality or of fairness thus reduces to the question of how best to distribute these primary goods. Rawls, like most modern political and legal theorists, is a social utilitarian who transforms the question of the equality of legal or political rights into the question of the more or less equal distribution of substantive goods.[118] The question of political equality reduces to the question of social equality. Whether one is entitled to something is not a question of right or of desert. It is a question of utility or of what is more or less socially expedient.[119]

THE PROBLEM OF TUTELARY DEMOCRACY

There is little doubt that to the extent democracies promote equal rights to the acquisition of the fruits of this earth, the inequality of fortunes that results from the inequality of natural endowments may breed resentment and despair. That same equality that creates vast hopes, Tocqueville warned, makes individuals weak; what is new in modern democracy is not the spectacle of obsession, fear and agitation at the prospect of never attaining or losing wealth, but that an entire people now suffers from it.[120] The vulnerability and impotence, combined with the impatience to achieve wealth quickly, so characteristic of commercial republics, renders their citizens prone to give themselves over to the first power that promises to preserve comfort and well-being. The state, which is this sanctuary, not only possesses the authority to protect all collective interests because only it has the authority of consent (represented in the 'sovereignty of the people'), but also because industry, which creates 'new and complicated relationships', exposing people 'to the great and sudden alternatives of abundance and misery', requires regulation and surveillance that only government can provide.[121] The great threat to liberty in modern democracies is a bureaucratic or administrative despotism that originates in fear and that develops into an intricately complex web of relationships that links virtually every aspect of society to the state. Tocqueville described the situation where men think they 'have adequately guaranteed the liberty of individuals, when they have delivered it to the national power', where 'free will' will be enclosed in a smaller and smaller circle because the state, 'after having taken each individual into its powerful hands', will 'extend its reach over the whole of society, covering its surface with a network of complicated, minute and uniform petty rules'.[122] Above individuals will be raised

> an immense and tutelary power, alone charging itself with the assurance of their happiness and looking out for their lot . . . providing for their security, foreseeing and assuring their needs, facilitating their pleasures, leading their principal affairs, directing their industry, regulating their estates, dividing their inheritances [and eventually] wholly removing from them the trouble of thinking and difficulty of living.[123]

Tocqueville presented a caricature of advanced democratic society, one where the prerogative of acting was delivered to the state in the name of the 'indefinite perfectibility of man',[124] in the name, in other words, of the infinite perfectibility of equality. The danger to modern democracies is a behavioural or social technology intent on making society over in the image of an equality that always remains just beyond our reach. Since human nature and natural rights are denied by modern social science, there are no limits to human perfectibility and there are therefore no limits to the behavioural modification of society in the name of equality. The levelling of society by equality, Tocqueville said, 'presents the image of an ideal and always fugitive perfection to the human mind'.[125] We see this image in the day-to-day practice of affairs. It is inherent in that fundamental division of liberal political thought, between those who believe that people are more or less the products of nature and those who believe they are more or less the products of society. If people are the products of society, social problems are 'systemic'. They are not natural or part and parcel of the human condition. Politics, in this latter case, reduces to the politics of perfection. More and more 'systemic barriers' are sought to be eliminated because social problems originate in the 'system'. The system is perfected only when it accords with the ideal of equality, as conceived, from time to time, by our social planners, the sociologists, activists, political scientists, law professors. Of course, the ideal is never attained, the system never perfected. Equality always remains 'fugitive'.

The endless pursuit of greater equality requires an ever distending marriage of society to the state and the concomitant elimination of private life and self-government. The systemic model of politics suggests, in fact, that there is no real private life. There is no real freedom. Individuals are the products of their environment, their thought included. At the same time that advocates of the systemic model tell us that individuals are the products of their environment, post-modernists and deconstructionists, their intellectual acolytes, tell us that thought is the instrument of prejudice and control, the subjugated victim of power. More precisely, thought is the subjugated victim of competing wills to power. The only truly liberated thought is thought that is noncommittal, open to all possibilities, no longer the subject of any instrument of domination. The corollary to the systemic model of politics is the intellectual model of openness, a model which results in silly practical consequences, in nihilism.

CONCLUSION

Regardless of how we conceive affirmative action, human rights legislation and section 15 of the Charter, it is clear, in the case of all three initiatives, that government is the vehicle charged with bringing about greater equality. All three initiatives, with their expanding rhetoric and augmenting legislative and constitutional refinements, draw a certain parallel to that 'network of complicated, minute and uniform petty rules' Tocqueville admonished was the consequence of the desire for equality of conditions becoming a consolidated social state. Social reformers of all stripes appeal to government to smooth over the inconsistencies in private action that have not yet been regulated by the technology of equality. Open-ended invocations, such as Gibson's statement that although there 'are undeniable limits to the degree of equality that can be achieved by [human rights legislation] those limits have not yet been reached, or even approached',[126] are commonplace. We hear them all the time. And, in fairness, they are not limited to social reformers. Even those who believe that government should not interfere in private affairs always seem to find an exception when it concerns their own affairs; they too, as Tocqueville predicted, look to attract government to their side, all the while denying that it should assist others.[127]

The benefits of eliminating discrimination and disadvantage are obvious. The indiscriminateness that policies such as affirmative action, human rights legislation and section 15 jurisprudence facilitate is not. To the extent that social distinctions between groups are embraced as the product of discrimination, regardless of the causes of these discriminations, the meaning of equality is lost. Distinctions that originate from the differences in choices, capacities, interests, desires, intelligence, determination, competence, and inclinations of individuals and groups are not necessarily morally arbitrary. Nor are they necessarily morally culpable. As long as political or individual liberty is conceived as the right to pursue one's self-interest, desires or needs, liberty will always be commensurate with a great inequality. To eliminate such inequality under the pretext of eliminating 'discrimination' or in the name of 'social equality' may not only stretch the meaning of equality beyond its ostensible limits, but encroach upon that liberty that is the benchmark of liberal democracies and the constitutional theory that guides them. As Thomas Sowell has pointed out, there is a difference between equality of *process* and equality of *result*. Equality of process is within the capacity of man. Equality of result is not. It requires more intellectual and moral capacity than man has. Not that it is impossible to reduce or eliminate specific instances of inequality. It is not. Only, the processes involved in doing so may create other inequalities, specifically, inequalities of political power. Attempting to equalize economic and social result may lead to greater, and more dangerous, inequalities of political power.[128]

In law, as elsewhere, claims to special knowledge usually lead to demands for political power or political change in light of that special knowledge. In Canada, affirmative action, human rights policy, and the constitutional protection of equality have established the existence of rights on the basis of imperceptible causes of social circumstance, social differences, and group affinities. The judicial construction of section 15 now makes individual rights conditional upon the type of group to which one belongs. As a recent editorial in the *Globe and Mail* observed, section 15 itself has become an affirmative action program, the main section, 15(1), protecting individual rights, being interpreted in light of section 15(2), which promotes group rights.[129]

Equality rights under affirmative action, human rights, and section 15 are now formulated on the basis of approximation and imprecision. In a recent decision of the Ontario Court of Appeal, the late Justice Tarnopolsky, following human rights jurisprudence and the *Andrews* interpretation of section 15, suggested that in applying public policy to private scholarships, the courts will have to engage in 'an equality analysis' that differentiates between beneficiaries on the basis of group characteristics: 'In such an analysis, attention will have to be paid to the social and historical context of the group concerned . . . as well as the effect of the restrictions on racial, religious or gender equality, to name but a few examples.'[130] The difficulty with Justice Tarnopolsky's formulation is the capacity of the court to engage in such an investigation. If the 'equality analysis' is not to be a farce or mere pretext under which the opinions of special interests are adopted without scrutiny, the court will have to distinguish between amorphous groups, such as 'races', 'creeds', 'colours', and 'religions', distil the vast literature that has attempted to trace the genealogical, sociological, and historical development of such groups, compare the economic, political and perhaps even biological or psychological relationships between such groups, and eventually arrive, more or less holus bolus, at a determination as to which of the groups deserves special or differential treatment. The task will be duly complicated by the obvious fact, enunciated by Justice Robins, that public policy tends to change. 'The public policy of the 1920s is not the public policy of the 1990s.'[131] The question arises: are courts capable of such a task?

Probably not. And the result will be what it has been in numerous human rights and section 15 decisions, namely, courts' adopting policies on the basis of dominant or fashionable opinion rather than on the basis of concrete evidence. The rules of evidence in litigation are intended to search for truth between parties, not truth in general.[132] Social scientific facts of the kind required in equality rights litigation search for truth in general. They are impervious to close judicial scrutiny.

Finally, the issue of equal rights protection in Canada concerns not merely the integrity of the judiciary. It concerns the broader issue of Canadian citizenship. When the process that was intended to remove the protection of equality from partisan, political disputes, itself becomes consumed by partisanship and ideology, meting out economic and legal benefits on the basis of dubious generalizations about groups, the relationship between the individual and the group that has characterized Canadian pluralism becomes inverted. No longer is the individual identified as an individual, but as a member of a group with fixed characteristics and interests. The very group-based distinctions that determined political rights and privileges in non-democratic regimes, and that the modern democratic state was intended to overcome, resurface as the basis of political rights. Has Canadian democracy then been transformed into a status regime?

Ultimately, we must ask, how far do affirmative action, human rights policy, and section 15 jurisprudence have to be taken before the demands of equality will be met? If these initiatives increase social and political antagonism, dividing Canada into an archipelago of self-seeking, self-serving minority identities, perhaps it is time to reconsider their efficacy.

NOTES

I would like to thank James W. Ceaser, William Evans, and Freya Godard for their comments on earlier drafts of this paper.

1 Rainer Knopff, *Human Rights and Social Technology: The New War on Discrimination* (Ottawa: Carleton University Press, 1990), 216.

2 Mary Ann Glendon, *Rights Talk: The Impoverishment of Political Discourse* (New York: Free Press, 1991).

3 F.L. Morton, *Morgentaler v. Borowski: Abortion, the Charter, and the Courts* (Toronto: McClelland and Stewart, 1992), 311.

4 Alan C. Cairns, *Charter versus Federalism: The Dilemmas of Constitutional Reform* (Montreal and Kingston: McGill-Queen's University Press, 1992), 4.

5 Ibid., 7.

6 Harvey Mansfield, *America's Constitutional Soul* (Baltimore: Johns Hopkins University Press, 1991), 86.

7 *Andrews v. Law Society of British Columbia*, [1989] 1 S.C.R. 143, at 154. See also *R. v. Turpin*, [1989] 1 S.C.R. 1296, at 1333, Wilson J., writing for a unanimous court, repeating this statement verbatim.

8 *R. v. Swain*, [1991] 1 S.C.R. 933, at 992.

9 See David J. Bercuson and Barry Cooper, *Derailed: The Betrayal of the National Dream* (Toronto: Key-Porter, 1994), 33: 'To favour liberal individualism is not to deny the importance of groups and collectivities in liberal democracies. After all, freedom of association is an important component of individual freedom. The question is not whether one is for or against groups and collectivities but whether and to what extent they should be given legal and constitutional status and recognition—especially since we know from long experience that special legal status for some groups will always generate ill-will among others; it is not a recipe for comity among one's fellow citizens.'

10 See, for instance, *R. v. Turpin*, [1989] 1 S.C.R. 1296 (Wilson J. writing for the Court): 'A finding that there is discrimination [under section 15(1)] will, I think, in most but perhaps not all cases necessarily entail a search for disadvantage that exists *apart from and independent* of the particular legal distinction being challenged' (at 1332, emphasis added).
    There is significant disagreement in academic commentary about whether independent disadvantage should be a required element of proof of discrimination in a section 15 action. See Peter Hogg, *Constitutional Law of Canada*, 3rd edn (Toronto: Carswell, 1992), 1173–6.

11 Glendon, *Rights Talk*, 171-2: 'Our rights-laden public discourse easily accommodates the economic, the immediate, and the personal dimensions of a problem, while it regularly neglects the moral, the long-term, and the social implications. . . . [T]he new rhetoric of rights is less about human dignity and freedom than about insistent, unending desires. Its legitimation of individual and group egoism is in flat opposition to the great purposes set forth in the Preamble to the Constitution: "to form a more perfect Union, establish Justice, promote the general Welfare, and secure the Blessings of Liberty to ourselves and our Posterity".'

12 See Knopff, *Human Rights and Social Technology*, 205, and Hannah Arendt, *The Human Condition* (Chicago: University of Chicago Press, 1958), 45: 'To gauge the extent of society's victory in the modern age, its early substitution of behavior for action and its eventual substitution of bureaucracy, the rule of nobody, for personal rulership, it may be well to recall that its initial science of economics,

which substitutes patterns of behavior only in this rather limited field of human activity, was finally followed by the all-comprehensive pretension of the social sciences which, as "behavioral sciences", aim to reduce man as a whole, in all his activities, to the level of a conditioned and behaving animal.'

13 Neil Postman, *Technopoly: The Surrender of Culture to Technology* (New York: Vintage, 1993), 9. Postman here is describing Innis's theory.

14 See Alan C. Cairns, 'Ritual, Taboo, and Bias in Constitutional Controversies, or Constitutional Talk Canadian Style', in Alan C. Cairns, *Disruptions: Constitutional Struggles from the Charter to Meech Lake* ed. Douglas E. Williams (Toronto: McClelland and Stewart, 1991), 199. See also F.L. Morton's and Rainer Knopff's contribution to this volume, as well as Robert Martin's final chapter in this volume.

15 Mansfield, *America's Constitutional Soul*, 94, emphasis in original.

16 Nathan Glazer, *Affirmative Discrimination: Ethnic Inequality and Public Policy* (New York: Basic, 1975), 197.

17 Martin Heidegger, *The Question Concerning Technology and Other Essays*, trans. William Lovitt (New York: Harper and Row, 1977), 12.

18 Ibid., 26–8.

19 Ibid., esp. 3. See also Michel Foucault, *The Archaeology of Knowledge*, trans. A.A. Sheridan Smith (New York: Pantheon, 1972), 183: '[K]nowledge is defined by the possibilities of use and appropriation offered by discourse. . . . [T]here is no knowledge without a particular discursive practice; and any discursive practice may be defined by the knowledge that it forms.'

20 Jacques Ellul, *The Technological Society*, trans. Robert K. Merton (New York: Vintage, 1964), 79.

21 Jacques Ellul, *The Technological System*, trans. Joachim Neugroschel (New York: Continuum, 1980), 293–4.

22 See Knopff, *Human Rights and Social Technology*, 183-209.

23 Thomas Flanagan, 'The Manufacture of Minorities', in *Minorities and the Canadian State*, eds Neil Nevitte and Allan Kornberg (Oakville: Mosaic, 1985), 107.

24 The distinction between stigmata and life-cycle and life-style criteria has been recognized, to some extent, in the legal doctrines of bona fide occupational qualification (BFOQ) and requirement (BFOR), defences to human rights violations that have applied predominantly to life-style and life-cycle criteria. See, for instance, the BFOQ and BFOR defences provided under the Saskatchewan Human Rights Code, S.S. 1979, c. S–24.1, s. 16(7) (applying to sex, disability, and age), the Ontario Human Rights Code, R.S.O. 1990, H.19, s. 24(1)(b) (applying to age, sex, record of offences, and marital status) and the Yukon Human Rights Act, S.Y. 1987, c. 3, s. 9 (applying to criminal record, criminal charges, sex, and 'other factors establishing reasonable cause for the discrimination').

25 Flanagan admitted that his three-part division of discriminatory prohibitions was inexact. Marital status and family status, life-cycle criteria, for instance, overlap with life-style criteria in so far as they are acquired by personal choice. Citizenship, which Flanagan listed as stigmata, is generally inherited but may be voluntarily assumed, thus corresponding to life-style and some life-cycle criteria. Similarly, homosexuality, criminal behaviour, and even poverty have been

explained as biologically based and not voluntarily acquired, thus suggesting that sexual orientation, criminal record, and other social and economic criteria should be categorized as stigmata.

Dale Gibson has argued that Flanagan's method fails to explain adequately why precisely the element of choice is relevant to distinguishing legitimate from illegitimate forms of discrimination. '[W]hy should it be more acceptable to discriminate against someone who has chosen to be associated with a particular group than one who had no choice in the matter? Flanagan offers no such explanation.' ('Stereotypes, Statistics and Slippery Slopes: A Reply to Professors Flanagan and Knopff and Other Critics of Human Rights Legislation', in *Minorities and the Canadian State*, 130.)

26 [1985] 2 S.C.R. 536. This case is usually referred to by the complainant's last name, O'Malley.

27 [1985] 2 S.C.R. 561.

28 [1985] 2 S.C.R. at 547.

29 Ibid.

30 Ibid., 551.

31 Walter Surma Tarnopolsky and William Pentney, *Discrimination and the Law* (Toronto: De Boo, 1989), Nov. 1994, 4–56.7.

32 Ibid., 4–56.2.

33 See Knopff, *Human Rights and Social Technology*, 118: 'Although the battle against categorization has been waged in the name of individual treatment, its paradoxical result is radically to depersonalize the individual by stripping away all his recognizable characteristics. . . . Far from promoting individual treatment, this depersonalization actually undermines it.

'Under Canadian legislation and its amplifying regulations and guidelines, it has become unlawful for an employer to request a photograph from an applicant; to inquire into age or sex; to ask if the applicant is married, has children or plans to have children; to require a medical examination; to inquire into any facts that might have a bearing on religion or ethnic origin. . . .

'. . . . The protection of human rights has come to mean the deletion of information, reducing applicants to abstract dossiers.'

34 Christopher P. Manfredi, *Judicial Power and the Charter: Canada and the Paradox of Liberal Constitutionalism* (Toronto: McClelland and Stewart, 1993), 136–7.

35 [1989] 1 S.C.R. 143.

36 Ibid., 164.

37 Section 15(1) provides that 'Every individual is equal *before* and *under* the law and has the right to the equal *protection* and equal *benefit* of the law without discrimination. . .' (emphasis added).

38 [1989] 1 S.C.R. at 181.

39 Ibid., 182.

40 McIntyre borrowed this phrase from a famous footnote in *United States v. Caroline Products*, 304 U.S. 144, at 152–3, n. 4 (1938).

41 Joel Bakan, 'Constitutional Interpretation and Social Change: You Can't Always Get What You Want (Nor What You Need)', in 70 *Can. Bar Rev.*, 307, at 311, n. 7, emphasis in original. Bakan qualified this observation, suggesting that the Court's ostensible deference to looking at the actual equality of actors may belie a more fundamental commitment to formal equality, manifest in its holding that the Charter 'protects individuals only *from* state action' rather than requiring 'the state to protect individuals *through* its action'.

    '[S]ection 15 [on Justice McIntyre's reading in *Andrews*] is reactive to "the application of the law". It cannot be relied upon to enjoin the state to pass laws or create programs that are aimed at ensuring "equality between individuals or groups within society".' At 316, emphasis in original.

42 Manfredi, *Judicial Power and the Charter*, 152–3.

43 Gibson, 'Stereotypes, Statistics and Slippery Slopes', 126.

44 See Knopff, *Human Rights and Social Technology*, 99 and 106.

45 See Herman Belz, *Equality Transformed: A Quarter-Century of Affirmative Action* (New Brunswick, NJ: Transaction, 1992), 51.

46 See Rainer Knopff, 'What do Equality Rights Protect Canadians Against?' *Canadian Journal of Political Science* 20, no. 2 (1987): 265.

47 Rainer Knopff, 'The Statistical Protection of Minorities: Affirmative Action Policy in Canada', in *Minorities and the Canadian State*, 103.

48 On the transformation of the meaning of discrimination from a concept signifying invidious intent to one signifying adverse impact, and the implications of this for a legal order based upon individual rights and responsibilities, see Belz, *Equality Transformed*.

49 Knopff, 'The Statistical Protection of Minorities'.

50 Gibson, 'Stereotypes, Statistics and Slippery Slopes', 133, emphasis in original.

51 Ibid., 132.

52 Ibid., 134.

53 Mansfield, *America's Constitutional Soul*, 85.

54 Raymond Aron, *Les Désillusions du progrès: Essai sur la dialectique de la modernité* (Paris: Calmann-Levy, 1969), 22. The translation is my own.

55 Ibid.

56 See Hannah Arendt, *On Revolution* (Markham: Penguin, 1965), 109. See also Mansfield, *America's Constitutional Soul*, 139.

57 Allan Bloom, *The Closing of the American Mind* (New York: Simon and Schuster, 1987), 30.

58 Leo Strauss, *Natural Right and History* (Chicago: University of Chicago Press, 1953), 3–8.

59 *What is Political Philosophy?* (Chicago: University of Chicago Press, 1959), 27.

60 Strauss, *Natural Right and History*, 6.

61 Stanley Rosen, *Nihilism: A Philosophical Essay* (New Haven, Conn.: Yale University Press, 1969), xiii.

62 See Bercuson and Cooper, *Derailed*, 36: 'Historically, the language of rights was developed in Europe as part of the liberal strategic plan to dethrone the claim that certain types or classes of people—namely, aristocrats and priests—had a natural or revealed right to rule. That is, the language of rights was developed to defend individuals against the tyrannical pretensions of groups, and against the civil strife that was inevitably produced by contested group-based claims to rule.'
    Although there are no longer group-based claims to rule, the group-based claims to special legal and constitutional status in equality rights litigation may create a form of civil strife not entirely unrelated to the sort of civil strife referred to here by Bercuson and Cooper.

63 Tocqueville, *De la Démocratie en Amérique* (repr., Paris: Garnier-Flammarion, 1981), II, 174. Hereafter referred to as *Democracy in America*. All translations are my own.

64 Ibid., I, 57.

65 See Ward E.Y. Elliott, *The Rise of Guardian Democracy* (Cambridge, Mass.: Harvard University Press, 1974).

66 Tocqueville, *Democracy in America*, I, 333.

67 Ibid., I, 334.

68 Ibid., I, 279.

69 Ibid., I, 66.

70 Ibid., I, 54.

71 Ibid., I, 64.

72 Ibid., I, 334.

73 Ibid., I, 115.

74 Ibid., II, 119.

75 Ibid., II, 123.

76 Ibid., I, 115–16.

77 Ibid., II, 395.

78 Ibid., I, 335.

79 Ibid., II, 361.

80 Ibid., II, 50.

81 Ibid.

82 See ibid., II, 394–7.

83 Ibid., II, 50.

84 See F.L. Morton and Rainer Knopff, *Charter Politics* (Scarborough, Ont.: Nelson, 1992), 237–8.

85 Tocqueville, *Democracy in America*, II, 394–5.

86 See Friedrich A. Hayek, *The Constitution of Liberty* (Chicago: University of Chicago Press, 1960), 232: 'Those who pursue distributive justice will in practice find themselves obstructed at every move by the rule of law. They must, from the very nature of their aim, favor discriminatory and discretionary action. But, as they are usually not aware that their aim and the rule of law are in principle incompatible, they begin by circumventing or disregarding in individual cases a principle which they often would wish to see preserved in general. . . . [T]he ultimate result of their efforts will necessarily be, not a modification of the existing order, but its complete abandonment and its replacement by an altogether different system—the command economy.'

87 Tocqueville, *Democracy in America*, II, 394–5.

88 Ibid., II, 394.

89 Ibid., II, 397.

90 See ibid., esp. I, 54, and I, 334–5.

91 Marc F. Plattner, 'Capitalism', in *Confronting the Constitution*, ed. Allan Bloom (Washington, DC: AEI Press, 1990), 314, at 331.

92 See Glendon, *Rights Talk*, 16.

93 Tocqueville, *Democracy in America*, II, 9.

94 Ibid., II, 87.

95 Ibid., II, 84.

96 Ibid., II, 16

97 Ibid., II, 17.

98 Ibid., II, 85.

99 Ibid., II, 18–19.

100 Ibid., II, 173.

101 Ibid., II, 162.

102 Ibid., II, 17.

103 See Thomas L. Pangle, *The Ennobling of Democracy* (Baltimore: Johns Hopkins University Press, 1992), 4: 'Few educated citizens of our time dare to endorse "natural rights" or even the "rights of man". Property rights, which stood at the core of the Enlightenment conception of the rights of man, are looked upon with great skepticism by today's constitutionalists. Above all, reason itself, and the universalism implied in rationalism, is more and more viewed with distrust. At the popular level, this distrust is animated by the sharp suspicion that rationalism may be the source of "sexist", "Eurocentric", inhumanly utilitarian, and technologically driven exploitation.'

See also, Allan Bloom, *Giants and Dwarfs* (New York: Simon and Schuster, 1990), 315–16: 'Hardly anyone would be willing to defend as truth the natural right teachings of the founders of liberal democracy or of their philosophical masters, as many, for example, defend Marx. The state of nature and the natural rights deriving from it have taken their place beside the divine right of kings in the graveyard of history.'

104 (1991) 29 *Osgoode Hall L.J.*, 411, at 416.

105 Peter W. Hogg, 'The Charter of Rights and American Theories of Interpretation', (1987) 25 *Osgoode Hall L.J.*, 87, at 89.

106 'On Being a Positivist: A Reply to Professor Vaughan', 417.

107 See ibid., 416.

108 See Martin Diamond, 'Democracy and *The Federalist:* A Reconsideration of the Framer's Intent', in *American Political Science Review* 53 (1959): 52. See also Harry V. Jaffa, *Crisis of the House Divided: An Interpretation of the Issues in the Lincoln-Douglas Debates* (Chicago: University of Chicago Press, 1982) and *How to Think about the American Revolution: A Bicentennial Celebration* (Durham, NC.: Carolina Academic Press, 1978).

109 Frederick Vaughan, 'On Being a Positivist: Does it Really Matter?' (1991) *Osgoode Hall L.J.*, 399, at 403.

110 'On Being a Positivist: A Reply to Professor Vaughan,' 415–17.

111 Tocqueville, *Democracy in America*, II, 167.

112 Ibid., II, 120.

113 Arendt, *On Revolution*, 30.

114 Alexander Hamilton, John Jay, and James Madison, *The Federalist Papers*, intro. Clinton Rossiter (New York: New American Library, 1961), no. 10, 78.

115 My argument here regarding distributive justice and the interpretation of Rawls relies in large measure on Marc Plattner's essay 'Capitalism', in *Confronting the Constitution*, esp. 330-3; George Grant's *English-Speaking Justice* (Toronto: Anansi, 1985), 13–47; and Allan Bloom's *Giants and Dwarfs*, 315–45.

116 John Rawls, *A Theory of Justice* (Cambridge: Harvard University Press, 1971), 15.

117 Ibid., 62, 92–5 and 396. '[T]he index of well-being and the expectations of representative men are specified in terms of primary goods. Rational individuals, whatever else they want, desire certain things as prerequisites for carrying out their plans of life. Other things equal, they prefer a wider than a narrower liberty and opportunity, and a greater rather than smaller share of wealth and income' (p. 396).

118 Grant, *English-Speaking Justice*, 24–5.

119 In the context of redistributive justice, however, why limit things to the redistribution of primary goods? Does a system of perfect substantive equality not require the redistribution of natural goods—talents and endowments, for instance—as well as primary goods? If the most important things in life are those that 'money can't buy', do we not have to redistribute these things as well? The logic of substantive equality would seem to compel such an outcome. (See Bloom, *Giants and Dwarfs*, 329.)

120 *Democracy in America* II, 172–3.

121 Ibid., II, 375.

122 Ibid, II, 386.

123 Ibid., II, 385.

124 Ibid., II, 43.

125 Ibid., II, 44.

126 Gibson, 'Stereotypes, Statistics and Slippery Slopes', 137.

127 Tocqueville, *Democracy in America*, II, 360, n. 1.

128 Thomas Sowell, A *Conflict of Visions* (New York: William and Morrow, 1987), 121–2, 128.

129 '[T]he courts have decided that the promotion of equity among groups, rather than the protection of the rights of individuals, is the main purpose of Section 15. This, despite the clear reference in Section 15 to "every individual is equal".' *Globe and Mail*, 14 July 1993, A20.

130 *Canada Trust Company v. Ontario Human Rights Commission* (1990), 74 O.R. (2d) 481, at 514.

131 Ibid., 497.

132 Donald L. Horowitz, *The Courts and Social Policy* (Washington, DC: Brookings Institution, 1977), 50.

8

What's the Evidence?
The Use the Supreme Court of Canada
Makes of Evidence in Charter Cases

John T. Pepall

The coming into force of the Charter of Rights and Freedoms in 1982 launched a mass of speculation as to what it might mean. It was suggested immediately that the courts would have to rely on evidence in deciding whether legislation should be struck down under the Charter. While not unprecedented in Canada,[1] the use of evidence in constitutional cases is an American practice, and speculation drew on American precedents. The Brandeis brief, long revered in law schools, was always referred to. Louis Brandeis, several years before his appointment to the United States Supreme Court, had filed government studies and other material to support the constitutionality of employment standards legislation specifically protecting women.[2] The practice became common in American constitutional practice and, with its apparent promise of litigating political issues, has been attractive to Canadian law professors and their more impressionable students.

Also rehearsed was a distinction between, on the one hand, adjudicative facts, the ordinary facts in litigation—who did what to whom and with what effect—proved by conventional evidence and tested by cross-examination, and, on the other hand, legislative facts, general social facts on which it might be thought legislatures should rely in making laws and which would be established in Charter cases by different kinds of evidence, subject, if only for practical reasons, to less rigorous testing.[3] One of the grounds for the distinction between adjudicative and legislative facts was the suggestion that with legislative facts all that was necessary was to establish a reasonable basis for legislative action. For that purpose more lax standards of admissibility and less rigorous testing of the evidence might be indicated. If the purpose of leading evidence was simply to show what the legislature was trying to do, and thus to explain away any apparent infringement of rights, the scrutiny of the evidence and the role assumed by the Court would be limited.

The early years of speculation have been superseded by more than 10 years' experience with Charter litigation. Evidence has been used to explain what the Charter's rights and freedoms must mean, whether they have been infringed, and what remedies there may be.[4] But the consideration of whether impugned legislation can be, in the words of section 1 of the Charter, 'such reasonable limits prescribed by law as can be demonstrably justified in a free and democratic society', has been the commonest and most important use of evidence.

An examination of the more significant cases in the Supreme Court of Canada in which evidence was, or might have been, introduced to help the Court pass judgment on the work of the legislatures does not reveal settled principles or practice. But three uses of evidence for the Court are apparent. The Court has effectively used a call for and the availability of evidence to enhance and protect its authority and power. First, by calling on evidence the Court has helped to protect itself from blatantly imposing its political opinions on the legislatures. Second, by insisting that it decides, on evidence, whether legislation can be justified, rather than simply satisfying itself that there was a reasonable basis for the legislation and deferring to the institutionally competent and democratically accountable legislatures, the Court reserves for itself unrestricted power. Finally, by purporting to base its decisions on evidence in particular cases, it has reserved to itself the freedom to revisit every political issue.

The first significant reference in a Supreme Court of Canada judgment to evidence in Charter cases came in 1984 in *Skapinker*.[5] Skapinker, a South African citizen at the time he was to be called to the Ontario bar, objected to the requirement in paragraph 28(c) of the Law Society Act that persons called to the bar be Canadian citizens or British subjects. Estey J., having decided that Skapinker's rights had not been violated, nonetheless commented on the case that the Law Society would have had to make to justify the citizenship requirement if the Court had decided that it did violate Skapinker's rights. He described the material that the Law Society would have relied on as minimal. It consisted of reports of government studies of professional organizations and a survey of the requirements in other jurisdictions. He insisted that more would be expected in the future:

> As experience accumulates, the law profession and the courts will develop standards and practices which will enable the parties to demonstrate their position under s. 1 and the courts to decide issues arising under that provision. May it only be said here, in the cause of being helpful to those who come forward in similar proceedings, that the record on the s. 1 issue was

indeed minimal, and without more, would have made it difficult for a court to determine the issue as to whether a reasonable limit on a prescribed right had been demonstrably justified.[6]

In the light of what has been looked at in later cases it must be understood that it was the bulk rather than the character of the evidence that seemed deficient to Estey. Moreover, the deficiency would not have prevented the Court from deciding whether a reasonable limit had been justified, as Estey seems to say, but simply from deciding in favour of the limit, something he appeared inclined to do but wanted evidentiary cover for.

Almost a year later Wilson J. in *Singh*[7] expressed disappointment at 'the limited scope of the factual material brought forward by the respondent in support of the proposition that the Immigration Act's provisions constitute a "reasonable limit" on the appellant's rights'. She quoted Estey from *Skapinker*.[8] The appellant refugee claimants argued successfully that the Act, in denying them an appeal to the Immigration Appeal Board unless the board was of the opinion that the denial by the Minister of Immigration could likely be overturned, denied them security of the person without regard for the principles of fundamental justice, contrary to section 7 of the Charter. It was contended for the Minister of Immigration that the UN High Commissioner for Refugees had approved Canada's procedures, that Commonwealth and Western European countries offered no right of appeal, and that the Immigration Appeal Board, already under strain, would be unreasonably burdened by a requirement for an oral hearing in every case. What exact factual material would have been satisfactory is unclear, as Wilson doubted that 'utilitarian' considerations could be allowed to prevail over the Charter rights that she held had been infringed.[9] She placed more reliance on a task force report and a speech by an Appeal Board chairman, which contained merely political comment more to her taste. The utilitarian results of the Court's decision were a huge backlog of refugee claims, tens of thousands of claimants in welfare limbo, a raft of new patronage appointments, public lack of confidence in the refugee program and a legal aid crisis.

The exact evidentiary character of the material needed to justify a limit under section 1 of the Charter remained vague. But the celebrated *R. v. Oakes*,[10] in which Chief Justice Dickson attempted to codify the requirements for a section 1 justification, seemed to call for something like evidence in the received sense. Before outlining the requirements of 'pressing and substantial concerns', 'rational connection', 'minimal impairment', and 'proportionality' on which a whole scholastic industry has since been built, the Chief Justice held that the onus of proving justification is on the party seeking to uphold the limitation and that the civil standard of proof by a 'preponderance of probability' applies.

By speaking of onus and a standard of proof, which are concepts of the law of evidence, the Chief Justice called on evidence as the principal basis for the justification of limits to Charter rights. It was not surprising that he should do so. But it was not necessary. Justification could have been left as a matter of argument, with legislative history and some evidence of political or economic context as an adjunct of legal argument. Reading the Court's reasons, this is often all that seems involved. But the Chief Justice said 'cogent and persuasive' evidence would generally be necessary and, whether or not it has been cogent and persuasive, his wish to have evidence has generally been granted.

Dickson's consideration of evidence in *Oakes* does not much help to show how evidence should be used. Oakes challenged section 8 of the Narcotic Control Act, which put the onus on the accused of showing that possession, once proved by the Crown, was not for the purpose of trafficking. The Court held that this reverse onus was contrary to the presumption of innocence required by paragraph 11(d) of the Charter. The Crown argued that any infringement of the right to be presumed innocent was justifiable under section 1.

Dickson was satisfied that Parliament's desire to fight drug trafficking was substantial and pressing on the basis of government reports from the fifties and seventies, international conventions, and legislation in other countries. Reasonable people might judge that a recent leading article from *The Economist* was as good evidence, and more cogent and persuasive, to the contrary.

Having satisfied himself of Parliament's pressing and substantial concern on doubtful evidence, the Chief Justice then struck down the reverse onus provision without further examination of evidence by holding that there was no rational connection between possession of a narcotic and possession for the purpose of trafficking. The implicit characterization of the legislation as irrational seems unfair to its framers. The provision did not simply deem possession to be possession for the purpose of trafficking, which might arguably be irrational. It placed an onus on anyone proved to have been in possession of a narcotic to prove, on the balance of probabilities, that it was not for the purpose of trafficking. The question was not therefore whether 'the possession of a small or negligible quantity of narcotics does not support the inference of trafficking',[11] but whether the reverse onus would help the fight against drug trafficking. On this specific point, which the Court does not even seem to have grasped, no evidence was considered and its absence or insufficiency went unremarked.

After the elaborate analysis and solemn talk of cogent and persuasive evidence, the determinative finding came too easily. The case could have been decided on brief reasons without the encouragements to Charter scholasticism and an inflation of constitutional evidence. The consideration of evidence in *Oakes* demonstrated that the use of evidence would be strongly determined by the circumstances of the specific case and the positions taken by the parties. The Court purported to endorse Parliament's concern about drug trafficking on the basis of doubtful evidence when it was never seriously in issue. It then rejected the instrument by which Parliament attempted to address its concern by reasoning without evidence, no attempt being made to consider how the instrument might work.

References to legislation in other countries and international conventions have been common since the earliest attempts to justify legislation under section 1. It has been argued that if legislation like that impugned under the Charter is tolerated in other nice countries, it must be a reasonable limit demonstrably justified in a free and democratic society. The references in *Oakes* were intended only to show that the object of the impugned legislation was 'substantial and pressing' and not to justify the specific impugned legislation. The logic of attempts to justify impugned Canadian legislation by showing similar legislation in other putatively free and democratic countries is dubious. But they present little problem of getting evidence as the foreign legislation can generally simply be filed without controversy. The analysis in *Oakes* shows that, as always seemed likely, justification by foreign legislation alone will not work. But as *Oakes* itself demonstrates, foreign legislation can still, strangely enough, be accepted as evidence to satisfy one or another of the *Oakes* criteria for justification.[12]

As *Oakes* illustrates, the use made of evidence by the Court in Charter cases will be determined by the judges' preconceptions. In ordinary trials the judge has no preconceptions about the facts and must rely entirely on the evidence to decide where the cars were at the time of the accident, who shot whom, where the money went, or why the machine would not work. In Charter cases judges appear to invoke evidence or pass it by depending on how it suits their arguments. It is often difficult to determine from the Court's logorrhoeic reasons exactly what evidence they considered and what they made of it. Ordinary cases often turn entirely on the facts, and judges' reasons review the evidence in detail and make findings expressly based on it, particularly on issues pertaining to credibility. The credibility of the reports and studies relied on in Charter cases is never made an issue.

Oakes implied a readiness to weigh up the merits of legislation in light of political findings based on evidence. A few months before, in *Operation Dismantle*,[13] Dickson J. (who became Chief Justice between the argument of the case in February 1984 and judgment in May 1985) firmly refused to be drawn into political judgments, dismissing them as matters of speculation. The appellants alleged in their statement of claim that cruise missile testing would violate the section 7 right to security of the person and life because, *inter alia*:

> verification of the extent of this nuclear weapons system [would be] impossible; with the impossibility of verification, the future of nuclear weapons control . . . [would be] completely undetermined as any such agreements become practically unenforceable; the testing . . . would result in making Canada more likely to be the target of nuclear attack; a 'Launch on Warning' system would be necessary in order to respond to the cruise missile . . . increasing the likelihood of either a preemptive strike or an accidental firing; the cruise missile [would] have the effect of a needless and dangerous escalation of the arms race, thus endangering the lives and security of all people.[14]

The usual approach in deciding whether to strike out a statement of claim, the issue in *Operation Dismantle*, is to assume that the allegations in the statement of claim are true and decide whether they could support any claim at law. Dickson decided the case on the novel basis that the allegations made by the appellants simply could not be proved:

> Since the foreign policy decisions of independent and sovereign nations are not capable of prediction, on the basis of evidence, to any degree of probability, the nature of such reactions can only be a matter of speculation; the causal link between the decision of Canada to permit the testing of the cruise and the results that the appellants allege could not be proven.[15]

In later cases the Court has been ready to hear and make findings on evidence no less intractable than what might have been led by Operation Dismantle and on issues no less speculative than those raised by it. While the dismissal of its claim came as relief to sensible people, the reasoning was unsatisfactory. Had the Court chosen to impose some limits on the imperial powers the Charter grants it, conceding that it cannot properly deal with certain kinds of issues, it would have been a healthy development.[16] But in deciding the case on a kind of finding of fact, for which no evidence was considered necessary, or even possible, the Court showed that it was not prepared to set any limits on its powers beyond its energy and interests.

By 1986 what evidence could be led to justify a limit under section 1 of the Charter remained a matter of speculation and lobbying. While seized with *Operation Dismantle*, Chief Justice Dickson, addressing a Bar Association meeting in Edmonton in February 1985, had invited counsel to: 'become more imaginative in their presentation of factual material in constitutional litigation. . . . While I cannot pre-judge the evidence the Court will deem relevant and admissible in a particular case, I urge all counsel in constitutional litigation to offer the Court, *as evidence*, any material they deem useful to the questions at hand [emphasis added].'[17] With this encouragement it might have been expected that some Charter litigation would have degenerated into a battle of the social scientists, like the battles of psychiatrists in criminal cases or social workers in custody cases. But generally a mass of dull paper has been dumped on the Court without controversy, being matter for argument between counsel and picked over by the judges.

In *Thomsen*,[18] *Hufsky*,[19] and *Ladouceur*[20] the respective accused drivers argued successfully that their right not to be arbitrarily detained under section 9 of the Charter had been infringed. But the Court accepted in justification several volumes filed by the Crown as evidence of the seriousness of impaired driving and unlicensed and uninsured driving and the need for breathalyzer tests and random checks to deal with them. Though these considerations may justify the legislation being attacked and go some way beyond judicial notice, the show of bringing an open mind to be persuaded by evidence is not credible. The Court was making political judgments. On such issues lack of existing opinion is improbable. Judging by the questions asked by Sopinka J. in *Ladouceur*, the evidence, for the assembly of which the case had been adjourned for a year in the Ontario Court of Appeal, did not itself compel the Court's conclusion:

> Although the statistics are voluminous, there is no evidence as to whether during the relevant period police officers were actually exercising the 'roving random stop' power. For example, was the percentage of accidents involving unlicensed drivers realized notwithstanding the fact that police officers were employing this method of enforcement? If it was, presumably it is only since s. 189a(1) was enacted in 1981. What were the percentages before this method was used? How many motorists who were perfectly law-abiding were stopped for every one that was committing some violation? On the other hand, if the police have not been using this method and this case is an isolated incident, what is the evidence that police officers consider that this power is essential to effective enforcement?[21]

Some other questions might be asked. Did the legislature do wrong in giving the police the power being challenged without exhaustive evidence to satisfy Sopinka? Sopinka, in a minority of four, held that the 'roving random stops' in question in Ladouceur could not be justified. Was Sopinka asking the questions because of a principled requirement for evidence or because he did not like the police having the power and just wanted to strike down this particular bit of legislation? In later cases Sopinka was prepared to be much less demanding of the evidence.

In the cases dealing with Quebec's language legislation at the end of 1988,[22] the Court accepted material simply attached to the Quebec attorney general's factum in the Court of Appeal. It ranged 'in nature from the general theory of language policy and planning to statistical analysis of the position of the French language in Quebec and Canada'.[23] Excusing the irregular way in which it had been submitted, the Court, in *Ford*, commented that:

> . . . the parties did not appear to be taken by surprise . . ., but showed themselves fully prepared to argue the merits of the material. . . . The material is of the kind that has been invited and considered by the Court in other cases involving the application of s. 1 of the Charter, without having been subjected to the evidentiary testing of the adversary process. It is material that is treated similarly to treatises and articles in other judicial contexts.[24]

The printer Singer, in *Devine*, attacked some of the material as biased or misleading and submitted other statistical analysis. The Court said 'due regard' should be given to this. But what is remarkable in the cases is the readiness of the Court to accept the whole of Quebec's linguistic national policy 'without [its] having been subjected to the evidentiary testing of the adversary process'. Because the Court struck down the outright ban on English signs and Quebec reacted strongly, invoking the notwithstanding clause, the public believed that the Court had condemned Quebec linguistic nationalism. In fact it had endorsed it, only balking at the outright ban on languages other than French on signs, holding that it failed to meet the proportionality test in *Oakes*.

The French-language decisions illustrate the artificiality and evasiveness of the Charter evidence practice. In accepting Quebec's language policy the Court had not only to accept the statistics it submitted 'without [their] having been subjected to the evidentiary testing of the adversary process'. It had also to accept Quebec's 'general theory of language policy and planning' and the value placed on Quebec's language and culture as against other affected values. By discussing 'materials' or 'evidence' the Court obscured the fact that it had to and did make political judgments beyond anything determined by the general language of the Charter itself.

In the *Irwin Toy*[25] case, a toy manufacturer argued that Quebec's ban on advertising directed to children was a denial of freedom of expression. Having already forced itself to accept that argument by its inclusion of 'commercial expression' within freedom of expression in *Ford* and *Devine*, the Court was ready to consider social science evidence justifying the ban. Irwin Toy argued that studies done after the legislation was enacted could not be relied on to justify it. It seemed to contend that legislation should be reviewed like an administrative decision: only what was before the legislature when it enacted the legislation—an extended legislative history—could be considered. The Court could only go so far as to look for some justifiable intention at the time of the enactment. While it wondered 'why the Attorney-General did not tender in evidence certain reports and studies that were used by the government both in enacting the legislation and subsequently in reviewing its operation', the Court was content 'to assess the constitutionality of the legislation on the basis of the material that was filed'.[26] The material included 'studies post-dating the enactment of the [legislation] and upon which the government did not rely in adopting [it].'

> In showing that the legislation pursues a pressing and substantial objective, it is not open to the government to assert post facto a purpose which did not animate the legislation in the first place (see *R. v. Big M Drug Mart* (1985), 16 D.L.R. (4th) 321, [1985] 1 S.C.R. 295).[27] However, in proving that the original objective remains pressing and substantial, the government surely can and should draw upon the best evidence currently available. The same is true as regards proof that the measure is proportional to its objective: see *R. v. Edwards Books and Arts Ltd* (1986), 35 D.L.R. (4th) 1 [at p. 41], [1986] 2 S.C.R. 713 [at p. 769]. It is equally possible that a purpose which was not demonstrably pressing and substantial at the time of the legislative enactment becomes demonstrably pressing and substantial with the passing of time and the changing of circumstances.[28]

The result seems to be that the legislation must have had an objective when it was passed that can be justified when the matter comes before the Court, but that it does not matter whether that objective could be justified when the legislation was passed. Legislation may come to be justified some time after it is passed as its objective becomes pressing and substantial or the proportion between the objective and the measure shifts. It should also follow that legislation once justifiable may in time cease to be.[29]

The implication of these principles is that the Court may be asked to revisit any issue on the grounds that circumstances have changed since it last upheld or struck down any particular legislation. Indeed, it should not be necessary to argue that circumstances have changed. As the Court claims to decide the issues on evidence, it should be enough to say that there is evidence that the Court has not previously considered. While Irwin Toy has had its chance to rebut the Crown's evidence, any other toy maker, or children's advocate, who wants to challenge the Quebec legislation should be free to do so.

On this analysis, the claim to decide section 1 issues on evidence must largely preclude any final settlement of constitutional jurisprudence as the Court pushes its way through the first wave of Charter cases. Cases decided on evidence are generally binding only between the immediate parties.

By 1989 the Court's appetite for evidence in Charter cases seemed to have become an addiction. In *MacKay v. Manitoba*,[30] MacKay challenged provisions of the Manitoba Election Finances Act for the subsidization of candidates' elections expenses. He contended that the use of tax monies, to which he was obliged to contribute, to support candidates with whose opinions he disagreed and the 10 per cent of votes requirement for the subsidy as a barrier to small or new parties, infringed his freedom of expression. The case was apparently pursued with more enthusiasm than thought, and no facts were put before the Court beyond the legislation itself. The government of Manitoba was content that it should proceed on that basis, and the judge at first instance and the Manitoba Court of Appeal held that there was no infringement of freedom of speech.

Before the Supreme Court of Canada the attorneys-general of Canada and Ontario intervened and took the position that there was no factual basis for dealing with the appeal. Cory J. agreed and delivered a homily on the need for evidence in Charter cases:

> In light of the importance and impact that these decisions may have in the future, the courts have every right to expect and indeed to insist upon the careful preparation and presentation of a factual basis in most Charter cases. The relevant facts put forward may cover a wide spectrum dealing with scientific, social, economic and political aspects. Often expert opinion as to the future impact of the impugned legislation and the result of the possible decisions pertaining to it may be of great assistance to the courts. Charter decisions should not and must not be made in a factual vacuum. To attempt to do so would trivialize the Charter and inevitably result in ill-considered opinions.[31]

For a Court that dismissed Operation Dismantle on the basis that its allegations about international politics could simply never be proved, the readiness to be persuaded of the future impact of impugned legislation and the result of possible decisions is remarkable. Also remarkable is the contrast between the demand for the careful preparation and presentation of a mass of factual material and wide-eyed acceptance of any social scientific opinion without 'the evidentiary testing of the adversarial process'.

MacKay's counsel argued that neo-Nazis might get 10 per cent of the vote and be entitled to public funding. Cory would have none of this without evidence. But it is not clear what help evidence would be. Did Cory mean that only when a neo-Nazi actually had 10 per cent of the vote and was about to receive public funds would freedom of expression be in danger? Or would some specific probability of a neo-Nazi getting 10 per cent of the vote testified to by some dubious political scientist have decided the case?

MacKay's case was simple enough. Even Cory dealt with a large part of it as presented:

> The appellants also argued an issue that does not require a factual foundation. It was said that the statutory funding of candidates could, whenever a losing candidate or candidates received 10% of the vote, force a taxpayer to support a candidate whose views are fundamentally opposed to that of the taxpayer. This enforced support of a contrary view was said to infringe the taxpayer's right to freedom of expression. I cannot accept that contention. The Act does not prohibit a taxpayer or anyone else from holding or expressing any position or their belief in any position. Rather, the Act seems to foster and encourage the dissemination and expression of a wide range of views and positions. In this way it enhances public knowledge of diverse views and facilitates public discussion of those views.[32]

But by 1989 the Court had become so used to buffering its decisions in masses of evidence that it would not fully deal with *MacKay*.

In 1990 and 1991 the Court became increasingly confident and ambitious in dealing with political issues. Although it upheld mandatory retirement provisions in universities[33] and hospitals,[34] it struck down a provision of the Unemployment Insurance Act that restricted benefits for people over 65.[35] While upholding bans on hate propaganda in the Canadian Human Rights Act,[36] it overruled limits on political activity by public servants.[37] In all of these cases quantities of evidence were before the Court, but it is hard to tell from its reasons how much evidence was relied on.

Merv Lavigne's unsuccessful attempt to have struck down the requirement that he pay dues to the Ontario Public Service Employees Union in order to keep his teaching job at a community college[38] demonstrated how far politics cloaked in evidence could go. Lavigne objected that his dues were being used to support the New Democratic Party, disarmament campaigns, and other causes. None of the judges thought Lavigne's right to freedom of expression had been infringed by his being forced to contribute funds to support causes he disagreed with. Wilson J. relied on *Mackay*. Only three of the judges thought Lavigne's right to freedom of association had been infringed. But all of the judges held that whatever rights or freedoms might have been infringed, the dues requirement could be justified under section 1. LaForest J., who had held that Lavigne's freedom of association was infringed, nevertheless insisted that he could not even be allowed an opt-out for dues not spent strictly on collective bargaining, having evidently been persuaded by the evidence of the following:

... there is evidence to support the view that the cause of unionism has been advanced by the NDP. The respondents referred to the role that the party played in the establishment of medicare, pensions, and unemployment insurance, and of what unions would have had to give up in the way of demands in other areas in order to get medical coverage from employers, private unemployment insurance coverage, and so on. In the light of the foregoing, it is inconceivable that support of the NDP could be considered irrelevant to the union's obligation to represent those who pay dues to it. But the important point is that if individuals can 'opt out' of supporting the NDP, the unions will have much fewer dollars to support it.[39]

It was never in the cards that the Supreme Court of Canada would take on the unions over the use of compulsory dues for political purposes, something that people with more political *nous* than the National Citizens' Coalition, which backed Lavigne's case, would have known. This was all the more so after the Court had repeatedly held in 1987 that freedom of association did not include a right to strike, despite alarming dissents by Dickson and Wilson. But the readiness to find political facts on which to base its decision shows a Court acknowledging no bounds to its political competence.

In more recent cases there have been comments that might be read as indicating that the Court had developed a more modest conception of its competence and might be ready to defer slightly to the legislatures. These cases might even be read as saying that the Court would be satisfied with a 'reasonable basis' for impugned legislation. In *Dickason*,[40] yet another lengthy and inconclusive treatment of the issue of mandatory retirement, Sopinka J. (dissenting) says:

> The first question in this appeal is the meaning to be ascribed to the phrase 'reasonable and justifiable.' I agree with the board of inquiry, the courts below and my colleagues that the jurisprudence developed with respect to s. 1 of the Charter is a useful guide in applying s. 11.1 of the I.R.P.A. There is also substantial agreement that in determining whether the proportionality factor has been met, the Court should not defer to the decision of an employer in the same way as in the case of a governmental actor. The rationale for this approach in the latter case is that in dealing with governmental actors, it is often difficult, if not impossible, to prove in the ordinary way whether a particular measure will in fact achieve its objective. Accordingly, if Parliament ... had a reasonable basis for concluding that the measure would achieve its objective, that is ordinarily a basis for concluding that there is a rational connection between the measure and the governmental objective. Accordingly, although the government could not prove that advertising toys on television had a manipulative effect on children, nor that hate propaganda actually promoted hatred against an identifiable group, nor that pornography caused harm to women, the fact that there was sufficient evidence to provide a reasonable basis for the legislature to adopt the impugned legislation in aid of its objective was sufficient to save it.[41]

There is no reason to conclude from this that the Court will not, as it has done readily for 10 years, put itself in the place of the legislature. The point in *Irwin* where the Court would not second-guess the legislature was the age

limit of 13 for a ban on advertising. *Irwin* followed *Edwards*,[42] a Sunday shopping case, in which Chief Justice Dickson accepted the exception for stores
with seven employees or less, saying:

> . . . I do not believe that there is any magic in the number seven as distinct
> from, say, 5, 10, or 15 employees as a cut-off point for eligibility for the
> exemption. In balancing the interests of retail employees to a holiday in
> common with their family and friends against the s. 2(a) interests of those
> affected the legislature engaged in the process envisaged by s. 1 of the Char-
> ter. A 'reasonable limit' is one which, having regard to the principles enunci-
> ated in *Oakes*, was reasonable for the legislature to impose. The courts are
> not called upon to substitute judicial opinions for legislative ones as to the
> place at which to draw the line.[43]

Clearly, in these cases the Court had no different idea of its own on where
to draw the lines and might as likely as not have done so at 13 years and seven
employees. It was not so much deferring to the legislatures as condescending
to them, leaving them the details to work out. Contrary to the implication of
Sopinka's comments in *Dickason*, the Court seemed satisfied in *Irwin* that
advertising toys on television did have a manipulative effect on children. It was
only unsure at what age this ceased to be a pressing and substantial concern.

In *Keegstra*,[44] the Alberta school teacher was charged with wilfully promoting hatred against an identifiable group under subsection 319(2) of the Criminal Code. The defence argued that the provision infringed Keegstra's
freedom of expression and, in addition, by putting the onus on him to prove
the truth of his teaching, infringed his right to be presumed innocent. There
was a real difference of opinion between the majority and the minority in the
Court over whether the hate propaganda provisions of the criminal code
would be effective to combat racial hatred, an objective all agreed was pressing and substantial. The minority was persuaded by the argument that the
prosecution of hate propagandists can give their views free publicity and
encourage a public suspicion that there may be something to what the propagandists say because it is suppressed. Though a newspaper report of Ernst
Zundel's relishing his Court battle was referred to, this did not appear to be
an argument for which evidence was considered necessary. The minority was
also impressed with the argument that the use of an anti-hate law in pre-
Hitler Germany did no good. 'Historical evidence' was relied on for this
argument. But Chief Justice Dickson, writing for the majority, simply
brushed aside this argument, most pertinently observing that post-war Germany had enacted new anti-hate legislation. Typically, *Keegstra* is a rambling
political discussion given an air of detachment by both the *Oakes* jargon of
'minimal impairment', etc., and the citation of many authors putatively
learned in the law and other subjects. It is clear, however, that in the end the
Court decided whether it liked the legislation, without any deference to the
legislature. Contrary to Sopinka's claim in *Dickason*, that the case did not
depend on the government proving 'that hate propaganda actually promoted

hatred against an identifiable group', Dickson held: '[I]t would be difficult to deny that the suppression of hate propaganda reduces the harm such expression does to individuals who belong to identifiable groups and to relations between various cultural and religious groups in Canadian society.'[45]

Keegstra contained a statement by Dickson of a common recent theme of flexibility in the use of the *Oakes* criteria:

> The analytical framework of *Oakes* has been continually reaffirmed by this Court, yet it is dangerously misleading to conceive of s. 1 as a rigid and technical provision, offering nothing more than a last chance for the state to justify incursions into the realm of fundamental rights. From a crudely practical standpoint, Charter litigants sometimes may perceive s. 1 in this manner, but in the body of our nation's constitutional law it plays an immeasurably richer role, one of great magnitude and sophistication.[46]

This typically vain and self-serving comment on the Court's chief source of power cannot be read as indicating a readiness to defer to the legislatures. Rather it is an announcement of the Court's refusal to be bound by the straitjacket it might have fashioned for itself in *Oakes*. A rigid application of *Oakes* might have obliged the Court to strike down legislation it liked when the evidence it called for was not forthcoming.

In *Butler*,[47] in which the owner of an adult video store in Winnipeg challenged the obscenity provisions of the Criminal Code, Sopinka J. did find that the government could not prove that pornography caused harm to women. He referred to the conflicting conclusions of reports in Canada and the United States. Nevertheless he was prepared to uphold freshly interpreted obscenity legislation on the basis of the possibility of harm. But again there is no basis for the suggestion, encouraged by his own comment in *Dickason*, that he was deferring to Parliament. Clearly, he thought that the evidence of the possibility of harm was enough and that the obscenity law as he reinterpreted it was worth having to guard against the possibility of harm. He would not have deferred to Parliament if he had not thought so. If he had taken the trouble to follow *Oakes* closely enough to speak of standard of proof, perhaps he would have been prepared to find that, on the balance of probability, pornography does cause harm.

The Supreme Court of Canada's call for and acceptance of a mass of doubtful political evidence and its casual use of it has simply illustrated the incapacity of any court satisfactorily to exercise the power that the Court so complacently holds. A proper use of evidence would limit its quantity and use to showing that the legislature was reasonably addressing a problem and not simply contemptuous of rights and freedoms. It would see the Court expressly relying on evidence in its reasons or expressly rejecting it as unhelpful and unwanted. It would subsume evidence within an extended legislative history and allow the Court to speak once on the validity of legislation rather than leaving it open for fresh evidence or changed circumstances. Most importantly it would require the Court expressly to limit its own absolute power.

NOTES

1 P.W. Hogg, 'Proof of Facts in Constitutional Cases', 26 U.T.L.J. 386 (1976).

2 *Muller v. State of Oregon* (1908), 208 US 412.

3 K.C. Davis, 'An Approach to the Problems of Evidence in the Administrative Process' (1942) 55 *Harvard Law Review* 364.

4 Carl Baar, 'Criminal Court Delay and the Charter: The Use and Misuse of Social Facts in Judicial Policy Making' (1993) 72 C.B.R. 305 is an interesting discussion of the use and abuse of evidence in the *Askov* fiasco, although biased by Baar's interest as a part-time researcher in the field of Court delays and the source of much of the evidence.

5 *Law Society of Upper Canada v. Skapinker* (1984), 9 D.L.R. (4th) 161, [1984] 1 S.C.R. 357.

6 Ibid., D.L.R. 182; S.C.R. 384

7 *Re Singh and Minister of Employment and Immigration* (1985), 17 D.L.R. (4th) 422, [1985] 1 S.C.R. 177.

8 Ibid., D.L.R. 467; S.C.R. 217.

9 Ibid., D.L.R. 469; S.C.R. 218.

10 *R. v. Oakes* (1986) 24 C.C.C. (3d) 321, 26 D.L.R. (4th) 200, [1986] 1 S.C.R. 103.

11 *Oakes* C.C.C. 350; D.L.R. 229; S.C.R. 142.

12 Even more dubious is the logic of appeals to international conventions (see *Keegstra* and *Butler* in notes 43 and 46 below). But as these may be considered part of the law of Canada, they may be left out of a consideration of the role of evidence.

13 *Operation Dismantle v. The Queen* (1985), 18 D.L.R. (4th) 481, [1985] 1 S.C.R. 441.

14 Ibid., D.L.R. 485; S.C.R. 448.

15 Ibid., D.L.R. 488; S.C.R. 452.

16 Uncharacteristically, Wilson J. seemed ready to accept a presumptive limit on the Court's power to review 'governmental action which concerns the relations of the state with other states . . .' (D.L.R. 490; S.C.R. 518).

17 Quoted by Brian G. Morgan in 'Proof of Facts in Constitutional Litigation', notes for an address at the University of Toronto Faculty of Law Constitutional Litigation Programme on 26 February 1986. The papers were revised and published as Robert J. Sharpe, ed., *Charter Litigation* (Toronto, 1987). Morgan drops the quotation from Dickson, but Katherine Swinton cites it in 'What do the Courts Want from the Social Sciences?' Swinton and Morgan's chapters, and John Hagan's 'Can Social Science Save Us? The Problems and Prospects of Social Science Evidence in Constitutional Litigation' are a good representation of the state of knowledge and speculation in 1986. For the practitioner no more is known now.

18 *R. v. Thomsen* (1988), 40 C.C.C. (3d) 411, [1988] 1 S.C.R. 640.

19 *R. v. Hufsky* (1988), 40 C.C.C. (3d) 398, [1988] 1 S.C.R. 621.

20 *R. v. Ladouceur* (1988), 56 C.C.C. (3d) 22, [1990] 1 S.C.R. 1257.

21 Ibid., C.C.C. 27; S.C.R. 1265.

22 *Ford v. Quebec (Attorney General)* (1988), 54 D.L.R. (4th) 577, [1988] 2 S.C.R. 712 and *Devine v. Quebec (Attorney General)* (1988), 54 D.L.R. (4th) 641, [1988] 2 S.C.R. 790.

23 *Ford*, D.L.R. 626; S.C.R. 777.

24 Ibid., D.L.R. 626; S.C.R. 776.

25 *Irwin Toy Ltd. v. Quebec (Attorney General)* (1989), D.L.R. (4th) 577, [1989] 1 S.C.R. 927.

26 Ibid., D.L.R. 619; S.C.R. 985.

27 This is not exactly what *Big M* says. There Ottawa had legislative jurisdiction to pass the Lord's Day Act only if it was criminal law enforcing a religious obser-vance. If it was that, according to the Court, it offended the religious freedom pro-vision in paragraph 2(a) of the Charter. If the Lord's Day Act only established a secular day of rest, the basis on which Ottawa tried to justify it, it was not within Ottawa's legislative jurisdiction.

28 *Irwin Toy*, D.L.R. 618; S.C.R. 984.

29 In *Butler* (note 47 below) and *R. v. Zundel* (1992) 95 D.L.R. (4th) 202, [1992] 2 S.C.R. 357, the Court added to the confusion, arguing with itself over whether there could be a shift in emphasis giving new constitutional life to legislation without the shift in purpose rejected in *Big M*. A shift in emphasis allowed obscenity legislation for the protection of women in *Butler*, but the argument that section 181 of the Criminal Code could now be considered anti-hate legislation was rejected.

30 (1989), 61 D.L.R. (4th) 385, [1989] 2 S.C.R. 357.

31 Ibid., D.L.R. 388; S.C.R. 361.

32 Ibid., D.L.R. 392; S.C.R. 366.

33 *McKinney v. University of Guelph* (1990), 76 D.L.R. (4th) 545, [1990] 3 S.C.R. 292, and *Harrison v. University of British Columbia* (1990), 77 D.L.R. (4th) 55, [1990] 3 S.C.R. 451.

34 *Stoffman v. Vancouver General Hospital* (1990) 76 D.L.R. (4th) 700, [1990] 3 S.C.R. 483.

35 *Tétrault-Gadoury v. Canada (Employment and Immigration Commission)* (1991), (4th) 81 D.L.R. 358, [1991] 2 S.C.R. 22.

36 *Canada (Canadian Human Rights Commission) v. Taylor* (1990), 75 D.L.R. (4th) 577, [1990] 3 S.C.R. 892.

37 *Osborne v. Canada (Treasury Board)* (1991), 82 D.L.R. (4th) 321, [1991] 3 S.C.R. 69.

38 *Lavigne v. Ontario Public Service Employees Union* (1991), 81 D.L.R. (4th) 545, [1991] 3 S.C.R. 211.

39 Ibid., D.L.R. 638; S.C.R. 337.

40 *Dickason v. University of Alberta* (1992), 95 D.L.R. (4th) 439, [1992] 2 S.C.R. 1103. *Dickason* is not a Charter case, but the Court proceeded on the basis that the 'reasonable and justifiable' defence provided for in the Alberta Individual's Rights Protection Act was equivalent to section 1 of the Charter and embarked on an *Oakes* analysis.

41 Ibid., D.L.R. 482; S.C.R. 1195.

42 *R. v. Edwards Books and Art Ltd* (1986), 35 D.L.R. (4th) 1, [1986] 2 S.C.R. 713.

43 Ibid., D.L.R. 51; S.C.R. 781.

44 *R. v. Keegstra* (1990), 61 C.C.C. (3d) 1, [1990] 3 S.C.R. 697.

45 Ibid., C.C.C. 52; S.C.R. 767.

46 Ibid., C.C.C. 28; S.C.R. 735.

47 *R. v. Butler* (1992), 89 D.L.R. (4th) 449, [1992] 1 S.C.R. 452.

9

Disclosure after
Stinchcombe

Gerald Owen

Before 1982 I was one of those who thought the Charter of Rights and Freedoms—or rather, judicial review of legislation—was a bad idea. But I left law practice for journalism when Charter cases were still just climbing up to courts of appeal and the Supreme Court of Canada. In early 1992 I found myself doing some law journalism. I wondered Rip-van-Winkle-ishly how things had gone with the Charter. Could I fairly say to anybody, 'I told you so'? Chance let me look at the Charter in action in one area where the Supreme Court had just made an important decision. Here at least, the consequences turned out to be more comic than tragic.

This decision had to do with William Stinchcombe, an Alberta lawyer charged with breach of trust. For my purpose here, what matters is that his former secretary spoke to the police. Oddly enough, though she told them things that would have helped him, she refused to speak to his lawyer. The prosecutors did not pass what she had said on to the defence, because it was not evidence they wanted to bring. The defence complained, knowing she had said something good.

This dispute got up to the Supreme Court of Canada. In November 1991, Mr Justice John Sopinka said that a prosecutor has to disclose 'relevant information'—not just the damning stuff. This is now the leading case on 'disclosure', that is, on what the Crown has to tell (or show) the defence before trial.

A SUPERFLUOUS DOCUMENT

R. v. Stinchcombe[1] may well be the most important event in Canadian criminal law since the Charter (or so one senior Ottawa Crown attorney has said). And for that matter, it is one of the Charter's main effects. In a book called *Contempt of Court*,[2] Carsten Stroud, a relentlessly hip journalist with excellent police sources, says that *Stinchcombe* severely, perhaps fatally, hampers the ability of the police to solve crimes, because they have to uncloak their informants. But no, they don't have to do that—unless an informant is going into the witness box, in which case his or her name comes out anyway. And in fact few if any disasters have ensued. The subsequent history of disclosure does, however, show various interesting symptoms of the times, and some unforeseen consequences.

The Charter forces judges to make decisions about matters they don't know about and can't find out about—they can't launch royal commissions to look into the prudence of the acts of Parliament (and of legislatures) that they have to evaluate. As a result their decisions often feel like fog. But the Charter also comes up in a sphere they are acquainted with: the processes of courts. Here they can get some grip on things or some footing in their own experience.

On the other hand, where (as here) the Charter is more or less harmless, it may well be superfluous. Disclosure rules could have been made by several means, without any talk of constitutional rights. For one thing, higher courts have 'inherent jurisdiction' over their own processes, a power that is said to arise from 'the very nature' of a court, or perhaps from ancient royal prerogative. Roughly speaking, this is common law; it does not come from an act of any Parliament or legislature, let alone from anything like the Charter.

Judges (or else committees controlled by them) have statutory powers to make rules of procedure. For criminal cases, the higher courts are given this power by s. 482 of the Criminal Code. In particular, a superior court can regulate the duties of its officers, in other words, all the lawyers who appear there. That means it can regulate prosecutors and the way they disclose or withhold information. And again, disclosure rules could have been made by statute—added to the Code. But I admit that attempts by statutory drafters (and Parliament itself) to pin down the meaning of, say, 'relevant information' might have been worse than judge-made law, which is often stated quite informally.

Stinchcombe is not like a statute. It furnishes some principles. Disclosure litigation, I think, has actually calmed down since it was decided. Few cases after it have shed much light on the substantive (and substantial) questions about what should be disclosed or what can be withheld.

LOGISTICS

Instead, the cases often illustrate clerical and administrative difficulties. *Stinchcombe* is an example of one institution making a large commitment on behalf of another. The courts have no power of the purse. But here they have added greatly to the expenses and labours of prosecutors and police.

The strain is noticeable in the poorer parts of the country. For example, in rural Saskatchewan the RCMP has a hard time coping with all the photocopying that disclosure demands. And it is no accident that the Atlantic provinces have produced several decisions about photocopying. In one Newfoundland case,[3] the Crown offered a prisoner access to thousands of documents concerning himself and would have let him copy them out longhand, but would not allow any photocopying. Similarly, a Newfoundland defence lawyer was told to come to a police station, where he could take notes and read the documents aloud into a tape recorder but not make photocopies.[4] Again in Newfoundland, a Crown attorney met with a defence lawyer (and a private detective, for some reason) in the courthouse law library in St John's, and showed him the documents (not all, as it turned out) but wouldn't let him take detailed notes.[5]

The judge didn't think that was enough and said there is a right to photocopies—normally at least. But after that, the Newfoundland Crown attorneys came out with a policy saying that defence lawyers would get copies only if they signed a stringent agreement not to let anyone except their clients see the documents, and even they would not be allowed to take copies away.

This policy gave rise to a case in which a Legal Aid staff lawyer, working in Harbour Grace, Nfld, refused to sign the agreement. He was allowed about three minutes at a courthouse in Whitbourne, Nfld to look through the file. (He was there on another matter.) The judge hearing this latter case remarked that disclosure seemed to have actually tightened up in Newfoundland since *Stinchcombe*. When I raised this with the Crown attorney and the defence lawyer involved, I was surprised that they both thought it was true, at least outside St John's. Province-wide policies had been set down in writing since the Supreme Court of Canada made its pronouncements, whereas before, in smaller places, disclosure was given on the basis of trust built up between prosecutors and the local defence bar.[6]

In a case in Truro, N.S., a judge agreed with a regional Crown policy, saying it was enough to let the defence lawyer come to the Crown's office and do the photocopying there himself. Here again the defence lawyer was on the staff of Legal Aid. He told me that Legal Aid could not afford to pay a lawyer to travel to another office to stand around and work at a copying machine. So Legal Aid would no longer take on criminal cases until the accused person had obtained disclosure himself. This means that someone who may be inclined to violence and who is certainly displeased at being charged has to visit the prosecutor's office, deal with the staff there, and do clerical work.[7]

PAPER GLUT

This prevalence of clerical problems makes sense in a way, because things that get disclosed (or withheld) are mostly papers. And paper breeds paper. When a year had passed since *Stinchcombe*, I asked some criminal lawyers what effects it had had. One Crown attorney told me that previously he had received perhaps half a dozen letters a year. Now about one a day was coming in. A criminal lawyer's life had become more like a civil lawyer's, he said. Perhaps it is no coincidence that John Sopinka used to be a leading civil litigation lawyer. (Carsten Stroud confidently asserts twice that he is a former criminal defence lawyer, strongly implying that he is biased accordingly.)

With pardonable exaggeration, a defence lawyer, Alan Whitten, the chair of the criminal justice section of the Ontario branch of the Canadian Bar Association, said in early 1994 that disclosure might turn the criminal bar into 'bigger paper pushers' than real estate solicitors.[8] Civil practice of course has a lot of paper partly because business and commerce have. But also because of procedural rules, disclosure, or 'discovery', is well settled in private lawsuits. Each side has a right to know the case it has to meet. 'Production of documents' is an important part of civil discovery.

In this light, the fairness of criminal law disclosure is evident. People in criminal law (mostly judges and defence lawyers) now repeatedly say that the day of 'trial by ambush' or 'trial by surprise' is past. Prosecutors should not set traps lest they disable an accused person from answering charges. Inevitably, this hampers the Crown's cross-examination. Indeed cross-examination would lose much of its point if there were no surprises at all for witnesses.

THE INFORMATION AGE

But more broadly, I believe that *Stinchcombe* is part of movement away from drama, away from face-to-face encounters, from personality, from shocks and sudden flashes of insight. For all the talk—usually complaints—about this being a post-literate age, it may be all too literate. There is a powerful trend toward trying to reduce experience to information, documentation, and abstraction.

Among the crucial documents to be disclosed are 'will-say' statements. They contain what police officers expect Crown witnesses to say. Naturally, they are often wrong. 'Hope-they-will-say' would be more accurate. Police officers must now more consistently render their own experience into writing, too. As a logical consequence of disclosure, police officers now have 'a duty to make careful notes', or so says a consensus report on the whole subject, chaired and led by G. Arthur Martin, a revered former judge and defence lawyer.[9]

The Charter itself is another part of this trend. It is an attempt to turn principles into abstract formulas on paper. If life is turned into atoms of information, then one can feed them into a supposedly logical system of general rules, and all—or much—will be well. Something of this character belongs to law and the rule of law at all times. Legality is always somewhat rationalistic.

But this characteristic is heightened by the Charter, which is a higher law; it is the law about the laws.

I keep speaking about paper, but the glut of information of modern times is one great reason for information technology. Photocopying and other processes (including word processors) breed more and more paper, which creates a need for new techniques to handle the 'flow', and to store and also destroy documents. So let 'paper' stand also for disks, microchips, videotapes, and so forth. I am speaking here about criminal trials in the age of mechanical reproduction generally. Criminal law is comparatively new to all this; only now are advanced filing systems beginning to emerge.

Information theory believes in units called 'bytes'. Mr Gradgrind, the caricature of a utilitarian in Dickens's *Hard Times*, was a great believer in Hard Facts. His twentieth-century equivalents are less confident, but they still believe that experience can at least be *hardened into* units of information. Lawyers, for the most part, are fully capable of scepticism about the clarity of facts. But the Chief Justice of Canada, Antonio Lamer, is arguing that full disclosure means that preliminary inquiries are no longer necessary. Defence lawyers do not need to prepare for trial by confronting the prosecution's main witnesses face to face, they can just read their will-says.[10] But because disclosure supplies a collection of documents, of course it does not reveal the natures of the witnesses. The defence learns many ingredients of the case it has to meet under *Stinchcombe*, but it does not learn the real drama: the Crown's strategy, tactics, and arguments, in other words what the Crown will actually do and say.

Depersonalization, then, is an aspect of these trends that can hurt the defence as much as the prosecution. I will now turn to another way in which *Stinchcombe* may rebound on defendants.

SELF-INCRIMINATION

'Relevant information' means (as I have said) more than the evidence the Crown wants to bring forward at trial. It means whatever might help answer a question that is in dispute: a question that could at least partly decide the case.

In a civil lawsuit, the two (or more) sides set down their basic contentions in documents. Then they have to exchange whatever 'relevant' papers they may have. But in criminal cases, the defendant does not have to say anything more specific than 'guilty' or 'not guilty'. Consequently, the Crown often does not know what is in dispute, because it does not know what the defence's arguments are. It can try to assemble evidence to show that whatever happened had all the necessary elements that add up to a certain crime. It can then supply this in documentary form. In other words, it cannot know what could help the person who has been charged unless it knows what his defence is. A disclosing prosecutor has to guess the other side's argument, its 'theory' of the facts—even its evidence.

The Crown may guess wrong. So the defendant's lawyer often has to ask for specific things, or reveal in general terms what his argument is. Either he has to lighten the Crown's burden of proof and yield some part of his client's right to keep quiet—or else not make some requests, and be content with incomplete disclosure.

This is not disastrous or scandalous. But it does eat away at what is held to be a sacred liberty of the subject, the right to remain silent and perhaps the right to be presumed innocent as well. At least one prosecutor says the time has come for 'reverse disclosure'. So far, *Stinchcombe* makes a criminal trial more like a civil one, but in a one-sided way.

MORE SIDE-EFFECTS

Fuller disclosure has other curious consequences. I have been saying that it is a sort of 'civil-ization' of criminal law. But it does carry some gruesome possibilities. Crown witnesses may be murdered in jail when their intended testimony gets down on paper (though prosecutors can withhold information if they have cause to expect that). And on aesthetic—that is, more or less pornographic—grounds, witness statements and photographs of victims can get circulated and read by prisoners, or pasted up on cell walls.

There have been some attempts to expand the scope of disclosure—even, in one case, to facts not yet in the hands of the police. The defence wanted to send along its own pathologist to digging up of a body (that might not be found at all) of someone who might have been a murder victim. The judge didn't go for this.[11]

Sensational murders generate a mass of information; the killings of children and young girls are rather like the Kennedy assassination. The much-publicized disputes over the prosecution of Guy-Paul Morin for the murder of a child called Christine Jessop have had a lot to do with non-disclosure about other suspects, about leads that were hardly followed up. And some months before the arrests of a certain Paul Teale *né* Bernardo and Karla Homolka, a Crown attorney wondered aloud to me what would have to be disclosed if there were ever any charges for the murder of a teenage girl called Kristen French: every well-meaning crank call from the public?

If an accused person is a career criminal, should every 'occurrence report' (a police term) ever mentioning him be supplied? Or every such report about victims and witnesses who were pro criminals too? Or even on a place—a bar or a billiard parlour—that is a hangout for a group of pros?

One odd twist is that Mr Justice Sopinka said in *Stinchcombe*, apparently rather casually, that the trial judge is the one to review the Crown's performance of the disclosure duty, if need be—forgetting, perhaps, that at the vital early stages of the process there is no such person for the defence to turn to.

An interesting weakness of dealing with disclosure by judge-made rules—whether under the Charter or the common law—is that Crown attorneys and judges don't really have the authority to tell the police what to do. Only Parliament and the provincial legislatures have such powers. So this may be an argument for dealing with such matters through statutes and regulations governing police forces.

USE AND ABUSE

In spite of all these problems and in spite of the broad-brush style in *Stinchcombe*, Mr Justice Sopinka took a moderate view of what should happen if the Crown has not told all it should have. For the Crown, the worst result is a 'stay of proceedings', which has much the same effect as an acquittal. From the cases that have come to my attention, it appears that there have been fewer stays because of non-disclosure since *Stinchcombe*. Things may have got quieter. Disputes seem to be getting settled at early stages, or at least they are not often reaching the surface, in the form of judges' written reasons.

In short, we cannot fairly accuse the Supreme Court of Canada of obstruction of justice. *Stinchcombe* supplies some principles without taking away Crown discretion. Most Crown attorneys are quite reasonable people.

But one notable stay of proceedings is certainly a symptom of the times.[12] I have heard that the Vancouver Crown attorney involved, Wendy Harvey, was already known as a 'loose cannon'. She had been warned, it is rumoured, that she was heading for trouble in her single-minded resolve to get sexual assault convictions. (For the most part, disclosure works rather smoothly in British Columbia.) In the case of *R. v. O'Connor*, a former Catholic bishop was the alleged villain, charged with sexual assault. (Canada has abolished the previous offences of rape, indecent assault, and so on.) The alleged victims were aboriginal Canadians, former pupils—'inmates' might be a better word—of a residential school in Williams Lake, B.C.

The Associate Chief Justice of British Columbia had ordered the Crown to disclose various kinds of information connected with all the therapists, counsellors, psychologists, and psychiatrists concerned. Ms Harvey found his order 'socially unacceptable and unworkable', so she didn't obey it. And as for certain interview transcripts that were not passed on, she said later that she might have dreamt that she had supplied them to the defence. The lack of 'computer literacy' of another Crown had been another obstacle, it was said.

The trial judge, Mr Justice Allan Thackray, said that although there had been no grand design to subvert justice, the excuses for non-disclosure were 'limp'. Senior Crown attorneys were looking into the matter. The prosecutors admitted that they could not assure the court that full disclosure had been made. The judge agreed with the defence lawyer that there was now a certain 'aura' around the case. To allow the prosecution to go ahead would tarnish the court's integrity, so he stayed it, while recognizing that many people would be outraged.

Later, the B.C. Court of Appeal brought the case back to life by lifting the stay, but it did not excuse Ms Harvey.[13] The case at least illustrates the risk that a charge may never be dealt with on its merits because of disclosure duties—when, that is, bad disclosure lets slip some other vice, some high-handedness, some overreaching.

Another example arose from an excessive cosiness with a star witness. Luciano Pietrorazio of Hamilton, Ont., is a career criminal who took such an active part in one investigation that he may have concocted his testimony entirely from police theories. The police gave him a free holiday from jail, putting him up for some weeks in a motel, where they could go over the case together. When he went back to prison, his cell became a library of their papers.[14]

But in *O'Connor* we glimpse what looks like modish fanaticism. This is a reminder of something obvious: abuses of process can be committed on all sides—left and right—and all sides should fear them and want remedies.

Justice and injustice in legal procedure existed before 1982. They will doubtless outlive the Charter.

NOTES

1 [1991] 3 S.C.R. 326; 68 C.C.C. (3d) 1; [1992] 1 W.W.R. 97.

2 Carsten Stroud, *Contempt of Court* (Toronto: Macmillan, 1993), 337–40.

3 *R. v. Fleming*, 12 Mar. 1992 (Nfld S.C.).

4 *R. v. Luff*, 11 C.R.R. (2d) 356; 101 Nfld & P.E.I.R. 260; 321 A.P.R. 260 (Nfld C.A.).

5 *R. v. Vokey*, (1992), 72 C.C.C. (3d) 97; 10 C.R.R. (2d) 360; 14 C.R. (4th) 311; 102 Nfld & P.E.I.R. 275; 323 A.P.R. 275 (Nfld C.A.).

6 *R. v. Mercer*, 5 Nov. 1992 (Nfld. S.C.).

7 *R. v. Dohan* (1992), 116 N.S.R. (2d) 134; 320 A.P.R. 134 (N.S.S.C.).

8 Panel at the Canadian Bar Association—Ontario Annual Institute of Continuing Legal Education, as quoted by Eugene McCarthy in *The Lawyers Weekly*, 18 Feb. 1994, 13.

9 *Report of the Attorney General's Advisory Committee on Charge Screening, Disclosure and Resolution Discussions* (Toronto: Ontario Ministry of the Attorney General, 1993), 151.

10 Interview with the Chief Justice by David Vienneau in *Law Times*, 29 June 1992, 1 and 3 (also referring to his speech of 10 June 1992 to the Montreal Kiwanis Club and a letter written to the Prime Minister 'because of protocol'); remarks by the Chief Justice at the Canadian Association of Provincial Court Judges meeting, Regina, Sask., 19 Sept. 1992. I have also heard that Lamer was a leading spirit in the Law Reform Commission of Canada's *Study Report on Discovery in Criminal Cases*, 1974, which made the same argument.

11 *R. v. Irwin*, 2 Dec. 1992 (B.C.S.C.).

12 *R. v. O'Connor* (1992), 18 C.R. (4th) 98 (B.C.S.C.).

13 *R. v. O'Connor*, not yet reported (30 March 1994, B.C.C.A.).

14 *R. v. Buric*, 10 March 1993 (Ont. C.J. Gen. Div.).

10

Penumbras for the People: Placing Judicial Supremacy under Popular Control

Scott Reid

> If the Court is to serve as the keeper of the community's conscience, who is to keep the Court's conscience?
>
> Sidney Hook, *The Paradoxes of Freedom*

Since 1982, an enormous power shift has taken place in Canadian politics. Following the proclamation of the Canadian Charter of Rights and Freedoms, the judicial arm of government in general, and the Supreme Court of Canada in particular, began to exercise sweeping powers to disallow all legislation found to be in conflict with the rights listed in the Charter.

In general, the Canadian public has embraced this turn of events with enthusiasm, if not with a great deal of sophisticated understanding. However, a small number of scholars have taken the contrary view that the practical effect of the Charter, and of the courts' ability to interpret it as they see fit, is likely to produce worse public policy than would otherwise have prevailed.

The analysis of these scholars is reviewed in this chapter. In general, this analysis is mordant and insightful, albeit gloomy. However, most solutions proposed by Charter sceptics to the problem of judicial supremacy are not practical. In particular, remedies based on revitalizing section 33 of the Charter tend to hinge on the unlikely premise that the infamous 'notwithstanding' clause can be brought into public favour.

This chapter reviews a range of critiques of the Charter, as well as the solutions proposed by its critics. An alternative method of making section 33 more palatable is also suggested. This solution involves investing the power of legislative override in the only institution that commands more popular respect than the court system—the popular will itself.

THE RISE OF JUDICIAL POWER SINCE 1982

No observer of the Canadian political system would seriously contest the asser-tion that the courts have become vastly more powerful since the proclamation of the Constitution Act in April 1982. Nor is there much debate over the sources of this new power. Partly it rests in the Canadian Charter of Rights and Freedoms, which granted broad constitutional protection to the individual rights of all Canadians and to the collective rights of certain enumerated groups within society. By necessity this grant of enumerated rights involved the transfer of broad powers to the bodies charged with interpreting the Charter. This is particularly true given the vague wording of certain Charter rights.

Another source of power came from within the courts themselves. After 1982, the courts experienced a significant psychological shift, characterized by a new willingness to disallow legislation. The courts might easily have chosen to treat the Charter with caution, extending section 1 (which states that the fundamental rights laid out elsewhere in the Charter will be 'subject only to such reasonable limits prescribed by law as can be demonstrably justi-fied in a free and democratic society') so broadly as to render the Charter largely meaningless. They did not do so.

The political importance of this new-found judicial 'will to power' is not to be underestimated. After all, it is not inconceivable that the justices of the pre-Charter Supreme Court could have interpreted Diefenbaker's 1960 Bill of Rights much more broadly, disallowing large numbers of federal laws. The judges of the 1960-82 era chose not to do so. It is even imaginable that in the absence of either 1982's Charter or 1960's bill, the court could have embraced the concept of an 'implied bill of rights'. This idea, which surfaced repeatedly in court decisions between the 1930s and the 1980s, held that since the pre-amble to the British North America Act declared the new constitution to be 'similar in principle to that of the United Kingdom', any law repugnant to the civil liberties enjoyed in Britain in 1867 would be unconstitutional.[1]

The ability of courts to create rights in practice where none previously existed on paper is limited only by the imaginations of supreme court justices. Even in Switzerland, which has no constitutionally entrenched bill of rights, the confederation's supreme court has chosen to interpret the constitution's sole enumerated right (to equality before the law) very broadly, thereby disal-lowing certain cantonal legislation. In 1990 the Swiss Federal Court managed to interpret this right as guaranteeing women the right to vote in the half-canton of Appenzell Inner Rhodes, despite a clear statement elsewhere in the constitution that the equality clause does not extend to voting rights.[2]

Similarly imaginative rulings could have been made by Canadian courts before 1982, and occasionally they were, in judgments on matters relating to jurisdictional disputes between Ottawa and the provinces. But on the whole, there can be little doubt that 1982 is the fundamental watershed in both legal and psychological terms.

CHARTERPHILIA AND CHARTERPHOBIA

In broad terms, there are two schools of thought on the affect of the Charter on Canadian politics. The members of these two schools have been styled 'Charterphiles' and 'Charterphobes'. More politely, they may be referred to as Charter admirers and Charter sceptics. Although the schools differ in their views of the Charter itself, the main source of dispute between them is whether it is beneficial to invest the courts with unchecked control over the interpretation and application of Charter rights. This complete control has been described as creating a situation of 'judicial supremacy', in which ultimate political power is shifted, not to the constitution itself, but to the institution that possesses a monopoly on its interpretation. Charter admirers tend to see this supremacy as the guarantee, in practice, of the elevation of the constitution to a position of legal supremacy. Charter sceptics view judicial supremacy as the nullification of constitutional supremacy.

THE CASE FOR JUDICIAL SUPREMACY

The popular view among English-speaking Canadians is that the judicial supremacy that has existed since 1982 is a positive step in the country's political evolution (the predominant view of judicial supremacy differs in French Canada, owing to the different light in which Supreme Court rulings striking down aspects of Bill 101 are regarded). The dominant opinion among anglophones seems to be based upon the assumption that legislatures are the arm of government most likely to introduce oppressive or rights-infringing measures. Therefore, the unlimited ability of the courts to review legislative actions removes the power to oppress from legislatures and in effect causes it to disappear.

Historically, the fear of legislative oppression is well founded. From New Brunswick in 1871 and Manitoba in 1890 to Quebec in 1977, it has been provincial legislatures that have adopted measures offensive to the rights of their linguistic and religious minorities. In the 1940s it was the Parliament of Canada that authorized the internment of Canadian citizens of Japanese origin. By comparison, the courts appear—at least at first glance—to be free of any such stains. A closer look shows that the courts upheld Manitoba's unconstitutional 1890 English-only laws, tolerated racially exclusive voting laws in the pre-1960 era, and collaborated in the Japanese internments in the Second World War. But these facts are not widely known. Thus, most Canadians would probably find little to object to in the words of a 1982 federal government pamphlet, which states that 'constitutional entrenchment of a Charter of Rights and Freedoms limits the power of both provincial and federal governments in favour of the rights of individual citizens. It gives people the power to appeal to the courts if they feel their rights have been infringed or denied.'[3] The predominant view holds that since the legislature and the executive are the only branches of government capable of violating individual rights, judicial oversight will limit the extent to which such abuse can take place. This view is a Canadian version of the belief, famously expressed by 'Publius' (Alexander Hamilton) in *Federalist Paper* 78, that

> The Executive not only dispenses the honors, but holds the sword of the community. The legislature not only commands the purse, but prescribes the rules by which the duties and rights of every citizen are to be regulated. The judiciary, on the contrary, has no influence over either the sword or the purse; no direction either of the strength or of the wealth of society; and can take no active resolution whatever. It may truly be said to have neither FORCE nor WILL.[4]

Nonetheless, even in Hamilton's day the argument that the judiciary can command neither sword nor purse was far from universally accepted. Elsewhere in *Federalist* 78 Hamilton felt constrained to argue that 'it can be of no weight to say that the courts, on the pretext of a repugnancy, may substitute their own pleasure to the constitutional intentions of the legislature.'[5] Hamilton was unable to offer any proof of this assertion, although he did argue that life tenure would permit judges to be freed from the financial and electoral considerations likely to produce corruption, demagoguery, and other such abuses of power in the legislative and executive arms of government.[6]

Today, Hamilton's arguments remain the intellectual foundation of the supporters of unlimited judicial power of interpretation over both the American Bill of Rights and Canada's Charter of Rights and Freedoms. The judiciary is widely counted on to act as a salutary brake against 'the momentary passions of the majority'[7] and mob rule. As the editor of the *Canadian Bar Review*, J.G. Castel, put it in a 1983 essay, courts can use the Charter to prevent basic rights from being 'set aside by a transient majority'.[8] To use a venerable Canadian phrase, the courts can be counted on to act as chambers of 'sober second thought'.

A second line of argument has been made in favour of unrestricted judicial supremacy. This argument holds that the function of legislatures is to enact measures beneficial to the aggregate well-being of the public. It can be expected that often these will be enacted regardless of the implications that they may have for the rights of individuals who happen to stand in the way of such policies. The function of the courts is to oppose policies enacted for the greatest good of the greatest number, whenever they conflict with rights enumerated in the constitution.

What this means in practice is that legislative and executive actions will tend to be utilitarian, whereas individual court rulings will tend to be anti-utilitarian. Any individual court action is therefore likely to be against the public interest, as the public itself conceives this interest; it is only in the long run that the utility of court actions will emerge, by providing a framework of rules in which utilitarian acts of legislatures are likely to be in the public's best long-term interest. Only a firmly established and widely respected judiciary can legitimately play this unpopular but critically important role. Alexis de Tocqueville seems to have been the first to express this idea. He writes,

> The courts of justice . . . alone can compel the elected functionary to obey without violating the rights of the electors. The extension of judicial power in the political world ought therefore to be in the exact ratio to the extension of the elective power; if these two institutions do not go hand in hand, the state must fall into anarchy or into servitude.[9]

The American legal scholar Ronald Dworkin expresses the same idea somewhat differently:

> For the most part we accept that in any democracy the majority *should* govern: we think that though institutional structures that insulate officials from public opinion are necessary in practice, they are undesirable in principle. But when constitutions declare limits to the majority's power, this democratic assumption is displaced: decisions are not supposed to reflect the will of the majority then.[10]

Dworkin's views and those of Canadian scholars who support him are described by Michael Mandel in his book *The Charter of Rights and the Legalization of Politics*. Mandel, who does not support these views, nonetheless summarizes them well. As he puts it, supporters of this line of thought embrace the belief that '[w]hile the collective welfare of the community is best left to the community to decide, through majoritarian, representative institutions, rights *against* the collective welfare are best determined by a judge who is insulated from the "demands of the political majority whose interests the right would trump".'[11] Against these pro-judiciary views are arrayed the arguments of the Charter sceptics.

THE CHARTER SCEPTICS: A BRIEF CARICATURE

The viewpoint of the admirers of judicial supremacy boils down in the end to a single assertion: on certain questions, judges are better decision makers than are elected politicians. Charter sceptics present a strong case for being doubtful of the superior wisdom of judges; their own case boils down to the assertion that on some matters currently under the jurisdiction of the courts, judges are not the best decision makers. To some degree, the sceptics have been caricatured by their intellectual opponents. Charter admirer Richard Sigurdson, for example, has labelled the sceptics 'Charterphobes',[12] presumably because the name is as unbecoming as the designation 'Charterphile', coined earlier by Rainer Knopff and F.L. Morton.

In a more serious vein, Sigurdson maintains that Charter sceptics tend to be strong supporters of either a generally left-wing or a generally right-wing vision of society, and that they may be placed, without too much distortion of their individual views, into what he calls 'left wing Charterphobe' and 'right wing Charterphobe' groups. He then argues that each of these two groups believes that its own vision of society has broad support among the electorate and could be more rapidly achieved if the courts were not empowered to place impediments in the way of majority rule.

According to Sigurdson, the most prominent left-wing critics of judicial supremacy in the interpretation of the Charter are Joel Bakan, Robert Martin, Andrew Petter, Alan Hutchinson, and Michael Mandel,[13] while the most prominent right-wing Charter sceptics are Rainer Knopff and F.L. Morton.[14] Presumably Peter Russell, Peter Hogg, and Christopher Manfredi could also be added to the right wing list, although Sigurdson does not mention them.

There is some validity to Sigurdson's broad description of the Charter-phobes. Much of the criticism both of the Charter itself and of its interpreta-tion and application by the judiciary is based on the assumption that less restrained majority rule is more likely to produce a generally more 'left-wing' or 'right-wing' policy environment than judicially restrained majority rule. Some specific examples of this view, from both the left and the right, are noted below. But the most profound criticisms of judicial supremacy are premised on a different assumption altogether. This assumption holds that, regardless of the ideological makeup of Parliament or of the Supreme Court, in many circumstances judicial decision making *by its nature* produces worse policies than decision making by elected politicians. This thought will be returned to later, after the more easily caricatured left-wing and right-wing objections have been dealt with.

The chief left-wing objection to the new powers of the judiciary is that it has failed to alter the Canadian power structure in a manner that will permit progressive or redistributive policies to be adopted. Mandel, for example, describes the enthusiasm with which the leaders of various traditionally dis-advantaged groups and causes have leapt on the Charter bandwagon but warns that 'legal politics is highly resistant to hijacking' by the partisans of progressive causes.[15]

As a case in point he reviews the story of Operation Dismantle's unsuccess-ful attempt to convince the Supreme Court that cruise missile testing was an infringement of the right, under section 7 of the Charter, to 'security of the person'. Pursuing this course of action caused the group to abandon what Mandel regards as a promising effort to force Parliament to hold a referen-dum on testing. By the time the court effort had failed, the group's resources were exhausted and the public's attention had turned elsewhere. If this result is typical of what the left can expect in court, much time and many dollars will be wasted in futile court challenges when they could be better employed in promoting progressive causes in the legislatures.

Other left-wing critics agree that repeated disappointment is exactly what progressive causes can expect to encounter in court. Andrew Petter observes that judges are drawn primarily from privileged groups within society, and can be expected to share, at best, the perspectives of a privileged class, ethnic group, or sex. At worst, judges will be active partisans of their own social groups.[16] Mandel makes the same point in a slightly different way. Judges are appointed by politicians. Naturally, politicians can be expected to take special care to appoint judges with beliefs similar to their own. Judicial decisions will thus reflect the views of the populace in a very approximate way, but only after a very long time lag and only after going through two filters (the nomination and appointment process by which judges reach office and the electoral process by which politicians reach Parliament). The judiciary is thus an inefficient forum for attaining social justice.

Another left-wing objection is raised by Petter and Alan Hutchinson in an article published in the *University of Toronto Law Journal*. They express concern that the Charter will be applied only to government violations of rights, owing to an artificial distinction between the public and private realms that has been created as a result of the entrenchment of individual rights in the Charter. This artificial distinction will have the effect of insulating from the scrutiny of the courts the inequitable distribution of private property, which is the chief source of injustice in Canadian society.[17] Similarly, Mandel worries that the protection of individual rights in the Charter has the effect of hurting rather than helping members of disadvantaged groups, since it subverts their more important collective rights. Members of these groups would be better served if it were only their collective rights that had been constitutionally entrenched.[18]

A number of right-wing objections focus on the detrimental effect of section 15 of the Charter, which entrenches a series of collective rights. Peter Russell objects that collective rights can be enforced only by redistributive measures and argues that 'deciding questions of distributive justice is an essential responsibility of political man'.[19] When distributive matters are placed in the hands of the courts, the question of distributive justice is removed from its natural home in the political realm.

Knopff and Morton argue that the entrenchment of collective rights can have serious consequences for individual liberties. In particular, they draw attention to the potential for the courts to interpret collective rights as requiring 'equality of outcome', rather than 'equality of opportunity'. This could lead to court-sponsored reverse discrimination in favour of historically disadvantaged groups. Knopff finds it particularly ironic that the language of individual rights has been appropriated by forces that have no respect or even tolerance for individual liberties, and is being used to suppress these traditional freedoms.[20] A 1993 editorial in *The Globe and Mail* expresses similar misgivings:

> In one area, in particular the Charter's equality guarantees, the Court has openly declared its bias. The right to equal protection and benefit of the law does not, according to the Court, apply to every individual, though Section 15(1) of the Charter says so explicitly. Rather, the Court says it will hear equality-rights cases according to which group the individual belongs to. Equity among groups has replaced equality among individuals. . . . as

former Justice Bertha Wilson has put it, 'while Section 15 speaks in terms of a right to equality, it really addresses the problem of inequality.' We await similar group-contingent interpretations of freedom of speech and the right to a fair trial.[21]

Morton states a further objection to collective rights. It is impossible to list all disadvantaged groups within society in the Charter of Rights and Freedoms. Some are included and therefore are guaranteed a sympathetic ear in court, whereas others, which may be equally disadvantaged, have been over-looked and now must take a permanent back seat. Indeed, their non-recognized status may cause them to face greater hurdles, in a world where group rights are increasingly important and individual liberties increasingly circumscribed, than would have been the case if the Charter had enumerated only individual rights. He warns that there is already evidence that the groups that have achieved recognized status are attempting to reinforce their superior status by preventing the recognition of other groups, while groups that have been left on the outside are clamouring for enumeration in the Charter.[22]

Christopher Manfredi states this problem a different way:

> [T]he substitution of collective rights for individual rights does not really solve anything. One can speak of the collective right of communities, or of the collective rights of specific groups within a community, but it will always be necessary in a heterogeneous, pluralist society to resolve disputes among these equally strong competing claims. Moreover, in most instances there will be more than one principled way to resolve a particular dispute. What occurs in Charter adjudication is that the Supreme Court uses its considerable discretion to employ one principle rather than another.[23]

This is the basis of the objection by 'right-wing charterphobes' to the Charter's usurpation of powers that otherwise would be exercised through the legislature. The concern with the decline of democracy induced by the Charter is therefore not quite as cynical or calculating as critics like Sigurdson have suggested, and is not exclusively bound up in the belief that legislatures are more likely than courts to produce conservative, right-wing, or low-tax policies.

SYSTEMIC FLAWS IN JUDICIAL SUPREMACY

The most profound criticism by the Charter sceptics cannot be characterized as either left- or right-wing. Rather it concentrates on the nature of judicial decision making and maintains that the courts are inherently unsuitable, or even incompetent, to make good decisions about public policy. Courts are designed as chambers of adjudication rather than as parliamentary bodies. All of their internal workings suit them to resolve disputes on a case-by-case basis rather than to make decisions with wide-ranging policy implications.

For example a court is bound by its mandate to regard all matters in terms of rights, rather than in terms of the public good. Utilitarian considerations therefore are beyond the scope of the courts. Principles rather than facts are supposed to guide their deliberations. In practice, of course, courts do give at least some consideration to the practical consequences of their decisions. Elaborating on the practical effects of judicial decisions is one of the chief functions of interveners in Charter cases. Nonetheless, questions of principle rather than questions of policy must predominate in court judgments if the courts are not to become overtly legislative bodies.

The result, as even the fiercest defenders of unchecked judicial review will admit, is that many Charter cases have the effect of harming rather than helping the public interest, simply because they force governments to adopt less efficient policies in order to avoid violating the Charter. Very often, this is a cost worth bearing, compensated for by the fact that legislative abuses of Charter rights will have been prevented. Nonetheless, the wider the purview of the courts, the wider the areas of public policy in which the final decisions will be rendered by bodies that are precluded from showing 'an explicit concern with cost-benefit analysis'.[24] Clearly there are vast areas of public policy where such a decision-making process is simply inappropriate. These are the areas which the Charter sceptics would like to see reserved to the legislative and executive arms of government.

For Charter sceptics, therefore, the real question is one of boundaries: where do the matters best suited to rule-based, non-utilitarian decision making end, and where do the matters best suited to the utilitarian, end-based decision-making processes of the legislature begin? There is no simple answer, but a few outlines can be traced. Much judicial decision making involves the rendering of *proscriptive* rulings, which forbid governments or individuals from undertaking certain activities. In a complex welfare state, however, governments willingly take on positive obligations to provide education, health care services, and a range of other benefits. If these are distributed inequitably the results may be appealed as an infringement of constitutionally protected rights. If the courts rule in favour of the appellants in such a situation, judges will then find it necessary to issue *prescriptive* rulings, including instructions on how governments must act in order to end or redress these errors. This sort of ruling is easily recognized in the United States Supreme Court's famous judgment in *Brown v. Board of Education*.

A brief review of some of the desegregation rulings that have followed *Brown* indicate some of the perils of prescriptive rulings. The initial desegregation ruling was a source of public dispute at the time, but today it is widely respected. However, the removal of formal barriers to school integration in the 1950s and 1960s did not produce the expected racial integration of American schools. As a result, a series of later decisions led to the imposition, by the courts, of specific solutions. The most famous of these was busing, in which children were daily transported miles from their homes in order to attend racially mixed schools. Parents in the white middle class were horrified, and many enrolled their children in private schools to avoid seeing them bused to academically inferior schools in the decaying urban cores. In the end busing failed to achieve its goal, at a cost of billions of dollars.

More recently, a federal district court has attempted to impose a different detailed solution to the problem of racial segregation. The judge in *Jenkins v. Missouri* (1987) instructed the Kansas City School District to desegregate through the creation of 'magnet schools' in the inner city and through a vast program of infrastructure improvements, including the construction of new schools, the purchase of the most modern computer equipment and the hiring of the finest educators money could buy—including the former head coach of the Soviet Olympic fencing team. This program was intended to drive academic achievement levels in the ghetto skyward, thereby encouraging parents from the city's predominantly white suburbs to enrol their children voluntarily in schools in black neighbourhoods. Half a decade later, the program had cost $1.3 billion, much of which had been provided by permitting infrastructure conditions and teaching standards to drop in schools across the state. When the administrators of the school district expressed doubts about their ability to pay for the program, the court ordered them to raise taxes. When the construction of magnet schools ran over budget in 1991, the judge appropriated 10 per cent of the state's $700 million education budget to pay the bills. Meanwhile, drop-out rates in Kansas City had continued to rise, the schools had not become more integrated, and median scores on mathematics and reading tests in the magnet schools had declined.[25]

Somewhere between the widely acclaimed Brown decision and the widely reviled *Jenkins* decision, the line had been crossed between what most members of the public would probably have regarded as acceptable and unacceptable judicial exercise of prescriptive rulings. At some point, the courts had moved from adjudicating in the proactive manner unavoidable in a complex modern state to actually legislating in place of elected politicians. With the problem defined, the practical question becomes, what is the best practical method of keeping each arm of government on its side of the policy wall?

PROPOSED SOLUTIONS TO THE PROBLEM OF JUDICIAL SUPREMACY

The proposed solutions to the problems caused by the judiciary's new-found powers can be divided into four categories. The first category contains solutions that are largely technical and mostly minor in scope, usually involving adjustments to court procedures. These solutions tend to be favoured by observers who consider the problems arising from unchecked judicial review to be fairly limited.

The other three categories are normally advocated by observers who regard these problems as more serious. One involves changes to the process by which judges are appointed. Another involves redrafting the rights entrenched in the Charter so that they will be less subject to judicial re- or mis-interpretation. The final category involves a variety of proposals to strengthen or improve the legislative override clause in section 33 of the Charter, popularly known as the 'notwithstanding' clause.

CATEGORY NO. 1: PROCEDURAL SOLUTIONS

The scholars who have proposed procedural or incremental improvements to the way in which the court system is organized tend not to be the fiercest critics of the dangers of judicial supremacy. Usually they simply feel that the process of judicial review could be improved. Some of the most interesting ideas to emerge in this area are put forward by David Beatty in his book *Talking Heads and the Supremes*. Beatty acknowledges the criticisms by Charter sceptics like Paul Weiler and Peter Russell and declares his intention to address the 'institutional and structural characteristics of the courts which, in [Charter sceptics'] minds, render judges ill-equipped to perform [the] task [of judicial review].'[26] His proposals for change are based on a comparative study of the internal workings of the supreme courts of a series of countries. Beatty recommends that the Canadian court's method of reviewing cases be replaced by that of the German supreme court, by which each case undertaken by the court is researched by one of its members before it is presented to the court as a whole. The file prepared by the first justice is then circulated among all the others before the case is discussed by the whole court. Only at this time is each justice asked to state his or her opinion as to whether the constitution has been violated. Beatty maintains that 'in assigning one person the primary responsibility for the initial researching and writing up of a case, [the] system is obviously highly efficient. As a practical matter it will minimize the waste and duplication that plagues the current system in which, on occasion, three and even four different judges might have the same research done on a case.'[27] More important, the system would keep justices from staking out positions before they are in possession of all the facts of a case.

Another of Beatty's suggestions is for the court to produce a single document listing and explaining the reasons behind a judgment, rather than the current practice of having each justice writes his or her own document. Frequently the logic in one justice's report is so greatly at odds with that of the other justices that it is hard to believe they were sitting on the same court and examining the same evidence. Under the collegial, single-document approach preferred by Beatty, each justice would be forced to justify his or her reasoning to all of the other justices on the court. Judgments would be freed of the rather stretched logic that sometimes finds its way into the reasoning of judges who are attempting to give their opinions the maximum possible legislative effect.[28]

This approach would also probably lead to greater consensus among justices. F.L. Morton notes that the court is unanimous in 80 per cent of its non-Charter decisions but only in 64 per cent of Charter decisions, and that the percentage of cases in which justices supported individual Charter claims has ranged from a low of 23 per cent (Justice McIntyre) to a high of 53 per cent (Justice Wilson).[29] If judges were forced to justify their ideas to one another in the course of writing a single joint judgment, much of this dissent and the bad legal theory to which it gives rise would be removed.

It is quite clear that Beatty's reforms are intended to strengthen the Supreme Court, permitting it to execute its new political role more effectively, rather than to shift power away from the Court. The same can be said of all other proposals in this category. This is certainly the case in an essay by Dale Gibson entitled 'Judges as Legislators: Not Whether but How',[30] in which the author—who is no great admirer either of judicial supremacy or of the quality of Supreme Court judgments[31]—presents a series of proposals by which the court can act more efficiently in its quasi-legislative capacity. Gibson favours enlarging the court, which would increase its potential to be representative. He also recommends enlarging the research staff available to each justice, and emphasizes that since they are legislators in practice, justices should also have access to poll data and social science expertise.

Former Justice Bertha Wilson has also said that she favours increasing the court's ability to draw on resources not now available to it. In particular, she favours increasing the range of permissible evidence in Charter cases and liberalizing the rules for interventions, so that justices will have a clearer idea of the practical consequences of their rulings.[32]

Andrew Heard notes that most Charter cases brought before the Supreme Court are reviewed by panels of seven or fewer justices. As the number of justices declines, the influence on decisions of random factors involved in the individual perspectives of each justice begin to rise. The chances of decisions being made that do not reflect the consensus of the court's full wisdom increase. For this reason, he would like to have all cases heard by all nine justices.[33]

This proposal raises its own problems, since it would either reduce the capacity of the court to hear new cases or would reduce the amount of time that each justice would be able to devote to learning the particulars of each case. The result of the latter might be shoddy judicial workmanship. On the other hand, Charter cases are still a relatively small proportion of all the cases heard by the Supreme Court, so the increase in the total amount of work for each justice would not be overwhelming.

With the exception of Heard's proposal, each of these suggestions points to the Supreme Court's becoming more and more a legislative rather than a purely adjudicative body. By placing more resources in its hands, the reformers might discover that they had not so much improved the quality of the decisions emanating from the court as whetted the court's appetite for new cases.

CATEGORY NO. 2: SOLUTIONS BASED ON REWRITING THE CHARTER OF RIGHTS

If one of the crucial problems with judicial interpretations of the Charter of Rights is the ambiguity of the rights it enumerates, an obvious solution is to define these rights more precisely. This seems to have been the intention of the 'distinct society' clause of the Meech Lake Accord, which would have extended the interpretation of section 1 of the Charter in Quebec in matters relating to the protection of the French language.[34] Similarly, an effort was made in the Charlottetown Accord to expand section 1 by instructing the courts to interpret the Charter with Quebec's distinctive character and Canada's multicultural nature in mind.

Some efforts to introduce new rights into the Charter show a keen awareness of the dangers of constitutionally entrenching rights that have been written to sound grand rather than to be easily justiciable. The Reform Party's proposed property rights amendment is a good example. The wording of the amendment is deliberately narrow, calling for the 'right of every person to the use and enjoyment of property, both real and personal, and the right not to be deprived thereof except by due process of law [and] unless that law provides for just and timely compensation.' This is less inspiring but also a good deal less nebulous than the right to 'life, liberty and property' that nearly made its way into the American Declaration of Independence. The precise wording is designed to prevent the right from being interpreted by the courts to limit environmental or social legislation, to deny the right to collective bargaining, or to oppose native land claims.[35]

This is reminiscent of the situation in the United States, where every constitutional amendment enacted since the Bill of Rights (except the Fourteenth and Fifteenth Amendments) has been so clearly and narrowly worded 'that legislatures simply do not contravene the principles they contain'.[36]

However, as in the United States, there is no way of undoing the vaguely worded rights already in the Charter. The prospect of constitutional amendments successfully modifying either section 1 or any of the rights in sections 2–23 now seems remote, with two failed constitutional accords behind us and the present Prime Minister determined to keep the constitution 'in the refrigerator'. Therefore this solution appears to have little utility.

CATEGORY NO. 3: SOLUTIONS BASED ON CHANGES TO THE APPOINTMENT AND TENURE OF JUDGES

The emphasis of solutions in this category is on making the court system more representative of the will of the people. One of the best-known proposals for changes in the appointment processes is David Beatty's suggestion that Canada adopt nominating procedures similar to those employed in Germany, where each of the two houses of the federal parliament has complete control over half the appointments to the country's supreme court. Beatty rejects as inadequate the American system, in which the Senate is empowered to turn down a presidential nominee but not to make nominations of its own, since the real power in the appointment process lies with the nominator rather than with the ratifier. Quoting American constitutional scholar Laurence Tribe, he warns that any American president 'with any skill and a little luck can . . . with fair success, build the court of his dreams'.[37] Instead, Beatty suggests that

> the West German model could either be transplanted in its entirety, or adapted as required, to the federal scene. A committee of the House of Commons, for example, could easily be struck to undertake the search, screening, and selection of candidates for appointment to the Court. . . . [H]owever, in order to maximize the democratic integrity of the Court, it would clearly be preferable if . . . the provinces were involved directly.[38]

Beatty also recommends that changes be made to justices' tenure, since this would keep them from falling behind the times or representing points of view more in keeping with those of the long-departed prime minister who appointed them than with views currently held by most of the Canadian public. He observes that members of supreme courts in most European countries are appointed for fixed terms averaging between 9 and 12 years. The German system, which he seems to prefer, uses 12-year non-renewable terms.[39]

Fixed tenure turns out to be a fairly common proposal. Donald Smiley once proposed that the constitution should be amended to replace the mandatory retirement age of 75 with a requirement that the median age of justices should not exceed 60. Every time another judge celebrated his or her sixtieth birthday, the oldest member of the court would be required to step down in favour of an appointee under the age of 60.[40] Like Beatty's proposal, this is intended to keep the court from becoming out of step with society.

Michael Mandel devotes an entire chapter of his book, *The Charter of Rights and the Legalization of Politics in Canada* to a review of the literature on what he calls 'minimizing the unrepresentative nature of judicial review'. His conclusion is that despite the ingenuity of Smiley and others it will never be possible to produce a Supreme Court that is truly representative. Partly that is because most of the credible candidates for judicial appointment are wealthy white males. He asks, 'How far can representativeness go? Judges still have to be lawyers with some prominence in the profession, and the profession is still almost entirely the domain of the white and the upper class.'[41]

There is some truth in this. When a proposal was made during the negotiations that eventually produced the Charlottetown Accord to reserve one seat on the Supreme Court for an aboriginal Canadian, it was discovered that there were fewer than 10 candidates who either qualified to meet the chief technical criterion for appointment (ten years' service at a provincial bar or on the bench of a lower court) or who would qualify in the foreseeable future. Moreover, even a superficial examination of the proposals for changing the appointment process reveal that they would probably do little to change the representativeness of the courts. For example, Beatty's proposal to appoint judges for 12-year terms would change nothing at all. Since 1875, the average term served by a Canadian Supreme Court justice has been 13.2 years. Among judges appointed since the mandatory retirement age was imposed, the average length of term has been 11.4 years.[42]

Solutions in this category tend to focus on making the court more representative, which means in practice that these solutions attempt to make the court less likely to place itself in opposition to the legislative arm of government. But this begs the vital question. Is not an independent judiciary, which is capable of single-handedly opposing the wishes of parliamentary majorities, the whole point of judicial review? Presumably the Supreme Court *should* be composed of individuals whose point of view is in some respects different from that of the people and of the people's elected tribunes.

With this in mind, it is easy to sympathize with Manfredi, who observes that in making changes to the appointment process and the internal workings of the court, Beatty and others are essentially transforming the Supreme Court into another legislative chamber. 'This would give Canada three such bodies, each accountable to the public in a different way . . . . [the] third chamber, to be styled the Supreme Court, would be indirectly accountable to the public through the appointments process.'[43] At the end of all this discussion, one is left with the feeling that nothing has really been achieved. As Manfredi notes, it is true that changes to the system by which appointments are made to the Supreme Court 'may enhance the legitimacy of judicial review, but they cannot legitimate judicial supremacy'.[44]

CATEGORY NO. 4: SOLUTIONS BASED ON THE SECTION 33 OVERRIDE

Authors who regard the problem of judicial supremacy as particularly serious tend to believe that measures designed to make the court function more effectively in its supreme role will simply fail to address the problem of the court's new function in Canadian politics. Their desire to check this supremacy through the use of the Charter's notwithstanding clause, which permits Parliament and the legislatures to override judicial decisions, is explained by Peter Russell:

> In a nutshell, the argument about the substance of decision-making is as follows. Judges are not infallible. They may make decisions about the limits and nature of rights and freedoms which are extremely questionable. There should be some process, more reasoned than court-packing and more accessible than constitutional amendment, through which the justice and wisdom of these decisions can be publicly discussed and possibly rejected. A legislative override clause provides such a process.[45]

On its face, this is a simple enough solution: legislatures that do not approve of judicial decisions rendered under section 2 or Sections 7–15 of the Charter may simply pass a measure re-enacting the statutes nullified by the Court.

Many Charter sceptics therefore feel that section 33 is serviceable in its present form. Michael Mandel, Peter Hogg, Rainer Knopff, and F.L. Morton each have specific misgivings about the form or wording of the override, but nevertheless assert that legislatures should feel free to use the section, as now worded, when they feel that the courts have made a decision that is not in the public interest.[46]

From a strictly legal point of view, this argument is solid, but politically it is impractical. The problem, of course, is one of legitimacy. Even as the Charter was being debated in late 1981 there was substantial opposition to the inclusion of an override, which was thought by its opponents to nullify the rights laid out in the Charter. One MP even voted against the Constitution Act in the House of Commons specifically because he objected to the clause.[47] This opposition remained relatively muted when the first use was made of section 33 in a 1986 Saskatchewan law.[48] The Lévesque government's inclusion of a section 33 provision in each law it passed after 1982 did not help the section's reputation outside the province, but the real crisis of legitimacy for section 33 did not come until 1988, when it was used to pass the Bourassa government's new sign law, Bill 178, notwithstanding its violation of the Charter right to freedom of speech.

After this date, the notwithstanding clause became the constitutional *bête noire*, not only of strong civil libertarians, but also of most English-speaking Canadians. The risks involved in invoking the override, which had seemed so slight to Premier Grant Devine of Saskatchewan in 1986, shot up exponentially. Any politician who dared to use the clause now, or even to mention it in a favourable light, risked being branded an enemy of human rights. By 1993 the clause had become so repugnant to most English-speakers that even the Bourassa Liberals—who had lost the support of anglophone voters as a result of their use of the clause—chose to enact a new, milder sign law under which section 33 would not have to be invoked, rather than to use the clause to re-enact Bill 178.

The crisis of legitimacy for the clause has been so profound that one scholar has gone so far as to predict that Canada's next great constitutional battle will be fought over amending the Charter to remove section 33. But since the section offers the only realistic method by which other actors in society can hope to counteract judicial supremacy, some Charter sceptics have set themselves the task of seeking a method by which it can be used without causing a crisis of legitimacy for the government that invokes it.

Peter Russell argues, in an article entitled 'Standing up for Notwithstanding', that the legitimacy of section 33 might be improved if its limits and hence its ability to be used for the purpose of abusing rights, were circumscribed:

> If we do anything to section 33 of the Charter, we should reform it, not abolish it. There is need to overcome by constitutional amendment that part of the Supreme Court's decision in *Ford [v. A.-g. Quebec]* which permits standard-form overrides without any obligation on the legislature to identify the specific legislative provision which in its judgment needs protection or the right or freedom which in its view should not be given priority.[49]

In another article, Russell and Paul Weiler argue that the section might have more legitimacy if it were amended so that a specific use of the clause would not come into force until it had been enacted twice: once before and once after a general election.[50] The election would therefore become a sort of referendum on the government's specific use of the notwithstanding clause.

Christopher Manfredi suggests that the section's legitimacy could be strengthened if it were modified in two ways. First, as currently worded the section can be used to pre-empt judicial review of statutes. If applied in the manner that the Lévesque government used it in 1982–85, section 33 not only ends the problem of judicial supremacy, but also the possibility of judicial review. Potentially, whole classes of rights wind up being less well protected than they were before 1982.

Second, Manfredi recommends that the section be amended so that court decisions can be overridden only by extraordinary parliamentary majorities. He cites with approval the federal government's 1991 proposal to modify the section so as to require a three-fifths majority rather than a simple majority vote in order to override a court decision.[51]

In general, it is easy to see how these proposals are motivated by genuine considerations of concern for the rule of law and for limiting the dangers of legislative tyranny. It is very difficult, however, to believe that any of them would actually bring sufficient legitimacy to section 33 to permit governments to employ the notwithstanding clause without suffering dire political consequences. Even the authors of these suggestions admit as much. Manfredi, for example, acknowledges that 'none of these changes is likely to satisfy the most adamant opponents of section 33.'[52] Michael Mandel is also unenthusiastic. He notes that any attempt to open an intelligent discussion of the merits of the notwithstanding clause will probably fail, 'since superficiality tends to characterize discussion of the Charter, [and] supporters of s. 33 . . . are far outnumbered by the detractors'.[53] Knopff and Morton are reduced to wishing out loud that Supreme Court justices would more openly admit that their decisions are legislative in character, since this would help to overcome the public's misconception that court decisions represent the impartial voice of the constitution itself.[54]

The politically weak position of the Charter sceptics is shown by the fact that they feel compelled to limit their attempts to reform section 33 to reducing its scope or the ease with which it may be used. They seem to be motivated by the hope that by immediately surrendering some territory to their opponents, they will be able to gain the popular legitimacy that their arguments currently lack. The dynamics of constitutional politics suggest that they will almost certainly fail. Section 33 is certainly widely reviled, but it is not currently the top item on anybody's political agenda. Should it rise to the forefront, the voices of those who advocate limited and practical-minded tinkering with the details of the section will quickly be swept aside by the more charismatic and urgent voices in favour of simply abolishing it altogether. Although he was almost certainly being insincere when he spoke on the issue, the rhetorical power of Brian Mulroney's condemnation of the notwithstanding clause is not quickly forgotten, and could easily be mimicked by more credible spokesmen:

The government of Canada surrendered a notwithstanding clause in 1981–1982, which said, in effect, 'We hereby guarantee Canadians their fundamental right to language, to religion and to association, but, by the way, we forgot to tell you, these fundamental rights can be overridden if the Premier of Prince Edward Island or Saskatchewan or Quebec decides that it is in his interest to take them away. . . .' A constitution that does not protect the inalienable and imprescriptible individual rights of individual Canadians is not worth the paper it is written on.[55]

It is not difficult to imagine how an attempt to amend section 33 could be hijacked. An amendment would require the approval, not only of Parliament, but also of the legislatures of seven provinces containing half of Canada's population. Thus, it could scarcely be attempted without convening a round of first ministers' constitutional meetings. Once the subject of section 33 had been broached, most first ministers would probably choose the politically expedient course of demanding that the override be completely abolished. The premier of Quebec would almost certainly oppose any move to do this, since it would limit his province's autonomy. But he might take advantage of the occasion to present a list of Quebec's historic grievances. Somewhere in the midst of all this activity, it is possible that section 33 might actually be amended in a comprehensible manner. Or it might not.

A SUPERIOR OPTION: DEMOCRATIZING SECTION 33

Since most efforts to reform section 33 seem doomed to snag on the insurmountable twin obstacles of lack of legitimacy and the complexity of the amending formula, an alternative must be sought. One way of overcoming the first hurdle is to invest the override power in some institution other than the legislative arm of government. To overcome the second hurdle, the ambitious goal of actually amending the wording of section 33 in the Constitution Act must be set aside in favour of the more modest but easily attained goal of altering the section legislatively.

It is curious that critics of judicial supremacy have failed to deal with the fact that the chief practical effect of their proposals to re-invigorate section 33 would be to move supreme power from the courts back to the legislatures. No matter what modifications to the section are dreamed up, this transfer will, in greater or lesser degree, still take place. This means that legitimacy will never be brought to the exercise of the override, unless there is a massive shift in public opinion away from the hegemonic belief that judges are wiser adjudicators than politicians.

Such a shift is unlikely to occur, particularly in view of the very poor record that many legislatures in Canada have had of actually representing the popular will. It is by no means clear why the people of any Canadian province would want to entrust the final say over what constitutes freedom of speech, freedom of religion, or 'security of the person' to institutions that cannot balance a budget. After Meech Lake, Charlottetown, and the GST, it is understandable that Canadians might question whether the government they elect one year can be counted on to legislate in a manner in keeping with the will of the people two or three years later. Since no obvious means exists to overcome this suspicion, it is unlikely that Canadians will at any point in the foreseeable future invest their politicians with the legitimacy they would need to make effective use of their section 33 powers.

As the 1992 referendum on the Charlottetown Accord showed, Canadians may be unwilling to vest supreme power in their politicians, but they have no fear of exercising the power to ratify or veto their own fundamental laws by direct means. If Canadians were willing to accept the legitimacy of a popular override on this vast package of constitutional amendments, it is entirely possible that they will feel comfortable using referenda to ratify or veto the Charter interpretations of the Supreme Court, which can carry the weight of de facto amendments to the constitution.

It would be an easy matter for Ottawa or any provincial government to draft a parliamentary resolution declaring its intention to exercise its section 33 rights only where so authorized by the people of the country (or province) by means of a referendum on the law in question. The resolution could state that if any law of that jurisdiction were struck down by the courts as infringing on rights guaranteed under the Charter, the offending provisions would automatically be submitted to the electorate for their consideration at the time of the next general election. Following such a combined referendum and election the new government would find itself under a moral obligation to use section 33 to re-enact all laws approved by the electorate and to let stand any court decisions not marked for override by the voters.

The Supreme Court has been striking down laws at the rate of 3.3 provincial statutes and 4.6 federal statutes each year.[56] This means that at the end of the average four-year life of a provincial government, voters in a typical province could expect to face between one and three referendum questions. The number of questions put to the electorate at every federal election would obviously be unmanageably high unless a mechanism were included in the override to permit the number to be whittled down. For example, a parliamentary committee could be charged with the job of selecting a set number of the most important statutes (say five, for the sake of argument) from among the 15 to 20 struck down by the courts during the term of a typical government, to be placed on the ballot at the time of the next election. Alternatively, referenda could be held at two-year intervals, as they are in many American states.

During the period between the handing down of any court decision that struck down a law and the successful use of the democratic override to review this decision, the judgment would of course remain in effect. This means that the electorate would have up to four or five years to assess the practical effects of each judgment, and could vote on it with greater insight (at least at the practical level) than was ever available to the judges who wrote the judgment.

This is the outline of the democratic override in its simplest form. Various provisions could be added to improve this basic model. For example, it might be desirable to emulate the Swiss referendum and initiative law, which permits two options to be placed on the ballot. Swiss voters then choose between two alternative laws: one or the other may be accepted, or both may be rejected, but only one can become the law of the land.[57] This could be done with regard to laws ruled invalid by the courts. The legislature might choose to present the voters with the old law, as well as with a redrafted alternative that perhaps makes an effort to conform in full or in part with the judges' interpretation of the Charter. Ratification of the redrafted law or the rejection of both the old and the new options by the electorate would signal a popular acceptance of the judicial interpretation of the relevant Charter rights. Ratification of the old law in unchanged form would send a clear message to the courts that their interpretation of the Charter is not in accord with that of the public.

If it were successful in returning legitimacy to section 33, the democratic override would certainly reduce the power of the courts to make arbitrary judgments as to the meanings emanating from the penumbras of various vaguely drafted Charter rights.

This is only one advantage of the override. A democratic override would also serve a vital purpose by educating the judiciary as to the community standards at work in the various provinces. As time went by and the override was repeatedly exercised, a body of evidence would be built, indicating for the benefit of the courts what constitutes a 'reasonable limit' on freedoms, such as is 'demonstrably justified in a free and democratic society'. Since the voting patterns would be different in each province that had chosen to exercise a democratic override provision, it would be possible to apply section 1 of the Charter differently to each province, according to the political culture of that province, as revealed by its voting record. The homogenizing influence of the Charter, of which Hogg and others warn,[58] would be reduced to levels more likely to be acceptable to Canadians.

At present, it is not an easy task for the justices of the Supreme Court to determine whether a law is genuinely deserving of section 1 exemption. This is particularly true when provincial laws are being challenged, since it is often the case that none of the judges come from the province in question. Judges are therefore faced with the choice of from time to time erring on the side of extending the definition of rights in a manner offensive to community standards, or of erring on the side of restricting rights through the too frequent or too extensive invocation of section 1. It appears that the court has chosen to err on the side of repeatedly broadening the definitions of rights, since in its first 100 decisions, section 1 was employed only 15 per cent of the time.[59]

A democratic override would bring an end to this problem. Whenever a vote was held, the electorate would be, in practice, redefining Section 1. Given that the debate would be free and the vote democratic, one can scarcely imagine a more suitable way of demonstrably justifying what constitutes a reasonable limit on rights in a free and democratic society. Just as, according to one Supreme Court justice, rights enumerated in the Charter gain meaning when the courts 'breathe life' into them,[60] the electorate would be able to breathe life into section 1.

The prospect of greatly expanding the scope of direct democracy raises some obvious concerns. The first is the danger that voters will be overwhelmed by the number of questions on their ballots and consequently will be unable to vote intelligently on any of them. When critics of direct democracy raise this objection, they normally do so by citing the example of the desperately confusing election referenda staged regularly in California. However, as laid out in this essay, the democratic override would lead to a situation in which the average ballot in a federal election would contain only six questions (five questions linked to the override and one vote for the MP). At the provincial level, the override would lead to ballots with no more than four questions, including the vote for the local MLA, and often as few as two questions.

This compares very favourably indeed to the situation in California, where each voter is called upon regularly to vote simultaneously for the president, the governor, a federal representative, a federal senator, a state representative, a state senator, elected judges, and a host of state, county, and special-purpose district representatives in addition to casting ballots on a large number of referendum questions. In November 1990, voters in Los Angeles County were allotted 10 minutes each in the voting booths to cast more than 100 votes at the state, federal, and local levels.[61] By contrast, voters in Switzerland's moderate and well-managed system of direct democracy cast ballots on 250 referendum questions between 1948 and 1990 at the federal level alone.[62] This amounts to an average of six referendum questions each year, or one every two months, for 40 years on end. The voters have had no difficulty acting intelligently on the majority of the questions put to them in this manner.

Of course, the most obvious objection to the extension of direct democracy is the potential for mob rule. James Madison's objection that systems of direct democracy 'have ever been spectacles of turbulence and contention' remains a potent fear today. The record, however, suggests that when voters are able to vote directly on complex issues, they educate themselves on the issues sufficiently to vote on the basis of a consistent set of values. They may not grasp all the subtleties of each measure before them (a problem also suffered by many elected lawmakers!), but they absorb enough to be able to cast their ballots as intelligent fiscal conservatives, social democrats, civil libertarians, etc. The process of self-education reduces the opportunity for politicians to practice demagoguery on an uninformed electorate.

As a result, the outcome of direct democracy in Switzerland has been the opposite of mob rule. Writing of the Swiss situation, Charles Blankart observes, 'Direct democracy through referenda tempers, rather than accentuates, majoritarian dictatorship. [Over time, it] contributes to the creation of a near consensus among the parties and interest groups involved.'[63] Bruno Frey and Iris Bohnet show that the use of referenda in Switzerland has permitted the opening of public dialogue on matters that were formerly out of bounds and has permitted moderate compromises to be developed in policy areas that had formerly been highly polarized.[64] In his book *Direct Democracy in Canada* Patrick Boyer shows how the 1942 referendum on conscription had the effect of producing a compromise where none had seemed possible previously: by showing the deep divisions in Canadian society, it permitted Prime Minister King 'to successfully prosecute the war effort and delay bringing in conscription for overseas service for two years'.[65] Similarly, the 1992 referendum on the constitution had the effect of defusing tensions that had threatened to rip the country apart. By contrast to this record, the decisions of the Supreme Court on issues as diverse as abortion and Quebec's sign law have repeatedly stirred up contention and caused polarization rather than consensus.

At the federal level there are numerous cases where the public interest would probably have been served by the democratic override process. These include the *Keegstra* case, in which hate literature laws were struck down on the basis of the freedom of speech provisions in Section 2(b) of the Charter, the *Singh* case, in which the section 7 right not to be deprived of 'life, liberty and security of the person . . . except in accordance with the principles of fundamental justice' was interpreted as giving each refugee claimant the right to appear before the body determining his or her status, and the *Askov* case, in which the section 11(b) right to a speedy trial was interpreted as meaning that all charges should be dropped against defendants who are not brought to trial within a limited time.

There are also many provincial cases where the democratic override would have proved useful. In some, like the mandatory retirement laws struck down in *Harrison v. U.B.C.* and *Stoffman v. Vancouver General Hospital*, referenda on the issue would cause a public dialogue on an important issue that has not gained enough public attention. Likewise, if voters had been given the opportunity to vote on the Lord's Day Act (struck down in 1985) or the Ontario Retail Business Holidays Act (struck down in *R. v. Videoflicks*, 1984, and rehabilitated in *Edwards Books v. the Queen*, 1986), they would have been given the opportunity to show whether or not they actually favoured a common day of rest. Under a democratic override on the Swiss model, voters could have been given a choice between the old, religiously based law, a new law providing for a non-sectarian common day of rest, and the wide-open shopping that has in practice been imposed by the courts.

The democratic override could also prove effective in defusing much more divisive situations arising from Supreme Court Charter decisions. This can be shown by reviewing the crisis precipitated by the court's ruling in *Ford v. A.-g. Quebec*, which struck down the sign law aspects of Bill 101. There is little need to review the calamity that arose from the ruling. Robert Bourassa's Liberal government had been bracing for the court's decision for months. Within days of the ruling, a new sign law, Bill 178, had been introduced in the

National Assembly. The new law contained some feeble hints at compromise with Quebec's anglophone community, but because Bill 101 had become such a potent symbol of Quebec's autonomy, it was politically necessary for Bourassa to appease the francophone majority by incorporating a clause in the law invoking section 33 of the Charter.

In English Canada the anger at this move knew no bounds. Bourassa's anglophone cabinet ministers resigned *en masse*.[66] In the subsequent provincial election, English-speaking voters turned away from the Liberals to the newly founded one-issue Equality Party; in ridings where the Equality Party ran candidates, two-thirds of anglophone voters chose it over the Liberals.[67] In Ontario, the timing of Bill 178 coincided with the introduction of the Peterson government's French Language Services Act. As a protest against the simultaneous expansion of French language rights in Ontario and the suppression of English language rights in Quebec, 12 per cent of all Ontario municipalities declared themselves unilingual. Meanwhile, the ratification of the Meech Lake Accord by the Manitoba legislature was halted as a direct response to the new law. The death of Meech Lake and the subsequent near-breakup of Confederation can, therefore, be directly attributed to Bourassa's ham-fisted use of section 33.

It is difficult to imagine that any process could have been more divisive than the one that grew out of the Bill 178 experience. Recourse to a democratic override, had one existed, certainly would have been less harsh. For one thing, a democratic override would have slowed down the whole process of creating a new law. Bourassa's Liberals had been forced to table their new law within days of the Supreme Court's decision because delaying any further would have permitted the Parti Québécois to seize control of the signs issue for its own partisan advantage. As a result, the short-sighted calculations of politicians subverted any chance for dialogue between Quebec's linguistic communities.

This would not have happened had the province adopted the policy of submitting all uses of the override to the electorate at the time of general elections. A year passed between the handing down of the Supreme Court's decision and the provincial election of 25 September 1989. In this interim period, parliamentary committees could have met, commissioners could have toured the province, passions could have cooled and a new law could have been drafted that embodied a compromise between all sides. The new law might even have looked very much like Bill 86, the 1993 law that has quietly replaced Bill 178.

Throughout the period in which a new law was being drafted, the provincial Liberals could have protected themselves from the wrath of the nationalists by observing that the voters would get their chance at the polls to choose either to implement the new law or to re-enact the overridden provisions of Bill 101. On election day itself, the government would have been insulated from any need to defend either the new or the old version of the language law, because the voters would have known that whatever party they elected would be obliged to adopt the language law selected by the people. By separating the politicians from the most heated issues and by slowing down the legislative process, the democratic override would have the effect of reducing the vote-winning potential of demagoguery for politicians seeking re-election. The critical mass necessary for majoritarian tyranny would therefore have dissipated.

CONCLUSION

The democratic override is far from being a complete solution to the problem of judicial supremacy. Its most obvious weakness is that it cannot be used to consult public opinion on the rights entrenched in sections 3 to 6 and 16 to 23 of the Charter, which are exempt from the existing legislative override. Nonetheless, it is probably the only realistic balance that Canadians can hope to apply to the process of judicial review. It would not be open to majoritarian tyranny, as is the unamended section 33, and it would not suffer from the consequent problems of legitimacy suffered by the notwithstanding clause in its present form. A democratic override would permit federalism and judicial review to exist in a comfortable balance and might even serve to open up to civilized debate certain areas of public policy that today seem hopelessly divisive.

As well, a democratic override could be introduced and exercised in any individual province without recourse to the messy seven-province formula for amending the Constitution Act, which could thus remain safely at the back of the icebox. The override could be enacted in any province by means of a simple resolution of the legislature and could be constitutionally entrenched for that province by means of an identical motion passed by Parliament in Ottawa under section 43 of the Constitution Act, which requires only the assent of Parliament and a single legislature. Similarly, Ottawa could unilaterally adopt the democratic override for the purposes of federal legislation by means of a motion passed under section 44 of the Constitution Act.

If the override were found to be popular and successful in one province, its use might well spread to other provinces. The experiences learned in the first province that adopted the override might permit other provinces to develop more refined versions, with some of the wrinkles ironed out.

This is how federalism is supposed to work. One constituent unit builds upon the experiences of the other, adapting its experiments to its own peculiar needs. This would be a refreshing change from the high-tension brinkmanship of constitutional amendments in Canada over the past 15 years.

NOTES

1 The concept was first raised by Chief Justice Duff in *Alberta Press Case* (1938), elaborated by Justice Abbott in *Switzman v. Elbling* (1957), and later dismissed by Justice Beetz in *A.-G. Canada and Dupond v. Montreal* (1978). The implied bill of rights is discussed briefly in Christopher Manfredi, *Judicial Politics and the Charter:*

Canada and the Paradox of Liberal Constitutionalism (Toronto: McClelland and Stewart, 1993), 31, 32 and in Peter Hogg, *Constitutional Law of Canada* (Toronto: Carswell, 1985) 636–8.

2 See Max Frenkel, 'The Communal Basis of Swiss Liberty', *Publius* 23, no. 2 (Spring 1993): 68, 69.

3 Government of Canada pamphlet cited in Michael Mandel, *The Charter of Rights and the Legalization of Politics in Canada* (Toronto: Wall and Thompson, 1989), 35.

4 'Publius' (Alexander Hamilton, John Jay, and James Madison), *The Federalist* (New York: Modern Library, 1937), 504. Emphasis in the original.

5 Ibid., 507.

6 Ibid., 508.

7 This is the phrase employed by Mandel in the *Legalization of Politics*, 48.

8 J.G. Castel, 'The Canadian Charter of Rights and Freedoms', *Canadian Bar Review* 61, no. 1 (1983): 1.

9 Alexis de Tocqueville, *Democracy in America*, trans. George Lawrence, ed. J.P. Mayer (New York: Harper and Row, 1966), 74.

10 Ronald Dworkin, 'Equality, Democracy, and Constitution: We the People in Court', *Alberta Law Review* 28, no. 2 (1990): 325. Emphasis in the original.

11 Mandel, *Legalization of Politics*, 52–3. Emphasis in the original.

12 Richard Sigurdson, 'Left- and Right-Wing Charterphobia in Canada: A Critique of the Critics', *International Journal of Canadian Studies* 7–8, (Spring-Fall 1993): 96.

13 Sigurdson, 'Charterphobia', 98.

14 Ibid., 102.

15 Mandel, *Legalization of Politics*, 55.

16 Andrew Petter, 'Immaculate Deception: The Charter's Hidden Agenda', *The Advocate* 45: 861.

17 Andrew Petter and Alan Hutchinson, 'Private Rights/Public Wrongs: The Liberal Lie of the Charter', *University of Toronto Law Journal* 38: 292.

18 Mandel, *Legalization of Politics*, 239.

19 Peter Russell, 'The Effect of a Charter of Rights on the Policy-Making Role of Canadian Courts', *Canadian Public Policy* 25, no. 1: 26.

20 Rainer Knopff, *Human Rights and Social Technology: The New War on Discrimination* (Ottawa: Carleton University Press, 1989), 213.

21 'Court Favourites', editorial, *The Globe and Mail*, 9 Nov. 1993.

22 F.L. Morton, 'The Politics of Rights', *The Literary Review of Canada*, May 1993, 14.

23 Manfredi, *Judicial Power*, 214–15.

24 Lorraine Weinrib, 'The Supreme Court of Canada and Section One of the Charter', *Supreme Court Law Review* 10 (1988): 486.

25 See 'The Cash Street Kids', *The Economist*, 28 Aug. 1993, 23–5, and Blake Hurst, 'Everything's Up to Date', *Reason*, Feb. 1992, 47.

26 David Beatty, *Talking Heads and the Supremes: The Canadian Production of Constitutional Review* (Toronto: Carswell, 1990), iii.

27 Ibid., 273–4.

28 I am indebted to Richard Schultz for pointing out that this proposal would impose a system similar to that employed by the Judicial Committee of the Privy Council in its pre-1949 constitutional decisions, and for drawing to my attention the fact that this method is regarded by some sources as having been problematic.

29 F.L. Morton, 'The Politics of Rights', 14–15.

30 Dale Gibson, 'Judges as Legislators: Not Whether but How', *Alberta Law Review* 25 (1987): 249–63.

31 See his scathing review of the history of judicial partiality in 'The Real Law of the Constitution', *Alberta Law Review* 28 (1990): 358–83.

32 Bertha Wilson, 'Decision-making in the Supreme Court', *University of Toronto Law Journal* 36 (1986): 242–4.

33 Andrew Heard, 'The Charter in the Supreme Court of Canada: The Importance of Which Judges Hear an Appeal', *Canadian Journal of Political Science* 24 (1991): 304–7.

34 F.L. Morton, Glenn Solomon, Ian McNish, and David Poulton, 'Judicial Nullification of Statutes under the Charter of Rights and Freedoms, 1982–1988', *Alberta Law Review* 23, no. 2 (1990): 424.

35 Reform Party of Canada, 'Why Do Reformers Want to Entrench Property Rights in the Constitution?' Caucus Issue Statement no. 21, 22 Feb. 1992.

36 Manfredi, *Judicial Politics*, 215.

37 Beatty, *Talking Heads*, 266.

38 Ibid. This system more closely follows the procedure used in the *Bundestag*, where appointments must be approved by a two-thirds majority of a special committee, than the procedure used in the *Bundesrat*, where the assembly as a whole must give a two-thirds vote in favour of ratifying each nomination.

39 Ibid., 271.

40 Donald Smiley, *The Canadian Charter of Rights and Freedoms* (Toronto: Ontario Economic Council, 1981), 55.

41 Mandel, *Legalization of Politics*, 43.

42 To obtain these totals, I added together the terms served by all Supreme Court justices (excluding those who are still serving) and divided the total by the number of justices. Source: Ian Bushnell, *The Captive Court: A Study of the Supreme Court of Canada* (Montreal and Kingston: McGill-Queen's University Press), 496–7.

43 Manfredi, *Judicial Power*, 192.

44 Ibid. Emphasis in the original.

45   Peter Russell, 'Standing Up for Notwithstanding', *Alberta Law Review* 29, no. 2 (1991): 295.

46   See, for example, Mandel, *Legalization of Politics*, 75-81; Peter Hogg, 'Federalism Fights the Charter,' in David Shugarman and Reginald Whitaker, *Federalism and Political Community: Essays in Honour of Donald Smiley* (Toronto: Broadview, 1989), 251–3; and Rainer Knopff and F.L. Morton, *Charter Politics* (Scarborough, Ont.: Nelson, 1992), 232–3. Knopff and Morton hint at a solution that would make the section 33 override more legitimate, although it would not take the direct route of modifying the section. They quote Roger Gibbins, who observes that if Canada's legislative process had more internal checks and balances, its decisions would have more popular legitimacy. This legitimacy presumably would extend to decisions to employ section 33. See *Charter Politics*, 232.

47   Svend Robinson of the New Democratic Party.

48   The political consequences of the Devine government's use of section 33 are described in F.L. Morton, 'The Political Impact of the Canadian Charter of Rights and Freedoms', *Canadian Journal of Political Science* 20, no. 1 (Mar. 1987): 45–9.

49   Russell, 'Standing Up for Notwithstanding', 302.

50   Peter Russell and Paul Weiler, 'Don't Scrap Override Clause—It's a Very Canadian Solution', *The Toronto Star*, 4 June 1989.

51   Manfredi, *Judicial Power*, 208–10.

52   Ibid., 209.

53   Mandel, *Legalization of Politics*, 75.

54   Knopff and Morton, *Charter Politics*, 231.

55   Brian Mulroney, House of Commons Debates, 6 April 1989, p. 153. For questions as to Mulroney's sincerity, see Mordecai Richler, *Oh Canada! Oh Quebec!: Requiem for a Divided Country* (Toronto: Penguin, 1992), 32. Richler notes that Mulroney was passionate in his condemnation of the section when speaking in English in the House, but curiously restrained in his French-language comments delivered to the media the same day.

56   This calculation is for the 1982–8 period. Morton, Solomon, McNish, and Poulton calculate that 80 decisions of the Supreme Court and the provincial courts of appeal have struck down all or part of a law or regulation, but that on a number of occasions separate decisions have struck down the same statute more than once. This leads to a total of 23 provincial statutes and 32 federal statutes under sections 2 and 7–15. Court of appeal decisions are included in their total only when they have not been followed by a successful appeal to the Supreme Court of Canada. See their article 'Judicial Nullification of Statutes', 398–405, 407–8.

57   The reality is a little more complex. This process applies to constitutional amendments but not to ordinary laws, which remain the monopoly of Parliament. However, the absence of judicial review at the federal level means that only a referendum can invalidate a law, by the process of passing a new constitutional amendment that clearly renders the existing law void. In short, the difference between constitutional and non-constitutional legislation in Switzerland is not so great as it first appears to be.

58   See, among others, Hogg, 'Federalism Fights the Charter', 249–50, 260.

59   Manfredi, *Judicial Power*, 38.

60   The reference is to Justice Dickson's comment, in *Mahé v. Alberta*, that the court must 'breathe life' into section 23 of the Charter, possibly by applying 'novel solutions' to the problem of minority official language education.

61   Bruno Frey and Iris Bohnet, 'Democracy by Competition: Referenda and Federalism in Switzerland', *Publius* 23, no. 2 (Spring 1993): 77.

62   Ibid., 73.

63   Charles Blankart, 'Public Choice View of Swiss Liberty', *Publius* 23, no. 2 (Spring 1993): 90-1.

64   Frey and Bohnet, 'Democracy by Competition', 76.

65   Patrick Boyer, *Direct Democracy in Canada: The History and Future of Referendums* (Toronto: Dundurn, 1992): 251. Emphasis in the original.

66   Three ministers resigned. Georges Mathews discusses the reasons why John Ciaccia, the Italian minister in Bourassa's cabinet, did not join his anglophone colleagues. See Mathews' book, *Quiet Resolution: Quebec's Challenge to Canada* (Toronto: Summerhill, 1990), 116.

67   For a description of the rise of Equality and its connection to Bourassa's use of the section 33 override in Bill 178, see Reed Scowen, *A Different Vision: The English of Quebec in the 1990s* (Toronto: Maxwell Macmillan), 101–2, 134.

PART III

Constitutional Theory

11

Theoretical Perspectives on Constitutional Reform in Canada

Barry Cooper

Now that the dust has begun to settle on the latest round of mega-constitutional discussions, Canadians can take stock of how, and perhaps why, the discussions failed and what, if anything, can be done. Recently several books have appeared that attempt to give an account of what went wrong. In this chapter I would like to suggest what light might be shed on this problem by political philosophy. I begin from the (surely uncontested) fact that Canadians have, to date, proved themselves incapable of establishing a constitutional regime embodying a reasonable degree of coherence.

It is true enough that Canadians have legal constitutional documents to which they can refer, a phalanx of highly trained constitutional experts, and a complex of more or less functioning political institutions. However, these are mechanisms for governance. They are both external and elemental, and as will become clear soon enough, Canada's constitutional problems are concerned less with questions of law than with the purpose or meaning of the country. One must consider the substance and not merely the form of the regime if one is to understand properly the extent of Canada's constitutional failures.

In one of the best analyses of what the author called mega-constitutional politics, Peter Russell discussed indirectly the question of constitutional substance when he asked the sobering question: Can Canadians Be a Sovereign People?[1] The origin of Russell's book, as with so many good books by scholars, was in the classroom. He was team-teaching a course at the University of

Toronto with the distinguished American constitutional scholar, Walter Berns, on the constitutions of Canada and the United States. One fine day Berns remarked, 'Peter, you Canadians have not yet constituted yourselves a people.' Russell was troubled by the remark and, as the years of futile constitutional negotiations went on, concluded that Berns was right.

But what did Berns mean? The word, constitution, is ambiguous in so far as it means both the act of constituting as well as the rules of governance that have been constituted. Regarding the latter meaning, things seem relatively clear and straightforward: constitutional government is government limited by law, chiefly by the safeguarding of civil liberties through obligatory procedural guarantees. The only form of government that, in this sense, is nonconstitutional is tyranny, but that sense of constitution is not what Berns meant and not what Russell took him to mean. Berns's usage bore the marks of his homeland, and more particularly, of the eighteenth-century founding of the American republic. His meaning was close to that enunciated by Tom Paine in *The Rights of Man*. 'A constitution,' said Paine, 'is not the act of a government, but of people constituting a government.' Later in this same tract Paine provided an alternative formulation: 'A constitution is a thing *antecedent* to a government, and a government is only the creature of a constitution.' This was Berns's meaning, and, as Russell observed, 'Canadians have never squarely faced the question whether they share enough in common to form a single people consenting to a common constitution.'

Now that Canadians clearly have failed in their attempt at constituting a regime it may be time to face squarely the question Russell has raised. The success of what the Americans quite properly call their founding is proof that they have been capable of forming a single people consenting to a common constitution. Canadians, never having undergone the experience of revolution, have never had the experience of making a sharp break with an imperial power and have never known the difficulties of founding a regime either. Nor, of course, have they experienced that 'public happiness', as John Adams called it, of founding a successful regime. On the contrary, throughout Canadian history (or at least until *very* recently) we have been particularly proud of our desire to maintain a symbolic continuity with the past, with the Crown, the Empire, and the Commonwealth. Among other things, it was said it was the British connection that distinguished Canadians from Americans.[2] It is for this reason, among others, that Canadians have on occasion turned to British constitutional history for insight into their own. After all, the Preamble to the British North America Act declared that the confederating provinces 'have expressed their Desire to be federally united into One Dominion under the Crown of the United Kingdom of Great Britain and Ireland, with a Constitution similar in Principle to that of the United Kingdom'.

The British, or more properly, the English, experience of constitutional development is important not simply because of Canada's historic legal and symbolic relationship to the imperial centre, but because English institutions have shaped modern notions of representation, parliamentary government, and constitutional government generally. An examination of the development of English institutions and of the successful creation of constitutional government will bring to light a pattern that can help us understand Canadian failures. Our concern is not with the constitutional history of England but with the interaction of sentiments, institutions, and symbolic and legal formulae that provide a meaning to the well-known events.

In England but also more generally, modern constitutionalism did not develop simply through the evolution of political institutions. Rather, political institutions were given a 'constitutional' meaning through the infusion of sentiments, doctrines, and purposes that had developed elsewhere. Typically, however, studies of the 'growth of constitutionalism' apply one or another a priori definition to the historical subject matter. One such approach is to declare that a constitutional order of government operates by means of a written constitution and is limited by a bill of rights. This approach leads to the unfortunate conclusion that England has no constitutional government. A second approach is less strict: governments are constitutional if they obey the rule of law and obtain the consent of the governed. But this one has the equally unfortunate consequence that nearly every government except the most arbitrary and oppressive tyranny would be included. Both approaches stress the existence or operation of the techniques of constitutional government: systems of representation, constitutional documents, regular elections, bills of rights, and so on. That such approaches obscure essential features of constitutionalism is indicated by the observation that political order is not simply one of law and procedure but also of purpose and meaning. In *The New Science of Politics*, Eric Voegelin addressed this problem.[3] 'Human society,' Voegelin wrote,

> is not merely a fact, or an event, in the external world to be studied by an observer like a natural phenomenon. Though it has externality as one of its important components, it is as a whole a little world, a cosmion, illuminated with meaning from within by the human beings who continuously create and bear it as the mode and condition of their self-realization. It is illuminated through an elaborate symbolism, in various degrees of compactness and differentiation—from rite, through myth, to theory—and this symbolism illuminates it with meaning in so far as the symbols make the internal structure of such a cosmion, the relations between its members and groups of members, as well as its existence as a whole, transparent for the mystery of human existence.[4]

The external aspect of politics exists because human beings participate bodily in the biological and physical world. A political order can accordingly be dissolved through the dispersion of the bodies of its members so that communication is impossible, through the enslaving or exterminating of its members, or perhaps by the destruction of only its politically visible members.

As far as the theory of political science is concerned, the physical existence of human society is less significant than the self-illumination of society by means of the symbolism mentioned above. In particular, ritual and myth provide a means for people to participate in the inner meaning of their social order, as well as in meanings that transcend their social order and that are conventionally referred to as religion.

Here one must make a distinction between the symbols of social self-interpretation and the theoretical symbols, or concepts, of political science. Following the procedure developed by Aristotle in the *Politics* (1280a ff), the latter are refined from the former by means of rational analysis. That is, symbols that express pre-theoretical meanings are part of the political reality studied by means of the theoretical concepts of political science. A constitution, I will argue, is both a symbol that expresses an important element of political reality and a term that can be critically clarified to the point that it can bear a limited theoretical meaning in political science.

If one considers only the external aspects of Canada's constitutional order, as has been done in political debate, in the media, and to a surprisingly great extent by our constitutional experts, one finds various proposals for altering or establishing political institutions, for new legal guidelines to assist in judicial interpretation, and so on. The cognitive value of much of this work is not negligible, but it assumes that the existence of Canada can be taken for granted, and few, if any, questions are asked about what makes Canada exist or what its political existence means. Even the controversial 'distinct society' clause in the Meech Lake Accord, section 2(b), declared that 'Quebec constitutes *within Canada* a distinct society.' Likewise, provisions that recognize the 'inherent right' of self-government that resides with aboriginal communities also specify that this right exists within Canada. The legal provisions of successive constitutional proposals, from the Victoria Charter of 1971 to the Charlottetown Accord of 1992 are, at least in principle, relatively clear, unambiguous, and unproblematic. It is for this reason that I have referred to the descriptive analyses as elemental. The same adjective would apply equally to most of the narrative accounts of the process of constitutional negotiation and failure. The conclusion to be drawn is that elemental analyses of political institutions, however necessary, provide insight only when the existence of Canada is not questioned. The question posed by Walter Berns to Peter Russell directs our attention to an internal symbolic and substantive, rather than external, elemental, and formal, sense of constitutionalism. That is, Berns's question directs us to consider what might be called questions of political existence.

We may approach the topic of Canada's existence by making the simple observation that at one time Canada did not exist. Some Canadians today fear, and others hope, that before long Canada will cease to exist. For the time being, however, Canada has a government whose legislative and administrative acts are domestically effective. That is, it is a power unit capable of acting both within an identifiable territory and, to a modest degree, outside it as well. Moreover, these actions are necessary to ensure the continued existence of the country. And finally Canada has an internal structure that enables some Canadians to exact obedience from others. This entire process, however, is contingent, not necessary. There is nothing about the existence of Canada that is given as a cosmic fixture. Voegelin has introduced the concepts of representation and articulation to describe 'this process in which human beings form themselves into a society for action'.[5] As a result of political articulation some persons can act on behalf of a society, and these people are its representatives. That is, articulation is the condition of representation in the sense that in order to exist a society must articulate itself, and it does so by producing a representative to act on its behalf.

I noted earlier that the development of English institutions is a model for the creation of constitutional government. The process of articulation from feudal to constitutional representation sheds some light by analogy on Canadian problems. This is not to suggest, as has been done on occasion, that Canada is in any sense a feudal society.

The first step towards the formation of an English political society was taken when the several tenants-in-chief transformed themselves from individual feudatories into the *baronagium*, a commune capable of collective action, as occurred on the occasion of the signing of Magna Carta. The growth of a new community substance was expressed in the act of communal self-constitution, was accompanied by new forms of representation, and was followed by similar acts by knights of the shire, burgesses, and proctors of the lower clergy. When summoned to the assembly of the realm, they all deliberated collegially in the same manner as the barons. The formation of these communes constitutes the process of articulation for action. In contrast, the mechanism of the representation of shires and boroughs by means of delegates, which has received much more attention from historians, is an external technique that inevitably develops when there exists an articulated reality that needs to be represented. In this instance the reality in question was the several newly constituted communes.

Constitutionalism in this context is less a term for the techniques of rule mentioned above than a symbol that expresses a complex of emotions and sentiments that emerged from the experience of constituting the articulate communes as meaningful political realities. Accordingly, the elemental understanding of constitutionalism, with its references to techniques of rule such as parliaments, elections, bills of rights and so on, is incomplete. The British Parliament, for instance, is not merely a mechanism for conducting the political affairs of the nation, but the instrument of action that has developed in tandem with the articulation of English society. As Voegelin remarked, the theoretical point illustrated by the English example is that 'the representatives of the articulate communes when they meet in council form communes of a higher order, ultimately the Parliament of two houses, which understands itself as the representative council of a still larger society, of the realm as a whole.'[6]

In thirteenth-century England the elements of a national unit of action were present in the articulation of the several communes, but there were also centrifugal tendencies.[7] The attendance of the lower clergy was difficult to enforce after the issuance in 1296 of the bull *Clericis Laicos*, which enjoined the lower clergy from paying taxes to the secular authorities; evidently merchants sought to treat separately with the king as well. Nevertheless, by the sixteenth century the amalgamation of the two higher estates, the lords spiritual and temporal, into a single upper house and of the two lower estates, the knights and burgesses, into a single lower house, was complete.

The institutional form of a bicameral legislature integrated the middle class into the English polity and prevented the articulation of a 'third estate', which caused such revolutionary havoc on the Continent. Specifically, the division of the nobility into the peerage and the gentry, and their distribution across both houses, meant that the style of the feudal nobility served as an independent factor in the integration of new political classes. In this way the old feudal liberties eventually were transformed into the liberties of the nation.

One preliminary conclusion to be drawn from the English evidence is that articulation and integration are both required for the formation of a single body politic. Articulation, that is, the growth of communal consciousness to the point where action becomes possible, without the institutional integration of the now articulate communes, is a recipe for fracture. On the other hand, integration without articulation may create the external formalities of a body politic, but it would be one without a substantive meaning. At best such a regime may amount to an alliance in defence of limited common interests. At worst it is simply another name for repression and dependency.

A second preliminary conclusion is that not all bodies politic are capable of constitutional government because not all societies are sufficiently articulated to bear the requisite institutions. The history of 'de-colonization' provides plenty of evidence that the adoption of a constitution is no guarantee of constitutional government, as does the fate of the wonderfully constitutional Weimar Republic. I will return to this question in my general conclusions.

A third preliminary conclusion has already been mentioned and follows from the conceptual distinction between the articulation of society and the devices used to operate such a society. These latter instruments—the written text of the law, the rules governing elections, the rights of citizens, and so on—are means to an end, not autonomous elements of political reality. For example, freedom of expression is rightly considered an essential element of constitutionality; it is given great prominence both in the US Constitution (First Amendment) and in the Canadian Charter (section 2). However, it remains an instrument promoting constitutional order only under conditions of social integration when it serves the purpose of securing consent. Abuse of freedom of expression, through subversive speech, pornography, and so on, is under these circumstances ineffective because society is strongly enough integrated that the disruptive effects of such expression are minimal. On the other hand, in a poorly integrated society, this same freedom of expression can promote distrust, disloyalty, and dissolution.

Using the language of political philosophy, one would say that it is the substantive, as distinct from the formal or procedural, issue of constitutionalism that concerns the articulation of society and the institutional integration of the articulate parts into a unit. In the English development one can see clearly enough the nature of these articulate parts. In the writ of summons of Edward I for the Parliament of 1295, for instance, the sheriff is enjoined to have 'elected' two knights from each country, two citizens from each city, and two burgesses from each borough who may be sent to Westminister with sufficient discretion and powers to act. What is missing is any notion of the people as an articulate community. On the contrary, the weight of representation lay with the king. 'Not only is the realm the king's,' wrote Voegelin,

> but the prelates, the magnates, and the cities are also his. Individual merchants, on the other hand, are not included in the representative symbolism; they are not the king's but always 'of the realm' or 'of the city', that is, of the whole or of an articulate subdivision. Ordinary individual members of the society are plainly 'inhabitants' or 'fellow-citizens of the realm'. The symbol 'people' does not appear as signifying a rank in articulation and representation; it is only used, on occasion, as a synonym for realm in a phrase like the 'common welfare of the realm'.[8]

The people are not, therefore, visible as the ultimate community of individuals. On the contrary, individuals were articulated politically by way of the communes or were of the realm as a whole.

It is important to bear in mind the fact that a person has political status only as a member of his (not her) commune or of the realm when we consider the famous dictum of Edward I, borrowed from the Justinian Code but issued in the writ to the bishops of 1295: 'that what touches all, should be approved by all.' Edward's dictum has, on occasion, been invoked in current constitutional debates.[9] In context, however, it referred to the specific problem of a 'common danger', namely the war preparations of the king of France, that had to be met by means provided in common. Not rights, therefore, but the duty of participation and aid in common affairs, especially the defence of the realm, was intended.[10]

The direction of articulation, from king through feudal communes to the middle classes, is clear. With the passage of the Great Reform Bill in 1832 the poorer sections of society and then women were absorbed into the political realm through the extension of the franchise for the Commons. Critics, beginning with Hegel,[11] have discussed the problem of the articulation of lower-middle-class citizens and of workers. The British 'solution' to this problem, at least before the administration of Mrs Thatcher, has been to idolize the institution of Parliament.[12] The Americans have, to a certain extent, also idolized their own constitutional document along with the virtues of 'Americanism'. Nevertheless, it was an American statesman, Abraham Lincoln, who first indicated that the process of articulation could proceed to the limit of the individual as the representative unit. Such is the significance of his evocative formula, 'government of the people, by the people, for the people', found in his Gettysburg address.[13] As Voegelin remarked, 'the symbol "people" in this formula means successively the articulated political society, its representative, and the membership that is bound by the acts of the representative.'[14] When a society becomes articulated down to the individual, it at the same time becomes representative of itself. Were such conditions to obtain in Canada, a positive response to Peter Russell's question, Can Canadians be a sovereign people? might be given.

The foregoing remarks lead to the conclusion that articulation is the condition for representation, whether in the mode of a king, a king and communes, or a fully differentiated democracy along the lines of Lincoln's evocation. As was noted above, the act of articulation that produces a representative ensures the continued existence of the particular political society. The historical depth of the concept of articulation includes the entire process by which political societies, from polis to empire, national state, republic, and confederation, rise and flourish, and decline and fall.

Many of the themes discussed so far were analysed by 'the most outstanding and original political writer in England in the fifteenth century', and 'the first to write a constitutional treatise in the English language', Sir John Fortescue.[15] Fortescue distinguished three types of regime and accounted for the origins of two of them.[16] The two fundamental concepts of Fortescue's political theory were the regal dominion (*dominium regale*) and the political and regal dominion (*dominium politicum et regale*).[17] For our purposes, it is not necessary to consider the derivation of the concepts[18] because our concern is with the meaning given the terms by Fortescue. That meaning is to be found in the use Fortescue made of the older terminology in developing his argument.

The two concepts have three purposes: (1) to distinguish two types of regime on the basis of their distinct origins, (2) to designate two phases in the development of government *per se*, and (3) to characterize two contemporary types of government, whatever their origin or position in a process of development, namely those of France and of England. The three purposes were not systematically distinguished and often overlap. The emphasis, however, is on providing an adequate account of the English polity, particularly as it had changed from the first to the second type of regime, that is, from a regal to a regal and political dominion, and of the superiority of the English to the French dominion.[19]

The *dominium regale* originates through the constitution of rule by force and ambition. The model founder is Nimrod, the mighty hunter, whose will establishes law. If the law is good, regal dominion may be an analogue to the kingdom of God. The doctrine, 'What pleases a prince has the force of law', is justified by the identification of the royal will with natural law; the subjects consent to regal dominion because they gain protection from other Nimrods.

The *dominium politicum et regale* is more advanced in the sense that political articulation has grown beyond the production of a representative king. In Fortescue's words, mankind had become 'more mansuete [that is, gentle] and bettir dispossid to vertu'[20] and so was prepared to enjoy a political and regal dominion. The change may occur by improvement, as in Rome, or a new foundation may begin immediately as a political and regal dominion, as occurred with England.[21] What is of interest here is not Fortescue's use of the conventional and static analogy, that a realm must have a ruler as a body must have a head, but his use of a dynamic one: the creation of a realm is analogous to the growth of a body from an embryo.

The concepts used to describe the process are 'eruption' and 'proruption'. In the first instance, as the physical body surges from an embryo, so the politically articulate realm erupts from the people.[22] The first 'eruption' of the people, then, articulates a realm where a prince rules *tantum regalitur* (merely regally). A second movement presupposes the existence of a realm sufficiently articulated as to be capable of further development towards 'gentility' and virtue. Specifically, Fortescue said, the kingdom of England prorupted into a political and regal dominion from Brutus's band of Trojans.[23] Fortescue's understanding here of the term 'people' carries two meanings. In the first instance, the embryonic people before its initial eruption or articulation into a realm is, he said, acephalous, headless, a mere trunk and not even a body, properly speaking, since a body must have a head. The second meaning of 'people' is synonymous with realm and refers to the politically articulate people.[24] One may conclude, therefore, that a realm is a politically articulate people, with king no less than baronage or commons contributing to its order.

Eruption and proruption are significant theoretical concepts because they draw our attention away from the legal formulae towards the actual social and political realities that constitute the different kinds of regime. 'But,' Voegelin observed, 'Fortescue went even further. . . . There was something about an articulated realm, an inner substance that provided the binding force of society, and this something could not be grasped by organic analogy.'[25] The limited usefulness of the analogy of an embryo and body is suggested in the following that Fortescue asked: Why did some embryonic people constitute themselves as a realm? Why did some realms, such as France, remain regal dominions while others, such as England, become political and regal? Fortescue recognized that, though there were no answers to such questions, it was nevertheless possible to describe the mystery of a political evocation.

Fortescue introduced the term *corpus mysticum*, mystical body, to symbolize the mysterious inner substance that bound a society together as politically articulate. The complete sentence, partially quoted earlier when I was introducing the concept of eruption, reads: 'Just as the physical body surges forth from the embryo, regulated by one head, so the realm erupts from the people, and exists as a mystical body governed by one man as head.' The transfer of the Christian symbol *corpus mysticum* to the field of secular politics indicates both the rising strength of national sentiments and the degree to which the imperial mystical body of Christianity, articulated into Church and Empire, had declined.[26] More important for our purposes, it suggests that the origin of the realm is to be found not in law or nature or a 'social contract', but in the forces of the soul that are expressed mythically through the evocation of a *corpus mysticum*. For Fortescue the mythical context was supplied by the founding of England by the grandson of Aeneas, the eponymous hero of the Britons, Brutus, and his wandering Trojans. This myth was, in different forms, adopted by several of the migration peoples from the Roman myth, just as the Romans had adopted it from the Greeks in order to achieve mythic equality with them. The *Aeneid*, in this context, is the Roman reply to the *Iliad*, and Fortescue's Brutus had a mythic pedigree equal to that of Aeneas, Achilles, and Odysseus.[27] Fortescue, in other words, lived sufficiently in the myth of the realm as to have no need or wish to scrutinize the actual evidence of the process of foundation.

The sacramental bond of the Christian community was the logos of Christ that dwells at the hearts of the members of the Christian *corpus mysticum*. The corresponding bond of the mystical body of the realm was termed by Fortescue the *intencio populi*, the support of the people. Just as the body natural has as its centre the heart, so the body politic, the mystical body of the realm, has as its centre the *intencio populi*, from which is transmitted to the head and to the members of the body as its nourishing bloodstream the political provision for the well-being of the people.[28] As Voegelin pointed out, 'The word "people" in this formula does not signify an external multitude of human beings but the mystical substance erupting in articulation; and the word "intention" signifies the urge or drive of this substance to erupt and to maintain itself in articulate existence as an entity which, by means of its articulation, can provide for its well-being.'[29] The conclusion to which we are drawn from Fortescue's argument is that the maintenance of a body politic requires not only the initial eruption of a people, which may or may not be followed by a proruption. More important perhaps, the maintenance of a body politic requires a common myth to animate the people as a whole so that they have as a collective purpose their own well-being.

A few hints at the appliability of the foregoing analysis to the Canadian situation must suffice.

I discussed the topic of constitutionalism in both the elemental or external and the substantive or existential sense. Following Voegelin, I argued that a description of the external constitutional procedures, however necessary, did not deal with the more fundamental question of the existence of a political society or of a regime. An examination of the conditions of existence of any political order brought into focus the related questions of articulation and the production of a representative. The question of social articulation, along with the problem of the meaning of any particular articulation, emerged as the most fundamental and most significant problem.

One clear implication of the argument is that the distinction between elemental and existential problems is of more than scholarly or methodological importance for an understanding of Canadian constitutional questions. To the extent that they have been confused, or that the distinction has been forgotten by politicians, journalists, constitutional experts, and even the public, this confusion will raise its own problems. The reason is as clear as it is simple: such confusions obscure the nature of political reality. Politics, including mega-constitutional politics in Canada, really does have an internal or substantive dimension of meaning and purpose as well as an external one of law and procedure. The former is expressed and illuminated by symbols, stories, rituals, myths, or, to use a well-publicized phrase, by a common or at least widespread 'vision' of the country. The latter is described conventionally in textbooks studied in political science departments and faculties of law. Both dimensions may be described through the concepts of political science.

We saw in the English example a process by which communes articulated themselves so as to be capable of political action. Later attempts at institutional and symbolic integration in England have proved less successful. The social relevance of communes, such as the aristocracy or the established church, are clearly less important for modern constitutionalism than the kind of articulation achieved in the United States, where the individual citizen is a representable unit. Other than some French-speaking Quebeckers and perhaps aboriginals, Canadians generally understand themselves as individual citizens rather than as members of one or another commune, notwithstanding the existence of so-called 'collective rights' in the constitution.[30] The chief impediment to constitutional development in Canada is not, therefore, the logical tensions within the constitution—as between individual and collective rights, for instance. Nor is it the historical tendency of Canadian governments to expand their purpose from the securing of citizens' rights to prescribing the manner of their exercise, a major consequence of which has been to transform independent and economically productive citizens into dependent pensioners.[31] However questionable such legal and economic developments may be, they could be changed with relative ease but for the greatest elemental impediment to constitutional development. Unfortunately, it is not an obstacle to be overcome but a lack, the presence of an absence. For mainly historical reasons, Canada lacks political institutions that can integrate individual citizens into a body politic. Not surprisingly it also lacks the symbols to express that integration.

The problem can be restated in Fortescue's terminology. To do so one might ask: Is Canada closer to what he meant by a *dominium regale* or a *dominium politicum et regale*? The answer depends on the extent to which Canadians have, in recent years, sought anything more or other from government than protection from frightening and predatory Nimrods. To the extent that Canadians have sought such protection, which is to a degree implied by governments' prescribing the manner in which citizens exercise their rights, one must also question whether such a goal can reasonably be attained. This is not to deny that there exist *bien pensants* who are of the opinion that Canadians have 'come of age' or whatever. But here, too, one must ask for evidence of our having 'prorupted' into a more virtuous regime. Somewhat anachronistically from the position argued by Fortescue, we could call this a constitutional regime. There is, of course, a considerable self-interpretation within Canadian society that we are indeed a constitutional regime. Politicians, journalists, and constitutional experts often have said so. But where is the substantive, not merely legal, expression of it? Where is the mythic evocation, Canada's *intencio populi*, the bond that sustains the mystical body politic?

The fact of the matter is this: there are no common myths, no widespread agreement to sustain a common 'vision' of the nation or even of citizenship.[32] Far from the *intencio populi* nourishing political provisions for the well-being of the people, the underground economy and widespread tax avoidance indicate that Canadians today have serious doubts about the value of even the external, formal, and legal constitution. And while they may long for a substantive and meaningful one, they also seem resigned to the fact that they are unlikely to obtain it. The truth of Walter Berns's observation to Peter Russell is plain: Canadians have not constituted themselves a people. Historically they have, until recently, existed in symbolic continuity with Britain. Now that the symbolism of Crown, empire, and what the Fathers of Confederation described as 'Home' have faded, Canadians are at a loss to discover the purpose of their living together.

Does it matter? To answer this question, by way of conclusion, we may examine briefly the work of a political thinker who considered the problem of articulation under conditions not of foundation and consolidation of a body politic, as Fortescue did, but during a time when an existing constitutional order was threatened with collapse. During the 1920s Maurice Hauriou elaborated a theory of articulation to account, *inter alia*, for the problems of the Third Republic.

In the *Précis de Droit constitutionnel*[33] Hauriou argued that government exercises legitimate power in so far as it is the representative of the state. The state, in turn, is the national community in which the business of the republic is conducted as rule. The first task of rule or of ruling power is the articulation of an unorganized collection of individuals and groups into a body politic capable of action. At the centre of the process of articulation, he said, was the governing idea, the *idée directrice*, that seeks to establish the state and to increase its power. The specific purpose of the ruler is to provide a concrete conception of the idea and to realize it by way of political institutions. A successful institutionalization occurs when a ruler is able to guide the process of achieving the governing idea and the citizens give a customary consent to the ruler's acts. Under such conditions the ruler is the representative of the governing idea and is able to exercise authoritative power on its behalf.

From this understanding of representation as the harmonious relationship between a guiding authority and support for the fact of actual power, Hauriou drew three conclusions about the relationship between the exercise of power by a representative and constitutional law. First, the force of representative power precedes its regulation by constitutional law; Canadians were reminded of this insight indirectly by the success of regionally based political parties in the 1993 federal election. The fact is that the regional articulation of Canadian political society simply has not found a means of expressing itself through constitutional formalities such as reform of the Senate or agreement on the relationship between Quebec and Canada. Second, power is legal in so far as it is institutionalized; in other words, in so far as a power has the authority of a representative it can make constitutional law. Here the failure of a series of constitutional packages, from the Victoria Charter to the Charlottetown Accord, indicated not simply the deficiencies of Canadian statesmanship but the lack of authority or of legitimacy of the parties to the process and even of the process itself. Canadian political society has become politically articulate down to the individual; Canada will be a self-representing body politic or nothing. Accordingly, Canadian citizens have simply refused to grant legitimacy to the procedures and practices that have been successful in the past and are often referred to by political scientists as 'élite accommodation'. Third, Hauriou concluded, the origin of constitutional law cannot be found in law but in the act that replaces more or less litigious conflict with ordered power.[34] In Canada, the end of the successive rounds of mega-constitutional negotiations, one may expect, will be followed by political, not legal or constitutional bargaining. The legal option simply cannot work because of the conflicting power configurations and the articulate political societies that give them legitimacy. It is as clear as anything in politics can be that a constitutional formula giving 'distinct' provincial status and powers to Quebec alone is not acceptable to, for example, British Columbia and Alberta. And just as clearly, Senate reform as advocated by the two western provinces is unacceptable to Quebec and evidently unacceptable to Ontario as well. So it seems likely that the only road to a genuine *modus vivendi* will come through political deals that frankly recognize low but solid interests and ignore high but mendacious ideals.

Hauriou's argument bears on the problems discussed in this paper because it draws attention to the fact that a representative is not merely a person or body of persons in a position of constitutional authority but is also the one who is capable of realizing the governing idea of the institution. In Fortescue's words, it institutionalizes the *intencio populi*. The government must be representative in the substantive or existential as well as the elemental sense. The implication is obvious. If a government tries to be representative in nothing but the legal-constitutional sense, a representative ruler in the existential sense will sooner or later make short work of it. 'Covenants without the sword,' Hobbes rightly observed, 'are but words.' And quite possibly the new configuration of rule in the existential sense may not be very representative in the constitutional sense. Canadians have had a glimpse of this already in the problems that the new political parties have had 'adjusting' to the rules, conventions and procedures of parliamentary government in the House of Commons.

Many of the recent mega-constitutional problems suffered by Canada result from the disjunction between our evident desire for constitutional representation in the elemental sense and the actual state of existential disintegration and rearticulation in which our society finds itself. But if anything is clear, it is that constitutional legalities cannot save representatives who are incapable of fulfilling their existential tasks. The 1993 Canadian election and the 1992 referendum on the Charlottetown Accord showed that clearly enough with respect to the informal institutions of rule, the political parties. It remains to be seen if the major components of the legal apparatus of rule, such as Parliament and federalism, suffer a similar fate.

NOTES

1 Peter H. Russell, *Constitutional Odyssey: Can Canadians be a Sovereign People?* (Toronto: University of Toronto Press, 1992).

2 To a degree, these institutional effects linger in popular attitudes and sentiments. See Seymour Martin Lipset, *Continental Divide: The Values and Institutions of the United States and Canada* (Toronto: C.D. Howe Institute, 1989) esp. chap. 12, 'Still Whig, Still Tory'.

3 Eric Voegelin, *The New Science of Politics* (Chicago: University of Chicago Press, 1952), chap. 1. The discussions of English constitutionalism also relied on chapter 19 of his unpublished 'History of Political Ideas: The English National Polity'.

4 Voegelin, *The New Science*, 27.

5 Ibid., 37.

6 Ibid., 39.

7 There was, of course, nothing necessary in the historical development of England as a political order where kingship was balanced by the articulation of the communes. See the apposite remarks of S.B. Chrimes in his 'Introduction' to *English Constitutional Ideas in the Fifteenth Century* [1936] (New York: American Scholar Editions, 1966), xvii–xviii.

8 Voegelin, *The New Science*, 39.

9 See, for instance, James Tully, 'Diversity's Gambit Declined: The Justice of Multilateral Constitutional Negotiations', in Curtis Cook, ed., *Constitutional Predicament: Canada after the Referendum of 1992* (Montreal and Kingston: McGill-Queen's University Press, 1994).

10 The phrase *quod omnes tangit ab omnibus approbetur* appears in the Writ of Summons of Edward I to the Archbishop and Clergy, reproduced in William Stubbs, ed., *Select Charters and Other Illustrations of English Constitutional History*, 5th edn, (Oxford: Clarendon, 1884), 485.

11 See Hegel, 'The English Reform Bill', trans. T.M. Knox, in Z.A. Peiczynski, ed., *Hegel's Political Writings* (Oxford: Clarendon, 1964), 295–330.

12 See the remarks of Arnold J. Toynbee on the 'idolization of an ephemeral institution', in this instance 'the Mother of Parliaments', in *A Study of History*, vol. IV (Oxford: Oxford University Press, 1939), 414–18 and on 'idolatry and pathological exaggeration', 635–9.

13 This is not to deny that the same sentiments can be found in the *Declaration of Independence*; it means, however, that the War between the States was fought, in some respects, in service to, or in order to actualize, the constitutional principles of the Declaration. See, for example, the arguments of Harry V. Jaffa, 'Another Look at the Declaration' in his *American Conservativism and the American Founding* (Durham: Carolina Academic Press, 1984), 18–25, or his *How to Think about the American Revolution* (Durham: Carolina Academic Press, 1978). See also Jaffa, *Crisis of the House Divided* (Chicago: University of Chicago Press, 1959), 268ff; and Eva Brann, 'A Reading of the Gettysburg Address', in Leo Paul S. de Alvarez, ed., *Abraham Lincoln, The Gettysburg Address, and American Constitutionalism* (Dallas: University of Dallas Press, 1976), 43–5.

14 Voegelin, *The New Science*, 40.

15 A.E. Levett, 'Sir John Fortescue', in F.J.C. Hearnshaw, ed., *The Social and Political Ideas of Some Great Thinkers of the Renaissance and the Reformation* (London: Dawsons, 1925), 61; and Caroline A.J. Skeel, 'The Influence of the Writings of Sir John Fortescue', *Transactions of the Royal Historical Society*, 3rd Series, 10 (1916), 77. See also William Holdsworth, *Some Makers of English Law* (Cambridge: Cambridge University Press [1938] 1966), 59–60.

16 The best guide to his thought is still Chrimes, *English Constitutional Ideas in the Fifteenth Century*, chap. 4, esp. 309–13 and 319–24. See also R.W.K. Hinton, 'English Constitutional Theories from Sir John Fortescue to Sir John Eliot', *English Historical Review* 75 (1960): 410–25; James L. Gillespie, 'Sir John Fortescue's Concept of Royal Will', *Nottingham Medieval Studies* 23 (1979): 47–65; Norman Doe, 'Fifteenth-Century Concepts of Law: Fortescue and Peacock', *History of Political Thought* 10 (1989): 257–80; and Mary Pollingue, 'An Interpretation of Fortescue's *De Laudibus Legum Angliae*', *Interpretation* 6 (1976): 11–47. There is also an interesting discussion of Fortescue's arguments, undertaken for a somewhat different purpose, in Donald W. Hanson, *From Kingdom to Commonwealth: The Development of Civic Consciousness in English Political Thought* (Cambridge, Mass.: Harvard University Press, 1970), esp. chap. 7.

17 The third, the political dominion, *dominium politicum*, elected its ruler or rulers, who in turn governed according to laws instituted of the people. For details see Chrimes, 309; Hinton, 413; and Doe, 58. See also C.H. McIlwain, *The Growth of Political Thought in the West, from the Greeks to the End of the Middle Ages* (New York, Macmillan, 1932), 357–8. So far as the immediate topic is concerned, this third concept can be ignored.

18 See, however, the exhaustive treatment by Felix Gilbert, 'Sir John Fortestcue's "Dominium Regale et Politicum"', *Medievalia et Humanistica* 2 (1944): 88–97.

19 Paul Janet, *Histoire de la science politique*, 2 vols, 3rd edn, (Paris: Vrin, 1913), 11, 144.

20 Fortescue, *The Governance of England* [Oxford: Claredon, 1885], ed. Charles Plummer (New York: Hyperion, 1975), 112.

21   See in particular Fortescue's *De Laudibus Legum Angliae*, ed. S.B. Chrimes (Cambridge: Cambridge University Press, 1942), chap. 12–13. Additional quotations below are from chap. 13.

22   '*Hoc ordine sicut ex embrione corpus surgit phisicum sic ex populo erumpit regnum.*'

23   '*Sic namque regnum Anglie quod ex Bruti comitiva troianorum quam ex Italie et Grecorum finibus perduxit, in dominium politicum et regale prorupit.*'

24   In *The Governance of England*, 112, Fortescue speaks of the founding by Brutus from 'grete comunaltes' the inarticulate people, of 'a body pollitike callid a reawme, hauynge an hed to governe it'.

25   Voegelin, *The New Science*, 43.

26   For an account of the history of the symbolic, mystical body see Ernst H. Kantorowicz, *The King's Two Bodies: A Study in Medieval Political Theology* (Princeton: Princeton University Press, 1957), Chap. 5, esp. 193–232.

27   See Plummer's note to his edition of *The Governance of England*, 185–6.

28   Chrimes translated *provisionem politicam* as political forethought, which is certainly possible; I prefer political provision because, in addition to forethought, it had the connotation of material prosperity, which was a central theme of *The Governance of England*, chap. 8–11.

29   Voegelin, *The New Science*, 44.

30   For an analysis of this problem see Jose Woehrling, 'Minority Cultural and Linguistic Rights and Equality Rights in the Canadian Charter of Rights and Freedoms', *McGill Law Journal* 31 (1985): 50–92; F.L. Morton, 'Group Rights versus Individual Rights in the Charter: The Special Cases of Natives and the Quebecois', in N. Nevitte and A. Kornberg, eds, *Minorities and the Canadian State* (Oakville: Mosaic, 1985), 83–4.

31   For an elaboration of this development in connection with the American constitution, see Harvey C. Mansfield, Jr, *America's Constitutional Soul* (Baltimore, Johns Hopkins University Press, 1991), 30–4, 55–9, 74–5, 93–7, 189–92, 197–200. See also David J. Bercuson and Barry Cooper, *Derailed: The Betrayal of the National Dream* (Toronto: Key Porter, 1994).

32   I have discussed some aspects of this question in the following articles: 'Western Political Consciousness', in Stephen Brooks, ed., *Political Thought in Canada* (Toronto: Irwin, 1984), 213–38; 'The West: A Political Minority', in N. Nevitte and A. Kornberg, eds, *Minorities and the Canadian State* (Toronto: Mosaic, 1985), 203–20; and 'Looking Eastward, Looking Backward: A Western Reading of the Never-Ending Story', in C. Cook, ed., *Constitutional Predicament: Canada After the Referendum of 1992* (Montreal and Kingston: McGill-Queen's University Press, 1994), 89–107.

33   Maurice Hauriou, *Précis de droit constitutionnel*, 2nd edn (Paris: Sirey [1929] 1965), 64–5, 72–4, 78ff.

34   Hauriou, *Précis*, chap. 1. This interpretation of Hauriou's thesis was guided by Voegelin's discussion in *The New Science*, 48–51. See also Voegelin, *The Nature of the Law, and Related Legal Writings*, vol. 27, *The Collected Works of Eric Voegelin*, ed. R.A. Pascal, J.L. Bagin, and J.W. Corrington (Baton Rouge, La.: Louisiana State University Press, 1991).

12

'Political Correctness' and the Constitution: Nature and Convention Re-examined

Tom Darby and Peter C. Emberley

Today, for reasons peculiar to our time, Canadians and other citizens of the western world usually think of constitutions exclusively as written documents that outline the legitimate and illegitimate uses of power. This narrow perspective distorts the foundation of constitution making itself. Our preoccupation with written constitutions tells us much about ourselves and the time in which we live. Constitutions in their earliest conception and in most of their subsequent evolution were not thought of as political arrangements tied exclusively to language. Customs, rites, and rituals, for instance, were not expressed in written form.

In this chapter, we attempt to explain the preoccupation of Canadians with providing for political change through the revision of written constitutional documents. We argue that just as the cultural left attempts to change the way we think about the world by changing the language through which we think, so the advocates of constitutional reform often assume that Canadian politics can be changed through formal revisions to the constitution acts. Although there is no doubt that formal amendments to the constitution can change political structures and institutional arrangements, they cannot change the way Canadians think. In particular, they cannot change what Canadians believe about such things as justice and fairness and what is a good social order. The attempt to change Canadian political opinion through formal constitutional amendments reveals a naïvety about what can and cannot be achieved through the political process. It reflects a naïvety about the distinction between nature and convention.

This distinction was the pole-star of ancient and modern political philosophy, serving as the guiding principle for the liberal constitutionalism of Hobbes, Locke, and Montesquieu. Today the distinction is overlooked, if not entirely disregarded. The attempt to correct politics and to impose progressive moral and political reform on Canadians through the modification of language and through formal legal and political change—what we call 'political correctness'—disregarding the limitations of nature, is futile. Political correctness attempts to coerce Canadians into submitting to its ideas without regard to the natural limitations of political change and without regard to those experiences and opinions that form the ideological foundation of Canadian identity. The disregard for this foundation explains much of the confusion about the constitutional and public policy proposals that have been foisted on Canadians and that Canadians have refused to accept.

In this essay, we examine the problems caused by political correctness and the demands it makes on the Canadian constitution and politics generally. First, we investigate recent Canadian examples that illustrate how the ideological offerings of political correctness clash with Canadian political traditions. Second, we investigate the relationship between nature and convention. What exactly was meant by these terms in ancient and modern political philosophy, and how are they related to sound political order? Third, we examine how words in the English language have been transformed by political correctness to further its artificial, ideological agenda. Fourth, we explore the implications of political correctness for Canada and the effect it has had on language, Canadian constitutionalism, and politics generally.

DESPERATE AND CONFUSED ATTEMPTS

In 1987 Teneng Jahate, a Gambian woman, was sent to jail in France for allowing her daughters to be circumcised, as custom in Gambia mandates. Jahate claimed that she did not know it to be a crime. In her Gambian village, the rite ensured virginity, chastity, and a dowry. Rough estimates put the number of circumcised African women in France at 25,000. The French government, upholding the World Health Organization's ban on female circumcision, has not looked favourably on the practice. Since 1988, 10 cases of 'voluntary mutilation' have come before the courts.

The issue is not confined to France. After some Ottawa doctors were asked by African families to perform clitoral circumcisions on their daughters, the Ontario medical establishment drafted a policy forbidding the operation. In so doing, they were confirming widespread Western objection to the tribal practice. Efua Dorkenoo, a member of the Foundation for Women's Health, Research and Development (FORWARD), expressed the characteristic judgment: 'It is an issue of gender and human rights abuse.' She added, 'but it may take some time before we can convince African women of this.'[1] Richard Mosley, senior general counsel in criminal and family law policy for the federal justice department, contributed a further element to the charge of rights violation: 'A child cannot consent to be mutilated and a parent cannot provide consent for a child to be mutilated.'[2] Charles Kayazze, head of the Ottawa African Resource Centre, linked the practice to male domination, charging that female circumcision 'was the ultimate oppression of women. . . . The bottom line is, this is men controlling women, controlling their sexuality and their desires.'[3]

Some African women have seen the issue otherwise. 'Circumcision,' in the opinion of Kenyan Poline Nyaga of London's Brent Council, 'should be allowed as a right to all British women, particularly for African families who want to carry on their tradition while living in this country.'[4] The Canadian African Women's Organization published an article defending female circumcision as a 'personal and delicate matter', arguing that parents had a 'right' to choose to circumcise their children if they wished. 'Our organization is not pro or against the practice,' Louisa Dourado president of that organization states. 'We are saying they should have a choice, parents have to decide.'[5] Another board member exclaimed, 'I don't think you have a right to tell us to do otherwise.'[6]

A similar cultural clash is occurring in the Indian community in Canada. With the availability of such sex-determination tests as amniocentesis, as well as the medical process of separating the Y-chromosome sperm out of semen, modern medicine has made it possible to choose the sex of one's child. Among Indians, male children are widely favoured. Girls are considered a liability, mainly because of the burden of providing their dowries, but also because, once married, they belong to their husband's family and do not attend to their own parents in their old age. Gender clinics in India are candid when they target their client group: 'Spend 500 rupees now to save 50,000 later'. In Canada, they have been no less so. Not only financial reasons underlie the preference for males. There are also religious reasons: the Hindu cycle of reincarnation decisively depends on the male first-born. Few Indo-Canadians have opposed the tests. Nonetheless, other Canadians have been quick to object. Judy Rebick, former president of the National Action Committee on the Status of Women, expressed her outrage: the practice, she charged, is 'absolutely terrifying' . . . 'blond, blue-eyed babies will be the next step.'[7] The Indian community does not agree. Dr Vibhuti Patel of Women's University in Bombay states that the attraction to amniocentesis is that 'now we can go for pre-selection, so we don't have to confront the messy business of guilt and shame.'[8]

And then there is yet another Canadian example, the more recent one of Nada, the Saudi woman who has become a symbol of the debate over whether women fleeing persecution because of their sex should be given the status of political refugees. After reversing himself because of pressure from women's lobbies, the then Minister of Immigration, Bernard Valcourt, pronounced on Nada's new status. The next day the head of the refugee board issued guidelines telling members of the board to consider following suit for other women who are persecuted because of their sex. Ironically, this minister and the government in power at the time of this ruling were the same ones that wrote the Charlottetown Accord, a document centred on con-sociational, as opposed to natural or human, rights—a document centred on convention rather than on any transcendent notion of nature.

Illustrative of the confused, strange, and troubling issues arising in our world, these are cases that are now confronting Canadians daily. For some Canadians, the solution to these problems is clear. The old compass points are still very much available. Richard Mitchell of Iroquois Falls, for instance, writes in the Ottawa *Citizen*:

> It is part of the Canadian reality that all (aboriginal included) of us or our ancestors came here from somewhere else and in every case left something in order to create something better. We will never be able to achieve that if we keep looking over our shoulders to where we came from, rather than focusing on where we are going to. We cannot become apologists for being essentially European-based culturally and ethnically. That is a Canadian reality. And it is the European concept of human rights (Magna Charta-French Revolution) that has attracted so many non-European people to Canada to become 'Canadians'. We all have a dish to offer to the Canadian cultural smorgasbord but only that which is palatable to our established culture, a culture based on the equality of all its citizens regardless of race or sex.[9]

For other Canadians, multicultural tolerance, and even full redress of all past wrongs, must take precedence. Differential treatment, special incentives, wide-ranging modification of education, and other demands are being made to correct a multiplicity of social problems. The boundaries between law, psychology, sociology, and biology must be dissolved to give way to a new style of politics and a new justice.

Into what perspective can we situate these complex issues? What does our future hold in light of the difficult demands being placed upon the formal structure of modern constitutional liberalism? What is the problem we must solve to overcome the inescapable pressures being placed upon us? What has caused our present disorder and confusion? There are a variety of answers.

Some analysts say that the language of the 1982 Charter of Rights and Freedoms is extravagant—especially the language pertaining to equality rights—and that we are now experiencing the results of that lack of moderation. Others point to lobbyists and special-interest groups, saying that they have become uncontrollable and unaccountable. Yet others maintain that important parts of the population—women, non-white races, homosexuals, ethnic groups, the handicapped—are being excluded from the political process. Some sense that our parliamentary process is flawed—only the checks and balances of a more republican system can prevent the excessive power of the Cabinet. Still others say that our house can be brought into order only if we turn our attention to being more globally competitive. And there is a demand for wholesale reform of our educational system, and the adoption of a curriculum that emphasizes problem solving and social issues.

Our emphasis is somewhat different. We put our current dilemmas and puzzling circumstances in a wider, theoretical perspective. Indeed, we suggest that our current state arises from a civilizational change.

The problems of culture and ethnicity, power and rights, authority and resistance are not new. Rather, they exemplify essential themes within the western political tradition. Answers to these problems characteristically have been linked to an account of order, which in turn is expressed through a primary political unit, be it empire or polis or nation-state. The ancient empires of Egypt and Mesopotamia reflected an understanding of the orderly whole evident in the linking of society with the divine cosmos. The Greek polis associated the human psyche with cosmic order. The Holy Roman Empire brought divine providence together with the life of the spirit. When the political unit broke down (as it did in the tenth century BC, the fifth century BC, the thirteenth century AD), the experience of order was simultaneously disrupted. Political, intellectual, and spiritual confusion arose, and power was realigned.[10]

We believe that we are living in a world undergoing such a re-alignment of power. The political unit that has dominated since the seventeenth century, the nation-state, is being attacked by powerful forces pushing at one and the same time outwards and inwards. Global processes of organization have had to respond to local assertions of autonomy. Multinational companies, for instance, have come into conflict with re-discovered regional or ethnic identities. Efforts at co-ordinating world-wide management of the environment have been hampered by opposing beliefs about mankind's relation to nature. No one voice can speak authoritatively; no voice is excluded from the new pluralism in political discourse, in which all voices, regardless of their message, must be heard.

One could summarize the dominant features of the contemporary world by saying that the focus of power is shifting away from the centre of the nation-state, away from the principle of order that has given that centre authority in the past. The experience of order that is underwritten by the nation-state and that legitimates a whole series of practices and institutions—the primacy of the free individual, limited but sovereign government, the rule of law, the autonomy of the judiciary, equality of opportunity, the guarantee of primary rights, and the political independence of the bureaucracy—is being dissipated. Accordingly, the point of those practices and institutions is being lost.[11]

Liberal constitutionalism, which is the characteristic feature of the nation-state, has been undermined. Although there is a long history of constitution making before the emergence of the nation-state, the distinctive characteristics of the nation-state gave us the form of the modern constitution. The nation-state was the political unit that attempted to link national identity with the formal, legal structure of modern constitutionalism.

Liberal constitutionalism was erected on the principle of the 'sovereignty of the law': all individuals and groups were equal before the law. Law had a monopoly of political power. The political relations between humans was dictated, not by birth or heritage, but by formal relations under the law. A constitution was intended to provide only the most minimal guarantees of the conditions pertaining to justice, the principles of right. The terms of a constitution could neither be exhaustive—because the application of general guarantees to particular circumstances demanded practical judgment or adjudication—nor could they advance a substantive notion of the good. National or multinational identities might supply the moral force or spirit behind the constitution, or a social diversity outside the constitution, but they could not constitute its substance. The elaborate artifice of the constitutional state in which the concrete particulars of individual and communal life were restricted to 'legal personalities' was the result of a prudent calculation of the disruptive consequences of permitting appeals to religious, ethnic, or cultural differences within a constitutional structure. It is not a mere curiosity that the historical period in which modern constitutions were developed followed on wars of religious intolerance, civil war, class antagonism, and rule by privilege.

There were good reasons for basing democratic participation on a system of representation, for not permitting bureaucrats to state publicly their political allegiances, and for making the judiciary accountable only to the letter of the constitution. All of these provided for wise government and a formal constitutional neutrality.

The contemporary re-alignments of power, however, have begun to challenge these practices and institutions. The extraordinary and inconsistent demands being placed upon the reform of constitutions and political practices reflects the radical fragmentation of order in our day. For those who see the shape of a new, fairer world emerging from these re-alignments, the institutions of the nation-state appear atavistic, oppressive, and out of line with the emerging 'social movements'. There is a groundswell of opposition to the practices and institutions of the nation-state. The very structure of the modern state is seen as exclusionary, discriminatory, unrepresentative, inefficient, and inflexible. The very principles underlying representation, legislative deliberation, and the primacy of individual rights—the principles of liberal constitutionalism—are all being challenged.

There have been great confusion and hard questions: Ought the unequal rights allocated under aboriginal cultural identity, for example, to be superseded by universal rights? Should the redressing of 'historical wrongs' be permitted to run roughshod over equality of opportunity? Should all representative political institutions correspond exactly to the statistical profiles of the population at large? Should the experiences of gender, race, sexual orientation, and cultural difference be permitted to re-arrange our notions of the family, marriage, political decision making, or education? An infinite variety of groups are making demands, each vying for special favour and recognition, and each assuming that its principle can establish a new political or social order.

We argue that beneath these questions lies a debate that has shaped most of the history of the Western world. Nothing is more puzzling in our current situation than the confusion associated with the relation between nature and convention. On the one hand, the appeals to race, gender, and ethnic identity are a return to letting the naturally given determine the relations of human society. The world-wide reorganization of commerce, rendering us into a single global consuming and labouring society, is seen in the most favourable light as analogous to the 'natural' processes of all organisms.[12] On the other hand, race, gender, and ethnic identities are being recognized as 'perspectives' or 'discourses', as conventional and thus arbitrary masks, mere instruments of power.

The question we ask is, How can we expect constitutions to be coherent documents that supply the ground of order for our political initiatives when we have lost our clarity about the proper relation between convention and nature?

ORDER AND DISORDER, NATURE AND CONVENTION

The question of what is by nature arises when laws, customs, and ways of human life are recognized as conventional. By conventional we mean what is based on agreement or force, what is artificial, arbitrary, and temporary. The natural is something that is permanent and that endures over time. When we speak of something as 'natural' or of 'natural right', we imply that there is an order or a measure apart from convention that allows us to assess convention. The works of human beings are less than what comes from this 'natural' order. Our laws and policies may be conventional, but they ought to accord with what is natural, that is, with what is not of our own making but which can guide our making.

Our laws and customs, invariably, are products of both nature and convention.[13] The insight that we are not the sole author of our ways is a radical one. It was first enunciated in the west by the sophists, who spoke up against the ancestral code, traditional religion, and particularly the prevailing forms of justice, all in the name of what is by 'nature'. We know of the sophist position primarily through the Platonic dialogues, where Socrates debates the sophists—opposing their view that the laws and conventions of the city are merely interests of the more powerful, instruments devised by the weak to protect themselves from the strong.

The sophists looked for a standard in nature. So did Plato. He looked for what was not merely arbitrary, temporary, or conventional. Nature, and especially human nature, supplied guidance about how humans ought to live. But here the similarity between Plato and the sophists ended. Though Plato agreed that there are ways by nature, he denied that an account of what we are 'naturally' could be expended by what we share with vegetative or animal life or with those humans who achieve only a part of what they are capable of. Plato spoke of the desire for justice, the passion for honour, man's sense of loyalty, and the perfectibility of men. Man had natural desires, such as the desire to know. To speak of man's desires as natural was, for Plato, to say that in pursuing the objects of their desires humans could complete themselves. Their nature was to become more fully human, which required the perfection of the sublime objects of their desires. Our experiences of justice, honour, and dignity were not temporary or arbitrary or mere cultural preferences. For Plato they were natural.

Plato's student Aristotle framed the relationship of nature to convention in a more formulaic manner, arguing that by engaging in politics or leading the life of reason, we were fulfilling our natural end. We were, in his words, actualizing the potential that is present in us and that defines the functions that are distinctive to the human species. The presence of these ends gives our human activities purposive order.

The term 'nature', as the ancients developed it, placed man in a 'cosmos'. Man participated in a cosmic order, which had both ends and limits. Nature also suggested that humans shared common characteristics and a common world. They were part of a greater whole. This whole transcended the historical and cultural particulars of a given people. To speak of natural justice, of acting in conformity with nature, of a soul harmonized with nature, or of natural happiness was to relate human doings to a purposiveness or order that was not of human making. What was right by nature entailed acting in concert with nature.

Thus in order to measure human order and political right, it was necessary to discover nature or what was natural. But ancient political philosophy was more complex than that. Once nature was discovered, she could not do her work unassisted. It should not be thought that either Plato or Aristotle was an idealist, expecting an unguided or spontaneous development of the human desire for order. Both insisted that the realization of nature's ends required much human effort and artifice. Man had to work in concert with nature; the work of reason in law and education and the use of habituation and of cultivated speech were necessary to shape and form the natural impulses. Aristotle was quite candid about how niggardly nature often appeared to be. Though 'nature does nothing in vain', much art is needed to improve nature. Nature's design gave human activity direction and purpose. Human judgment was required to see what this meant in the particular case. Both Plato and Aristotle recognized that the immediately given in nature is in need of considerable control and sublimation, by education and by the laws, if a political order is to exist at all. Nature inclines us as much towards bestiality as towards perfection. Convention and nature must be balanced, and only judicious statesmen, exercising both theoretical insight and practical judgment, can bring about a just polity.

Here is where our own understanding of nature has most radically departed from ancient thought. We do not believe nature is an orderly whole. Where we still use the term with any coherence, our meaning stems almost wholly from Rousseau, for whom nature referred to those spontaneous and primary impulses which, in our freedom from the corruptions of organized social life and from too much cleverness, provide us with 'sweet' sentiments. For us who are Rousseau's epigones, to do what is 'natural' is to give in to our first promptings, to our sentiments and passions. It is a small step from Rousseau to the view, generally held in the modern enlightenment, that our passions and interests pose no threat of disorder: a natural harmony of interests can be counted upon.

This romanticist view of nature, as primary and sweet, as a bucolic backdrop to social corruption, was obviously not countenanced for long historically (even if it still has a powerful allure for modern-day romanticists). Even Kant, so much a student of Rousseau's, found primary impulses to be ungovernable, selfish, and devoid of the purposiveness that defines distinctly human life, namely, moral choice. Kant dismisses primary impulses as 'unsociable' characteristics and the opposite of 'autonomous' conduct. Thus Kant makes an important modern distinction between the realm of necessity, which contains all the impulses of nature, and the realm of freedom, in whose domain humans express their capacity to carry out nature's purpose by transcending nature. To be 'moral', and make moral law the basis of political justice, demands that people suppress what is by nature and act according to imperatives that are wholly the product of practical reason.

Kant expresses his apprehensions about natural impulses with characteristic Protestant sobriety. De Sade, who had no such compunction, portrays nature in a wholly unadorned and unsentimental manner in its bacchanalian frenzy and ferocious power. De Sade, of course, revels in all the degeneracy, debauchery, violence, and excesses of sense and speech that are sanctioned by nature, but to recognize this is not to distinguish him from Rousseau and Kant. Rather, De Sade's writings simply expose the seamy underside of the 'natural' and an intolerance for institutional stability and the liberal principles of order. De Sade's tales of the perversions of the boudoir are similar to Rousseau's search for primeval nature and Kant's antipathy to fallen nature.

One could say that modern life is characterized by this paradox: on the one hand, we long for a lost, natural unity; on the other hand, we recognize the rapacity and destructiveness of nature, which must be suppressed if we are to have civil society.[14]

This is what we must appreciate today when we wish to understand modern constitutionalism, liberal democracy, and the nation-state. In the classic statement of modern politics by Hobbes and Locke, human beings, by nature, fear violent death and seek comfortable self-preservation. The modern experiment fails to explain the longings for justice or order described by Plato and Aristotle. On the Hobbesian reading, we are calculating and even rapacious animals, forever on the brink of mutual destruction by virtue of the partiality of our self-interest and our limitless pride. The natural inequalities of strength, intelligence, and ability are sources of dissidence, hostility, and conflict. An effectual justice can come to be only if this natural irascibility is controlled.

The architectural plans for civil society supplied by Hobbes and Locke provide a foundation for order, to be achieved through a process of de-naturing. Order and political right are predicated on radically artificial myths—the fiction of the 'state of nature' and an original 'social contract'—which legitimate the political authority's mandate to maintain peace and ensure the conditions necessary for prosperity. Civil society is thus wholly conventional; it is a fragile and vulnerable artifice, forever on the brink of dissolution under the powerful forces of nature. This artifice, while based on the low pedestal of the desire for peace and wealth, nonetheless supplies humanity with the small modicum of nobility that can be said to arise when the barbarism that can accompany the opening of the floodgates of nature is stemmed.

It should not be thought however that Hobbes and Locke, and their successors in America who built the first wholly modern state, abandoned nature as the standard for political order. Nor, more important, did they abandon the ancients' awareness of the need to balance nature and convention. In these early liberal thinkers, nature remains as that against which the artifice of civil society is directed. Nature is what we flee from: it is the *summum malum* guiding the work of skilled sovereigns, but it is still the beacon of political order. The basis of modern constitutional liberalism is neither abstract nor arbitrary. It takes its bearings from the concrete limits and possibilities supplied by nature.

Nowhere is this balance of nature and convention clearer than in the writings of Kant, who identified the moral basis of constitutional liberalism. Kant recognizes the moral imperative inherent in the modern nation-state. He announces that the demand for justice in modern life is achieved when people act in such a way that the maxims of their actions can be rendered into the form of universal law. Only with such a test, can the fairness we owe others—in transcending our narrow and partial, naturally given inclinations and by treating others as ends rather than as means—be actualized.

A century after Kant, however, Nietzsche argued that the ethos of forbearance, of giving way, of inclusion, of inoffensiveness at all costs, was a sign of spiritual exhaustion and weakness, in individuals as well as in regimes. He claimed that the origin of what we call justice was pity, and pity for Nietzsche was a sign of self-renunciation and the product of resentment. Pity arose out of impotence and guilt. Nietzsche felt it to be particularly noticeable where soft democratic mores, dictated by pity, shied away from making judgments, distinctions, and exclusions. Nietzsche's antidote to this weakness was the ethic of 'empowerment', an effort to reclaim the values of strength, creativity, and innocent play (the 'grand style') against the emasculated idea of justice as comfort that is manifest in mass society. Such a 'grand style', Nietzsche believed, required seeing 'beyond the little perspectives of good and evil' to a new mode of ruling, to a politics without limit.

Many of the strange contradictions of our time follow from our attraction to Nietzsche's dismissal of traditional ideas of nature and justice (evident in our language of 'empowerment', 'proactive', and 'creativity') and yet our equally fervent commitment to a residue of Kant's modern restatement of the grounds of justice. Our problem lies with the growing decay of the Kantian residue into a politics of pity and guilt. Here Kant's language of dignity is mortgaged to those low ideals of mass man that Nietzsche derided. The new 'identity' politics mistakenly sees itself as retaining the moral substance of Kant's thought, even as it adopts the corrosive Nietzschean teaching that there is nothing but power 'beyond the little perspectives of good and evil', that is, a politics without limit.

POWER AND LANGUAGE: ABSTRACT WORDS, DISFIGURED JUSTICE

If Nietzsche was right when he said that pity is the result of resentment and the enemy of justice, it is imperative to ask what this means. Resentment is the desire to find the conditions that result in some intolerable present and to eradicate them. In many ways, resentment is what animates modern social science, resting, as it does, on manipulating the future by uncovering and altering the principles that led to the present. Modern social science destroys nature and history by abolishing the traditional limits, as well as the traditional understanding, of political and social life. By doing so, it creates the conditions for reform, attacking and undermining common experience. Social science abstracts experience from the circumstances in which it occurs. Abstracting experience makes it more malleable, because it removes both temporal and spatial boundaries. It presents a false sense of control, which explains, in some measure, why so many predictive generalizations made by social scientists are inaccurate, if not often silly. Social science makes of the past what one wills it to be. Abstraction allows one to move things about, transform this into that, and increase one's control over one's natural and historical environment. It allows for incessant correcting of experience so as to have experience square with the flux of the will. This is nowhere illustrated more clearly today than our emphasis on language and the way it is being transformed.

Today we emphasize language because there is no common existential or experiential ground. There is no experiential ground because our experiences have become fragmented and heterogeneous. Both nature and convention, in all its varied manifestations, are under assault. Nature is under assault because of our technological prowess. We seek to control nature, and the idea that it could place any limitations on our activity is anathema to how we see the world. Convention is assailed because history is being revised to suit the agendas of various groups.

We have today language without content, what Hegel referred to as 'chatter'. Chatter is not benign. It may seem innocuous enough if we can give whatever meaning we want to words. But severed from their grounding in experience, the meaning of words has little or nothing to do with natural or historical referents and everything to do with power. In this condition, words are used to advance political agendas. Language without content has given political correctness the opportunity to flourish. 'Gender', 'sex', 'culture', and 'right', for instance, have all been transformed by the cultural left.

The roots of the word 'gender' are in Greek and Latin, the word genus designating a biological classification. Gender pertains to natural, biological differences related to sex. The differences related to sex today are denied by the advocates of political correctness, and with it 'sex' has been removed from the English lexicon. In the 1980s, in particular, the word 'sex' disappeared from the vocabulary of the more literate and informed and was replaced by the word 'gender'. Why?

There are probably two answers: First, sex no longer matters. The argument advanced by political correctness is that the divisions of nature—sex among them—are the result of either historical accident or political power. Like nature, sex is not fixed. It changes with time. Sex and the characteristics pertaining to it, like language, are historical and malleable.

The second answer is the opposite of the first: since sex is historical and malleable, it does not constitute mere differences within a specific species but rather a species difference in itself. Because of this species difference, the two sexes, cum species, live in two different experiential universes. Sex is an anachronistic term, referring to an old order where a single species was differentiated on the basis of arbitrary categorizations. According to political correctness, men and women are not privy to the experiences of the opposite sex. Sex constitutes universes as different for men and women as for dogs and cats. The word gender, specifying no particular sex, captures this difference. Hence it has replaced sex in the English lexicon.

The word 'culture' has also been transformed. Originally culture was conceived as a phenomenon identifying certain relations and practices that constituted groups of people. 'Culture' was applied to clans, tribes, and economic and political units. It was rooted in a specific locale. Cultures were bound to the earth, to nature's cycles, to agriculture, and to a collective memory. Culture often referred to nationalities.[15]

Today, when one speaks of culture one means something quite different. A cultured person is not thought to be some 'provincial' tied to a particular place, a particular set of practices, or some specific group into which he or she was born. On the contrary, a cultured person is cosmopolitan, a person of good taste who is at home anywhere, can adapt to an array of 'cultural practices' and can choose among them as if choosing flavours of ice cream. For cultural left, cultural practices can be understood only through the lenses of gender, race, and ethnicity. Culture seldom attaches to geography or locale.

In the writings of Plato, 'right' was tied to an idea of transcendental good. What was right was what was consistent with the natural order. This was the case in modern political philosophy as well. Hobbes and Locke do not speak of a transcendent order, but they do conceive right as attached to nature and the natural law. In the western world today, when one asserts a 'right', what one means is that one has both the will and the power to make right effective and legally actionable. Right equals power; it no longer has any attachment to what is good or to nature.

Other examples of words that have changed their meaning and that have replaced older words referring to common sense experience could be cited here. The point, in these few examples, is to illustrate that the old language, used to express social and political relations that were considered to be natural, has been replaced by purely conventional designations. In the next section we explain how political correctness has abandoned nature altogether and how this is reflected not only in language, but in the extraordinary demands made on constitutional reform and politics in general in Canada.

POLITICAL CORRECTNESS: ILLIBERAL, ANTI-POLITICAL POLITICS

The political artifice, which underlies modern liberal constitutionalism, and which used human nature as a guide for setting the limits to constitution making, sought to balance nature and convention. This balance has been disrupted. Pressures are being placed upon the Canadian constitution to create a plan for social reform that extravagantly exceeds the purposes or capacities of constitutions. The kinds of pressure we see today—the concentration of legislative power in the judiciary to advance various social mandates, a written constitution whose directives must cover all contingencies, the demand for a mode of representation that appears to be satisfied with nothing less than direct democracy (proportional representation in all public offices, referenda, and plebiscites), the insistence on legislative efficiency (abolition of the Senate, replacement of parliamentary supremacy with a committee system), the desire for parallel systems of justice for different cultures (self-government in all its forms), and special treatment of groups (affirmative action and employment equity)—reveal a misunderstanding of political order.

These pressures, we argue, have their origin in intellectual fantasies for which the shorthand name is 'political correctness'. These fantasies stem from a distortion of the relation of nature to convention that links the romanticism of Rousseau, the cynicism of de Sade, and the psychopathology of pity described by Nietzsche. Political correctness has targeted the very medium of understanding and of engagement between human beings—speech—as the object of a radical debunking of the order of the world. It is an attempt to cleanse speech of the hierarchies, judgments, and ambiguities that emerge from our everyday experiences. Political correctness attempts to put in place a fluid, artificial system of communication that by re-naming the world will alter its reality. Political correctness is a bid at world re-creation.

William Safire notes that the historical origin of 'political correctness' is the 1963 fragment of Chairman Mao Zedong's work, 'Where Do Correct Ideas Come From?' Mao asks, 'Do they drop from the skies? No. Are they innate in the mind? No. They come from social practice, and from it alone.'[16] In other words, political correctness begins with the assumption that our identities, relations, practices, and institutions are utterly arbitrary and reflect neither tradition nor a transcendent perception of the order of reality. The standards that support these structures are seen as only linguistic conventions, convenient tools serving an immediate purpose. It will not do, the advocates of political correctness state, to assume that any part of our being is naturally given. Underlying that confidence is the assumption that reality is how we perceive it and that language is the tool by which these perceptions are formed and changed.

Political correctness assumes that the every-day distinctions between higher and lower, noble and base, anger and loyalty, friend and enemy, self and other, are artificial. Human relations should have an authenticity that extends beyond the roles men and women have as members of society—as husbands and wives, mechanics and politicians, soldiers and poets, teachers and pupils, craftsmen and apprentices. These roles are conceived by political correctness as inauthentic and arbitrary.

Political correctness seeks a form of communication that massages political reality and smooths it over, eliminating those distinctions that we have come to identify with human existence—the difference between the animal and the human, between passion and reason, leisure and work, normality and disability, politics and administrative management, male and female. Its advocates seek to cleanse reality of common-sense distinctions. So certain are they of their cause that they are prepared to police the schools, the workplace, the media, and the family, expunging these of their delinquency.

The language of political correctness is that of victimhood and injury. It reminds us of the self-indulgence of the child described by Rousseau in *Émile*, the child who wants the world to bend to his way to the disregard of everything else. Political correctness seeks a world without pain, a world where no one has to pronounce judgments, no one must be ostracized, no one fails to live up to expectations, and everyone extends warm effusiveness to all others. Attempting to deny the burdens of existence, labour, and injustice at the hands of the stronger, presents us with a dream world.[17] By thinking that all injuries can be redressed, all future wrongs pre-empted, all human relations rendered 'rational', and all historical error eliminated, political correctness lives in an imaginary world. Ultimately, the aim of political correctness is the creation of a world that deprives humans of the very characteristics through which we express our responses to the contingencies of life—our acts of charity and of forgiveness, the desire for honour, and the exercise of righteous anger, compassion, and dignity.

There are two specific dangers that we see in the revolutionary fantasy of political correctness. The first is that a society that believes the message of political correctness displays supreme naïvety. Because of this, such a society will make itself vulnerable and susceptible to foolishness. When masses of men and women can be agitated and mobilized by the promise of a wholly new age and accept the illegitimacy of all traditional compass points, and when legislators and judges become receptive to engineering the law and the constitution to re-make the world, the result is that any desired fiction becomes a workable project.

Second, when political correctness penetrates the educational system and our fundamental laws, it promises to destroy the last bastions of independent thought and judgment. Education, traditionally understood, was an attempt to liberate the mind. Curricula were understood as frameworks beyond sectarian interest and compromise. Constitutions, in their original liberal meaning, were intended to provide formal and impartial rules of government. Neither curricula nor constitutions are considered to serve these functions by the advocates of political correctness. Curricula are hybrids of various programs of indoctrination; constitutions are to serve partisan, political interests.

In this sense, political correctness is profoundly illiberal and profoundly anti-political. Its agenda for social revolution is one that threatens to invoke all the excesses of the French Revolution. It originates out of a superficial understanding of our natural longings and a cynical reading of the conventions and artifices by which we have traditionally lived. Its ethos of victimhood is incapable of giving rise to those capacities of judgment and rule, thought and persuasive speech, which reality, always intractable, demands. Like all fashionable political projects, its interpretation of the political problem is superficial. The politically correct deceive us into thinking that the difficult work of politics is being undertaken, while in fact the real sources of injustice and disorder are being neglected. They demand ruthless measures and pretend the world admits of easy solutions. Reality, on the other hand, demands accommodating measures and balanced, continual solutions. What is tragic is that we are allowing the politics of political correctness to destroy what was coherent and balanced in our constitutional tradition.

NOTES

1   Helen Pitt, 'France Gets Tough on Circumcision of Young Girls', in *The Guardian* as reprinted in *The Ottawa Citizen*, 4 Mar. 1993, A8.

2   Sheri David-Barron, 'Drs Drafting Policy on Female Circumcision: Statement likely to forbid M.D.s to perform African ritual', in *The Ottawa Citizen*, 10 Jan. 1991, B7.

3 Sheri David-Barron, 'Female Circumcision: Practiced in Parts of Africa Has Foot-Hold Here', in *The Ottawa Citizen*, 10 June 1991, B1.

4 Ibid., 4 Mar. 1993, A8.

5 Sheri David-Barron, 'Female Circumcision Parents Rights: Group Says', in *The Ottawa Citizen*, 26 June 1991, B5.

6 Ibid.

7 Ibid., 11 Sept. 1992, A10.

8 Ibid., 14 Mar. 1993, B5. Dr Patel was, however, opposed to the use of the tests for this purpose.

9 Richard Mitchell, 'Sex Selection Clinic: Panic Unburdened by Fact' in *The Ottawa Citizen*, 18 Mar. 1993, A8.

10 Eric Voegelin, *Order and History*, vol. 1, *Israel and Revelation* (Baton Rouge, La.: Louisiana State University Press, 1956).

11 Mark Dickerson and Thomas Flanagan, *An Introduction to Government and Politics: A Conceptual Approach* (Toronto: Methuen, 1986), 27–35, 50–8.

12 Hannah Arendt, *The Human Condition* (Chicago: University of Chicago Press, 1963).

13 Leo Strauss, *Natural Right and History* (Chicago: University of Chicago Press, 1953).

14 Camille Paglia, *Sexual Personae* (New York: Vintage, 1991).

15 *The Encyclopedia of Philosophy*, vols. 1 and 2 (New York: Macmillan, 1967), 273–6.

16 William Safire, 'On Language', *New York Times Magazine*, Mar. 1991).

17 Eric Voegelin, 'The Eclipse of Reality', in Maurice Natanson, ed., *Phenomenology and Social Research* (The Hague: Martinus Nijhoff, 1973), 185–94.

13

Reconstituting Democracy: Orthodoxy and Research in Law and Social Science

Robert Martin

Throughout Canada's interminable constitutional debates a central role has been played by academics. Many of these academics have been law teachers; some have been social scientists. An implicit assumption underlying the discourse of academics is that, to a substantial degree, what they are saying and writing is the result of detached, scientific study and research. But to anyone who has followed our constitutional debate, the degree to which the academics tend to say the same things must be striking. The academic contribution to the debate has involved far more orthodoxy than science. What follows attempts to shed some light on how this came about and to illustrate the extent to which orthodoxy has come to dominate academic discourse.

This chapter is an essay about intellectual corruption. It describes some of the pathology in academic social sciences and law. Truth, objectivity and the discipline of research methodology are being abandoned, replaced by nothing more than a determination to propagate orthodoxy.

One of the many conceits that afflict us is the belief that we are all free-thinkers. We recognize that people living in other times and other places have been constrained by received ways of thinking, but we like to see ourselves as liberated from these sorts of fetters. Having no sense of history, we imagine we are no longer governed by its rules.[1] In this we are wrong. Like all societies, ours has its own established way of thinking, its own orthodoxy. Unlike other societies, we tend to deny the existence of such things, which only makes them more difficult to grasp. Our orthodoxy, in common with other orthodoxies, serves to determine the limits of what may be thought about and how. It defines the subjects of acceptable discourse and the way those subjects may be approached.

Our orthodoxy is applied in a comparatively gentle fashion. We neither hang people nor burn them alive for thinking or giving voice to improper thoughts. But mild as they may be, there are sanctions and they both deter the faint-hearted and punish transgressors.

My aim is to draw attention to the ways in which our current orthodoxy affects research. Any orthodoxy will tend to define both the matters to be researched and how that research is carried out. I will begin by setting out the elements of the orthodoxy and then look at its explicit and implicit applications in shaping the way research is conducted.

My analysis will be confined to the fields of law and the social sciences, since these are areas I know something about. I also believe this emphasis can be justified on other than parochial grounds. Research in law and the social sciences tends to have a significant effect in the formulation of public policy; that is, the research done in these areas can have concrete results in all our lives.

The situation that I will describe with respect to law and social science is not unique and is by no means restricted to these areas. There is a generalized assault underway that is transforming long-standing notions of what is acceptable and what is not in research methodology. As a result, the utility and the very legitimacy of research are being undermined.[2]

OUR ORTHODOXY

It is difficult to state the content of our reigning orthodoxy. It is difficult both because it is of recent origin and because there are no generally accepted, canonical statements of it.[3] We have no Thirty-Nine Articles to turn to. This is not to say that no one has attempted formal statements of the orthodoxy. The Rae government in Ontario and many, many Canadian universities have attempted to formally define different aspects of the orthodoxy. I will return to these statements later, but will, for now, attempt to set out what I take to be the central elements of the orthodoxy.[4]

RELATIVISM

The starting point in understanding our orthodoxy is its commitment to relativism—intellectual, cultural, and moral.[5] A paradox is immediately apparent. How can one have an orthodoxy based on relativism? There are two answers. First, I am only trying to set out the elements of the orthodoxy, not defend it. It is shot through with inconsistencies and contradictions. Second, it is essential to understand that the practitioners of the orthodoxy apply it to all ideas except their own. The soundness of relativism is assumed; relativism itself is not subjected to relativistic analysis.

Relativistic thought rejects any notion of absolutes. Intellectual relativism, the manifestation most relevant for present purposes, contains a number of sub-elements. Most important, it denies the existence or even the possibility of objective truth. The very notion of truth is chimerical; to purport to seek it is to obscure other and probably sinister motives. Since the study of the actual world and the concrete experiences of real human beings in it could lead to brushes with something that might look like objective truth, devotees of orthodoxy tend to be attracted to the abstract. And since there is no truth, all ideas, hypotheses, and assertions are, by definition, equal. Discriminating amongst ideas is seen to be as invidious as discriminating amongst human beings.

As we shall see, the denial of the possibility of objective truth carries with it some disturbing implications. Two are especially important. While nonrelativists generally understood that achieving or expressing truth was difficult, they did grasp that the distinction between truth telling and lying was salutary. While we might never be able to agree on the truth, we did understand what lying was about. But once we jettison the notion of truth, we also abandon the corollary notion of lies. To the relativist, the distinction between seeking the truth and telling lies is meaningless. Furthermore, I think it was generally understood that no human being was capable of thinking in a completely unbiased fashion. But scholarship demanded that each individual strive to recognise and overcome his or her biases. Relativism makes that striving unnecessary.

SUBJECTIVITY

Since there can be no such thing as objective truth, practitioners of orthodoxy embrace subjectivity. What comes to matter in intellectual enquiry, then, is not objective facts, but subjective feelings. If you *feel* something, it must be so. And one person's feelings are as good as anyone else's.

I must affirm that there is both an objective physical world and concrete social reality and that both exist regardless of the vagaries of human subjectivity. To take a well-known example, this planet is round. Individual subjectivity cannot alter that fact. No matter how many human beings feel the earth is flat and no matter how passionately they may cling to that belief, it cannot change the planet's shape.[6]

Indeed, the orthodox view is that all assertions, whatever their content or character, are simply manifestations of subjectivity. Thus, no matter how long and how thoroughly I may have studied a subject, no matter how rigorous has been my attempt to understand it, anything I say about it is merely an expression of my subjective feelings. And my subjective feelings deserve no more nor less weight than those of anyone else.

This is a curious epistemology. At its logical extreme it denies the possibility of knowledge, or if that is overstating the matter, it places knowledge and ignorance on an equal footing. And there is a further problem for the scholar.

Expressions of subjectivity are, by definition, unverifiable, even untestable. Subjectivity demands the rejection of established tests for accuracy.

The orthodoxy also addresses the roots of subjectivity. The primary constituents of an individual's subjectivity are seen to be that person's sex, skin colour, and sexual orientation. Men think differently from women, blacks from whites, and homosexuals from heterosexuals. To be concrete, the orthodoxy would hold that the reason I think the way I do is that I am a white male.

When we combine the three elements of this fascination with subjectivity, we get a clearer sense of where the orthodoxy is taking us. There is no such thing as truth; there is only subjectivity; and subjectivity is simply a manifestation of a particular combination of ascriptive criteria. Thus, no assertion that I make requires either analysis or refutation on its own terms. It is simply me giving vent to my subjectivity. And since my subjectivity is nothing but a reflection of my sex and my colour and my sexual orientation, anything I assert can be accepted or rejected according to how one happens to feel about my sex, my race, or my sexual orientation. This is not only profoundly anti-intellectual; it is deeply disturbing in its political implications. Both meaningful discourse and the notion of equal citizenship in a political community are denied.

VICTIMOLOGY

Practitioners of orthodoxy claim to be profoundly concerned about the plight of victims. Victims, as a result, loom very large in orthodox expression. The key to social and intellectual legitimacy is to be a victim, or, if one has little or no personal experience of being a victim, to be a member of a recognized victim group. The list of such groups is extensive. There is, indeed, a place for everyone who is not an able-bodied, heterosexual, white male.

Perhaps the most important implication of victimology for the way the orthodoxy operates is that it obviates any need for the concrete analysis of real social conditions. All able-bodied, white, male heterosexuals are, by definition, wealthy and powerful. All other human beings are oppressed and exploited. Difficult and troublesome questions like class simply do not arise.

There is, further, no need for anyone to verify a claim to victim status. If you belong to a recognized victim group, you are a victim; if you don't, you're not. The need for evidence of anything is neatly dispensed with.

The orthodoxy exempts all members of recognized victim groups from critical analysis. Asking questions about the behaviour or beliefs or arguments of anyone who belongs to a victim group is called 'blaming the victim'.[7] The orthodoxy defines such behaviour as unacceptable.

It is equally unacceptable for someone who is not a member of a victim group to write about or discuss the experience or beliefs of someone who is. This is called 'appropriation of voice'.[8] In its more extreme forms, this attachment of the orthodoxy to solipsistic ways of thinking further denies the possibility of social thought or analysis. Men cannot understand, and therefore cannot write or think about, women; white women cannot understand 'women of colour'; heterosexual 'women of colour' cannot understand lesbian 'women of colour', and on and on.[9]

POLITICIZATION

The fourth element in the orthodoxy is the politicization of everything. Work, literature, social intercourse, and personal and family relations are all defined as inherently political. And this is an exceedingly polarized politics. Much of our intelligentsia, especially its members who belong to recognized victim groups, seem to feel constrained to behave as if they were permanently at war. Anger is the preferred mood. The rhetoric is that of implacable struggle and hostility. Rational discourse is not promoted in an atmosphere in which people define anyone who disagrees with them as the enemy and where everyone is at pains to establish the intensity of his or her own passion and commitment.[10]

I should stress again that the various elements of the orthodoxy are by no means consistent with each other. It is, to take an obvious example, logically impossible to be both a highly politicized champion of victims and a relativist. This does not seem to bother anyone.

CYNICISM

Running through the orthodoxy is a deep, almost reflexive, cynicism. Indeed, cynicism is the inevitable result of embracing the other elements of the orthodoxy. Principles, institutions, beliefs are taken to be nothing but smokescreens, fashioned for no other reason than to obscure the oppression of victims. Everyone who does not belong to a recognized victim group is presumed to lie most of the time. Attempts to explain events are dismissed as 'cover-ups'.

The major purveyors of cynicism are the mass media. Knavery and skullduggery are seen to be endemic. But this cynicism has no goal, no obvious end, and no critical purpose. It is empty and barren, cynicism for its own sake. It has become very popular amongst university lecturers.

EXPLICIT APPLICATION

In this section I wish to give some examples of ways in which the orthodoxy is formally and directly used to constrain discussion, analysis, and therefore research. To use legal terminology, I am talking about prior restraints—rules of conduct that seek to limit in advance what human beings may write or speak. The primary goal in creating and enforcing such rules is to threaten potential transgressors, to ensure compliance through intimidation. I will begin by talking about the state and then move on to the universities.

THE STATE

The state can directly affect intellectual discourse and research in two ways. It may seek to define social truth and it may prohibit certain forms of discourse.

The Canadian state has not historically been interested in setting out formal definitions of social truth. Ontario's new Employment Equity Act[11] is a remarkable and unprecedented departure from principle. Its Preamble states:

> The people of Ontario recognize that Aboriginal people, people with disabilities, members of racial minorities and women experience higher rates of unemployment than other people in Ontario. The people of Ontario also recognize that people in these groups experience more discrimination than other people in finding employment, in retaining employment and in being promoted. As a result, they are underrepresented in most areas of employment, especially in senior and management positions, and they are overrepresented in those areas of employment that provide low pay and little chance for advancement. The burden imposed on the people in these groups and on the communities in which they live is unacceptable.

> The people of Ontario recognize that this lack of employment equity exists in both the public and private sectors of Ontario. It is caused in part by systemic and intentional discrimination in employment. People of merit are too often overlooked or denied opportunities because of this discrimination. The people of Ontario recognize that when objective standards govern employment opportunities, Ontario will have a workforce that is truly representative of its society.

> The people of Ontario have recognized in the Human Rights Code the inherent dignity and equal and inalienable rights of all members of the human family and have recognized those rights in respect of employment in such statutes as the Employment Standards Act and the Pay Equity Act. This Act extends the principles of those Acts and has as its object the amelioration of conditions in employment for Aboriginal people, people with disabilities, members of racial minorities and women in all workplaces in Ontario and the provision of the opportunity for people in these groups to fulfil their potential in employment.

> The people of Ontario recognize that eliminating discrimination in employment and increasing the opportunity of individuals to contribute in the workplace will benefit all people in Ontario.

This Preamble is little more than a restatement of the governing orthodoxy as I have already set it out. But now the orthodoxy is officially proclaimed by the state to be true. Leave aside the fact that such studies as exist have found few distinctions in levels of unemployment or rates of pay between members of so-called 'visible minorities' and other Canadians.[12] We now know that members of the various victim groups mentioned do experience 'higher rates of unemployment' and 'more discrimination' than other people. How do we know these things to be true? Because the state says so. How do we know that 'employment equity' is good for us? Again, the state says so. How did we come to know these things? Was there a Royal Commission to determine the scope and intensity of discrimination in employment in Ontario? Of course not. The state simply knows.

The NDP government of Ontario also sought to prohibit certain forms of discourse. The most thorough and far-reaching attempt to place express limits on research and academic discourse in Canada is the 'Framework' document issued by the Ontario Ministry of Education and Training in October of 1993. There were, in fact, two documents—one called 'Framework Regarding Prevention of Harassment and Discrimination in Ontario *Universities*' and the other 'Framework Regarding Prevention of Harassment and Discrimination in Ontario *Colleges*'. The genesis of the two documents was 'the ruminations of Stephen Lewis. The extensive "letter" Lewis sent to the Premier, following his investigations into the causes of the Yonge Street mini-riot of May 1992, failed to reference a single piece of serious research.'[13] The fact that Lewis's report had no empirical foundation did not, of course, matter. It expressed the prevailing orthodoxy, painting Ontario as a place seething with racism. The government of Ontario has treated the report as if it were divine revelation. Both 'Framework' documents note, as background, that Stephen Lewis 'recommended' such measures. No further justification, apparently, is required.

The university 'Framework', which was identical in all material respects to the colleges 'Framework', announced there was to be 'zero tolerance' of 'harassment' and 'discrimination' and then went on to set out norms of conduct that all Ontario universities were required to adopt. These were to apply to faculty, staff, and students at universities as well as to people who had contracts with universities and even to casual visitors. They were to embrace conduct both on and off university campuses, including at social functions and over the telephone. Persons were prohibited from engaging in 'harassment' or 'discrimination' or from 'creating a negative environment'. The 'Framework' purported to define such activities, relating all of them to the list of prohibited grounds of discrimination set out in the Ontario Human Rights Code, that is: race, ancestry, place of origin, colour, ethnic origin, citizenship, disability, age, marital status, family status, the receipt of public assistance, record of provincial offences, or pardoned federal offences. Harassment was said to involve

> one or a series of vexatious comments or conduct related to one or more of the prohibited grounds that is known or might reasonably be known to be unwelcome/unwanted, offensive, intimidating, hostile or inappropriate.

> Examples include gestures, remarks, jokes, taunting, innuendo, display of offensive materials, offensive graffiti, threats, verbal or physical assault, imposition of academic penalties, hazing, stalking, shunning or exclusion related to the prohibited grounds.

The 'Framework' suggested, further, that creating a 'negative environment' amounted to 'poisoning the work or study environment'. I mention this to illustrate our increasing difficulty in distinguishing between the abstract and the concrete. The authors of the 'Framework' clearly believed there was an actual thing that could be described as a 'poisoned learning environment'.

The punishments that universities were to be required to impose on transgressors were to include 'verbal or written apology, written reprimand, barring contractors from future bids, barring from campus, transfer, demotion, suspension, mandatory training/education, dismissal or expulsion'.

It must be evident that the 'Framework' would have precluded most discussion of anything involving human beings in universities. Nonetheless, the 'Framework' was approved by the Ontario Conference of University Faculty Associations and the president of the Canadian Association of University Teachers.[14] Since the 'Framework' was not initially made public, few people knew of its existence. More people heard about it, however, and opposition began to develop, culminating in a critical piece in the *Globe and Mail* by Robert Fulford.[15] On 10 February 1994, Dave Cooke, the Ontario Minister of Education and Training, withdrew the university 'Framework'. The colleges 'Framework' is still in effect.[16]

There are also some provisions of the general Canadian law that could affect the way research is carried out.

Section 319 of the Criminal Code prohibits the wilful promotion of hatred. While there have only been three prosecutions under this section,[17] it is conceivable that persons might be intimidated from doing research. Professor J. Philippe Rushton of the University of Western Ontario was subjected to a police investigation in 1989 for having expressed certain conclusions arising from his research, but the then Attorney General of Ontario refused to agree to a prosecution of Rushton.

The law of civil defamation might also be employed to sanction or discourage different kinds of research. There is widespread belief in Canada in 'libel chill', the notion that fear of being sued for libel may discourage the publication of heterodox ideas. The belief in 'libel chill' is much exaggerated, and I do not believe the law of libel influences research activities in Canada. I am only aware of one instance in this country where academic controversy led to a libel action.[18]

THE UNIVERSITIES

The 'Framework' document was sent to Ontario universities in October of 1993. Not one university administration spoke out against this document. It was only when others had brought the matter to public attention that the presidents of three of the province's twenty-odd universities added their voices. Indeed, the universities have been in the vanguard of imposing orthodoxy. It is the norm for universities today to have speech codes, formal statements that seek to define what may not be talked about on university campuses. The very existence of such codes is remarkable. Universities are supposed to be, or at least I had always thought they were supposed to be, places that by their very nature encouraged the widest possible inquiry and debate. It is evident that I have been wrong.

The University of Western Ontario's policy was typical. Its 'Race Relations

Policy', adopted in 1990, prohibited 'Racial Harassment', which it defined as 'unwelcome attention of a racially oriented nature, including remarks, jokes, gestures, slurs, innuendoes, or other behaviour, verbal or physical, which is directed at an individual or group by another person or group who knows, or ought reasonably to know, that this attention is unwanted'. The policy also required the hiring of a race relations officer. This official was made responsible for enforcing the policy, that is to say, for catching 'racists'. Inevitably, the policy was abused. A trivial accusation by a student against a professor led to a hearing, which in turn led to further hearings. Lawyers became involved, the matter spilled over into the press, and, in the end the university capitulated, with very bad grace, I might add, and paid the faculty member's legal bills and gave her a year's leave to make up for the time she had sacrificed to defend herself. The university also had the good sense to amend its race relations policy. In 1994 all references to direct enforcement of the policy against members of the university were deleted.[19]

The Canadian professoriate has shown itself to be about as cowardly as the people who run Canadian universities. The vast majority have quietly acquiesced in the imposition of controls on how they may think, speak, and write. It inheres in speech codes that they will be abused in ways that constrain discourse within the limits of orthodoxy. Abuses such as the one I have briefly described are not anomalies or aberrations. They are the natural result of these policies. Commenting on the case I described above, Western's race relations officer observed; 'I think that this case is reflective of what is happening on campuses across the country and it could happen with any [equity] policy.'[20] Professors who wish to avoid these sorts of difficulties will make sure they keep away from subjects or arguments which have been defined as incorrect. Intimidation, unfortunately, works.

IMPLICIT APPLICATION

In this section I will deal with the way the orthodoxy operates implicitly to shape the way research is carried out. Here I am concerned with how the orthodoxy works in people's minds to create an inclination or predisposition to address, or not address, certain issues and, more important, to reach certain conclusions about those issues. I will begin with some observations about the general effects of the orthodoxy and will then discuss four recent quasi-official reports that demonstrate the destructive effects the orthodoxy has had on research in Canada.

GENERAL OBSERVATIONS

The orthodoxy, I believe, works in people's minds to persuade them that the point of writing is not to seek truth, but to demonstrate to the world that one is firmly on the right side. And this, surely, has always been the effect of orthodoxies. An orthodoxy is a body of thought, a point of view, that becomes widely adopted. To diverge from the orthodoxy is to proclaim oneself to be an outsider, a heretic. It is vastly more comfortable and more useful to announce to the world that one thinks only correct thoughts. Orthodoxies are maintained, at the margin, through force and intimidation. But they survive and prosper from day to day on nothing more than the widespread fear invoked by the prospect of being caught thinking improper thoughts. In the extreme case one can affirm one's commitment to the orthodoxy simply by proclaiming one's status as a victim. In a recent journal article the writer announced: I am a white middle class Jewish radical lesbian feminist.[21]

Moving to a less extreme instance, in 1985 Professor Constance Backhouse of the Faculty of Law at the University of Western Ontario published an article about Clara Brett Martin, apparently Canada's first woman lawyer.[22] The article was adulatory, as was consistent with the author's avowed search for 'heroines'. And Clara Brett Martin did become something of a heroine: a number of feminist ventures were named after her, and the new head office for the Ontario Ministry of the Attorney General proudly displayed her name. Four years later a letter came to light that seriously damaged Martin's reputation. The letter, written in 1915, appeared to indicate that Martin held anti-Semitic views.[23] Serious doubts arose about Martin's status as a heroine and about Professor Backhouse, whose article had been largely responsible for Martin's posthumous rise to prominence. Much of a 1992 number of the *Canadian Journal of Women and the Law*[24] was devoted to soul-searching about Clara Brett Martin. Constance Backhouse contributed two articles to this number. She was clearly afraid that she herself might be accused of anti-Semitism. In the passage that follows she expresses her horror at the prospect of being seen publicly to be thinking improper thoughts. She is referring specifically to criticisms of her first article in the same number of the *CJWL*, an article in which she acknowledged Clara Brett Martin's anti-Semitism.

> As I read through the extensive, detailed, and carefully constructed critiques contained in the reports, what really seared into my consciousness were several lines which indicated that my article was 'apologist' for the anti-semitism of Clara Brett Martin and 'anti-semitic' itself.
>
> There is a certain 'weak-in-the-knees, wet-under-the armpit' adrenalin rush which visits me, and I suspect others, when I find myself characterized this way, or in parallel ways, in print. This seems to occur regardless of how supportively and thoughtfully the message is conveyed. And I want to emphasize, at this point, that I noticed, and appreciated, the care that had gone into framing the critiques. Nevertheless, my initial response was combined dismay and horror.[25]

This desire to demonstrate one's fealty to orthodoxy and the terror of expressing heterodox ideas make a powerful and, it seems, largely irresistible, combination.

Writers may openly proclaim that they have abandoned traditional methodological restraints. Again, I turn to Professor Constance Backhouse.

In 1991 she published *Petticoats and Prejudice: Women and Law in Nineteenth-Century Canada*, a collection of essays on legal history.[26] In the 'introduction' to the volume she stated expressly that her purpose in writing was to 'locate' 'heroines', to 'forge a new definition of "heroine" '.[27] As if to dispel any misunderstanding, Backhouse re-affirmed in 1992 that her aim indeed had been to create 'heroines'.[28] Perhaps it is unnecessary, but I must stress that to set out consciously to create 'heroines' (or 'heroes') is to abandon scholarly research and engage in nothing more than the production of propaganda.

The orthodoxy can also operate to suggest to its devotees that proof of their assertions is not needed, as long as those assertions are consistent with the orthodoxy. Some random examples will illustrate the point. Writing in the *Dalhousie Law Journal* in 1992, Professor Hester Lessard of the Faculty of Law at the University of Victoria pointed to the 'systemic racism implicit in legal reasoning based on precedent and in the rules of statutory interpretation'.[29] No explication was provided as to how exactly the fundamental methodologies of the legal system were 'racist'. No illustrations were offered. One might have thought the question whether any system based on following established approaches—precedents—was 'racist', would depend on whether the precedents relied on were or were not themselves 'racist', but no matter. The statement was simply assumed to be obvious, which it probably was to anyone who had adopted the orthodoxy. In a similar vein, Professor Rosemary Cairns-Way of the Faculty of Law at the University of Ottawa could inform readers of the *University of New Brunswick Law Journal* in 1993 that the doctrine of *mens rea*, the idea that you should not be convicted of a crime unless you actually meant to commit a crime, 'understood in law as neutral and objective, has been unmasked as partial, and as privileging a particular (male) viewpoint'.[30] Again, no examples to support this assertion were offered. The assertion was baldly stated as if it were unassailably correct. And, in a sense, it is. It is correct, because the orthodoxy says it is.

Abstractions are turned into concrete reality and then acquire an intellectual status that removes them from the normal constraints of critical discourse. The clearest example of this is 'patriarchy'. By its nature, the term is used metaphorically, suggesting a society and polity where men dominate in all spheres. It began its life as simply a conceptual device. But it has now been reified. It is assumed there is a concrete thing called 'patriarchy'. Its immanence, its characteristics, and its operation can also all be assumed.

Practitioners of orthodoxy feel free to make such factual statements as they please without the necessity of supporting them with evidence. Consider the following. In their 1993 book, *History of the Canadian Peoples*, the authors discussed the factors that created the Conscription Crisis of 1917. The generally accepted view is that the combination of a large military force in the field and very heavy casualties made it impossible for Canada to maintain its force solely on the basis of voluntary enlistment. The authors rejected this view and offered another, astonishing, analysis.

> The shortage of soldiers for the war effort was compounded by the exclu-
> sionary policies practised by the Canadian military. Despite the eagerness of
> some women to serve overseas, they were unwelcome on the front lines. The
> only official role for women in the armed forces was as nurses.
> When Indian, Japanese or African-Canadian men offered their services,
> they, too, were often turned away.[31]

No reference is provided for the assertion about women. Where did the
authors get their information? Notice also how they say '*some* women' were
eager for active service. How many is *some*? If the authors could establish that
there was more than one such woman, they could, presumably, claim their
assertion was accurate. But the reader has no idea. A single illustration is
given to support the assertion about 'Indian, Japanese or African-Canadian
men', but, again, no references are provided. Notice that such men were
allegedly turned away '*often*'. How many times is *often*? The authors conclude
this part of their book by referring to the 'racist sensibilities' of Canadian soldiers in the trenches. Once again, no evidence is offered.

The wildest assertions are made regularly with no apparent sense that
there is some sort of obligation to support what one says. Let me give one
more illustration. Professor Sheila McIntyre of the Faculty of Law, Queen's
University, ruminated on 'anti-feminism' in the *Bulletin* of the Canadian
Association of University Teachers in 1989.

> Consciousness of my own ill health caused me to register how many feminist
> scholars are struggling with serious illness. I know two other feminist legal
> scholars with rheumatoid arthritis. Among my academic acquaintances are
> feminists suffering from lupus, Epstein-Barr, serious insomnia, cancer, clini-
> cal nervous disorders, candida, and cluster migraines. Given how few femi-
> nist scholars there are, it is difficult to throw this off as mere coincidence.
> I think anti-feminism plays a significant role in triggering or aggravating
> such diseases, not least because acute stress and exhaustion have been med-
> ically linked to all these illnesses.[32]

It is not much of a step from obviating the need for any evidence to denying the existence of evidence that might possibly contradict one's point of
view. Here Professor Diana Majury of the Department of Law at Carleton
University explains why she refused to read a judicial decision that she was,
nonetheless, writing about.

> I have not read the Court of Appeal decision. Having read about it and heard
> about it, I chose not to put myself through the pain of reading it. The
> excerpts contained in the Supreme Court of Canada decision confirmed for
> me that I had made the right decision. I did experience reading these seg-
> ments as painful. This experience to me raises some very fundamental ques-
> tions about using legal forums to try to address problems of discrimination.
> Can a court decision itself be discriminatory because of the assumptions it
> brings to bear and perpetuates and because of the tremendous impact it can
> have on the disadvantaged group whose issue is before it?

I feel the need to add a footnote to this footnote because of the very negative response it triggered in at least two of the referees of this article. In the
words of one referee—'despite some astute observations about *Janzen*, the
discussion of *Janzen* is hampered (if not discredited) by the author's admission that she did not read the Court of Appeal decision in the case.' It was
suggested that I read the case and delete the footnote, or at least delete the
footnote. I find this response disturbing. It was difficult for me to write this
footnote knowing that some readers would see this as a flaw in my scholarship, if not in my character. But I felt it was important to acknowledge the
pain of doing this work, even the so-called 'academic' part of this work. And
it felt positive to acknowledge that I had made a conscious and deliberate
decision not to put myself through the particular pain of reading this particular decision. It was my way of diminishing the decision itself. I do not feel
that it hampered my discussion of the case, nor did the referee explain the
effect to me. If I had felt that not having read the Court of Appeal decision
somehow impeded my understanding of the Supreme Court of Canada decision, I would have read the Court of Appeal decision.

I understand that many will disagree with my decision—better to be fully
aware of everything said by the Court Appeal—the pain experienced is simply part of that full awareness. But I do not expect in the referee process of a
feminist journal to have the pain that I experience and about which I make
difficult choices in the context of my work discounted or rejected in the
name of 'credibility'.[33]

A well-known and highly serviceable methodological trick is to define one's
terms in such a way as to lead inexorably to the result one wants to achieve.
This is clearly not something invented by the practitioners of the current
orthodoxy. But neither have they eschewed it, which is one reason there continues to be vast debate over terminology. Despite this, I believe that Professor
Diana Majury, in another article, broke some new ground with the following.

I argue that it is in women's interest to refuse to subscribe to or commit
themselves to, any single meaning of equality. Feminist advocates need to
learn to use the equality discourse on behalf of women in as many and as
diverse situations as the term can bear. The needs and experiences of women
will dictate the meaning of equality in each particular context. It is these
needs and experiences which should be brought into the open and promoted, not some reified idea of equality.[34]

The logical conclusion from all this is a rejection of the idea that research
must be conducted in a manner that accords with methodological principles.
This, it seems to me, is what a new collection of essays, *Investigating Gender
Bias*, attempts to do.[35] As the book's title suggests, the task of research is not
to establish or define 'gender bias', for its existence is assumed, but to unearth
illustrations and examples of it. Professor Sheila Martin of the Faculty of Law
of the University of Calgary goes to the point of arguing that to ask for proof
of 'gender bias' is nothing more than to manifest 'gender bias'.[36]

It might be said that up to this point I have done little but raise a series of
aesthetic quibbles, and that I have neither established that the prevailing
orthodoxy has any particular effect on research nor that, if it does, there is

any great cause for concern. To address these matters I will leave off the listing of examples[37] and turn to four recent reports, each of which may well end up having concrete effects on the way we live.

FOUR REPORTS

The Wilson Report

In 1991 the Canadian Bar Association asked retired Supreme Court of Canada Judge Bertha Wilson to chair its Task Force[38] on Gender Equality in the Legal Profession. This committee published its report, *Touchstones for Change: Equality, Diversity and Accountability*, in 1993. The report concluded there was vast inequality between men and women in the legal profession, bias towards women in both the law itself and its practice, and harassment and oppression of female law students, lawyers, and even judges. But, given the committee's research methodology, its conclusions could not have been otherwise. Its research methodology was little more than applied orthodoxy.

In her 'introduction', Bertha Wilson affirmed her commitment to central elements of the orthodoxy. She stated:

A *white* view of the world is not neutral.
A *masculine* view of the world is not neutral.
A *heterosexual* view of the world is not neutral.[39]

The report talked of a 'glass ceiling',[40] as if this were a real thing and not a rhetorical flourish. Reified rhetoric like this is a useful methodological device for avoiding concrete investigation. Since the 'glass ceiling' is defined as being invisible, its existence can neither be proved nor disproved.

The methodological deficiencies in the Wilson report are apparent in the sections dealing with legal education.[41] In these sections, as in others, the report relied heavily on responses to questionnaires. Some serious methodological flaws immediately become apparent. The committee mailed questionnaires to all women teaching in Canadian university law schools and to an equal number of men similarly employed. There had been considerable advance publicity surrounding the Wilson committee and its work. Bertha Wilson and her politics were very well-known throughout the legal profession as a result of her judgments and the many speeches she had made. It is inconceivable to me that there was anyone, male or female, teaching in a law faculty in Canada who did not know what the Wilson committee was and, more important, the directions towards which it was predisposed. To put it bluntly, every recipient of the questionnaire must have known what the right answers were. Further, the respondents to the questionnaire were self-selected. Those who received the questionnaire who wished to return it to the committee did so; those who did not, didn't.

The questionnaire (which is not reproduced in the published version of the report) asked respondents to give subjective responses to a series of open-ended questions. They were asked, for example, whether colleagues and students gave 'appropriate weight' to their opinions. They were asked whether they had experienced, observed, or been made aware of unwanted teasing, joking, or comments directed at themselves or female colleagues by professors or students. The responses to questions such as this were then treated as proof of the accuracy of the facts asserted in them. If female professors felt their opinions were not given 'appropriate weight', the mere expression of that feeling was taken as proof that, indeed, their opinions were not receiving 'appropriate weight'. This methodology neatly avoids any questions about the content of these opinions and whether they merited 'appropriate weight', whatever that might mean.

The report is littered with unattributed anecdotal comments, the veracity and accuracy of which, since they were purportedly made by women, are assumed to be beyond question, but which certainly cannot be tested. Contentious assertions made throughout the report are given the authority of footnote numbers. When the footnote is consulted, it usually turns out to be a reference to an article by a noted feminist. For example, reference is made to an article by Professor Bruce Feldthusen of the Faculty of Law at the University of Western Ontario called 'The Gender Wars: "Where the Boys Are" '.[42] The article is pretentious, exaggerated, self-serving, and downright dishonest.

The report abounds with assertions like: 'A substantial percentage of women had heard professors make derogatory or sexist comments about feminists, at least occasionally.'[43] What is a 'substantial percentage'? What were the comments? What does 'at least occasionally' mean?

The report also makes assertions without offering any evidence at all, like 'Women, particularly junior faculty, are marginalised through poorly located offices.'[44] And, again, fundamental methodological questions are simply ignored. What is meant by 'marginalised'? According to what criteria was it determined that a particular office was 'poorly located'? Was a physical survey conducted of every law faculty building in Canada to determine which offices were 'poorly located' and the percentage of these offices occupied by female faculty members?

Where evidence is given to suggest a conclusion adverse to the orthodoxy, the evidence is rejected. The report notes on one page that the proportion of 'visible minorities' in law schools is twice the proportion of 'visible minorities' in Canadian society as a whole,[45] but on another page talks about 'discrimination' in law school admissions policies, asserting that the Law School Admission Test 'adversely affects students from non-Anglo-Saxon backgrounds'.[46] No evidence is presented for this assertion, but I suppose everyone knows how difficult it is for persons of Jewish or Scottish ancestry to get into law school.

In a more sinister vein, the report suggests in several places that criticism of or disagreement with feminism or feminist ideas should be regarded as a form of sexual harassment.

The Wilson report made sweeping recommendations for change. But the entire enterprise is a house of cards.

The Jury Selection Report

David Pomerant, who is a lawyer, began an investigation of multiculturalism and jury selection while working for the Law Reform Commission of Canada. When the Law Reform Commission was shut down in February of 1992, Pomerant was given a contract by the Justice Department to complete his research. The department published his report, *Multiculturalism, Representation and the Jury Selection Process in Canadian Criminal Cases* in 1994.

Pomerant stated the purpose of his research was to investigate 'the extent to which there is a need to reform the jury trial process to better reflect or accommodate the needs or aspirations of minorities in Canadian society'.[47] It seems not to have occurred to him that we have juries in criminal cases not to address the 'needs or aspirations' of anyone, but simply to determine whether the person accused of committing a crime is guilty or not guilty. But never mind. The report made numerous and far-reaching suggestions for change. Pomerant wished to see the adoption of expressly racial criteria in jury selection. The changes he recommended would transform not simply jury selection, but the meaning of citizenship in Canada. One would assume that compelling reasons for advocating such changes had been established. One would be wrong.

The entire report covers 80 pages. (There is also a six-page bibliography.) Only six pages were devoted to setting out the empirical basis—the social reality—that underlies the report's lengthy recommendations. Pomerant noted that the proportion of Canadians whose ancestors' origins were in Asia, Africa, Latin America, or the Caribbean has increased in recent decades—hardly much of a revelation. But are these Canadians and, in addition, aboriginal persons actually being excluded from jury service? Is there racial bias in the way juries are selected? The report was decidedly thin on evidence. There was a reference to the Rodney King trial in the United States, as if what happened to Mr King's assailants says something about the jury system in Canada. There was also discussion of the injustice visited on Donald Marshall in Nova Scotia.[48] And that's it. There are no more bits of evidence.

The report noted that inquiries into the justice systems and aboriginal peoples in Manitoba and Alberta had expressed 'concerns'. The fact that steps have been taken by the Attorneys General of Canada and Ontario to look into similar questions was treated as proof that a problem existed. Seventy-four pages of the report were then devoted to advocating detailed and fundamental changes in our jury system on the basis of one Canadian fact—the Donald Marshall case.

The Panel on Violence Against Women

The Panel on Violence against Women was established by the federal minister responsible for the Status of Women in August 1991. The panel was given a budget of $10 million in public funds. The panel's report, *Changing the Landscape: Ending Violence—Achieving Equality*, was published in 1993. It is a vast confidence trick.

On the first page of the report the panel openly abandoned any effort at objectivity and affirmed that it intended rather to look at the issues it was to address through 'a feminist lens'.[49] The panel stated: 'violence against women is seen as the consequence of social, economic and political inequality built into the structure of society and reinforced through assumptions expressed in the language and ideologies of sexism, racism and class.'[50] Why, one might ask, did the panel bother conducting any research at all? It could simply have stated the conclusions it had evidently reached before it began its inquiry and saved the Canadian people a lot of money.

There is a further methodological shortcoming concealed here. Because it adopted a 'feminist lens' the panel looked only at violence against women. This is sufficient reason for rejecting the report. If you do not investigate violence against men at the same time as you investigate violence against women, you cannot say anything meaningful about violence against women. There must be some context.

This difficulty did not deter the panel. It made recommendations covering every aspect of Canadian life. To take but one example, the panel decreed that all religions in Canada should revise their doctrine and teachings to bring them into line with the orthodoxy. Religions were admonished to 'review all basic materials, training programs, videos and texts used for religious and relationship instruction to eliminate sexist, racist and homophobic images and messages'.[51]

The Panel also recommended 'zero tolerance' of violence against women.[52] This is a phrase much-beloved amongst those who traffic in orthodoxy. If you are opposed to something, you must accept nothing short of 'zero tolerance' of it.

Like the Wilson report, the Panel's report is littered with anecdotal statements. These are appropriately horrifying. But, once again, they are unattributed and, therefore, unverifiable. Furthermore, the report is written in highly emotive language, language which suggests a reluctance to enter into careful investigation of social reality. The opening sentence of Chapter 1 states: 'Every day in this country women are maligned, humiliated, shunned, screamed at, pushed, kicked, punched, assaulted, beaten, raped, physically disfigured, tortured, threatened with weapons and murdered.'[53]

The passage just quoted points towards my main reason for describing the report as a confidence trick. This is its definition of 'violence', a matter that goes to the report's heart. The panel was supposed to investigate 'violence'. How, then, did it define violence? Let us not forget, of course, that 'violence' is not a neutral word. It is evocative and has decidedly negative connotations.

The panel decided that 'violence' had five aspects or 'dimensions'. The first two were unexceptionable—'physical violence' and 'sexual violence'. But then the panel added 'psychological violence'. I would have thought this was a semantical impossibility, but no matter. 'Psychological violence' was said to include 'the deliberate withholding of various forms of emotional support'. Then there was 'financial violence', which could occur when men 'withhold or maintain control over all or substantial amounts of money'. And, finally, there was 'spiritual violence', which might involve 'the exclusion of women from key positions in some religious institutions'.[54] I cannot avoid observing that many of the things the panel defined as 'violence' are part and parcel of the normal wear and tear of human life. With this definition of 'violence' how could the panel have reached any conclusion other than that violence against women in Canada was 'prevalent'? Indeed, I would venture to say that, on the basis of this definition, there is not a woman or man alive who has not been a victim of 'violence'.

The truly astonishing thing, however, is that having talked of the 'prevalence' of violence, having gone so far as to repeat the phrase 'war against women', in the very next paragraph of its report the panel stated: 'Despite a wealth of research in the area, we have only educated estimates of the prevalence of violence against women in Canada today.'[55] I take this as an admission that, even after cooking its definition, even after spending $10 million, the panel, at bottom, was relying on guesswork. More to the point, how on earth can recommendations based on 'educated estimates' be justified?

The Date Abuse Report

I have saved the worst for the last. In 1993 Professor Walter DeKeseredy and Professor Katharine Kelly of the Department of Sociology and Anthropology at Carleton University completed a very expensive report that was described as a national survey of 'date abuse' in Canada. The research was funded out of the Department of National Health and Welfare's Family Violence Prevention Division. This Division administers something called the Family Violence Initiative, as part of which it gives money to people like DeKeseredy and Kelly.[56] Press reports put the total cost of the project at $236,000. The questionnaire was completed by 3,142 students. A bit of simple arithmetic puts the cost to the taxpayer of each questionnaire at $75.11.[57]

The researchers administered questionnaires to groups of students in classrooms in post-secondary institutions in Canada. They concluded: 'Approximately 81.4% of the women reported having been victimized by at least one form of physical, sexual or psychological abuse during the year preceding the study.'[58] This sounds appalling, and it is, until we look at the way 'abuse' was defined for the purpose of the survey. The category 'psychological abuse' embraced 'insults or swearing', 'put you down in front of friends or family', 'accused you of having affairs or flirting with other men', 'did or said something to spite you', 'threatened to hit or throw something at you', and 'threw, smashed or kicked something', not, it should be stressed, the respondent, but *something*.[59] With this definition of 'abuse', what surprises me is not that 80 per cent of respondents said they had been abused, but that 20 per cent said they had not.

This report, or at least its aftermath, also demonstrates the power of orthodoxy to intimidate. David Hay of the University of Saskatchewan wrote an article analysing the methodology that DeKeseredy and Kelly employed in conducting their survey. Far from describing their report as the result of a fundamentally flawed, if not fraudulent, methodology, he praised their work as 'innovative and extensive' and contented himself with raising some minor methodological quibbles.[60]

CONCLUSION

The way people do research matters. It matters for a lot of reasons, but two seem specially important.

First, research is a crucial part of the intellectual project. The success or failure of that project depends on the integrity of the men and women involved and on the methods they use. If they abandon their own integrity and subvert their methods, they compromise not only research, but teaching and learning as well. They cease to be intellectuals and transform themselves into entertainers, which is relatively benign, or propagandists, which is not.

Second, research is also central to our democracy. The way we view ourselves and our society, the way we set our public agenda, and the way we address the various items on that agenda depend very much on the research of intellectuals. If the research is done shoddily or dishonestly or not at all, we compromise our ability to understand and address the challenges—constitutional and otherwise—that confront us, and eventually we sterilize our democracy.

NOTES

I would like to thank my colleague Robert Hawkins and my friend Jack Granatstein for their incisive comments. An earlier version of this paper was presented at the National Research Council of Canada symposium, 'Accuracy and Accountability in Scholarly Information', held in Montreal in August 1994.

1 See Christopher Lasch, *The True and Only Heaven: Progress and Its Critics* (New York, 1991).

2 A warning is sounded in Cynthia Crossen, *Tainted Truth: The Manipulation of Fact in America* (New York, 1994).

3 Anyone wishing to catch the flavour of the orthodoxy can do so by reading any issue of *Canadian Forum* or watching *Vision TV* for an hour or so.

4 In my opinion the fullest and most convincing statement of the reigning orthodoxy is found in Allan Bloom's *The Closing of the American Mind* (New York, 1987). For a succinct formulation, see Svi Shapiro, 'Postmodernism and the Crisis of Reason: Social Change or the Drama of the Aesthetic', *Educational Foundations* 5, no. 4 (1991): 53. The Canadian version of the orthodoxy is set out convincingly in John Fekete, *Moral Panic: Biopolitics Rising*, 2nd edn (Outremont, 1995).

5 Canada is, I believe, unique in being the only state in the world to have enshrined a commitment to relativism in its constitution. See section 27 of the Canadian Charter of Rights and Freedoms.

6 Deconstructionist thought has done much to promote subjectivity and a lot of other nasty habits. For a searching critique, see David Lehman, *Signs of the Times: Deconstruction and the Fall of Paul de Man* (New York, 1991).

7 William Ryan, *Blaming the Victim*, rev. edn (New York, 1976) is the origin of this bit of idiocy.

8 There is a large and bizarre literature on this point. Its flavour can be gleaned from Rosemary J. Coombe, 'The Properties of Culture and the Politics of Possessing Identity: Native Claims in the Cultural Appropriation Controversy', (1993) 6 *The Canadian Journal of Law and Jurisprudence* 249.

9 Madam Justice Bertha Wilson of the Supreme Court of Canada gave judicial blessing to this sort of thinking in her judgment in *Morgentaler, Smoling and Scott v. R.*, [1988] 1 S.C.R. 30.

10 Jean Bethke Elshtain's *Democracy on Trial* (Concord, Ont., 1993) is very good on the politicization of everything. Paul Fussell explains how we have come to adopt the rhetoric of warfare in *The Great War and Modern Memory* (New York and London, 1975).

11 S.O. 1993, c. 35.

12 Two studies by the now defunct Economic Council of Canada are relevant. See *New Faces in the Crowd: Economic and Social Impact of Immigration* (Ottawa, 1991) and *Earnings of Immigrants: A Comparative Analysis* (Ottawa, 1992).

13 Martin Loney, 'The Politics of Race and Gender', *Inroads* 3 (1994): 86.

14 See J.L. Granatstein, 'The Decline and Fall of Free Speech', *Literary Review of Canada* 3, no. 6 (1994): 9.

15 'Defending the Right to Be Offensive', *Globe and Mail*, 2 Feb. 1994.

16 I believe I was the first person to be publicly critical of the 'Framework'. See 'Ont. Universities Should Refuse to Adopt Minister's Vile "Anti-Racism" Policies', *Lawyers Weekly*, 17 Dec. 1993, 5.

17 See the analysis by the Supreme Court of Canada in *R. v. Keegstra*, [1990] 2 W.W.R. 1.

18 The belief in 'libel chill' is an important element in orthodox thought. The belief is set out in a self-serving and wildly overstated pamphlet by Kimberley Noble, *Bound and Gagged: Libel Chill and the Right to Publish* (Toronto, 1992). This is a superb example of orthodox writing in that Noble does not find it necessary to give a single reference to support her assertions.

19 An outline of the case can be found in Stephen Northfield, 'No Middle Ground', *London Free Press*, 20 Mar. 1993. Almost every Canadian university now has its very own horror story arising out of the enforcement of speech codes. A number of these stories are recounted in the article by Granatstein, 'Decline and Fall'. A full account of the suppression of speech at Canadian universities can be found in Fekete, *Moral Panic*, 199–318. The incident I described at the University of Western Ontario led to the creation of a committee to review the university's policy. This committee recommended significant changes in the policy. These were adopted towards the end of 1994.

20 Ibid.

21 Lynne Pearlman, 'Through Jewish Lesbian Eyes: Rethinking Clara Brett Martin', (1992) 5 *Canadian Journal of Women and the Law* 317 at 320.

22 'To Open the Way for Others of My Sex: Clara Brett Martin's Career as Canada's First Woman Lawyer', (1985) 1 *Canadian Journal of Women and the Law* 1.

23 I should confess that I made the letter public. See 'Clara Brett Martin's Canonization May Turn into an Embarrassment', *Lawyers Weekly*, 20 July 1990, 6.

24 Vol. 5, no. 2. The 'white middle class Jewish radical lesbian feminist' statement also came from this number.

25 'Response to Cossman, Kline and Pearlman', ibid., 351 at 352.

26 Constance Backhouse, *Petticoats and Prejudice: Women and Law in Nineteenth-Century Canada* (Toronto: 1991).

27 Ibid., 1 and 2. Indeed, this 'introduction' is not a bad statement of most elements of the reigning orthodoxy.

28 'Clara Brett Martin: Canadian Heroine or Not?', (1992) 5 *Canadian Journal of Women and the Law* 263.

29 'Equality and Access to Justice in the Work of Bertha Wilson', (1992) 40 *Dalhousie Law Journal* 35 at 49.

30 'Bill C-49 and the Politics of Constitutionalized Fault', (1993) 42 *University of New Brunswick Law Journal* 325 at 328.

31 Alvin Finkel and Margaret Conrad with Veronica Strong-Boag, *History of the Canadian Peoples*, vol. 2, *1867 to the Present* (Mississauga, Ont., 1993), 299.

32 Canadian Association of University Teachers, Bulletin, Mar. 1989, *Status of Women Supplement*, 3.

33 'Equality and Discrimination According to the Supreme Court of Canada', (1990–1) 4 *Canadian Journal of Women and the Law* 407 at 434.

34 'Strategizing in Equality', (1987) 3 *Wisconsin Women's Law Journal* 69 at 186.

35 Joan Brockman and Dorothy E. Chunn, eds, *Investigating Gender Bias: Law, Courts and the Legal Profession* (Toronto, 1993).

36 Sheila Martin, 'Proving Gender Bias in the Law and the Legal System', in ibid., 19.

37 An astonishing and very thorough list of similar examples from the United States is found in Christina Hoff Sommers, *Who Stole Feminism? How Women Have Betrayed Women* (New York, 1994).

38 We no longer, it seems, have committees; we prefer 'task forces'. The phrase originated in naval warfare. A task force, properly so-called, is a group of vessels assembled for a particular mission. Once the mission is completed, the task force is disbanded.

39 *Touchstones for Change: Equality, Diversity and Accountability* (Ottawa, 1993) (hereafter *Wilson Report*), 4.

40 Ibid., 137–43.

41 Ibid., 23-46, 155–76.

42 (1990–1) 4 *Canadian Journal of Women and the Law* 66.

43 *Wilson Report*, 33.

44 Ibid., 162.

45 Ibid., 25.

46 Ibid., 13.

47 *Multiculturalism, Representation and the Jury Selection Process in Canadian Criminal Cases* (Ottawa, 1994), 1.

48 Ibid., 4, 5.

49 *Final Report*, Ottawa, 1993, part one, 3.

50 Ibid.

51 Ibid., part five, 89.

52 Ibid., 23.

53 Ibid., part one, 3.

54 Ibid., part one, 7.

55 Ibid., part one, 8. It would be wrong to suggest that the Panel's report is the only, or even the most, misleading statement about the nature, scope, and extent of violence against women in Canada. See the useful article by Brian Lee Crowley, 'Sex, Lies and Violence', *Inroads* 3 (1994): 123. John Fekete gives a detailed dissection of the panel's report in his *Moral Panic*, 98–169.

56 Their report, in its original form, was not published in a journal. I will refer to it hereafter simply as *Report*. A published, although rather more restrained, version of the report can be found in *Journal of Human Justice* 4, no. 2 (1993): 25.

57 'What is "Abuse"? A Striking Survey Provokes a Heated Reaction', *Maclean's*, 22 Feb. 1993, 54.

58 *Report*, 13.

59 Ibid., 22.

60 'Methodological Review', *Journal of Human Justice* 4, no. 2 (1993): 53. Fekete comments on this study in *Moral Panic*, 70–97.

The 1995 Quebec Referendum, Liberal Constitutionalism, and the Future of Canada

Anthony A. Peacock

The 1995 Quebec referendum was held immediately before this book went to press. A few remarks about what it implies for Canadian constitutionalism and the future of Canada are appropriate.

After the referendum, there was significant speculation about the practical consequences of the close vote on sovereignty—would Prime Minister Chretien re-open constitutional negotiations, how would the vote affect the federal government's attempts to reduce the federal budget deficit and to deal with other matters of national concern, who would fill the vacancy left by the resignation of Premier Jacques Parizeau? As important as these practical issues are, the *theoretical* or *philosophical* problem of Quebec nationalism may be more salient over the long run. What does a vote for Quebec nationalism mean for liberal constitutionalism in Canada?

The movement toward Quebec nationalism—the nearly 50 per cent vote for Quebec sovereignty—represents a broader movement prevalent not only in Quebec, but throughout Canada and much of the western world. Many of those who voted 'no' and who wanted to keep Quebec a part of Canada no doubt subscribed to many of the same assumptions that moved Quebec nationalists. We might call these assumptions, and their policy implications, the politics of 'identity'. What is the politics of identity, and how is it distinguished from liberal constitutionalism?

Four years ago David Bercuson and Barry Cooper argued that one of the assumptions of modern nationalists, such as those in Quebec, is that language is not merely 'a means of communication' but 'primarily a symbol of identity'.[1] Writing 12 years earlier, and without Cooper or Bercuson in mind, Charles Taylor suggested that English Canadians who maintain 'that language is just a medium of communication' are 'crassly philistine'. They imply, on the one hand, 'that we should choose our media for greatest efficiency, and that English should therefore predominate,' or, on the other hand, that 'a society needs a minimum degree of unity and this precludes allowing wide rights to all minority languages.'[2] Taylor could call this English-Canadian disposition philistinism because, among other things, it failed to recognize that linguistic community could be a crucial condition of identity, a condition that might be considered indispensable to being recognized as a fully human subject.[3] If being recognized as a fully human subject required the maintenance and recognition of a language, as well as associated culture, then whatever means were necessary to preserve that language, including independent statehood, might be politically justifiable.

This argument assumes that identity is a legitimate source of political distinction and that language is a critical source of identity. Although there may be little doubt about the latter proposition, there is significant doubt about the former. How, we might ask, is government to be established on the basis of group identity? Ironically, it was for the purpose, among other things, of overcoming of group identities, in particular religious group identities, that liberal constitutionalism was founded. Religious factionalism was the principal reason for the doctrine of separating church and state, for ensuring that religion did not become, or remain, a source of political distinction.

Taylor emphasized that it was the erosion of earlier communities and sources of identity, perhaps above all religion, that paved the way for modern Quebec nationalism: 'people need a group identification, and the obvious one to take the place of the earlier forms is the one that springs to the attention of the speaking animal, namely, nationality based on language.'[4] Modern Quebec nationalism can be seen then as the offspring of a void created by the demise of traditional sources of identity such as religion and the local neighbourhood.

For the same reason that liberal constitutionalism does not tolerate an established church, however, it may not tolerate an established language/culture or ethnic identification. Such establishments are not only politically divisive, balkanizing the political community: they are contrary to the idea of democratic pluralism, the idea that in the public or political sphere no linguistic/cultural or ethnic group should dominate. In liberal democratic regimes, the political sphere must be linguistically, culturally, and ethnically neutral. It must allow people to say or express what they want, in the same way that it must allow people to believe what they want. If, for instance, an individual wants to advertise in English or French, or even Italian, he or she should have the freedom to do so, free of restriction from government.

The problem with this formulation is that in Canada outside of Quebec, the

English language and English culture dominate. There is no truly politically neutral sphere in English-speaking Canada, just as there would be no such sphere in an independent Quebec. If Quebec nationalism is illiberal for wanting to force people in Quebec to communicate in French and to preserve French culture, English-speaking nationalism is no less illiberal. What, we might ask, is the difference between Canadian nationalism outside of Quebec and Quebec nationalism?

The answer might be a rejection of the above statement: there is no such thing as English 'culture' outside of Quebec. Similarly, the English language is not a source of political identification for English-speakers—at least not to the extent that French is for French-speakers. As virtually every political commentator in Canada over the last generation has observed, English Canada is a nation without identity. As an editorialist put it two days following the 1995 referendum, English Canada in the twentieth century has been 'effectively deracinated'. Consequently, Canadians have talked 'endlessly about their identity crisis'.[5]

Whether in fact English-Canadian identity was ever based on race or ethnicity is a question that cannot be answered here. If it was based on a sense of Britishness, on the belief, as George Grant put it, 'that on the northern half of this continent we could build a community which had a stronger sense of the common good and of public order than was possible under the individualism of the American capitalist dream,'[6] then, as Grant eloquently pointed out, this belief was romantic and shallow. In the face of technological dynamism, it is questionable whether any particular nationalism can survive, particularly one that had been eclipsed historically by the middle of the twentieth century.

English Canada's identity crisis has the same principal source as Quebec nationalism: the abandonment of, or loss of faith in, liberal constitutionalism. Canadians have lost confidence in the capacity to achieve consensus on matters of the highest importance. The idea that through the deliberative process we could reach a common understanding, measuring and assessing social and political phenomena, and leaving to the private, politically irrelevant world 'cultural' differences seems to have been forsaken. In a very real sense, democracy has been turned on its head. Those very differences previously thought to be politically irrelevant are now the preconditions of political action, the springboards for new demands on the political community. Language and culture in Quebec, like gender, ethnicity, religion, and other group traits outside of Quebec, have become not only sources of identity, but conditions of political distinction. Policies such as official bilingualism, multiculturalism, affirmative action, and a judicial construction of the Charter that has constitutionalized a substantive, group-based conception of equality, have changed the way Canadians look at themselves and the sources of political judgment. Reason, as was pointed out in the introduction to this book, is now identified with status or power. It is considered to be a function of preference or will, not judgment. In political debate, what counts is not so much the content of what is being advocated as who is doing the advocating and where it is coming from. To scrutinize political issues independently of who is advancing them is anathema to mainstream political discourse, a discourse that understands politics as a clash between competing, sometimes incompatible, interests, but that seldom gets to the bottom of determining the legitimacy, illegitimacy, or outright silliness of the interests involved.

In brief, the danger of the politics of identity is that it may accentuate distinctions that are more artificial than real, more superficial than substantive. Beneath the veneer of Quebec nationalism, we might ask, is there any more substance than there is in the putatively effete nationalism of English-speaking Canada? If Quebec nationalism is as shallow as the current politics of identity in English Canada, which is incapable of providing any intellectual or moral cement on which to found or maintain a country, is there any wonder why Canadian politics, after so much time, is still unable to solve the riddle of unity?

The proximity of Quebec nationalism to a bald ethnic nationalism was illustrated perhaps most starkly by Premier Parizeau's instantly infamous remark that the referendum was lost on account of 'money and the ethnic vote'. Although identifying Quebec nationalism with a simple ethnic tribalism may be uncharitable, we have yet to be provided with a very persuasive argument that this is not what Quebec nationalism will degenerate into.

It would certainly be wrong and unfair to suggest that what is going on in Quebec is any different from what has been going on throughout much of the rest of Canada for at least a generation. But this only points up the necessity of reassessing the foundations of Canadian constitutionalism. 'The people of Canada', Peter Russell has observed,

> have not made a formal social contract here and now defining themselves and setting out their agreed-upon first principles of government. They have not covenanted together to produce a social contract that can be expressed in terms of formal constitutional law. But if for some time they carry on together developing a common constitutional tradition, it will turn out that they are after all the people of Edmund Burke, not John Locke, and that their social contract is essentially organic, not covenantal. Some of us might settle for that.[7]

For those of us who think that Burkean organic constitutionalism is an insufficient guide to a country too long mired in intellectual and political ambivalence, it may be time to chart out 'agreed-upon first principles of government'. If this proves impossible—which may well be the case—there may no longer be a social contract to worry about, no 'common constitutional tradition' to turn to. Such a development, however, might be easier to deal with than Canadians think. And it would certainly force a clarity in Canadian political thought that has yet to be seen and that is, arguably, long overdue.

NOTES

1 David Bercuson and Barry Cooper, *Deconfederation: Canada Without Quebec* (Toronto: Key Porter, 1991), 8.

2 Charles Taylor, 'Why Do Nations Have to Become States?' in *Reconciling the Solitudes: Essays on Canadian Federalism and Nationalism*, ed. Guy Laforest (Montreal and Kingston: McGill-Queen's University Press, 1993), 56. This essay originally appeared in 1979 in *Philosophers Look at Canadian Confederation*, ed. Stanley G. French (Montreal: L'Association canadienne de philosophie).

3 Ibid., 53.

4 Ibid., 42.

5 Barbara Amiel, 'Oh Canada! What Has Quebec Done?' in *The Wall Street Journal* (1 November 1995): A14.

6 George Grant, *Lament for a Nation: The Defeat of Canadian Nationalism* (Toronto: Macmillan, 1979), x.

7 Peter H. Russell, *Constitutional Odyssey: Can Canadians Become a Sovereign People?* 2nd edn (Toronto: University of Toronto Press, 1993), 235.

Notes on Contributors

BARRY COOPER is Professor of Political Science at the University of Calgary. He has published extensively in the areas of political philosophy, public policy and media studies, especially television. His recent scholarly works include *The End of History*, *Action into Nature*, and *Sins of Omission: Shaping the News at CBC TV*. In 1991 he wrote, with David Bercuson, the controversial best-seller *Deconfederation: Canada Without Quebec*. In 1994 he wrote, also with Bercuson, *Derailed: The Betrayal of the National Dream*.

TOM DARBY is Associate Professor of Political Science at Carleton University. Among his writings are *The Feast: Meditations on Politics and Time*, *Sojourns in the New World: Reflections on Our Technology*, and *Nietzsche and the Rhetoric of Nihilism* (ed.).

PETER C. EMBERLEY is Professor of Political Science at Carleton University. His articles on education, technology and ethics, and Rousseau have appeared in *Interpretation* and *Social Research* and edited volumes of essays. He is the author of *Values Education and Technology: The Politics of Dispossession* and *By Our Loving Own: George Grant and the Legacy of Lament for a Nation*. He is co-author, with Waller R. Newell, of *Bankrupt Education: The Decline of Liberal Education in Canada* and co-editor, with Barry Cooper, of *Faith and Political Philosophy: The Strauss-Voegelin Correspondence*.

H.D. FORBES is Professor of Political Science at the University of Toronto. He is the author of *Nationalism, Ethnocentrism and Personality: Social Science and*

Critical Theory and has edited *Canadian Political Thought*. He is working on a study of Trudeau and the Canadian electorate and is finishing a book on models of ethnic conflict.

RAINER KNOPFF is Professor of Political Science at the University of Calgary. He has published many articles on Canadian constitutionalism and political thought. He is the founding editor of the *Canadian Journal of Law and Society*, author of *Human Rights and Social Technology: The New War on Discrimination*, co-author, with F.L. Morton, of *Charter Politics*, and co-editor, with F.L. Morton and Peter Russell, of *Federalism and the Charter: Leading Constitutional Decisions*.

CHRISTOPHER P. MANFREDI is Associate Professor in the Department of Political Science at McGill University. His research interests centre on the politics of Charter litigation. He has published on this subject in the *Canadian Journal of Political Science, Canadian Public Administration*, and the *American Journal of Comparative Law*. He is also the author of *Judicial Power and the Charter: Canada and the Paradox of Liberal Constitutionalism*. His current research project examines the relationship between constitutional litigation and the politics of the formal amendment process.

ROBERT MARTIN is Professor of Law at the University of Western Ontario. He is a columnist for *The Lawyers Weekly*. He has published extensively in the fields of media law and Canadian constitutional law. His publications include *Personal Freedom and the Law in Tanzania, Critical Perspectives on the Constitution*, (ed.), *A Sourcebook of Canadian Media Law* (ed.), and *Controls and the Canadian Media* (ed.). He is a barrister and solicitor in Ontario and was a candidate for the NDP in London East in the federal elections of 1979 and 1980.

F.L. MORTON is Professor of Political Science and Co-Director of the Research Unit for Socio-Legal Studies at the University of Calgary. He is the author of *Law, Politics and the Judicial Process in Canada* and *Morgentaler v. Borowski: Abortion, the Charter, and the Courts*. He is also co-author, with Rainer Knopff, of *Charter Politics* and co-editor, with Rainer Knopff and Peter Russell, of *Federalism and the Charter: Leading Constitutional Decisions*.

GERALD OWEN practised law for five years before becoming managing editor and then editor of the *Idler*. From 1992 to 1995 he was a freelance journalist and a frequent contributor to *The Lawyers Weekly*. He is now managing editor of *Books in Canada*.

ANTHONY A. PEACOCK is a member of the Bar of Ontario and was educated at the University of Alberta, the University of Calgary, and Osgoode Hall Law School, York University. After articling and practising litigation for five years at Thomson, Rogers (Toronto), he moved to the Los Angeles area, where he teaches government at Claremont McKenna College. He is editing a book on voting rights.

JOHN T. PEPALL practices law at Abraham Duggan in Toronto. He was educated at Trent University, the University of Toronto, and Osgoode Hall Law School, York University. He was the Governor of Trent University from 1982 to 1985. He has published frequently in the *Idler* and was a Progressive Conservative candidate in the 1990 Ontario provincial election.

SCOTT REID is the senior researcher for the parliamentary caucus of the Reform Party of Canada. He is the author of *Canada Remapped: How the Partition of Quebec will Reshape the Nation and Lament for a Notion: The Life and Death of Canada's Bilingual Dream*.

KAREN SELICK is a partner in the law firm Reynolds, O'Brien, Kline and Selick, in Belleville, Ontario. She has been a regular columnist for *Canadian Lawyer* since 1990 and previously wrote columns for *The Lawyers Weekly* and *Canadian MoneySaver*. Her opinion pieces have also appeared in newspapers such as *The Globe and Mail*, the *Vancouver Sun*, the *Ottawa Citizen*, the *Financial Post*, the *London Free Press*, and *The Whig-Standard*.

BRADLEY C.S. WATSON was educated in Canada at the University of British Columbia and Queen's University Faculty of Law, in Europe at the Higher Institute of Philosophy of the University of Louvain, and in the United States at the Claremont Graduate School, from which he received his Ph.D. in political philosophy and American government. He practised law in Vancouver prior to moving to southern California, where he currently teaches in the Department of Government at Claremont McKenna College. He is working on a book examining the theory and practice of civil rights doctrines and their effect on liberal democracy.

Index

Aboriginal peoples, 50
Abortion, 65, 90, 91, 98
Activism of courts, xviii–xix, 74, 75–81, 91–4, 98–100, 193–5. *See also* Judicial supremacy under the Charter
Acton, Lord, 20, 21
Adjudicative facts, distinguished from legislative facts, 161–2
Adverse-effect discrimination, 127–8, 130, 131, 132, 135
Affirmative action: constitutional forms and the rule of law, 141–3; defence of, 132–3; group rights may conflict with individual rights, xx, 112–13, 136, 142, 151; 'hard' and 'soft', 126; and the problem of knowledge, 130, 140–1, 151–2; provides for 'positive' rather than 'natural' rights, 135–6; in the 'technology of equality', xx–xxi, 122–6, 130, 132–6, 150–2
African community in Canada, 234–5
Allaire Commission, 48
Amending formula: in Constitution Act (1982), 43–4, 209; importance of, 42
American Declaration of Independence, 147
Andrews case, 75, 129, 131
Anti-majoritarianism, 73–4
Arendt, Hannah, 148
Aristotle, 220, 240, 242
Arkes, Hadley, 89–90, 91
Aron, Raymond, 134, 135

'Articulation' of a society, xxiv, 221, 222, 223–4, 225–6, 227, 228; regional articulation in Canada, 229
Askov case, 58n12, 207

Backhouse, Constance, 258–9
Bakan, Joel, x–xi, 52, 129, 156n41
Beatty, David, 196–7, 198–9, 200
Beaudoin-Dobbie Committee (1992), 48, 49, 52
Beaudoin-Edwards Commission, 48
Bélanger-Campeau Commission, 48
Bercuson, David J., 153n9, 157n62, 271–2
Berns, Walter, 218, 228
Bhinder case, 127, 128
Bicameral legislature, 222
Big M case, 175n27
Bilingualism and Biculturalism, Royal Commission on (1963), 24, 27
Bilingualism, official, xiv, 24–6, 30–1, 33; and rights, 25–6
Bill 22 (Quebec), *see* Quebec: language laws
Bill 178 (Quebec), *see* Quebec: language laws
Bill C-60 (1978), 43
Bill of Rights (1960), 74, 84n51, 103, 187
Bills of rights, Hamilton's view of, 88–9
Blankart, Charles, 206
Bloom, Allan, viii, 158n103
Bohnet, Iris, 207
Borowski case, 86n76, 87n79

Bourassa, Robert, 32, 33, 42, 45, 207–8
Boyer, Patrick, 207
Brandeis, Louis, 161
British North America Act (1867), 24, 187;
    renaming of, xiii–xiv, 3–16
Brodie, Janine, 75
Brown case (US), 194
Butler case, 173, 175n29
Bygrave, Mike, 69

Cairns, Alan, vii, 45, 66, 123
Cairns-Way, Rosemary, 259
Canada Act (1982), 3, 4–7. *See also*
    Constitution Act (1982)
Canada Assistance Plan, 110
'Canada Clause' of Charlottetown Accord
    (1992), xiv, 10–11, 15n42, 41, 49–51, 56,
    57
'Canada Round' of negotiations, 56
Canadian Advisory Council on the Status of
    Women, 66
Canadian African Women's Organization,
    235
Canadian Bar Association, xi–xii; Ontario
    division, xii. *See also* Task Force on Gender
    Equality in the Legal Profession (1993)
Canadian Journal of Women and the Law, 258
Castel, J.G., 189
Charlottetown Accord (1992), xv, 12, 236;
    Canada Clause, xiv, 10–11, 15n42, 41,
    49–51, 56, 57; instruction to courts re
    interpretation of Charter, 198; as
    outgrowth of the Charter, xvi, 56;
    referendum on (1992), vii, xxiii, 3, 40–59,
    99, 100, 204, 207, 230; social charter, 41,
    51–6, 57
Charlottetown negotiations, viii, xii
Charter Canadians, xvii, 46, 66–7, 75, 77, 78,
    123–4, 129–30, 192–3
Charter of Rights and Freedoms (1982):
    constitutional protection for groups
    under, *see* Charter Canadians; distinctive
    features, 23–4; equality rights in, *see*
    Equality rights in the Charter;
    'fundamental freedoms' under, 106–7;
    maintains inequalities, ix–xi; negative and
    positive rights under, *see* Negative rights;
    Positive rights; 'notwithstanding' clause,
    see 'Notwithstanding' clause; property
    rights not mentioned, xx, 23, 117–18;
    rewriting, as solution to judicial review
    problems, 197–8; rights theory indicates
    flaws in, 109–19; shifts power from
    legislatures to courts, 24, 56, 64, 66, 75–6,
    99, 100, 115, 119–20, 131, 173, 178, 186,
    187; a threat to liberties?, *see* Collective
    rights and individual liberties; a unifying
    national idea?, 11, 23, 47, 65

Charter of the French Language, 45. *See also*
    Quebec: language laws
'Charterphiles', 65, 188–90
'Charterphobes', 188, 190–3
Christian, William, 8
Cité Libre, 29–30
Citizens' Forum on the Constitution, 48
Citizenship rights, universal, 42
Clark, Joe, 43
Clericis Laicos (1296), 222
Collective rights and individual liberties,
    xx–xxi, 89, 94, 100, 116–17, 119–20,
    123–4, 136–8, 142, 147–8, 151–2, 192–3
Conscription Crisis of 1917, 259–60
Consensus Report on the Constitution (1992), 47
Constitution Act (1867, formerly British
    North America Act, 1867), 4
Constitution Act (1982), 4, 66, 99; amending
    formula in, 43–4, 209; Charter, *see*
    Charter of Rights and Freedoms;
    development of, 42–3
Constitutional forms and the rule of law, xiii,
    141–3
Constitutionalism: external, *see* External
    constitutionalism; substantive, *see*
    Substantive constitutionalism
Constitution of the United States, viii, 89, 107
Constitutions: new expectations of, 40, 47,
    49, 238–9, 245, 247; and political
    correctness, 233–48; purposes of, vii–viii,
    40–1; reform not an answer to political
    conflicts, xv, 40–59; sources of
    constitutional difficulties, viii, xxiv–xxv,
    217–18, 228–30; as symbols, 5, 6, 49–50,
    220, 221, 228; traditional impartiality,
    238, 247
Constrained vision of human nature, 67, 70,
    72–3, 76–7
Contractarian thought, 148
'Conventional' and 'natural', *see* Nature and
    convention
Cooke, Dave, 256
Cooper, Barry, xxiv–xxv, 153n9, 157n62,
    217–32, 271–2
Corpus mysticum, 225–6
Cory, Peter de Carteret, 169, 170
Court Challenges Program, 110
Court Party, xvii, 63–87; Charter Canadians,
    66–7, 77, 78; élitism of, 68, 70–3, 80–1;
    postmaterialists, 68–9, 70, 71–2, 81; social
    engineers, 67–8, 70, 72, 73, 77, 81;
    'unifiers', 65–6; vs traditional judicial
    review, 73–80
Courts: activism of, xviii–xix, 74, 75–81,
    91–4, 98–100, 193–5; Charter increases
    power of, 24, 56, 64, 66, 75–6, 99, 100,
    115, 119–20, 131, 173, 178, 186, 187. *See
    also* Judges; Supreme Court of Canada

Criminal Code, 178, 256
Crown, importance in concept of Canada, 6–7, 10
Cultural clashes, 234–6
'Culture', meaning of word, 10, 244–5
Cynicism in orthodoxy, xxvi, 253

Darby, Tom, xxv–xxvi, 233–48
Date Abuse Report (1993), xxvii, 266–7
DeKeseredy, Walter, 266–7
Democracy: constitutional forms in, xiii; Crown as source, in Canadian conception, 6–7, 10; not synonymous with freedom, 115–16; problem of tutelary democracy, 138–50; and redistributive justice, 147–8; Trudeau's silence in early writings, 19–20
Democracy in America, see Tocqueville, Alexis de
Democratic élitism, 68, 72
Democratic override, xxiii, 186, 203–9
Devine, Grant, 201
Devine case, 167, 168
Dickason case, 171, 172, 173, 176n40
Dickson, Brian, 93, 98, 116, 163–4, 165–6, 172, 173
Disclosure, effects of Stinchcombe case, xxii, 177–85
Discrimination, 75–6, 112, 126, 151; adverse-effect, 127–8, 130, 131, 132; change in meaning of, 126, 132; grounds of, 127; Ontario government documents concerning, 254–6
'Distinct society', Quebec as, 46, 50
'Dominion', abandonment of term, 7–8
Dominium politicum et regale, 224, 225, 227
Dominium regale, 224, 227
Dred Scott decision (US), 92
Drybones case (1970), 84n51
Dworkin, Ronald, 190

Edwards Book and Art Ltd case, 116, 117, 172, 207
Élitism of the Court Party, 68, 70–3, 80–1
Ellul, Jacques, 125
Emberley, Peter C., xxv–xxvi, 233–48
Employment Equity Act (Ontario), 254
English experience of constitutional development, 218–19, 221–3
Entrenched rights, 42, 47, 73, 188, 209
Epstein, Richard, 118
Equality, 149, 150; 'economic equality' and 'equality of opportunity', 134–5; group-based conception of, 273; inconsistent with liberty, see Collective rights and individual liberties; Tocqueville's vision of, 139–41
Equality of process vs equality of result, 151
Equality Party, 208

Equality rights in the Charter, xx–xxi, 23–4, 112, 123–4, 136, 150–2; social equality replaces political equality, 122; technology of equality, 122–3, 124–38, 150–2
Estey, Justice, 162–3
Evidence in constitutional cases, xxi–xxii, 152, 161–76
External constitutionalism, 219, 220, 221, 222, 226, 227, 228, 229

Favreau, Guy, 36n34
Federalism: arguments for, 55–6; in Trudeau's early writings, 21
Federalist Papers, 77, 88, 189
Female circumcision, 234–5
Feminists, 66, 75, 78; Panel on Violence against Women (1993), 264–6
Filmon, Gary, 45
Finlay case, xix, 109–10
Flanagan, Thomas, 127, 154n25
Forbes, H.D., xiv, 17–39
Ford case, 167, 168, 207–8
Forsey, Eugene, 7, 10
Fortescue, Sir John, 224–6, 227, 228, 229
Founding peoples, 41–2
'Framework' documents for Ontario universities and colleges (1993), 255–6
Fraser, Blair, 24
Freedom, see Liberty
Freedom of association, 153n9
Freedom of expression, 222–3
Freedom of opinion, 144–5
Free market, Tocqueville's ideas on, 139, 140–1
French–Canadian nationalism, xiv, 20, 40, 41–2, 65, 271–4
Frey, Bruno, 206–7
Frye, Northrop, 27–8
Fulford, Robert, 256

Gettysburg address (Lincoln), 224
Gibbins, Roger, 212n46
Gibson, Dale, 76, 85n61, 130, 132, 133, 134, 135, 140, 150, 154n25, 197
Glendon, Mary Ann, 123, 124
Globalization of commerce, 237, 239
Globe and Mail, 151, 192–3
Godwin, William, 70
Government: separation of powers of branches, 115; as source of individual rights, 108–9
'Government generation', 74
Government intervention: positive activism of courts, xviii–xix, 74, 75–9, 81, 91–4, 98–100, 151–2, 194–5; redistributive justice, 140–1, 142, 147–8; social engineering, xvii, xxi, 67–8, 70–2, 73, 77, 81, 127–8, 129, 135, 149–52

Grant, George, 6, 7, 8, 17, 100, 273
Great Reform Bill (1832), 223
Groulx, Lionel, 20
Group affiliation, 136
Group rights may deny individual rights, xx–xxi, 89, 94, 100, 116–17, 119–20, 123–4, 136–8, 142, 151–2, 192–3
Grove, Frederick Philip, 6

Haig and Birch, 77, 78
Hamilton, Alexander, 84n47, 88–9, 94
Harassment, definitions of, 255, 257
Harvey, Wendy, 183, 184
Hate propaganda, 36n34, 172–3
Hauriou, Maurice, 228–9
Hay, David, 266–7
Hayek, Friedrich A., 114, 115, 142, 158
Heard, Andrew, 197
Hegel, Georg, 244
Heidegger, Martin, 125
Herrnstein, Richard, 71
Hitler, Adolf, 115
Hobbes, Thomas, 94–5, 229, 241–2, 245
Hogg, Peter W., 5, 8, 145, 146, 147
Holidays Act, 14n29
Homosexuality, 66, 77, 78
Hong Kong, 115–16
Hufsky case, 166
Human rights legislation, 123–4, 124, 126, 128, 150–2; knowledge presumed, 130–1; provides for positive rights, xix–xxi, 136
Hutchinson, Alan, 192

Idée directrice, 228
Identity, *see* National identity
Immigration policy, 28, 36n29, 38n47, 38n48
Indian community in Canada, 235
Individual freedom and collective rights, *see* Collective rights and individual liberties
Information age, and disclosure, 180–1
Inglehart, Ronald, 69
Innis, Harold, 125
Integration of a society, 222–3, 227
Intencio populi, 226, 228, 229
Interest groups, viii, xviii, 103, 239; Charter Canadians, xvii, 46, 66–7, 75, 77, 78, 123–4, 129–30, 192–3; constitutional litigation by, 79–80, 86nn73–5
Irwin Toy case, 168–9, 171–2

Jenkins case, 195
Johnstone, Cecilia, xii
Judges, *see* Courts; Supreme Court of Canada
Judicial activism, xviii–xix, 74, 75–81, 91–4, 98–100, 151–2, 194–5
Judicial Committee of the Privy Council, 74, 211n28

Judicial supremacy under the Charter: case against, 190–5; case for, 188–90; democratic override, xxiii, 186, 203–9; proposed solutions to problem of, 195–203
Judiciary, 'partisans' of, *see* Court Party
Jury Selection Report (1994), xxvii, 264

Kant, Immanuel, 241, 242, 243
Keegstra case, 172–3, 207
Kelly, Katharine, 266–7
Knopff, Rainer, xi, xvii, xviii, 63–87, 92, 100, 123, 131, 132, 133, 155n33, 190, 191, 192, 202
Knowledge, presumed by technology of equality, 130–1
Knowledge class, xvii, 68–9, 70–2, 73, 81, 125

Ladouceur case, 166
Lament for a Nation (Grant), 6, 7, 8, 17, 100, 273
Lamer, Antonio, xxii, 123, 181, 184n10
Language, 143; bilingualism, *see* Bilingualism, official; 'conventional' words replace 'natural' ones, 244–5; laws in Quebec, 32, 45, 46, 167–8, 207–9, 272, 273; of rights, 157n62; in the technology of equality, 125–6, 131–4
Lanning, Greg, xxii
Lasch, Christopher, 70, 71, 72, 83n30
Laskin, Bora, 84n51, 87n79
Lavigne case, 170–1
Law rationalizes power, ix
Law schools, xi, xii, xxiv, 147; as source of constitutional difficulties, ix
Lederman, W.R., 99
Legal Education Action Fund (LEAF), 66, 78
Legal positivism, 90, 91, 124, 143–7
Legal research, orthodoxy in, *see* Orthodoxy in academic discussion
Legislative facts, distinguished from adjudicative facts, 161–2
Legislative override, *see* 'Notwithstanding' clause
Lessard, Hester, 259
Leviathan (Hobbes), 95
Lewis, Stephen, 255
'Libel chill', 256, 268n18
Liberal constitutionalism, vii, xi, 57; and the 1975 Quebec referendum, 271–5; challenges to, xxv–xxvi, 237–8
Liberalism: self-expressive, 94, 97, 98; substantive equality inconsistent with traditional liberal democratic thought, 137; tradition of, 94–7
Liberty: collective rights and, *see* Collective rights and individual liberties; contrasted with equality, 137, 144, 147–8, 151; as

defined in the Charter, 118–19; freedom
not synonymous with democracy, 115–16;
'fundamental freedoms' under the
Charter, 106–7; individual freedom
ideological cement for US, 10
Life-cycle criteria for discrimination, 127, 154
Life-style criteria for discrimination, 127, 154
Lincoln, Abraham, 92, 223–4
Lipset, Seymour Martin, 11, 68–9
Locke, John, 95, 107–8, 241–2, 245
Lougheed, Peter, 42

Macdonald, John A., 13n18
MacGuigan, Mark, 4–5
McIntyre, Justice, 127, 128, 129
McIntyre, Sheila, ix, xxviiin23, 260
MacKay v. Manitoba, 169–70
MacKinnon, Catherine, ix
Madison, James, 148, 206
Magna Carta, 221
Major, John, 110
Majury, Diana, 260–1
Mallory, James, 68, 74, 80
Mandel, Michael, ix–x, 190, 191, 192, 199, 202
Manfredi, Christopher, xv–xvi, 40–59,
101n18, 128, 193, 200, 202
Mansfield, Harvey C., Jr., 97, 123, 125
Mao Zedong, 246
Marchand, Jean, 28
Martin, Clara Brett, 258
Martin, G. Arthur, 180
Martin, Robert, xi, xiii–xiv, xxvi–xxvii, 3–16,
249–70
Martin, Sheila, 261
Materialism, xxviin5
Meech Lake Accord (1987), 12, 45; 'distinct
society' clause, 46, 198, 220; failure of,
45, 46, 47–8, 56, 208; negotiations
leading up to, viii, 45; post-Meech
proposals for reform, 46
Mega-constitutional change, 41, 230
Memoirs (Trudeau), 17, 18, 22–3, 24, 26, 29,
32
Minority groups under Charter, xvii, 46,
66–7, 75, 77, 78, 123–4, 129–30, 192–3
Mitchell, Richard, 236
Modernity, 95
Montgomery, 118
Moral notion of rights, 139
Moral vision of Trudeau, xv, 17–39
Morin, Guy–Paul, 182
Morton, F.L., xi, xvii, xviii, 63–87, 92, 100,
123, 190, 191, 192, 193, 196–7, 202
Mulroney, Brian, 202–3, 212n55
Multiculturalism, xiv, 10, 24, 26–9, 31,
39n49, 144–5; cultural clashes, 234–6;
Jury Selection Report (1994), 264
Multi-ethnic states, 9–10, 11

Murray, Charles, 71
Myth, common, of a human society, 219–20,
226, 227; lacking in Canada, 10–12, 227,
228

National Anti-Poverty Organization, 54
National Citizens' Coalition, 80, 171
National identity, xv–xvi; Canada Clause
attempts statement of, xv–xvi, 49–50;
cannot be imposed by a constitution,
56–7; and the Charter of Rights and
Freedoms, 11, 23, 47, 65; and social
charter, 53, 56–7; 'unifying idea' lacking
in Canada, 10–12, 65, 227, 228, 274
Nationalism: Quebec, xiv, 20, 29–30, 40,
41–2, 65, 271–5; in Trudeau's early
writings, 20–1
National unity advocates, xvii, 65–6
Nation-state, power shift away from, 237–8
Natural inequalities (Tocqueville), 139–41
Natural rights, xx, 26, 90, 123, 124, 135–6,
142–4, 145, 146–7
Nature and convention, xxv–xxvi, 239–43;
'natural' words replaced by conventional
designations, 244–5; political correctness
distorts relationship of, 245–7
Nedelsky, Jennifer, 52–3, 54
Negative rights, xix, 104, 105–8, 109
New Democratic Party (federal), and social
charter proposals, 53–4
New Democratic Party (Ontario), xvi, 46–7,
114
Nietzsche, Friedrich, 97, 242–3
Nihilism, 136
Non-interpretivist approach to constitutional
interpretation, 78, 94–7
Non-utilitarian nature of individual court
actions, 189, 193–4
'Notwithstanding' clause, xxiii, 23, 44, 45, 46,
92, 113–14, 186, 200–3; democratizing,
203–9; Quebec language laws, 207–9

Oakes case, 98, 163–4, 165, 167, 173
O'Connor case, 183–4
Official Languages Act (1969), 24–5, 28
O'Malley, 127–8
Ontario provincial government: limits
research and academic discourse, 254–7;
and social charter proposals, 53
Operation Dismantle, 165–6, 169, 191
Opportunism, xiii
Oppositionist intelligentsia, 68–9
Ortega y Gasset, José, 72
Orthodoxy in academic discussion, xxvi–xxvii,
249–70; elements of, 250–3; explicit
application by government and
universities, 253–7; implicit application,
257–67

Orton, Helena, 75
Orwell, George, 112
Owen, Gerald, xxii, 177–85
Owram, Doug, 74

Padolsky, Enoch, 6
Paine, Tom, 218
Panel on Violence against Women (1993), xxvii, 264–6
Pangle, Thomas L., 158n103
Parizeau, Jacques, 271, 274
Partisan programs, xii
Peacock, Anthony, xx–xxi, 122–60, 271–5
Pelletier, Gérard, 18
'People' as a political symbol, 223–4, 225
Pepall, John T., xxi–xxii, 161–76
Perfectibility, see Unconstrained vision of human nature
Petter, Andrew, 191–2
Photocopying, xxii, 179, 181
Pietrorazio, Luciano, 184
Pigeon, J., 84n51
Plato, 239–40, 242, 245
Plattner, Marc, 142–3
Pluralism, 272; in Trudeau's vision, 31–2, 34
Political correctness, xxv–xxvi, 234, 244, 245–7; dangers of, 247
Political rights, 122, 138
Politicization in orthodoxy, xxvi, 253
Pomerant, David, 264
Populism, 67–8
Positive judicial activism, xviii–xix, 74, 75–80, 81, 91–4, 98–100, 151–2, 194–5
Positive rights, xix, 104, 105, 136, 138; in the Charter, 109–11
Positivism, 90, 91, 124, 143–7
Postman, Neil, 125
Post-materialism, xvii, xviii, xxviin5, 68–9, 70, 71–2, 73, 81
Post-modernism, 71, 72, 100
Power and language, 243–5
Power conflicts between social groups, ix
Prescriptive rulings, 194–5
Principle used to justify social arrangements, x
Private actions and public actions, ix
Programmatic liberalism, xii
Progressive Conservative Party of Canada, 99
Progressivism, xi
Property rights: absent in Charter, xx, 23, 117–18; 'negative form' of, 107–8; proposed Charter amendments concerning, 51, 53, 55, 198
Proscriptive rulings, 194
Provincial equality, 45
Public opinion as determiner of rights, 144, 145, 147, 152

Quebec: as a distinct society, 45, 46, 50; language laws, 32, 45, 46, 167–8, 207–9, 272, 273; nationalism, xiv, 20, 29–30, 40, 41–2, 65, 271–5; reaction to failure of Meech, 47–8; referendum (1995), 271–5; referendum on sovereignty-association (1980), 43

Racism, 38n47, 128; 'framework' documents in Ontario, 255–6; 'race relations policy' of University of Western Ontario, 256–7
Radwanski, George, 18
Rawls, John, 95, 97, 148
Realignments of power, 237–8
Rebick, Judy, 235
Redistributive justice, 140–1, 142, 147–8
Referenda: 1942 referendum on conscription, 207; 1992 referendum on the Charlottetown Accord, vii, xxiii, 3, 40–59, 99, 100, 204, 207, 230; Quebec referendum (1995), 271–5; on sovereignty-association (1980), 43; to ratify or veto Supreme Court interpretations, 204–9; use in Switzerland, 205, 206–7, 212n57
Reform Party: and opposition to bilingualism, 25; proposed property rights amendment, 198
Refugee status for women, 235–6
Regional concerns, xxv
Reid, Scott, xxii–xxiii, 186–213
Relativism, xiv, 250–1; in orthodoxy, xxvi
'Representation' in a society, xxiv, 221, 223, 224, 225, 226, 227, 228–30
Research and orthodoxy, see Orthodoxy in academic discussion
Responsible government, 63–4
Rights: become relative under substantive equality, 136–7; Canadian Bill of Rights (1960), 74, 84n51, 103, 187; Canadian Charter of, see Charter of Rights and Freedoms (1982); change in meaning of word, 143, 245; concept of, 103–4; entrenched, 42, 47, 73, 188, 209; 'fundamental', 90, 91; government as source of, 108–9; group rights may be inconsistent with individual liberties, xx–xxi, 89, 94, 100, 116–17, 119–20, 123–4, 136–8, 142, 151–2, 192–3; and 'guardian democracy', 138–50; 'language of', 88–102, 123–4; moral and immoral (Tocqueville), 138–9; natural, xx, 26, 90, 123, 124, 135–6, 142–4, 145, 146–7, 245; 'negative', xix, 104, 105–8, 109; not to be deprived of property, 107–8; and official bilingualism, 25–6; 'positive', xix, 104, 105, 109–11, 136, 138; social vs political equality rights, 122; technology of

equality, 122–3, 126–38; to liberty, 106–7; to life, 106; Trudeau's silence in early writings, 19; written bills of, 88–91
Rights talk, 123, 124
Romanow, Roy, 99
Rousseau, Jean Jacques, 96, 241, 246
Rule of law, ix, 141–3
Rules of evidence, xxi, 152, 165
Rushton, J. Philippe, 256
Russell, Peter, 41, 192, 200, 201–2, 217–18, 228, 274

Sade, Marquis de, 241
Schachtschneider case, 112–13
Schneiderman, David, x–xi
Scott, Craig, 52–3, 54
Scott, Frank, 7
Seaboyer case, 58n12
Section 1 litigation, xxi–xxii, 161–76
Section 15, *see* Equality rights
Section 33, *see* 'Notwithstanding' clause
Self-expressive liberalism, 94, 97, 98
Self-incrimination, 181–2
Selick, Karen, xix–xx, 103–21
Separation of powers, 115
Separatism, xiv–xv, 20, 29–30, 40, 41–2, 65, 271–5
Sexual preference, 77, 78
Sigurdson, Richard, 190–1, 193
Sin-crime distinction, 32, 38n43
Singh case, 163, 207
Skapinker case, 162–3
Smiley, Donald, 199
'Social and economic union' provisions, 41
Social articulation, *see* 'Articulation' of a society
Social charter, xvi, 51–6, 57; goals among proponents, 53–4; and national identity, 47, 53, 56–7; proposed, 46–7
'Social contract', 108, 242, 274
Social engineering, xvii, xxi, 67–8, 70–2, 73, 77, 81, 127–8, 129, 135, 141, 149–52
Social equality, 122
Social rights tribunals, 54
Social scientific research, orthodoxy in, *see* Orthodoxy in academic discussion
Social utility, Tocqueville's warning against, 140, 141
Socrates, 239
Sophists, 239
Sopinka, John, 167, 171, 172, 173, 177, 180, 182, 183
Sovereignty of the law, 238
Sowell, Thomas, 67, 72, 76, 83n30, 151
Spicer, Keith, 48
State: Court Party vs liberal view of state and society, 76–7; effects on research and academic discussion, xxvi, 254–6; the

national community, 228. *See also* Government intervention
Stereotypes and human rights, 128, 130
Stinchcombe case, xxii, 177–85
Strauss, Leo, 96, 136
Strayer, Barry L., 4
Stroud, Carsten, 178, 180
Structural injunctions, 75
Subjectivity as element of orthodoxy, xxvi, 251–2
Substantive constitutionalism, xxiv, 220, 223, 226, 227, 229–30; lacking in Canada, 217–18, 227–8, 230
Substantive equality, 124–6, 131–2; affirmative action, human rights legislation, and Section 15, 126–30, 132; inconsistent with traditional liberal democratic thought, 137; makes rights relative, 136–7
Substantive method, ix
Supreme Court of Canada, xviii, 42, 66, 74, 75–6, 78–80; appointment and tenure of judges, changes suggested, 198–200; and Charter of the French Language, 45; decisions on discrimination, 127–8; and provincial assistance programs, 59n29; referenda proposed on Charter interpretations, 204–9; suggestions for reform re Charter cases, 196–7; use of evidence in Charter cases, xxi–xxii, 161–76; nullification of laws by, 163–5, 167–9, 170, 204, 212n56
Supreme Court of the United States, 74, 194
Switzerland, xxiii, 187; referenda in, 205, 206–7, 212n57
Symbolism of human society, 212, 218, 219–20, 225–6, 227; 'people' as a symbol, 223–4, 225; symbols lacking in Canada, 10–12, 227, 228
'Systemic barriers', xxi, 127–8, 129, 135, 150

Tarnopolsky, Walter, 151–2
Task Force on Gender Equality in the Legal Profession (1993), xi–xii, xxvii, xxixn24, 262–3
Taylor, Charles, 272
Technology of equality, 122–3, 149; affirmative action, human rights, and Section 15!, 126–34; elements, 124–6. *See also* Social engineering
Thackray, Allan, 183
Third Republic, 228
Thomsen case, 166
Tocqueville, Alexis de, xx, xxi, 124, 190; equality may threaten liberty, 137; and tutelary democracy, 138–50
Tolerance in Trudeau's vision, 32–3

Transformation in assumptions about
   constitutional analysis, xii
Tribe, Laurence H., 90, 91, 92, 198–9
Trudeau, Pierre Elliott, xiv–xv, 65;
   constitutional reform under, 22–4, 33, 42,
   43; early writings (1950–1965), 18–21;
   economic policies, 19, 22, 33, 38n46;
   moral vision, xv, 17–39; and
   multiculturalism, 26–9, 33; and official
   bilingualism, 24–6, 30–1, 33; opposition
   to separatist nationalism, 29–30; pluralism
   of, 31–2
Truth, relativists deny possibility of objective,
   251
Tutelary democracy, Tocqueville and, 138–50

Unconstrained vision of human nature, 67–8,
   70–1, 72, 77; a danger to modern
   democracies, 149–50
'Unifiers', 65–6
Unifying idea for Canadian state lacking,
   10–12, 49–50, 65, 227, 228, 274
United States: Bill of Rights, 89, 90, 108,
   109, 120; Constitution, viii, 89, 107;
   success as a multi–ethnic democracy,
   9–10; Supreme Court, 74, 194

Universal health insurance, 54–5
Universities: 'framework' documents in
   Ontario, 255–6; imposition of orthodoxy
   by, xxvi, 256–7
University of Western Ontario, 256–7

Valcourt, Bernard, 236
Vaughan, Frederick, 147
Victimology, xxvi, 252–3
Victoria agreement (1971), 4, 42, 43
Voegelin, Eric, 219, 221, 223, 224, 226

Watson, Bradley C.S., xviii, xix, 88–102
Weiler, Paul, 201
Welfare state, 74, 141, 194
Whitten, Alan, 180
Wilson, Bertha, xi, 93, 98, 163, 197, 262
Wilson Report (1993), xi–xii, xxvii, xxixn24,
   262–3
Writers' Union of Canada, 49, 58n22
Writ of summons of Edward I (1295), 223
Written constitution, 83n44; dangers of a
   written bill of rights, 88–91;
   preoccupation with, 233, 245

Zundel, Ernst, 172